Kazunari Kakei

More than anything, I hope to keep drawing a manga that I myself enjoy working on. So it will be great if the people who read this enjoy it too! I draw each page with that wish in mind.

NORA: The Last Chronicle of Devildom is Kazunari Kakei's first manga series. It debuted in the April 2004 issue of *Monthly Shonen Jump* and eventually spawned a second series, *SUREBREC: NORA the 2nd*, which premiered in *Monthly Shonen Jump*'s March 2007 issue.

NORA
THE LAST CHRONICLE OF DEVILDOM

VOL. 1

STORY AND ART BY
KAZUNARI KAKEI

English Adaptation/Park Cooper and Barb Lien-Cooper
Translation/Nori Minami
Touch-up Art & Lettering/Wayne Truman
Design/Sam Elzway
Editor/Carol Fox

Editor in Chief, Books/Alvin Lu
Editor in Chief, Magazines/Marc Weidenbaum
VP, Publishing Licensing/Rika Inouye
VP, Sales and Product Marketing/Gonzalo Ferreyra
VP, Creative/Linda Espinosa
Publisher/Hyoe Narita

Printed in the U.S.A.

Published by VIZ Media, LLC
P.O. Box 77010
San Francisco, CA 94107

10 9 8 7 6 5 4 3 2 1
First printing, October 2008

www.viz.com

RATED T+ FOR OLDER TEEN

PARENTAL ADVISORY
NORA is rated T+ for Older Teen and is recommended for ages 16 and up. This volume contains violence, mild nudity and diabolical themes.
ratings.viz.com

SHONEN JUMP ADVANCED
Manga Edition

NORA
THE LAST CHRONICLE OF DEVILDOM

Volume 1: A Match Made in Hell

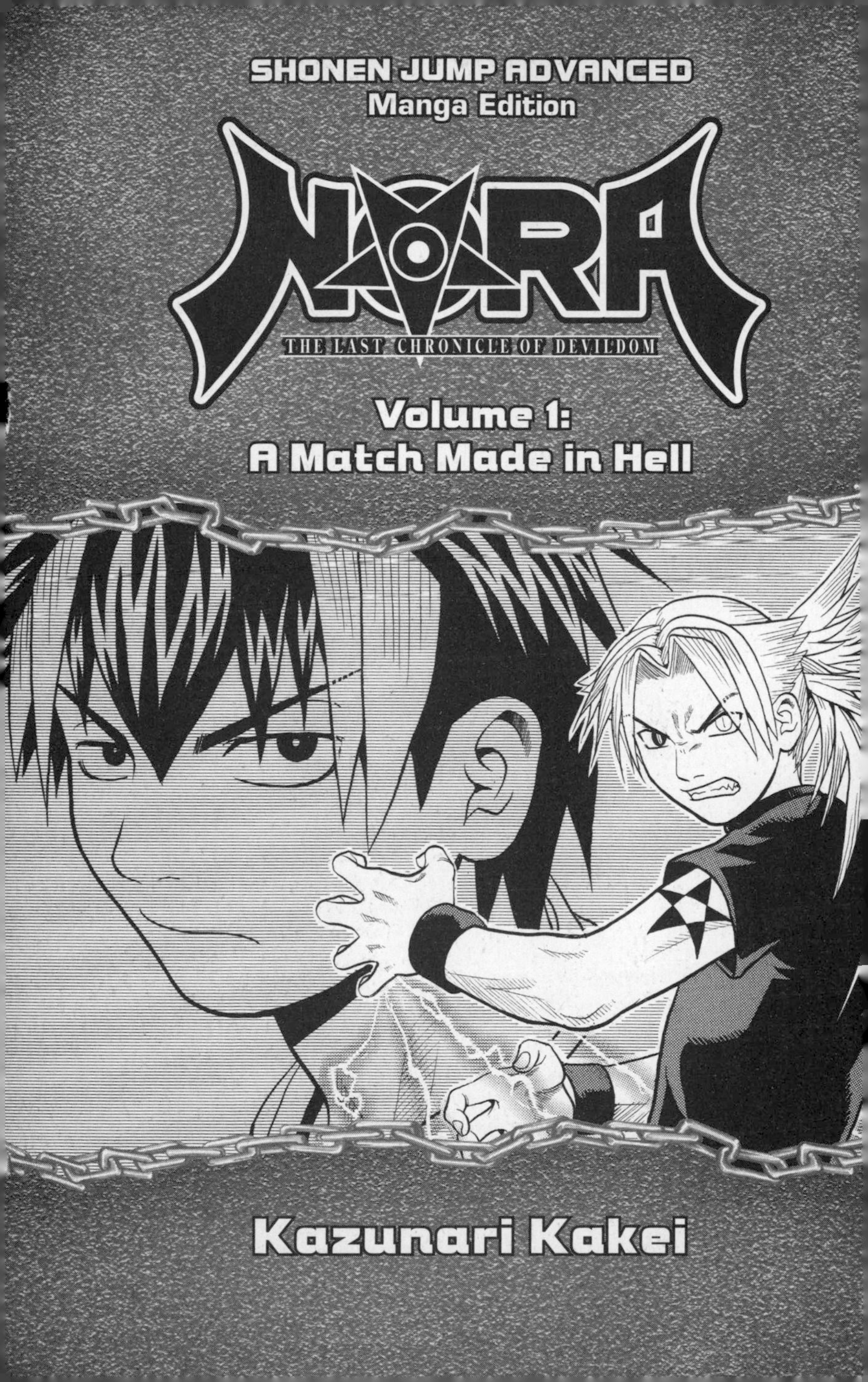

Kazunari Kakei

CONTENTS

A Match Made in Hell 5

Give and Take 67

The Watcher 113

The Price of Power........................159

Volume 1:
A Match Made in Hell

Story 1: A Match Made in Hell

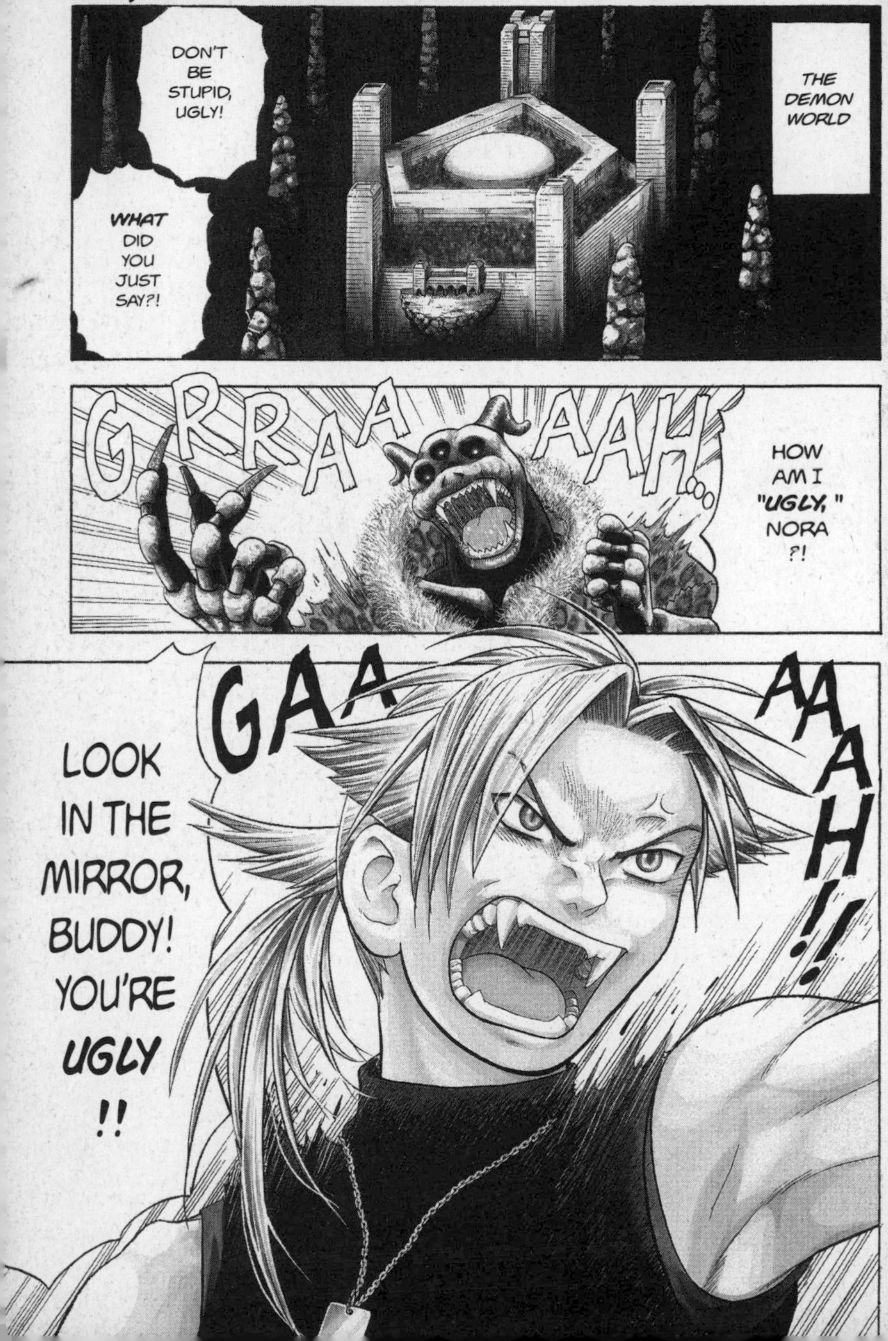
THE DEMON WORLD
DON'T BE STUPID, UGLY!
WHAT DID YOU JUST SAY?!
GRRAAAAAH...
HOW AM I "UGLY," NORA?!
AAAH!!!
GAA
LOOK IN THE MIRROR, BUDDY! YOU'RE UGLY!!

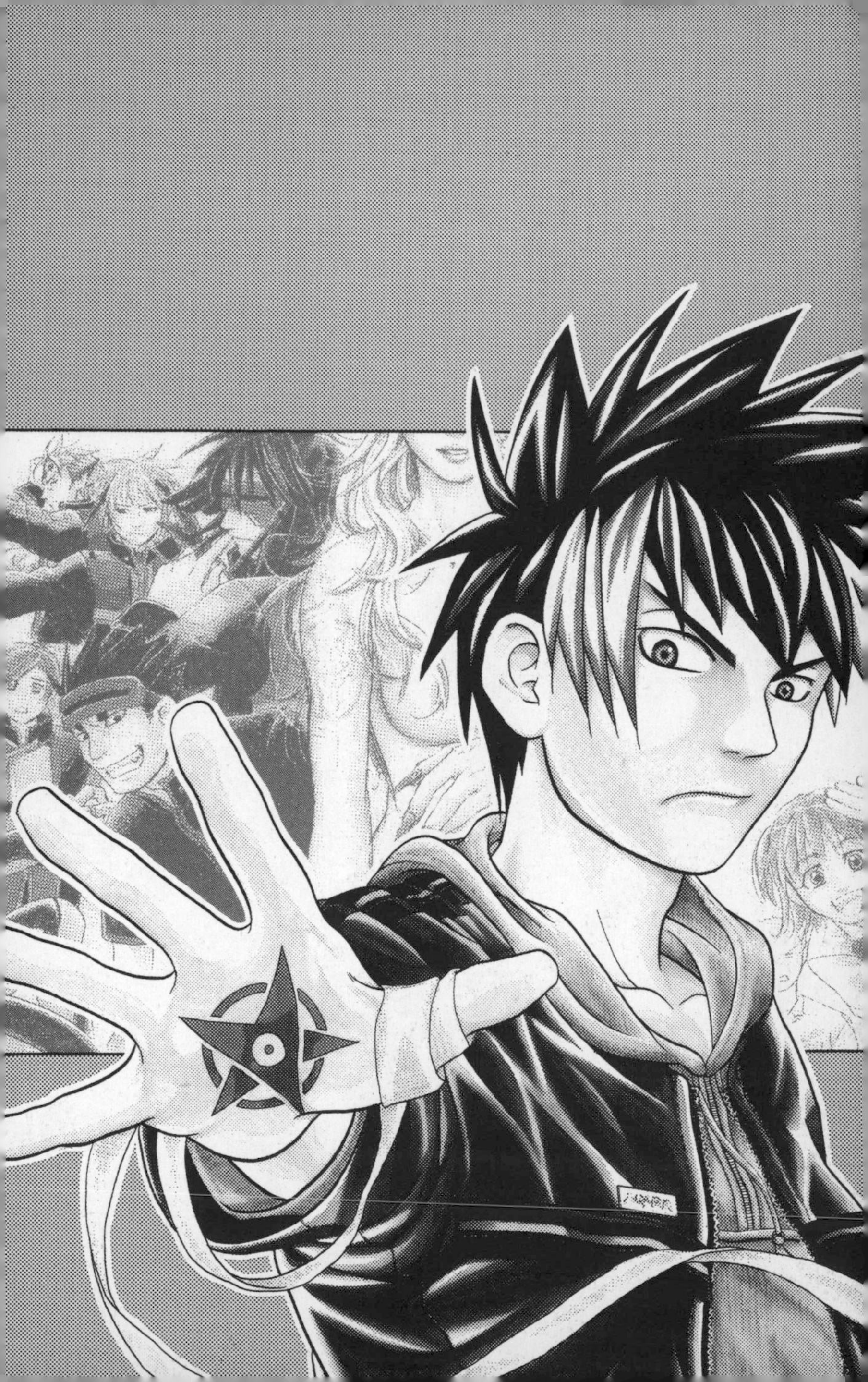

Story 1: A Match Made in Hell

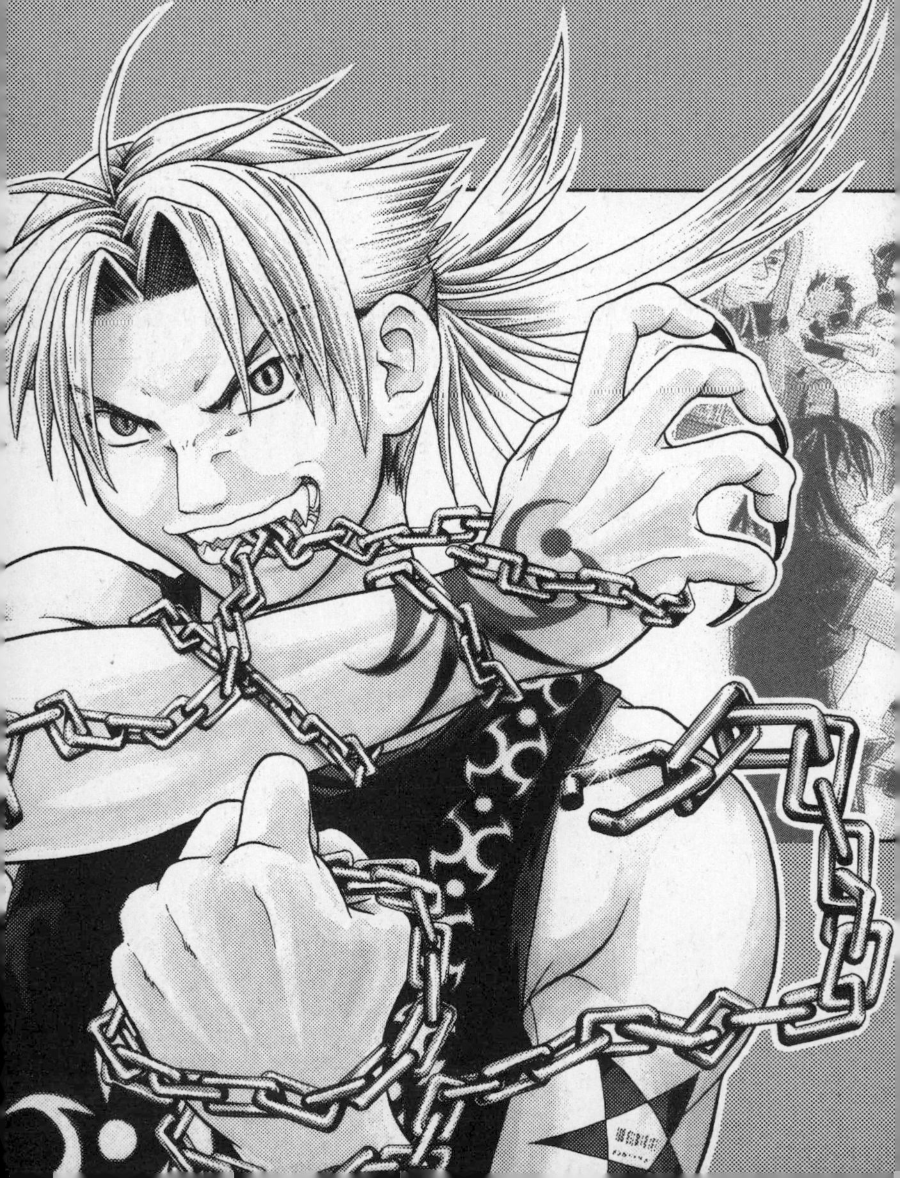

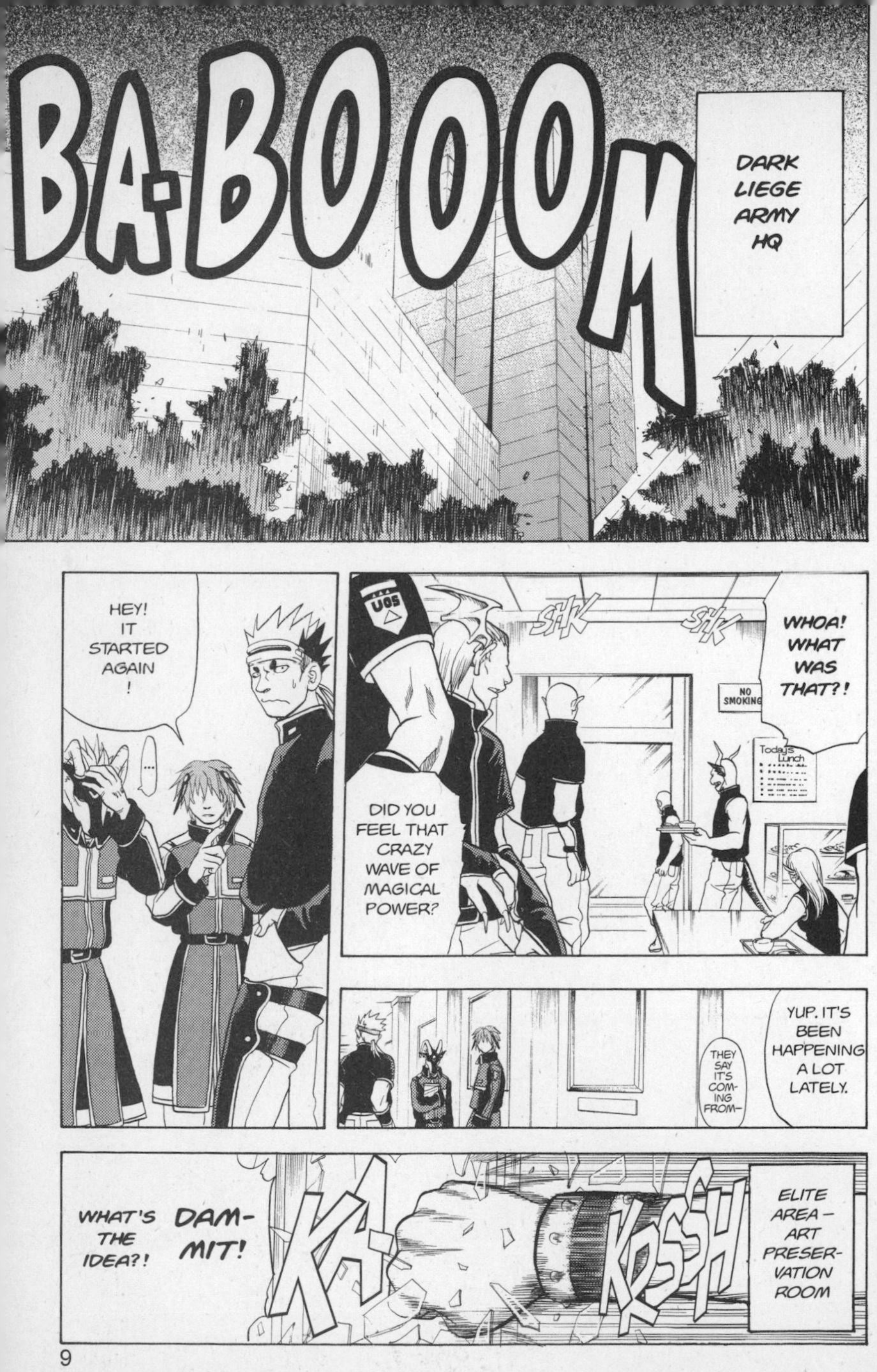
DARK LIEGE ARMY HQ
BA-BOOOM
SHK SHK
WHOA! WHAT WAS THAT?!
NO SMOKING
Today's Lunch
DID YOU FEEL THAT CRAZY WAVE OF MAGICAL POWER?
YUP. IT'S BEEN HAPPENING A LOT LATELY.
THEY SAY IT'S COMING FROM—
HEY! IT STARTED AGAIN!
...
ELITE AREA— ART PRESERVATION ROOM
KA-KRSH
DAM-MIT!
WHAT'S THE IDEA?!

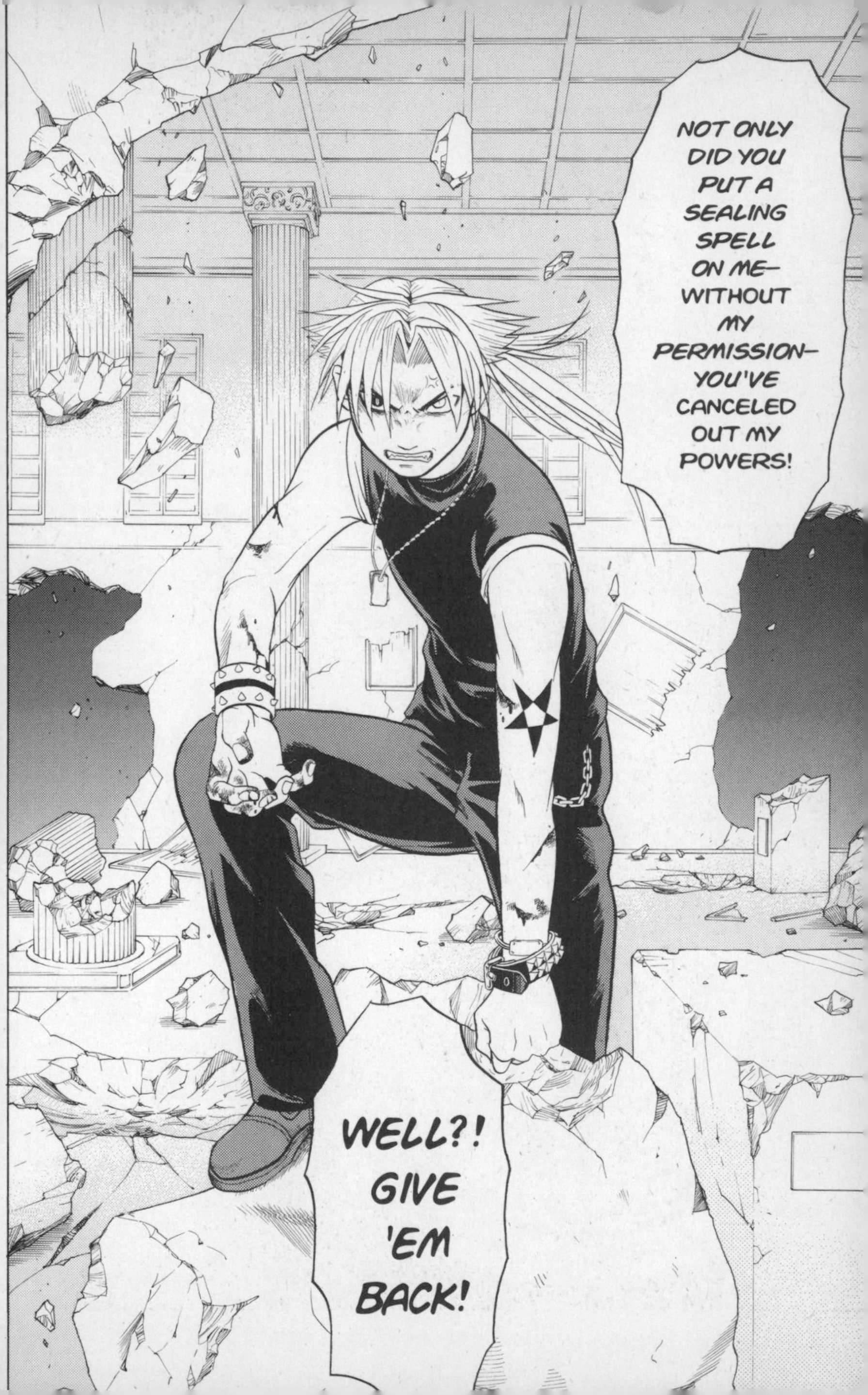
NOT ONLY DID YOU PUT A SEALING SPELL ON ME—WITHOUT MY PERMISSION—YOU'VE CANCELED OUT MY POWERS!
WELL?! GIVE 'EM BACK!

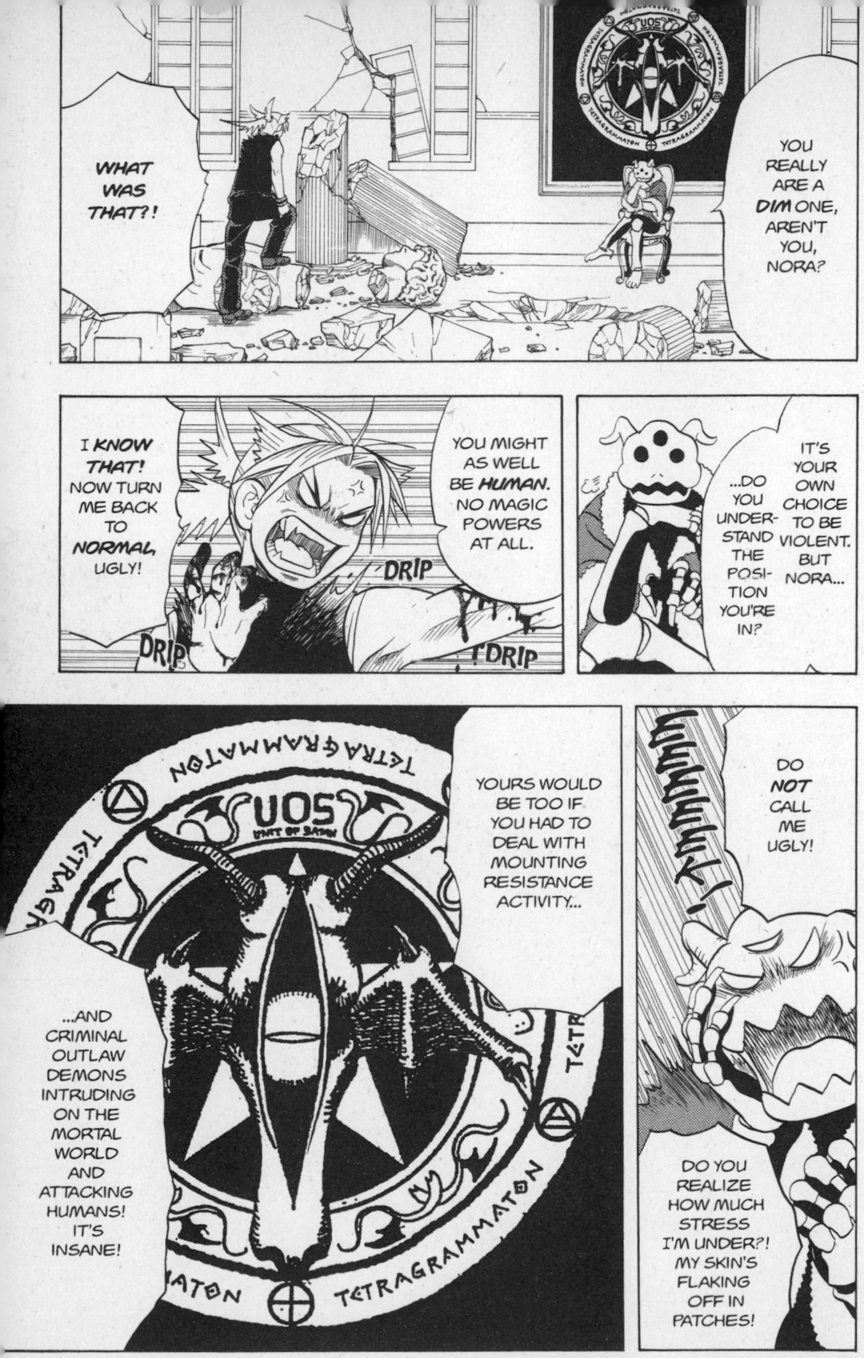

YOU REALLY ARE A DIM ONE, AREN'T YOU, NORA?
WHAT WAS THAT?!
IT'S YOUR OWN CHOICE TO BE VIOLENT. BUT NORA...
...DO YOU UNDERSTAND THE POSITION YOU'RE IN?
YOU MIGHT AS WELL BE HUMAN. NO MAGIC POWERS AT ALL.
I KNOW THAT! NOW TURN ME BACK TO NORMAL, UGLY!
DRIP
DRIP
DRIP
EEEEEEK!!
DO NOT CALL ME UGLY!
DO YOU REALIZE HOW MUCH STRESS I'M UNDER?! MY SKIN'S FLAKING OFF IN PATCHES!
YOURS WOULD BE TOO IF YOU HAD TO DEAL WITH MOUNTING RESISTANCE ACTIVITY...
...AND CRIMINAL OUTLAW DEMONS INTRUDING ON THE MORTAL WORLD AND ATTACKING HUMANS! IT'S INSANE!
UOS
UNIT OF SATAN
TETRAGRAMMATON

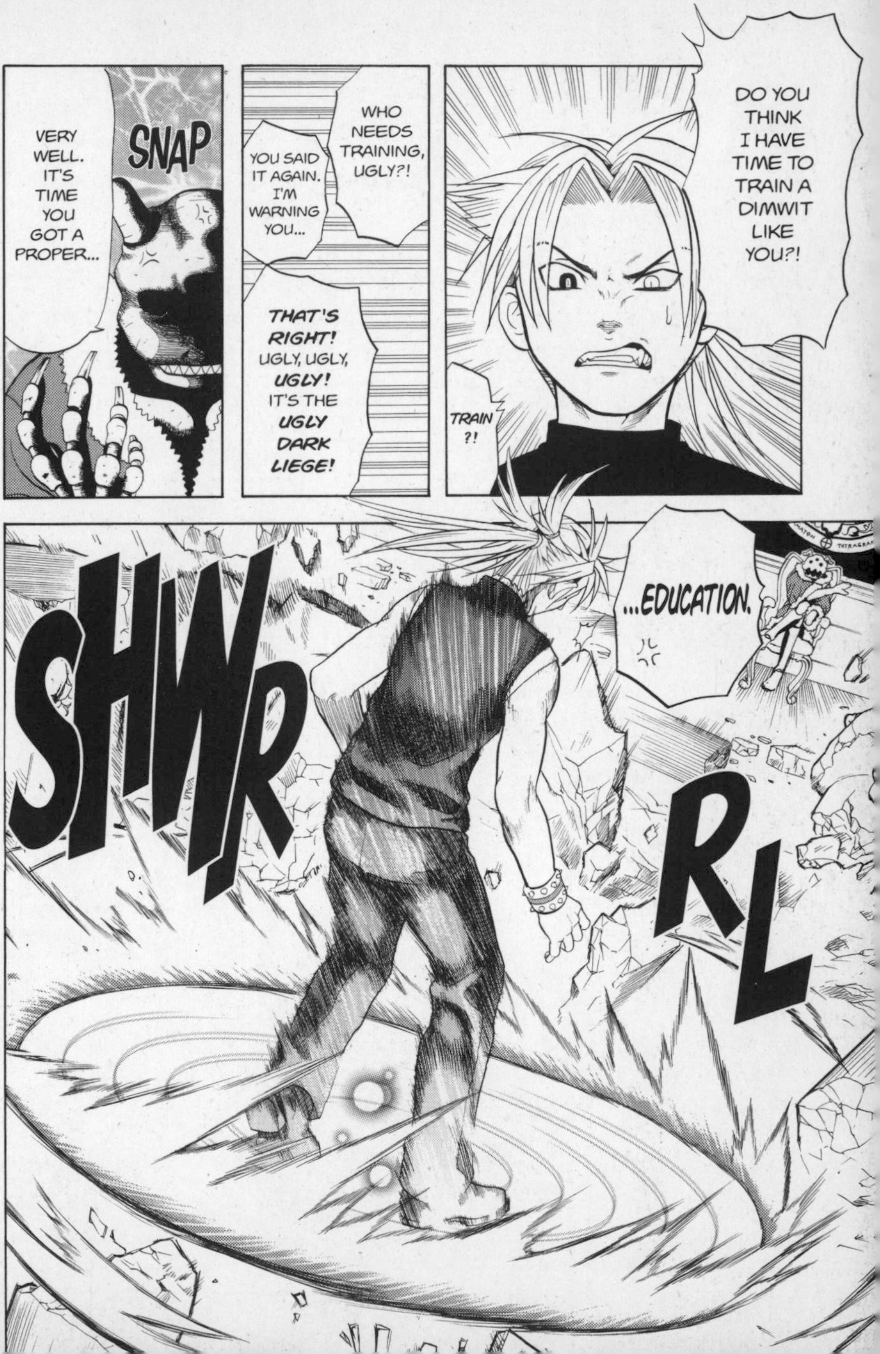
DO YOU THINK I HAVE TIME TO TRAIN A DIMWIT LIKE YOU?!
TRAIN ?!
WHO NEEDS TRAINING, UGLY?!
YOU SAID IT AGAIN. I'M WARNING YOU...
THAT'S RIGHT! UGLY, UGLY, UGLY! IT'S THE UGLY DARK LIEGE!
SNAP
VERY WELL. IT'S TIME YOU GOT A PROPER...
...EDUCATION.
SHWR
RL

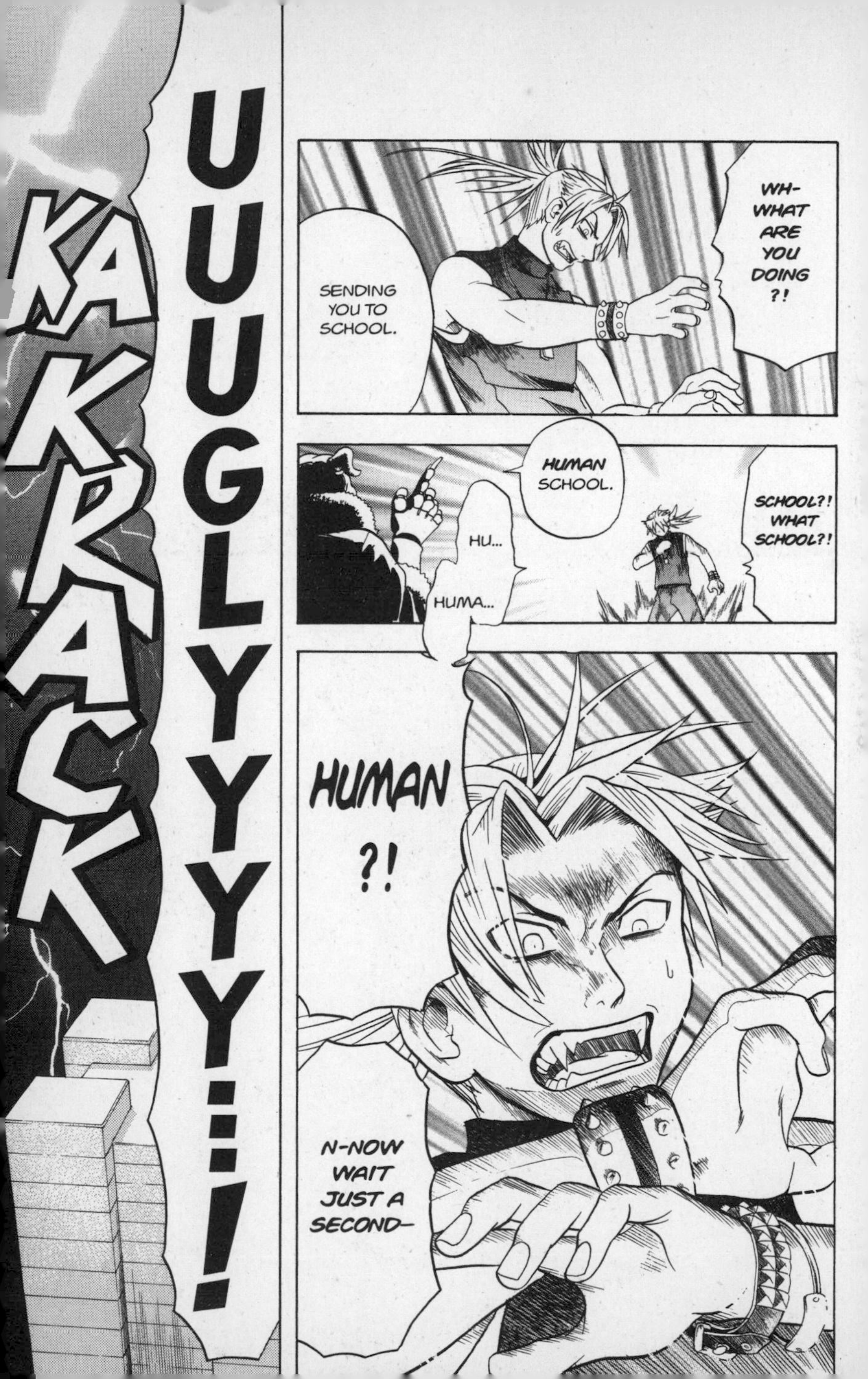
WH- WHAT ARE YOU DOING?!
SENDING YOU TO SCHOOL.
SCHOOL?! WHAT SCHOOL?!
HUMAN SCHOOL.
HU...
HUMA...
HUMAN ?!
N-NOW WAIT JUST A SECOND–
UUUGLYYYY!!!
KAKRACK

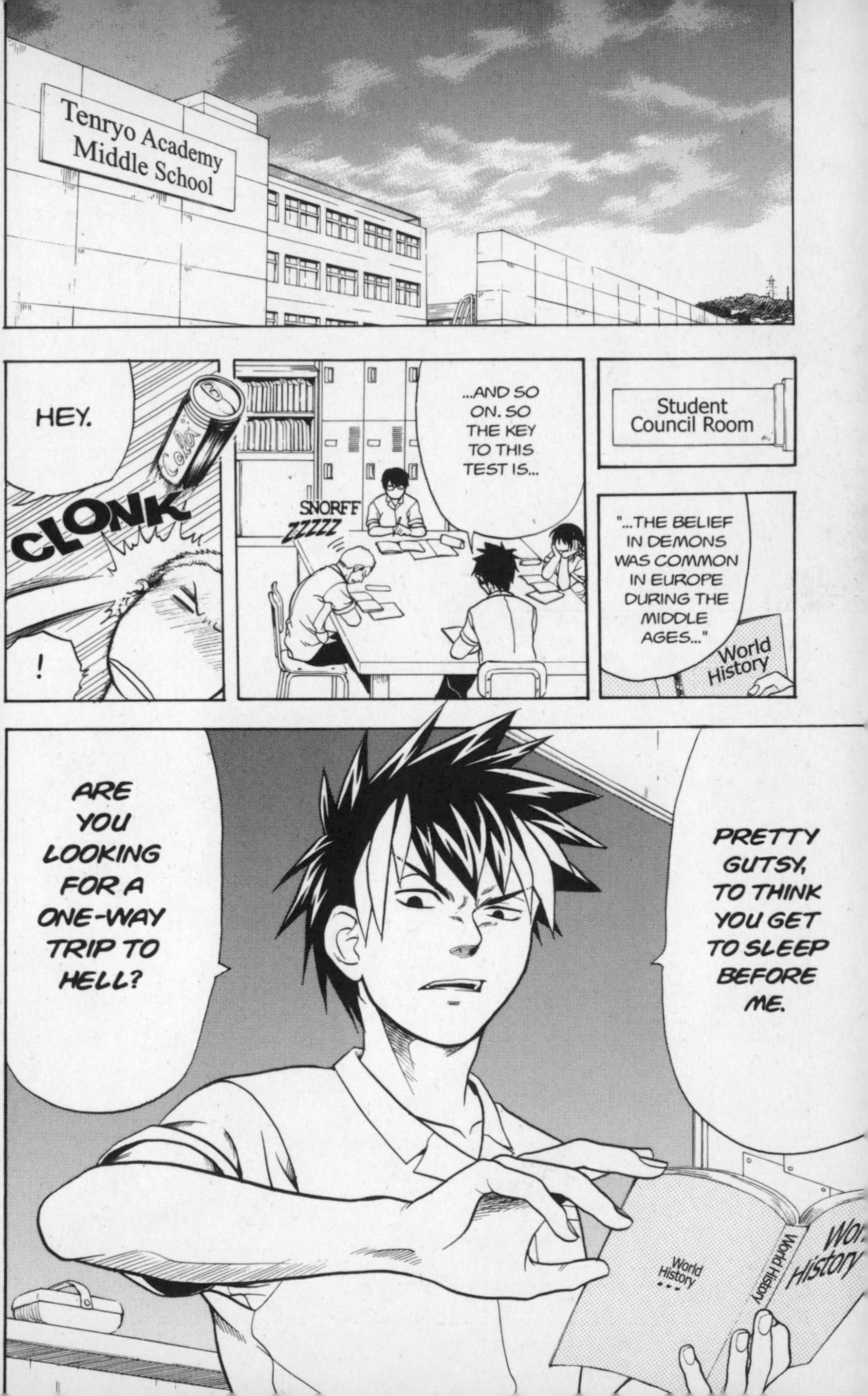

Tenryo Academy Middle School
Student Council Room
"...THE BELIEF IN DEMONS WAS COMMON IN EUROPE DURING THE MIDDLE AGES..."
World History
...AND SO ON. SO THE KEY TO THIS TEST IS...
SNORFF
ZZZZZ
HEY.
Cola
CLONK
!
PRETTY GUTSY, TO THINK YOU GET TO SLEEP BEFORE ME.
ARE YOU LOOKING FOR A ONE-WAY TRIP TO HELL?
World History
World History
World History

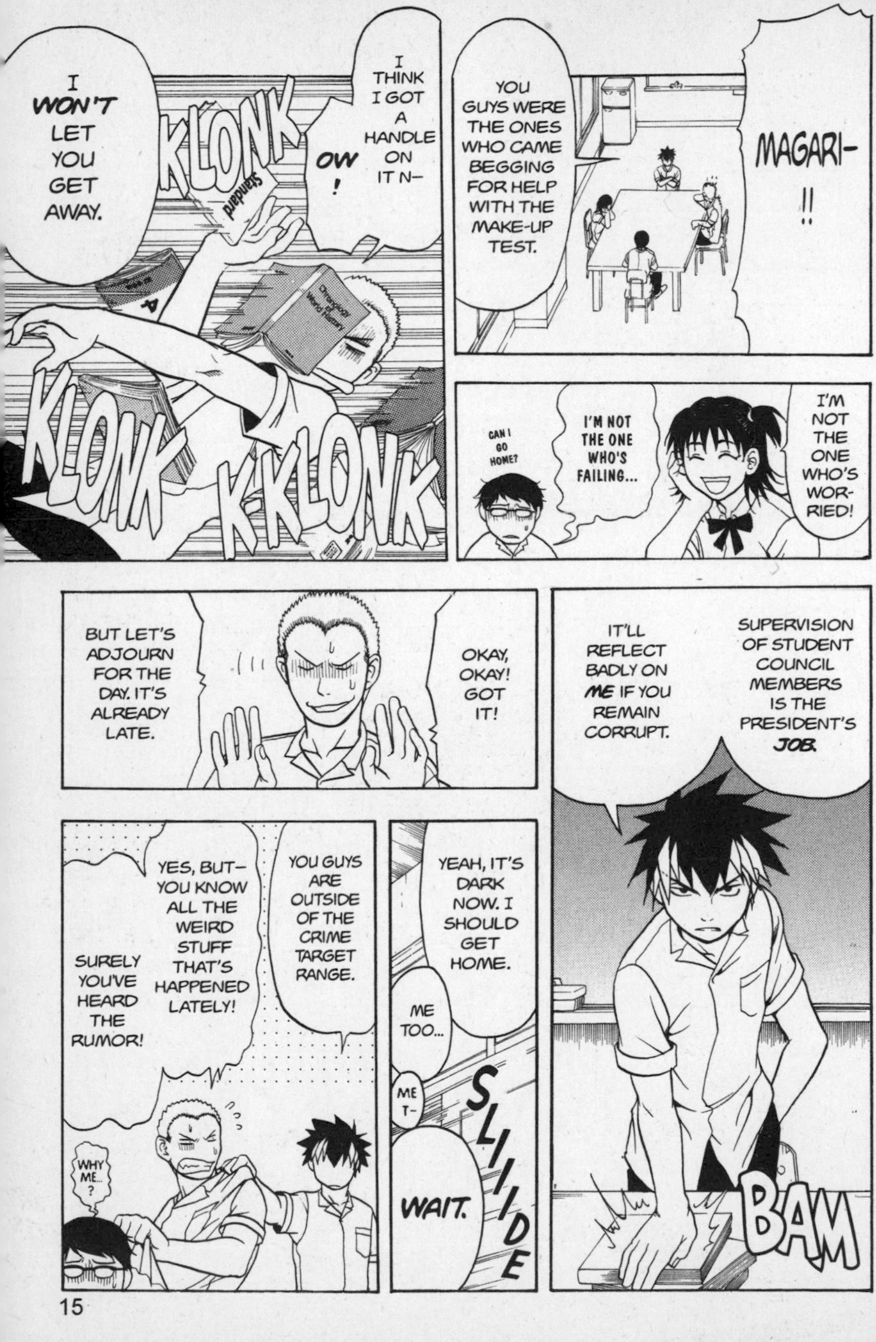
MAGARI-!!
YOU GUYS WERE THE ONES WHO CAME BEGGING FOR HELP WITH THE MAKE-UP TEST.
I'M NOT THE ONE WHO'S WORRIED!
I'M NOT THE ONE WHO'S FAILING...
CAN I GO HOME?
I THINK I GOT A HANDLE ON IT N-
OW!
KLONK
Standard
I WON'T LET YOU GET AWAY.
KLONK
K-KLONK
SUPERVISION OF STUDENT COUNCIL MEMBERS IS THE PRESIDENT'S JOB.
IT'LL REFLECT BADLY ON ME IF YOU REMAIN CORRUPT.
BAM
OKAY, OKAY! GOT IT!
BUT LET'S ADJOURN FOR THE DAY. IT'S ALREADY LATE.
YEAH, IT'S DARK NOW. I SHOULD GET HOME.
ME TOO...
ME T-
WAIT.
SLIIIDE
YOU GUYS ARE OUTSIDE OF THE CRIME TARGET RANGE.
YES, BUT— YOU KNOW ALL THE WEIRD STUFF THAT'S HAPPENED LATELY!
SURELY YOU'VE HEARD THE RUMOR!
WHY ME...?

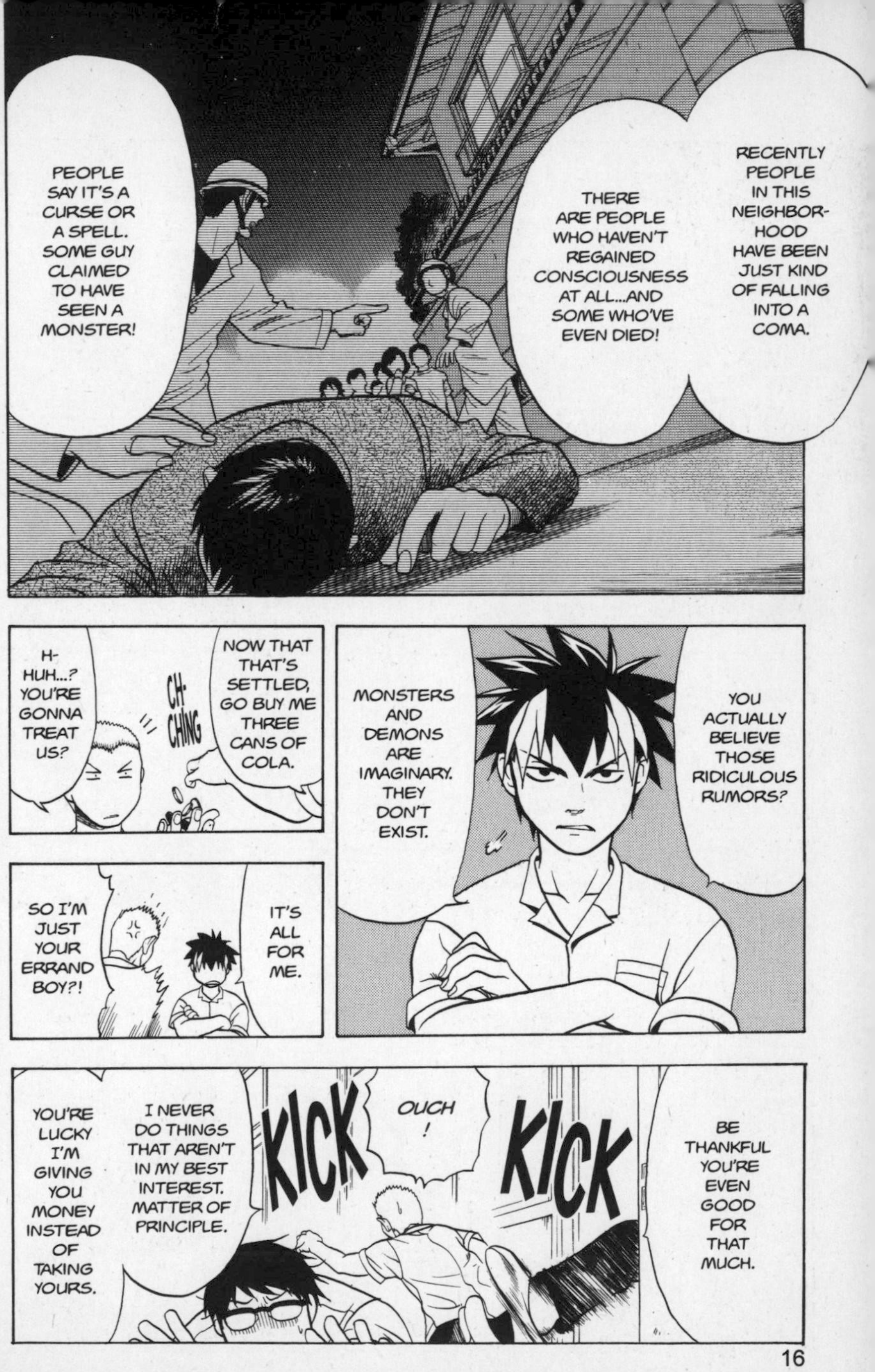
RECENTLY PEOPLE IN THIS NEIGHBOR-HOOD HAVE BEEN JUST KIND OF FALLING INTO A COMA.
THERE ARE PEOPLE WHO HAVEN'T REGAINED CONSCIOUSNESS AT ALL...AND SOME WHO'VE EVEN DIED!
PEOPLE SAY IT'S A CURSE OR A SPELL. SOME GUY CLAIMED TO HAVE SEEN A MONSTER!
YOU ACTUALLY BELIEVE THOSE RIDICULOUS RUMORS?
MONSTERS AND DEMONS ARE IMAGINARY. THEY DON'T EXIST.
NOW THAT THAT'S SETTLED, GO BUY ME THREE CANS OF COLA.
CH-CHING
H-HUH...? YOU'RE GONNA TREAT US?
IT'S ALL FOR ME.
SO I'M JUST YOUR ERRAND BOY?!
BE THANKFUL YOU'RE EVEN GOOD FOR THAT MUCH.
KICK
OUCH!
KICK
I NEVER DO THINGS THAT AREN'T IN MY BEST INTEREST. MATTER OF PRINCIPLE.
YOU'RE LUCKY I'M GIVING YOU MONEY INSTEAD OF TAKING YOURS.

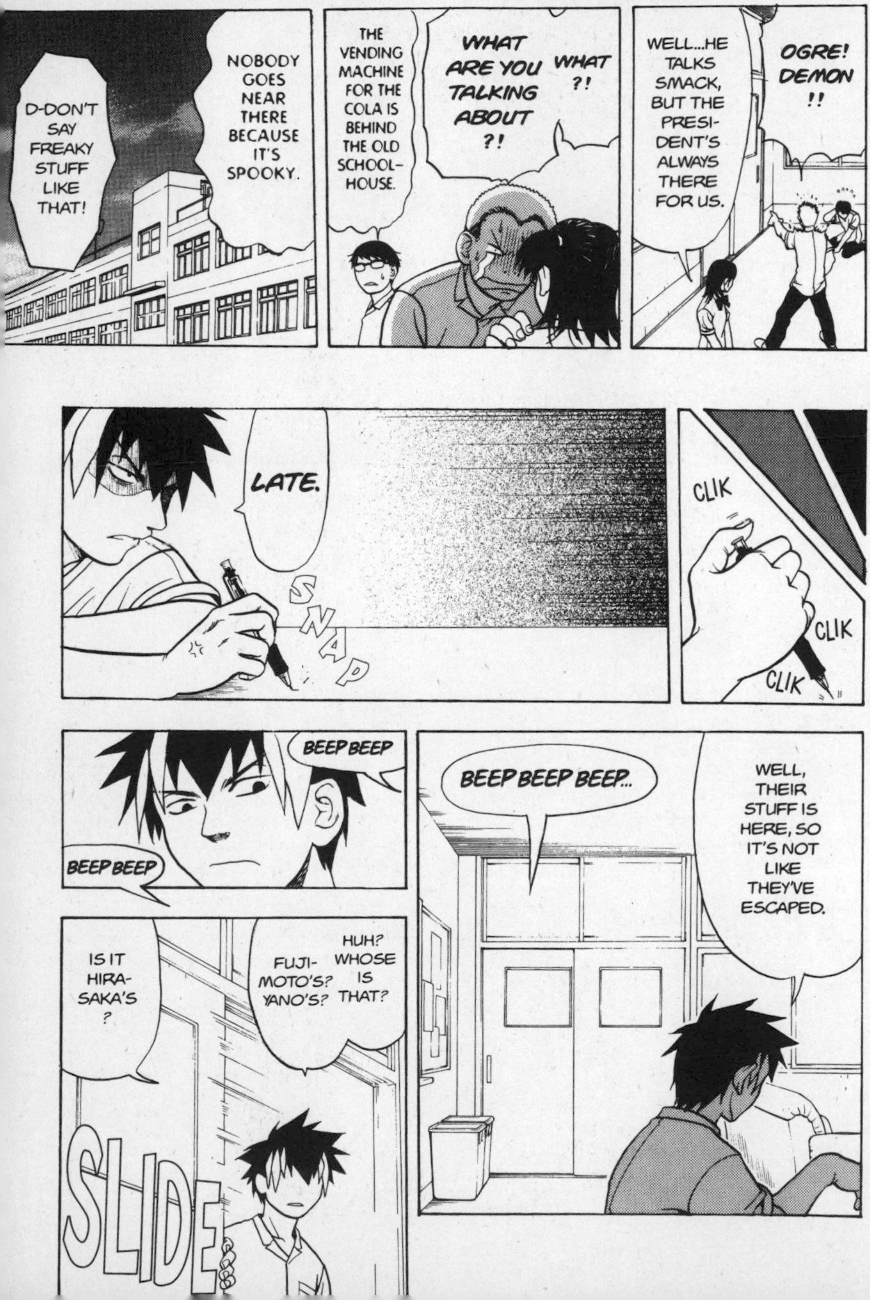
OGRE! DEMON!!
WELL...HE TALKS SMACK, BUT THE PRESI-DENT'S ALWAYS THERE FOR US.
WHAT?!
WHAT ARE YOU TALKING ABOUT?!
THE VENDING MACHINE FOR THE COLA IS BEHIND THE OLD SCHOOL-HOUSE.
NOBODY GOES NEAR THERE BECAUSE IT'S SPOOKY.
D-DON'T SAY FREAKY STUFF LIKE THAT!
CLIK
CLIK
CLIK
LATE.
SNAP
BEEP BEEP BEEP...
WELL, THEIR STUFF IS HERE, SO IT'S NOT LIKE THEY'VE ESCAPED.
BEEP BEEP
BEEP BEEP
HUH? WHOSE IS THAT?
FUJI-MOTO'S? YANO'S?
IS IT HIRA-SAKA'S?
SLIDE

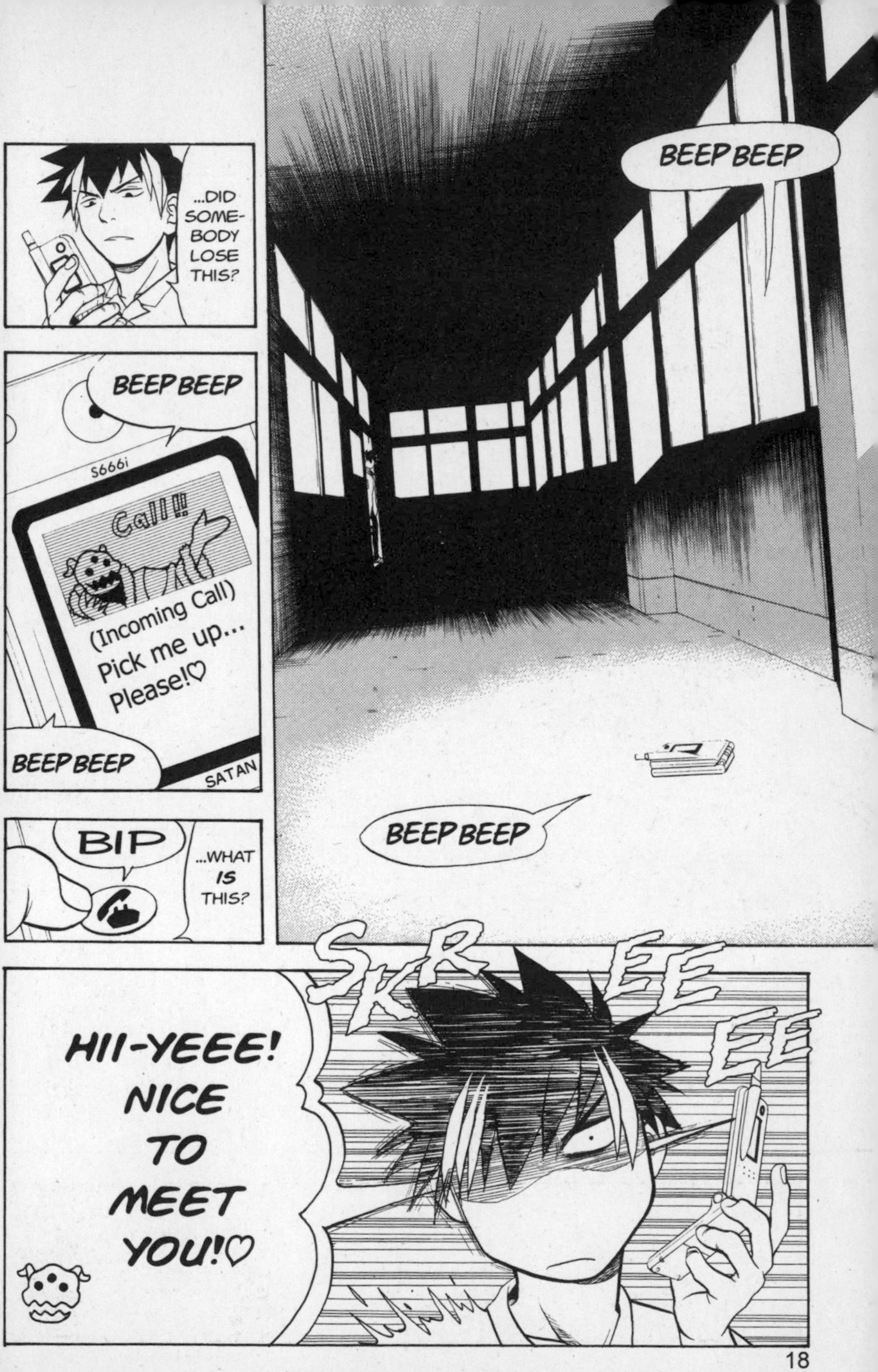
BEEP BEEP
BEEP BEEP
...DID SOMEBODY LOSE THIS?
BEEP BEEP
S666i
Call!!
(Incoming Call)
Pick me up...
Please!♡
BEEP BEEP
SATAN
BIP
...WHAT IS THIS?
SKREEEEEE
HII-YEEE! NICE TO MEET YOU!♡

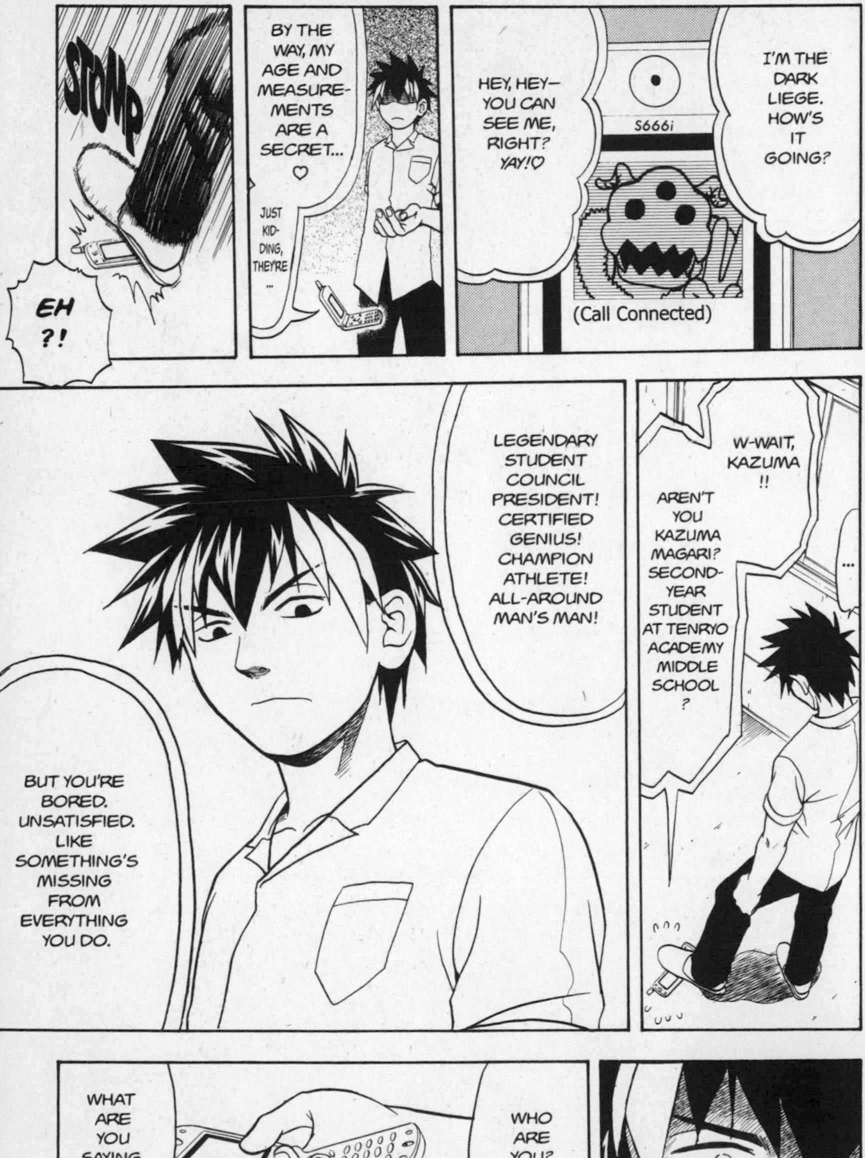
I'M THE DARK LIEGE. HOW'S IT GOING?
S666i
HEY, HEY— YOU CAN SEE ME, RIGHT? YAY!♡
(Call Connected)
BY THE WAY, MY AGE AND MEASURE-MENTS ARE A SECRET... ♡
JUST KID-DING, THEY'RE ...
STOMP
EH ?!
W-WAIT, KAZUMA !!
AREN'T YOU KAZUMA MAGARI? SECOND-YEAR STUDENT AT TENRYO ACADEMY MIDDLE SCHOOL ?
...
LEGENDARY STUDENT COUNCIL PRESIDENT! CERTIFIED GENIUS! CHAMPION ATHLETE! ALL-AROUND MAN'S MAN!
BUT YOU'RE BORED. UNSATISFIED. LIKE SOMETHING'S MISSING FROM EVERYTHING YOU DO.
WHO ARE YOU?
WHAT ARE YOU SAYING ?!

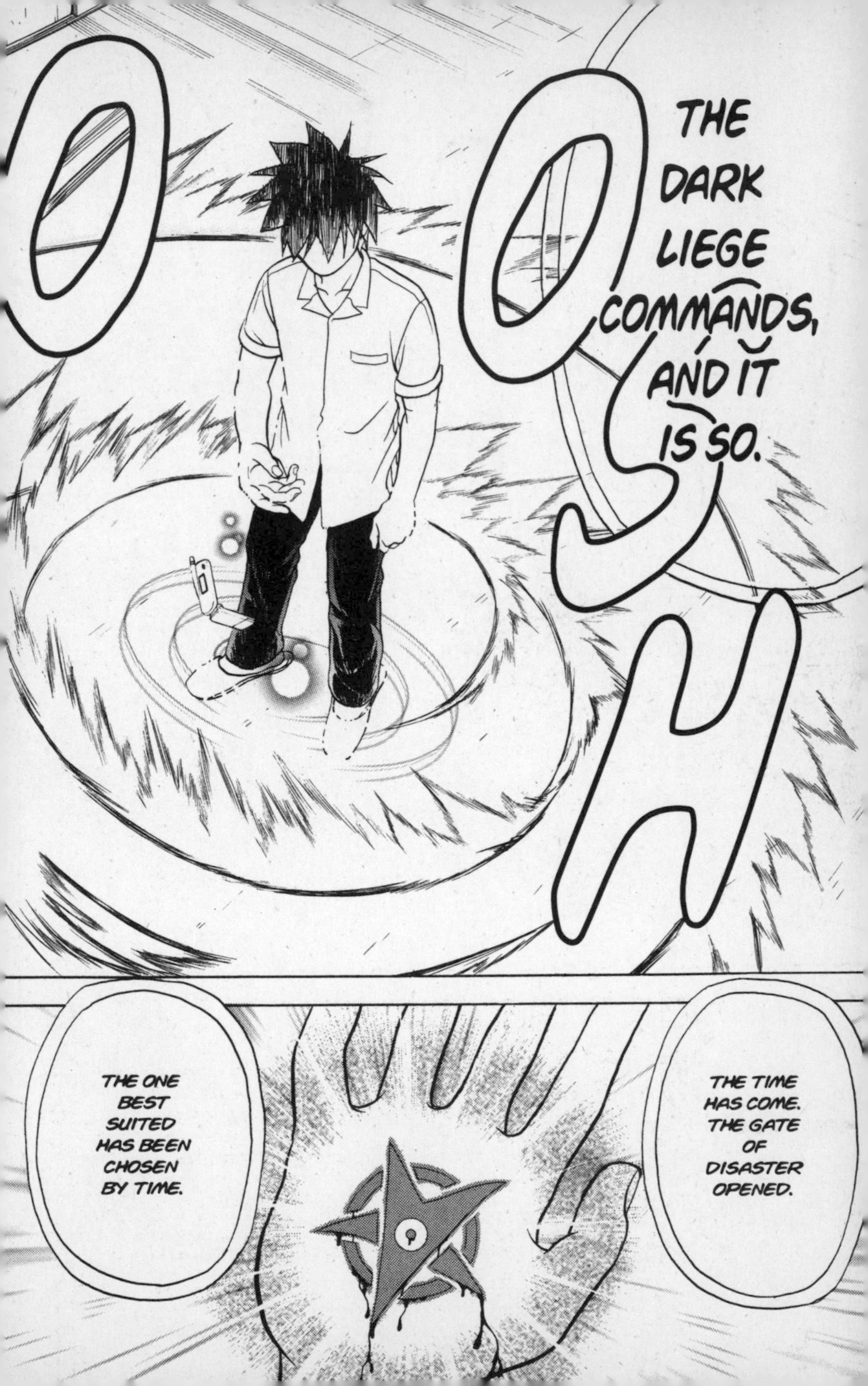
OOSH
THE DARK LIEGE COMMANDS, AND IT IS SO.
THE TIME HAS COME. THE GATE OF DISASTER OPENED.
THE ONE BEST SUITED HAS BEEN CHOSEN BY TIME.

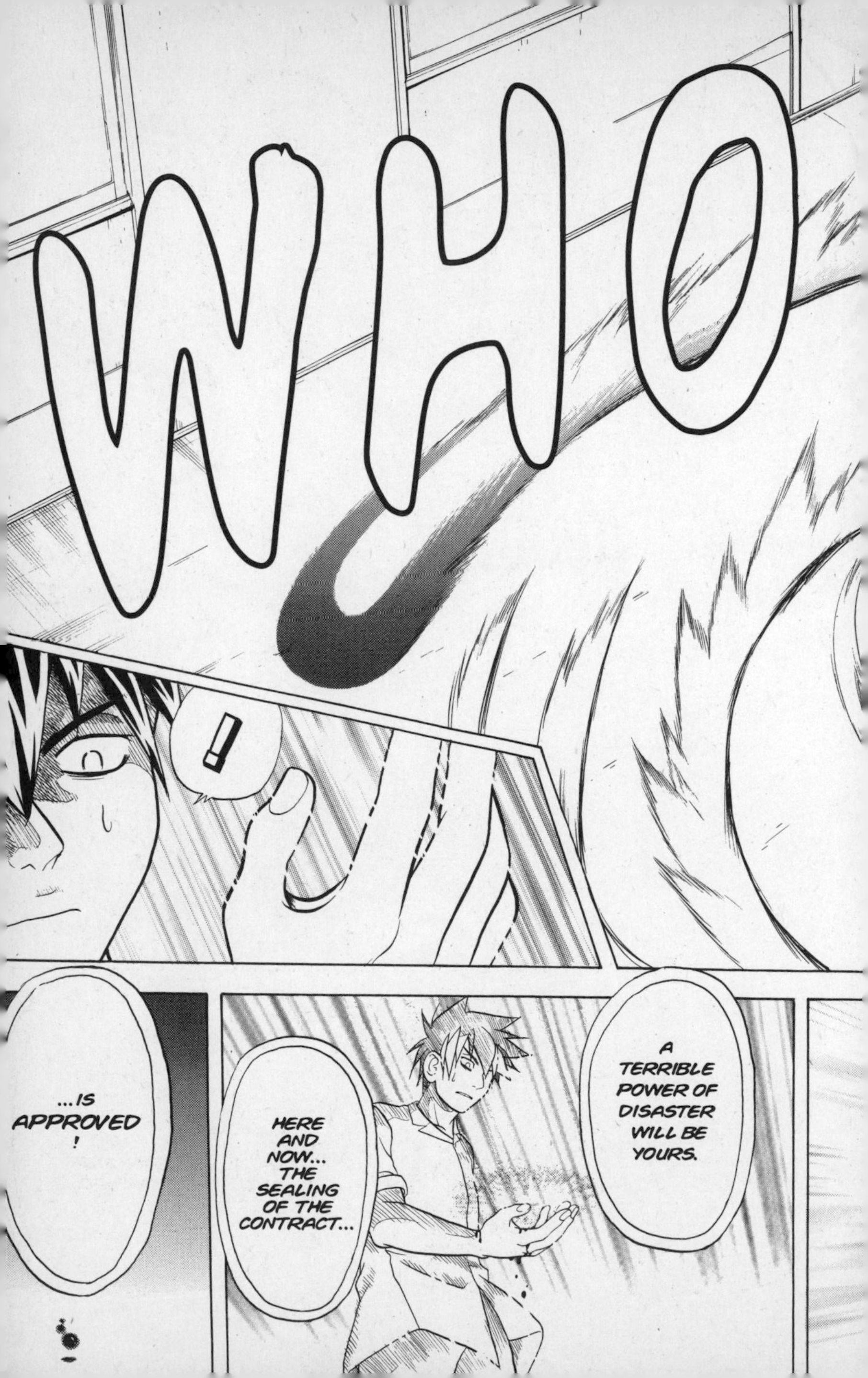
WHO
!
A TERRIBLE POWER OF DISASTER WILL BE YOURS.
HERE AND NOW... THE SEALING OF THE CONTRACT...
...IS APPROVED!

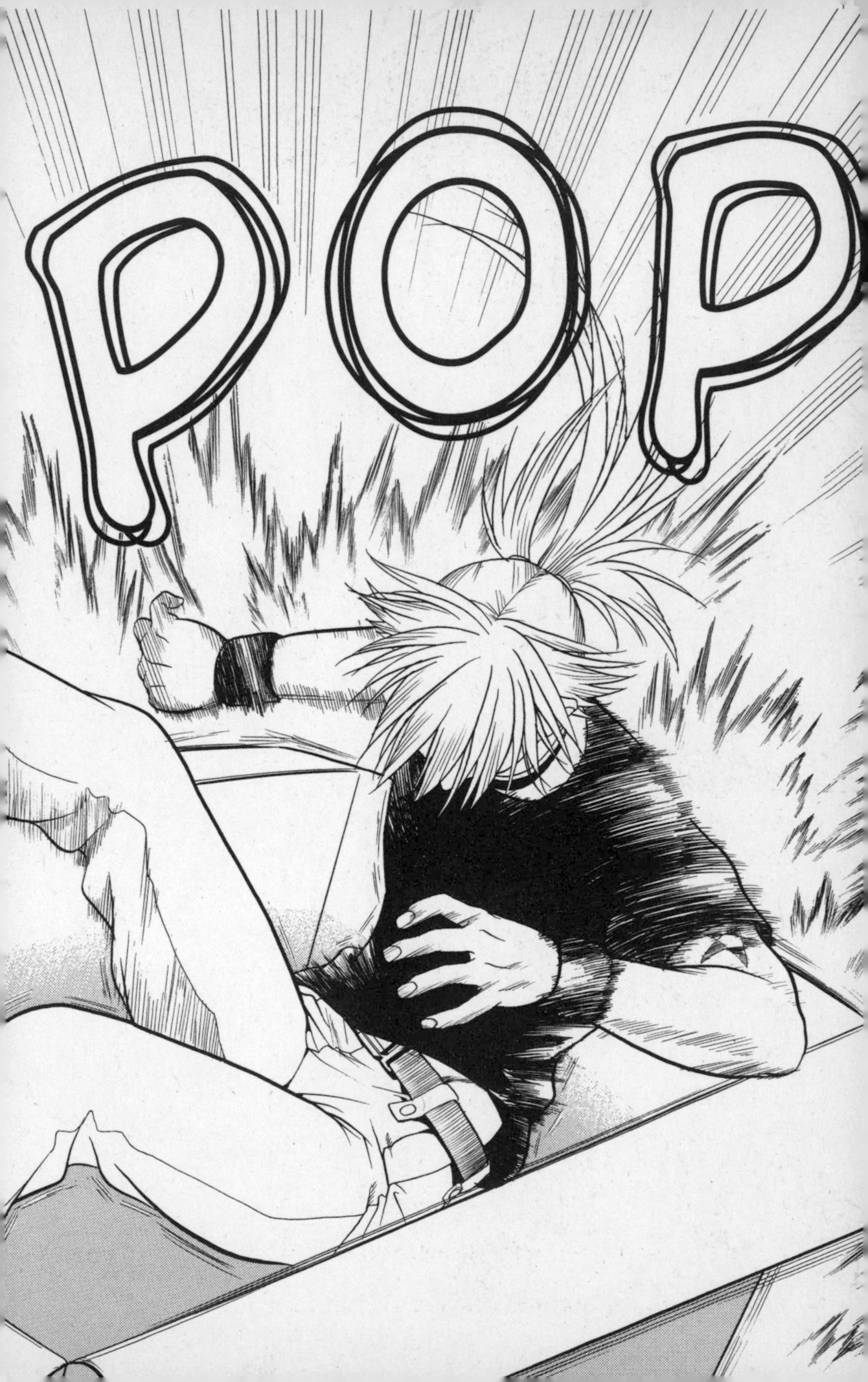
POP

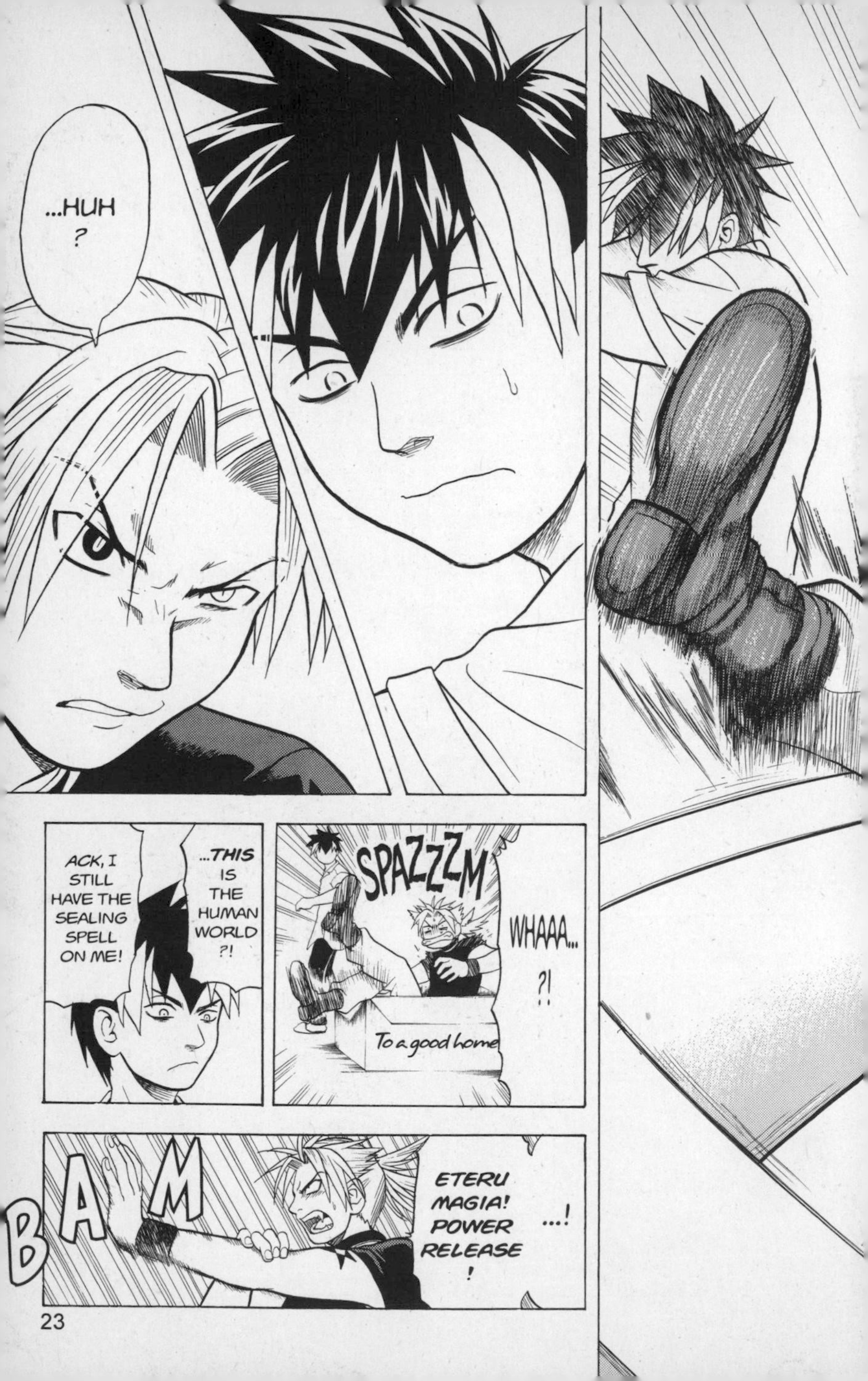
...HUH?
SPAZZZM
WHAAA...?!
To a good home
...THIS IS THE HUMAN WORLD?!
ACK, I STILL HAVE THE SEALING SPELL ON ME!
...!
ETERU MAGIA! POWER RELEASE!
BAM

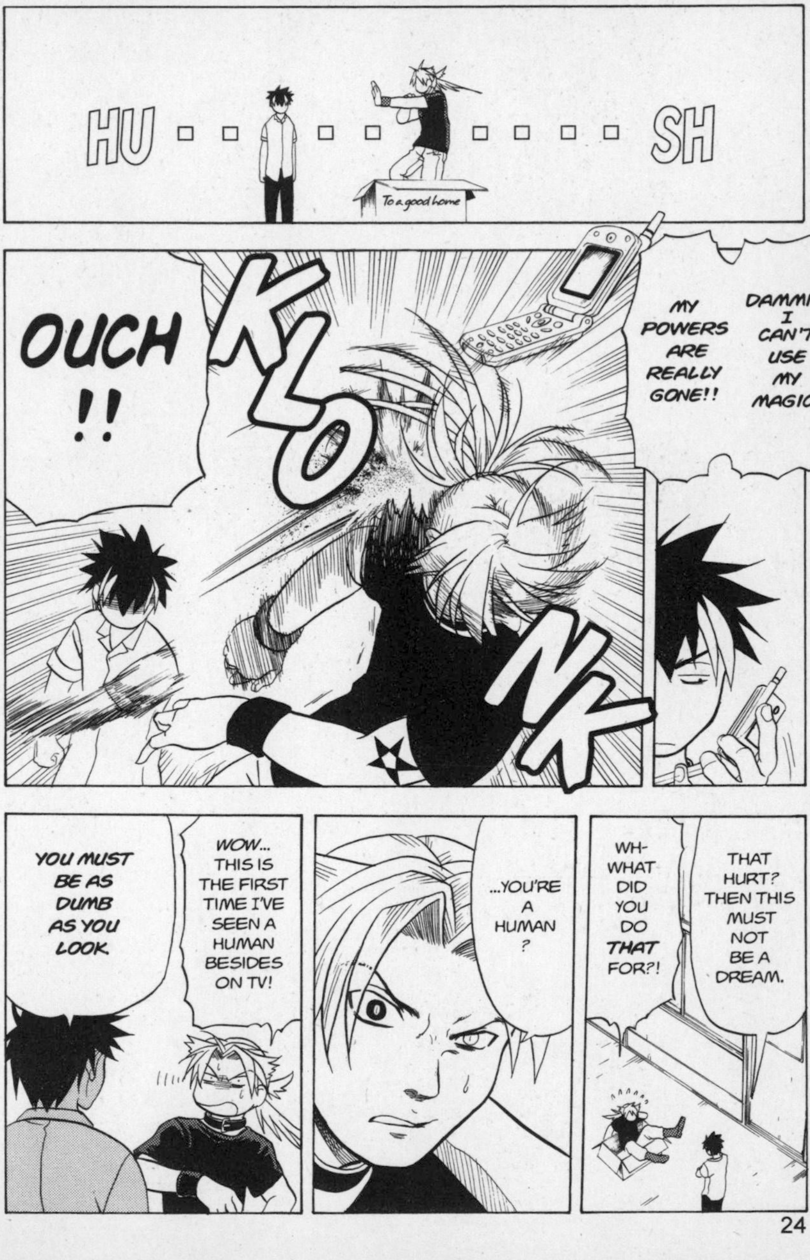
HU.........SH
To a good home
DAMMIT, I CAN'T USE MY MAGIC!
MY POWERS ARE REALLY GONE!!
KLONK
OUCH!!
THAT HURT? THEN THIS MUST NOT BE A DREAM.
WH-WHAT DID YOU DO THAT FOR?!
...YOU'RE A HUMAN?
WOW... THIS IS THE FIRST TIME I'VE SEEN A HUMAN BESIDES ON TV!
YOU MUST BE AS DUMB AS YOU LOOK.

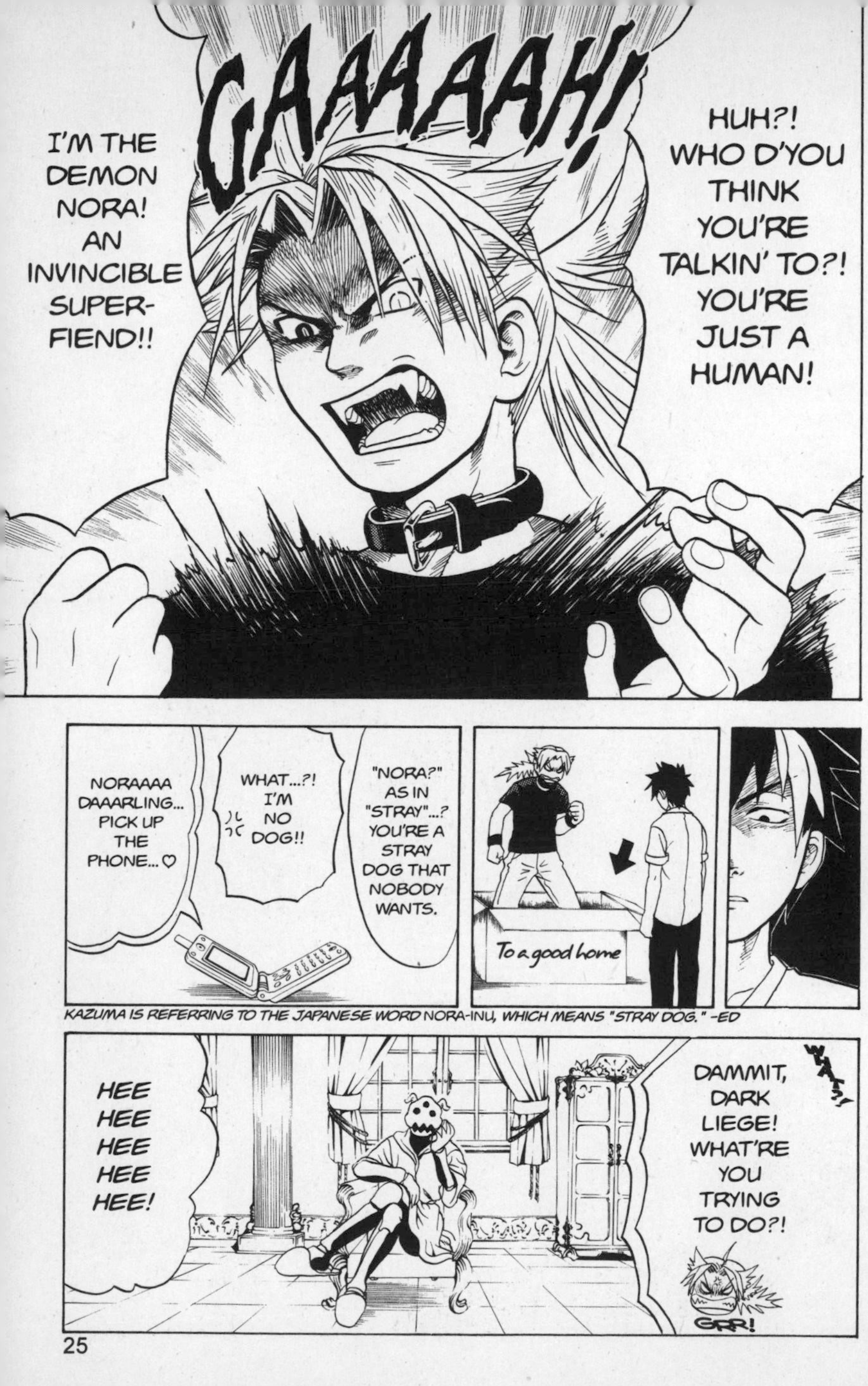
HUH?! WHO D'YOU THINK YOU'RE TALKIN' TO?! YOU'RE JUST A HUMAN!
GAAAAAH!
I'M THE DEMON NORA! AN INVINCIBLE SUPER-FIEND!!
To a good home
"NORA?" AS IN "STRAY"...? YOU'RE A STRAY DOG THAT NOBODY WANTS.
WHAT...?! I'M NO DOG!!
NORAAAA DAAARLING... PICK UP THE PHONE...♡
WHAT?!
DAMMIT, DARK LIEGE! WHAT'RE YOU TRYING TO DO?!
GRR!
HEE HEE HEE HEE HEE!
KAZUMA IS REFERRING TO THE JAPANESE WORD NORA-INU, WHICH MEANS "STRAY DOG." -ED

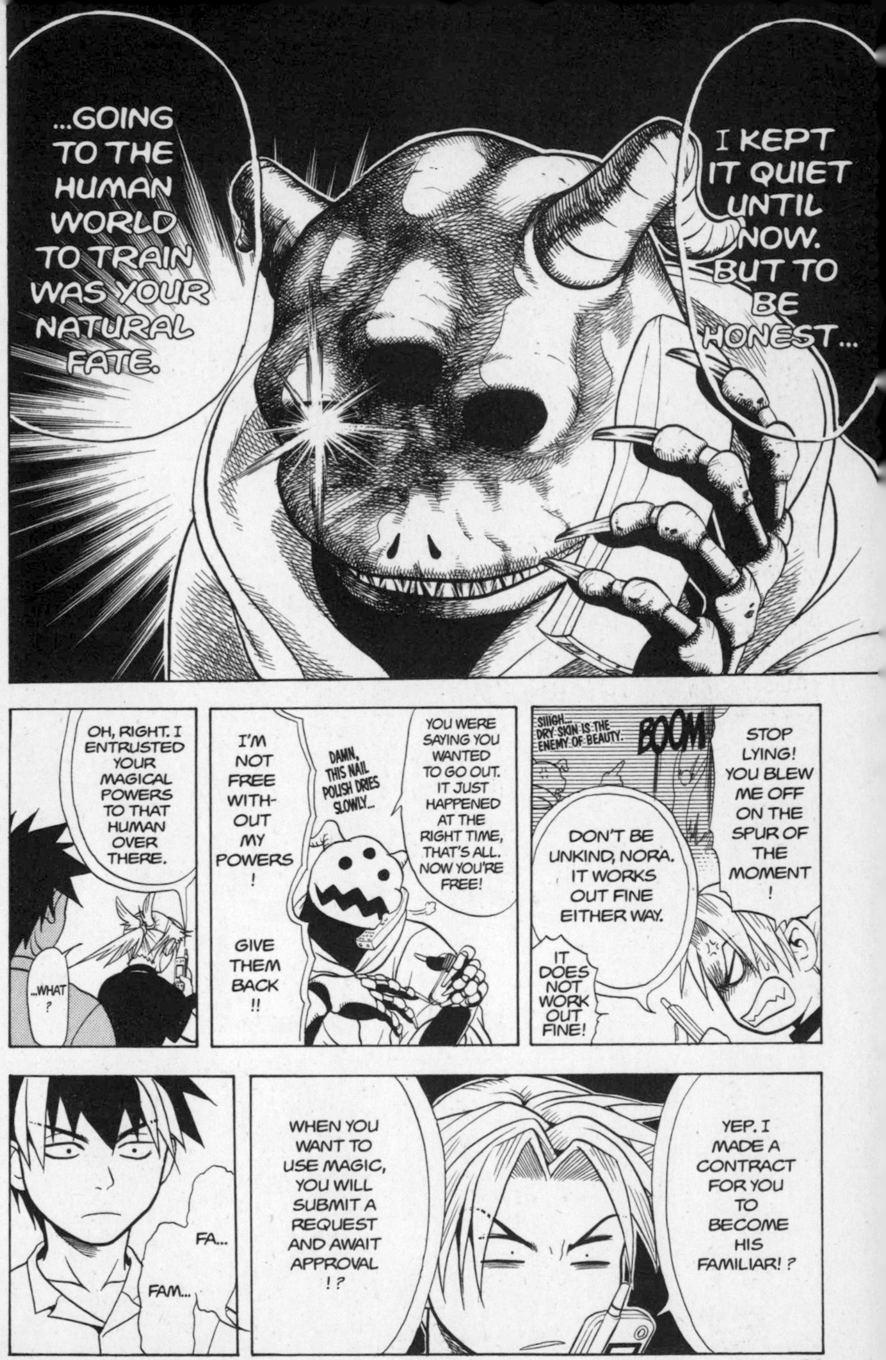
I KEPT IT QUIET UNTIL NOW. BUT TO BE HONEST...
...GOING TO THE HUMAN WORLD TO TRAIN WAS YOUR NATURAL FATE.
STOP LYING! YOU BLEW ME OFF ON THE SPUR OF THE MOMENT!
SIIIGH... DRY SKIN IS THE ENEMY OF BEAUTY.
BOOM
DON'T BE UNKIND, NORA. IT WORKS OUT FINE EITHER WAY.
IT DOES NOT WORK OUT FINE!
YOU WERE SAYING YOU WANTED TO GO OUT. IT JUST HAPPENED AT THE RIGHT TIME, THAT'S ALL. NOW YOU'RE FREE!
DAMN, THIS NAIL POLISH DRIES SLOWLY...
I'M NOT FREE WITHOUT MY POWERS!
GIVE THEM BACK!!
OH, RIGHT. I ENTRUSTED YOUR MAGICAL POWERS TO THAT HUMAN OVER THERE.
...WHAT?
YEP. I MADE A CONTRACT FOR YOU TO BECOME HIS FAMILIAR!?
WHEN YOU WANT TO USE MAGIC, YOU WILL SUBMIT A REQUEST AND AWAIT APPROVAL!?
FA...
FAM...

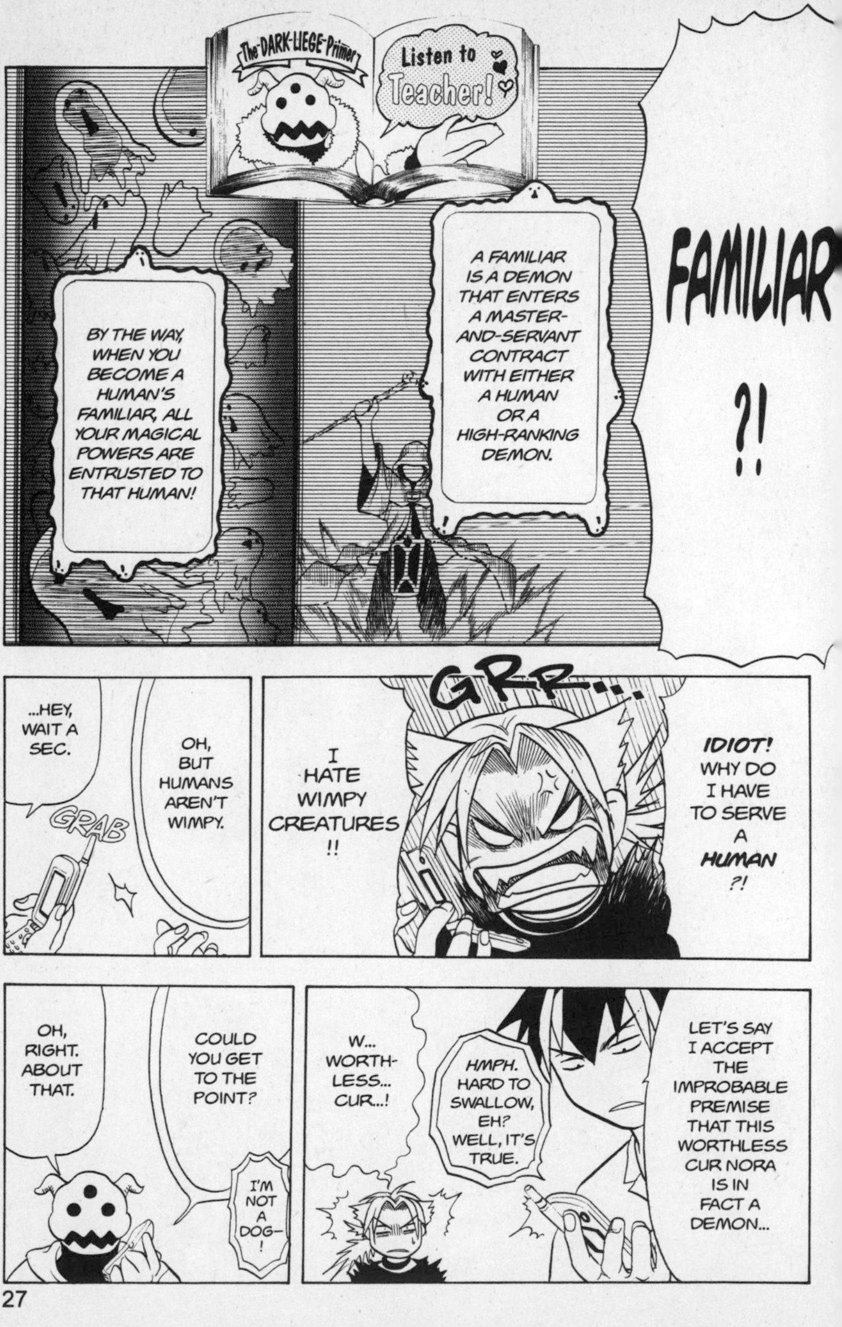
FAMILIAR
?!
The DARK-LIEGE-Primer
Listen to Teacher!
A FAMILIAR IS A DEMON THAT ENTERS A MASTER-AND-SERVANT CONTRACT WITH EITHER A HUMAN OR A HIGH-RANKING DEMON.
BY THE WAY, WHEN YOU BECOME A HUMAN'S FAMILIAR, ALL YOUR MAGICAL POWERS ARE ENTRUSTED TO THAT HUMAN!
GRR...
IDIOT! WHY DO I HAVE TO SERVE A HUMAN ?!
I HATE WIMPY CREATURES !!
OH, BUT HUMANS AREN'T WIMPY.
...HEY, WAIT A SEC.
GRAB
LET'S SAY I ACCEPT THE IMPROBABLE PREMISE THAT THIS WORTHLESS CUR NORA IS IN FACT A DEMON...
HMPH. HARD TO SWALLOW, EH? WELL, IT'S TRUE.
W... WORTHLESS... CUR...!
COULD YOU GET TO THE POINT?
I'M NOT A DOG-!
OH, RIGHT. ABOUT THAT.

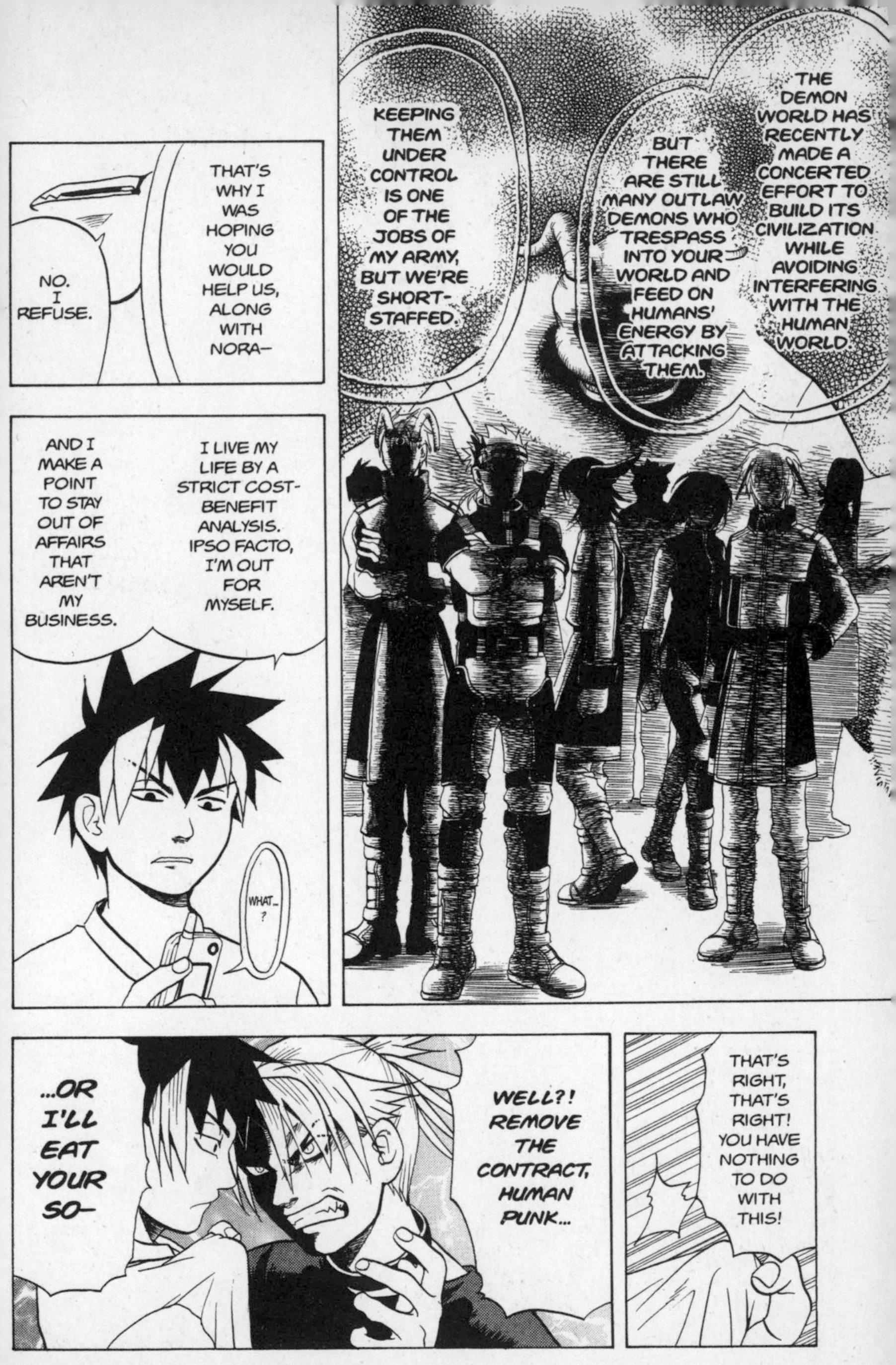
THE DEMON WORLD HAS RECENTLY MADE A CONCERTED EFFORT TO BUILD ITS CIVILIZATION WHILE AVOIDING INTERFERING WITH THE HUMAN WORLD.
BUT THERE ARE STILL MANY OUTLAW DEMONS WHO TRESPASS INTO YOUR WORLD AND FEED ON HUMANS' ENERGY BY ATTACKING THEM.
KEEPING THEM UNDER CONTROL IS ONE OF THE JOBS OF MY ARMY, BUT WE'RE SHORT-STAFFED.
THAT'S WHY I WAS HOPING YOU WOULD HELP US, ALONG WITH NORA—
NO. I REFUSE.
I LIVE MY LIFE BY A STRICT COST-BENEFIT ANALYSIS. IPSO FACTO, I'M OUT FOR MYSELF.
AND I MAKE A POINT TO STAY OUT OF AFFAIRS THAT AREN'T MY BUSINESS.
WHAT...?
THAT'S RIGHT, THAT'S RIGHT! YOU HAVE NOTHING TO DO WITH THIS!
WELL?! REMOVE THE CONTRACT, HUMAN PUNK...
...OR I'LL EAT YOUR SO—

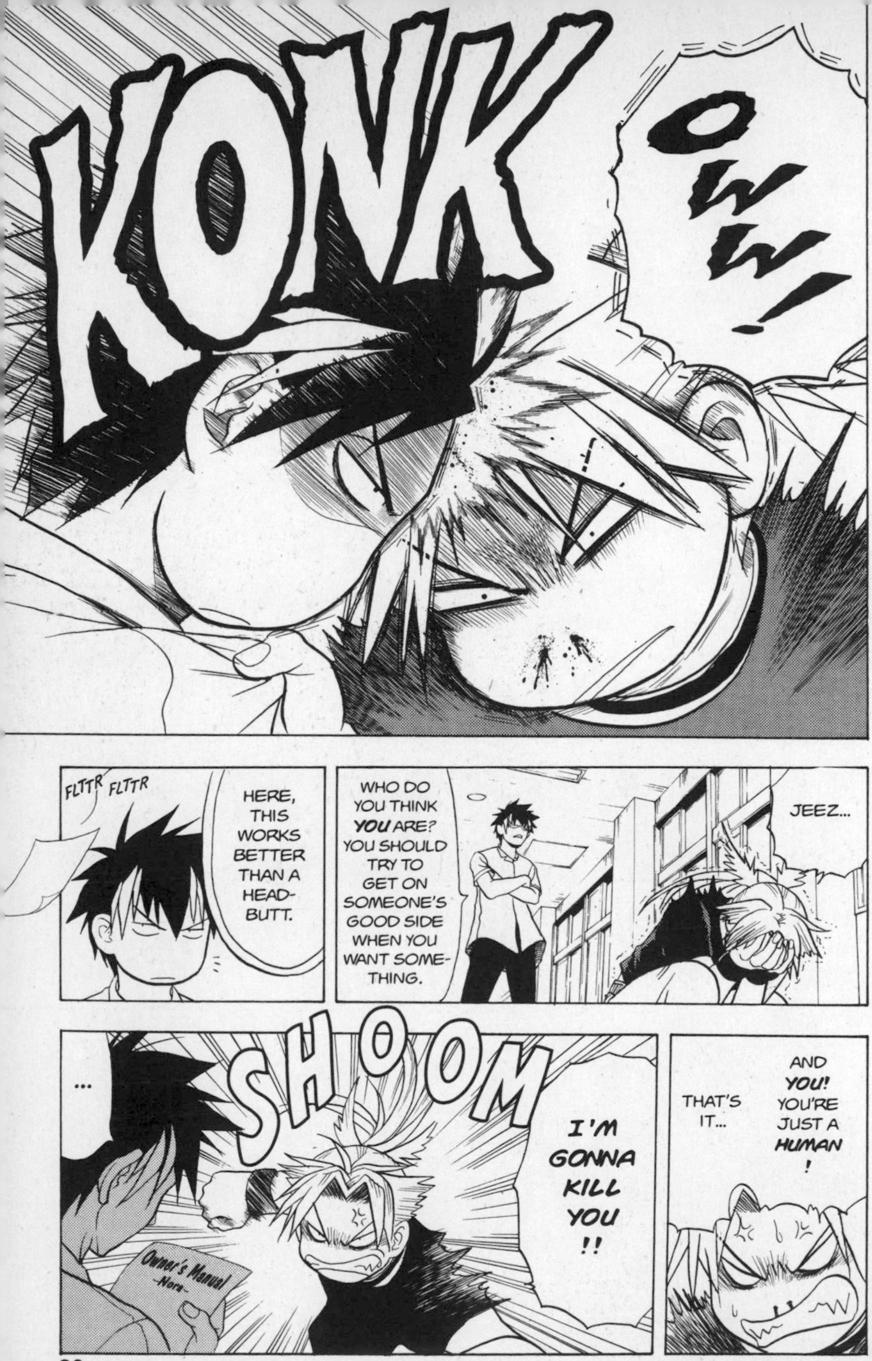
OWW!
KONK
JEEZ...
WHO DO YOU THINK YOU ARE? YOU SHOULD TRY TO GET ON SOMEONE'S GOOD SIDE WHEN YOU WANT SOME-THING.
HERE, THIS WORKS BETTER THAN A HEAD-BUTT.
FLTTR FLTTR
AND YOU! YOU'RE JUST A HUMAN!
THAT'S IT...
I'M GONNA KILL YOU!!
SHOOM
...
Owner's Manual
-Nora-

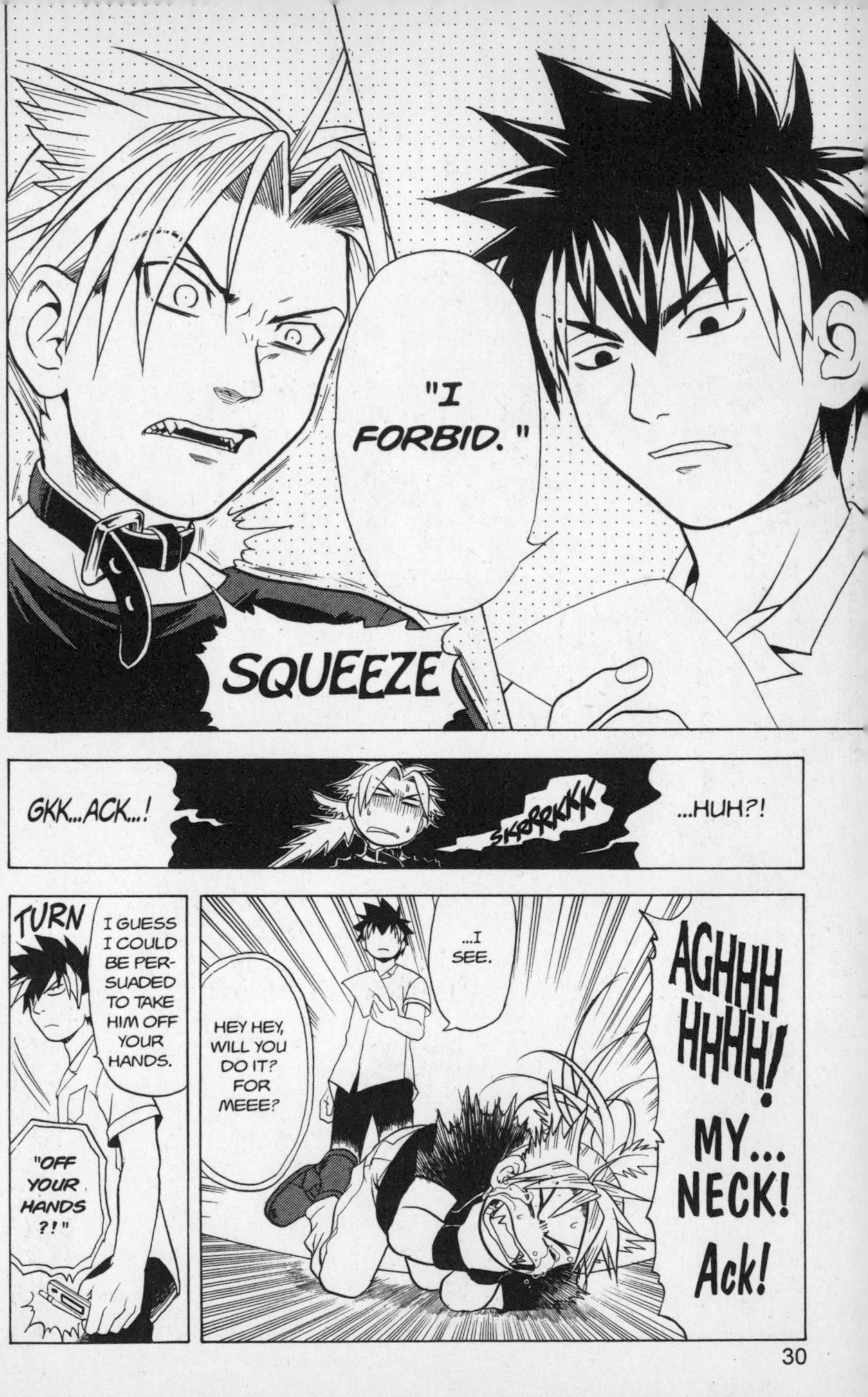

"I FORBID."
SQUEEZE
...HUH?!
SKRRRKKK
GKK...ACK...!
AGHHHHHHH!
MY... NECK!
Ack!
...I SEE.
HEY HEY, WILL YOU DO IT? FOR MEEE?
TURN
I GUESS I COULD BE PER-SUADED TO TAKE HIM OFF YOUR HANDS.
"OFF YOUR HANDS?!"
TURN

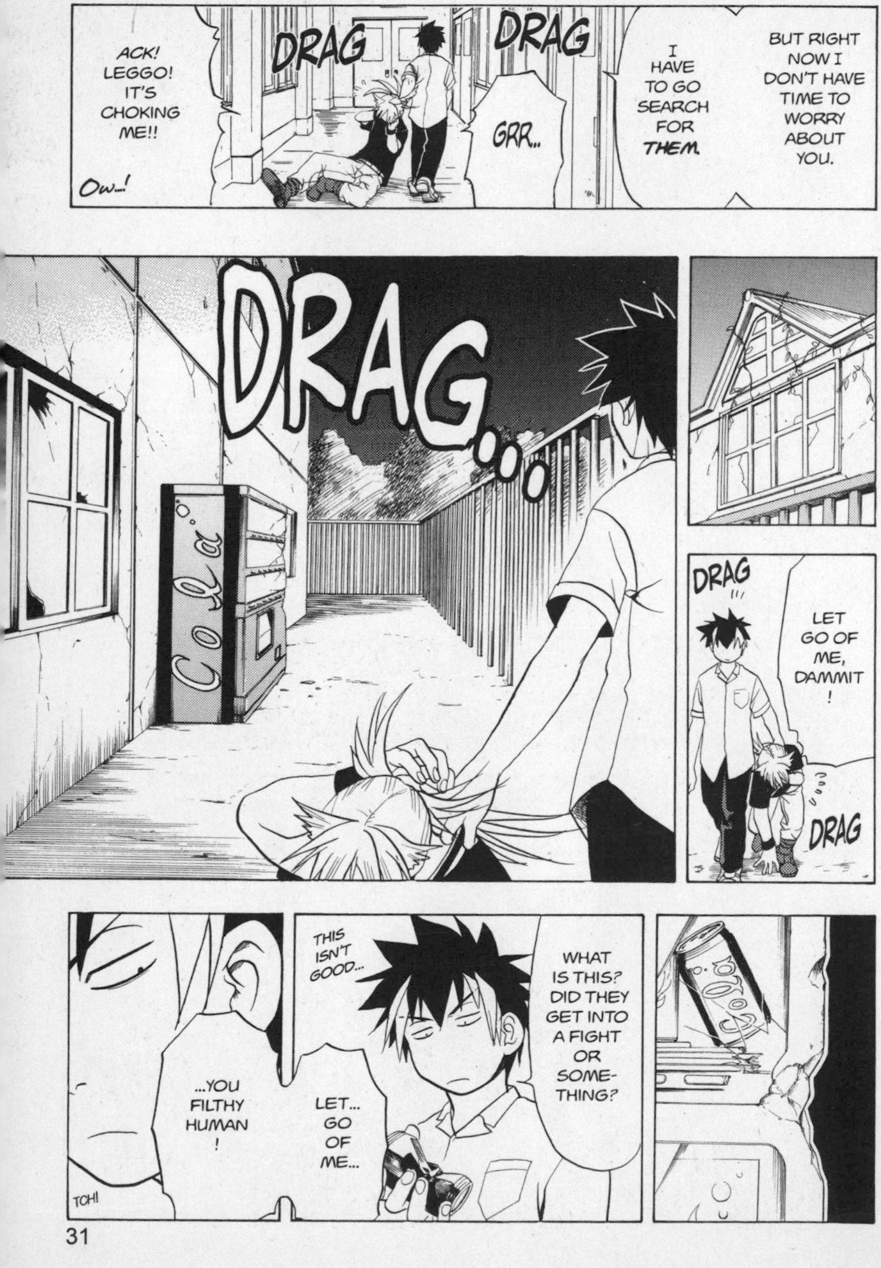
BUT RIGHT NOW I DON'T HAVE TIME TO WORRY ABOUT YOU.
I HAVE TO GO SEARCH FOR THEM.
DRAG
DRAG
GRR...
ACK! LEGGO! IT'S CHOKING ME!!
Ow...!
DRAG
LET GO OF ME, DAMMIT!
DRAG
DRAG...
Cola
WHAT IS THIS? DID THEY GET INTO A FIGHT OR SOMETHING?
THIS ISN'T GOOD...
LET... GO OF ME...
...YOU FILTHY HUMAN!
TCH!

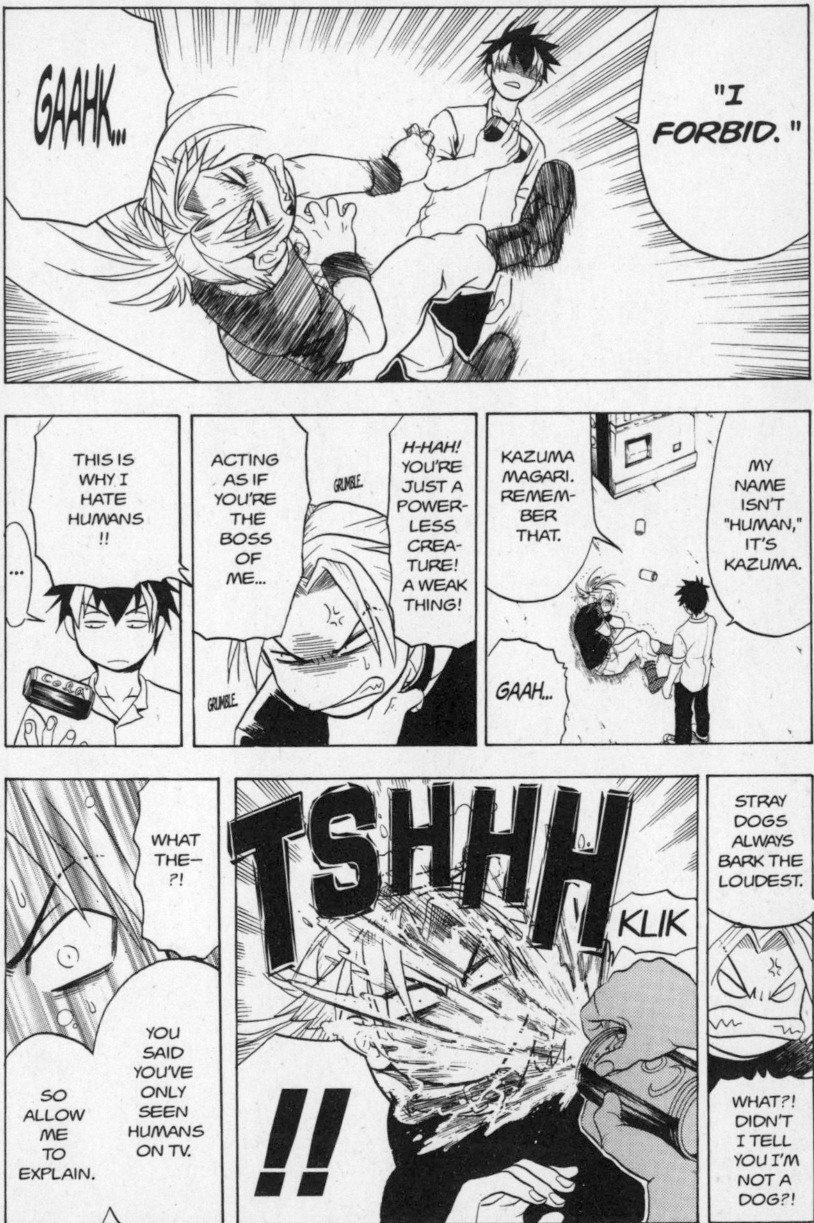
"I FORBID."
GAAHK...
MY NAME ISN'T "HUMAN," IT'S KAZUMA.
KAZUMA MAGARI. REMEMBER THAT.
GAAH...
H-HAH! YOU'RE JUST A POWERLESS CREATURE! A WEAK THING!
GRUMBLE
ACTING AS IF YOU'RE THE BOSS OF ME...
GRUMBLE
THIS IS WHY I HATE HUMANS!!
...
STRAY DOGS ALWAYS BARK THE LOUDEST.
WHAT?! DIDN'T I TELL YOU I'M NOT A DOG?!
TSHHH
KLIK
!!
WHAT THE—?!
YOU SAID YOU'VE ONLY SEEN HUMANS ON TV.
SO ALLOW ME TO EXPLAIN.

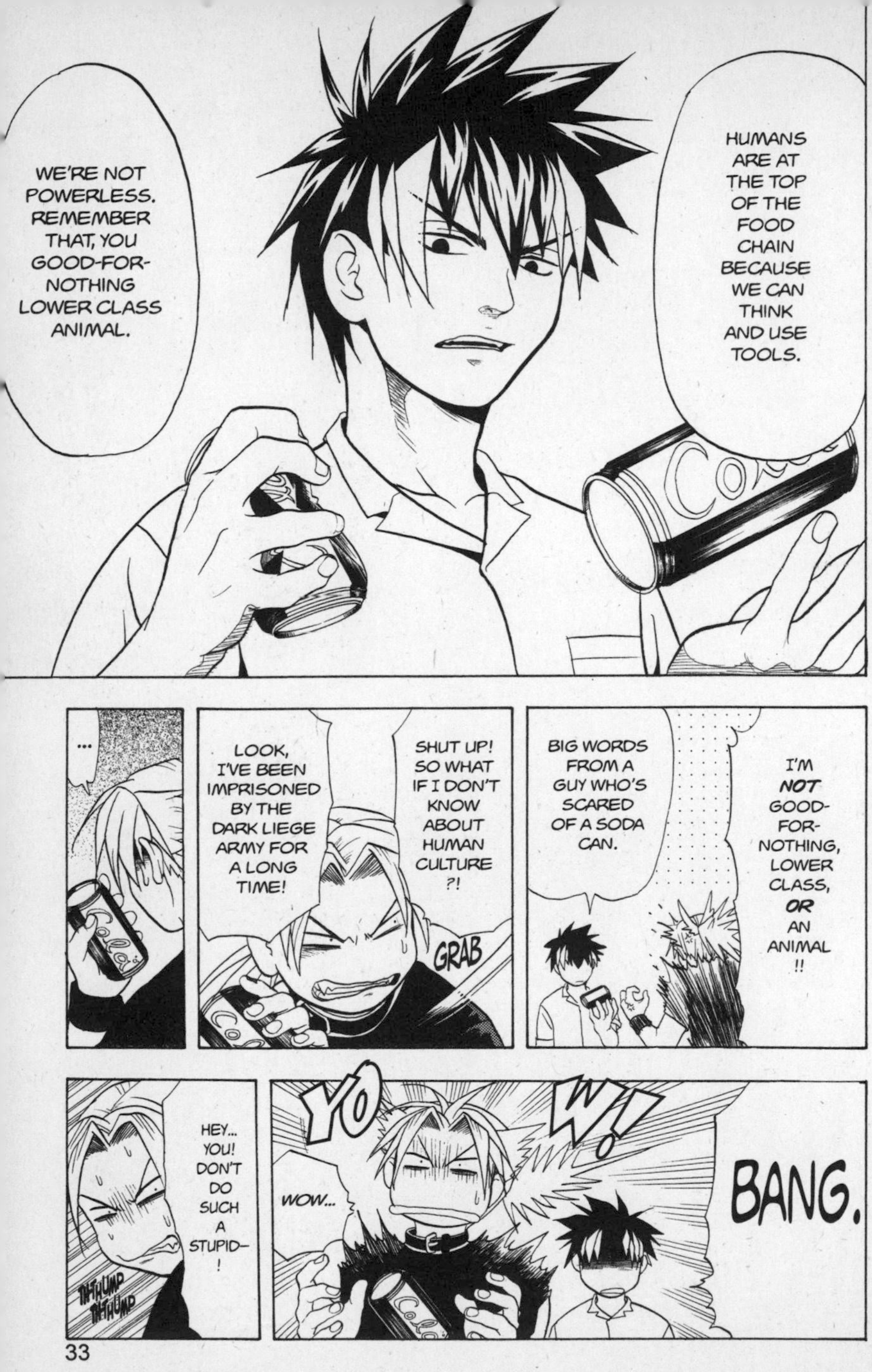
HUMANS ARE AT THE TOP OF THE FOOD CHAIN BECAUSE WE CAN THINK AND USE TOOLS.
WE'RE NOT POWERLESS. REMEMBER THAT, YOU GOOD-FOR-NOTHING LOWER CLASS ANIMAL.
I'M *NOT* GOOD-FOR-NOTHING, LOWER CLASS, *OR* AN ANIMAL!!
BIG WORDS FROM A GUY WHO'S SCARED OF A SODA CAN.
SHUT UP! SO WHAT IF I DON'T KNOW ABOUT HUMAN CULTURE?!
LOOK, I'VE BEEN IMPRISONED BY THE DARK LIEGE ARMY FOR A LONG TIME!
GRAB
...
YOW!
BANG.
WOW...
HEY... YOU! DON'T DO SUCH A STUPID—!
TH-THUMP TH-THUMP

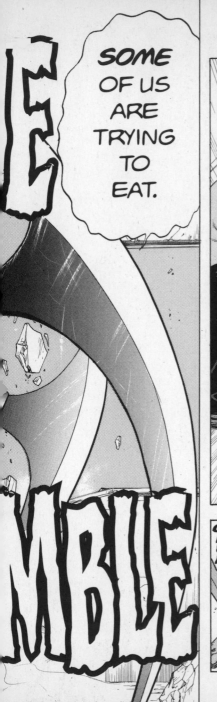

SOME OF US ARE TRYING TO EAT.

KABOOM

CRUMBLE

DO YOU MIND?

WHAT THE—?

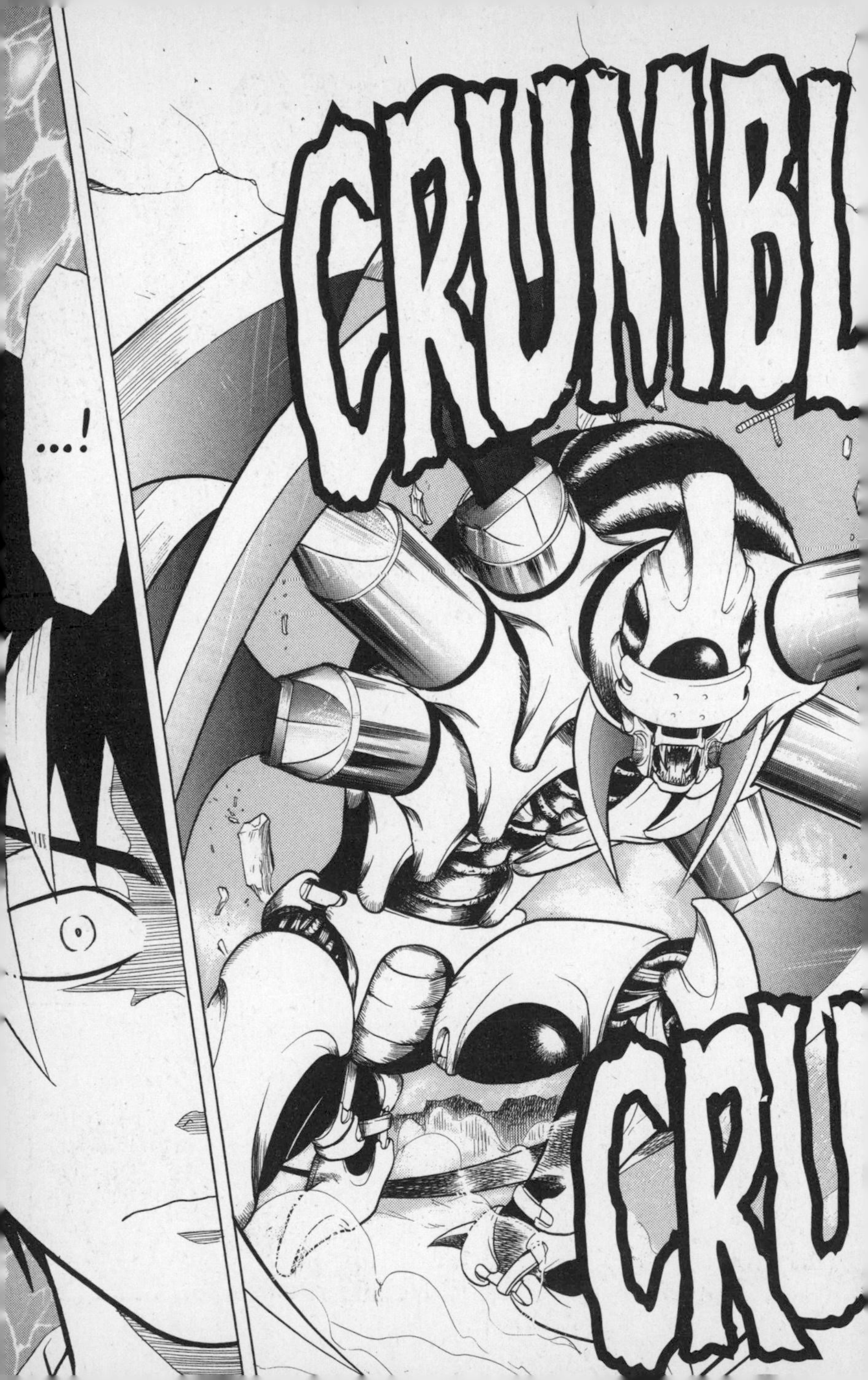
CRUMBL
...!
CRU

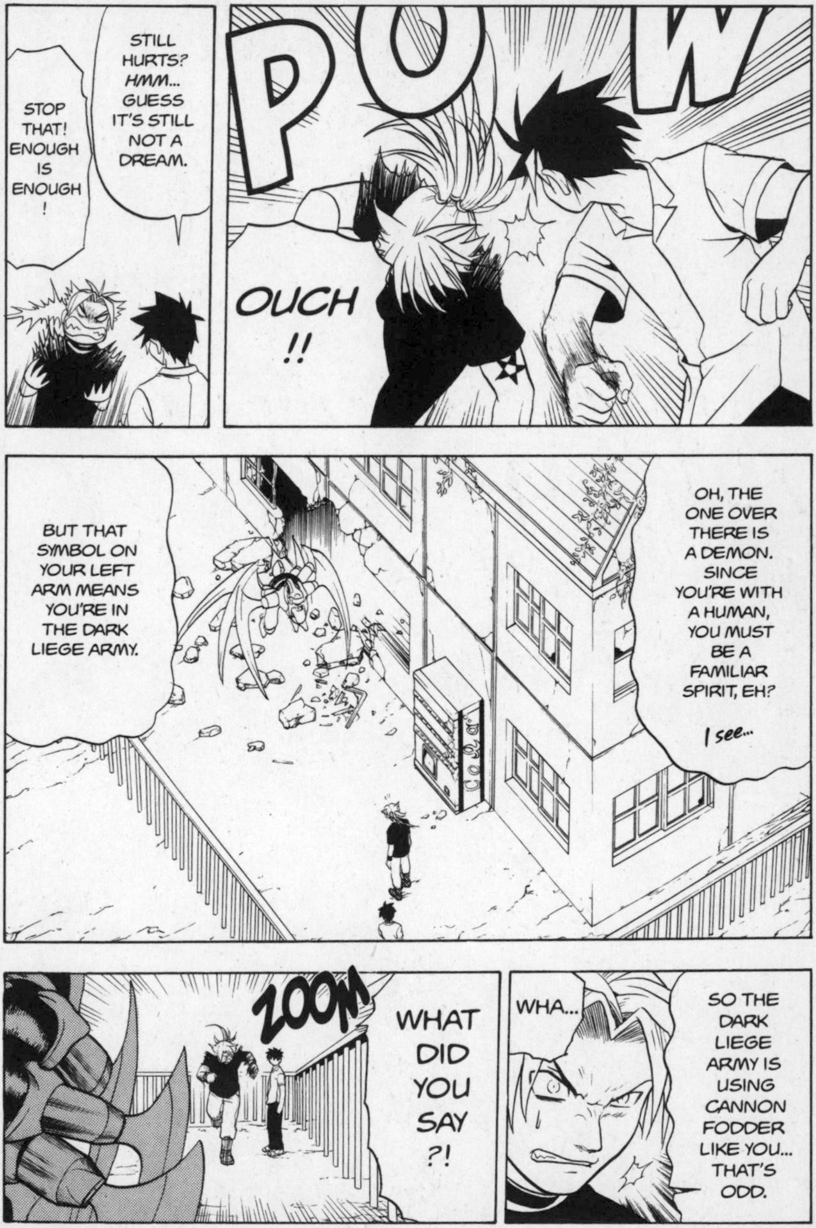
POW
OUCH !!
STILL HURTS? HMM... GUESS IT'S STILL NOT A DREAM.
STOP THAT! ENOUGH IS ENOUGH !
OH, THE ONE OVER THERE IS A DEMON. SINCE YOU'RE WITH A HUMAN, YOU MUST BE A FAMILIAR SPIRIT, EH?
I see...
BUT THAT SYMBOL ON YOUR LEFT ARM MEANS YOU'RE IN THE DARK LIEGE ARMY.
SO THE DARK LIEGE ARMY IS USING CANNON FODDER LIKE YOU... THAT'S ODD.
WHA...
WHAT DID YOU SAY ?!
ZOOM

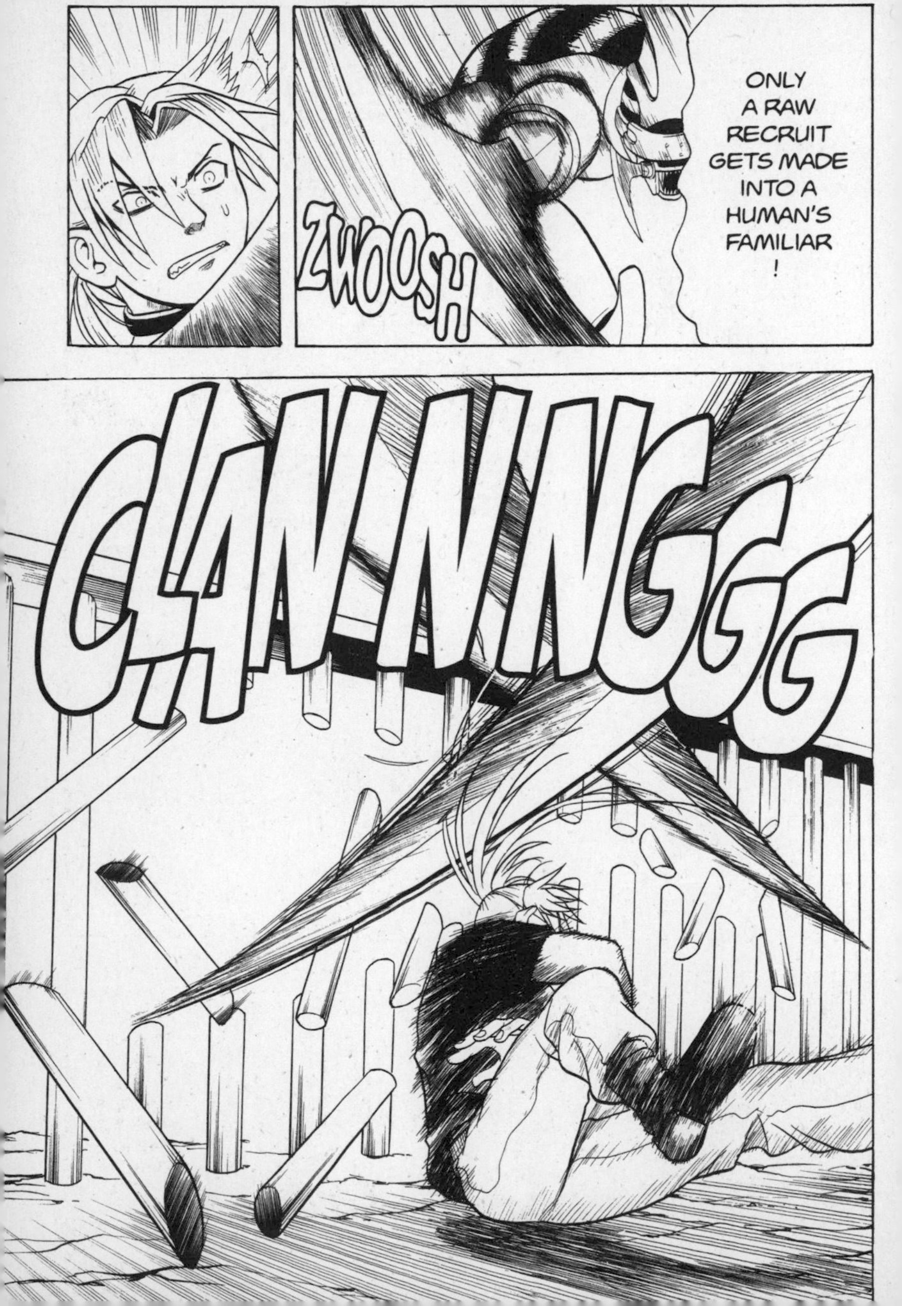
ONLY A RAW RECRUIT GETS MADE INTO A HUMAN'S FAMILIAR!
ZWOOSH
CLANNNGGG

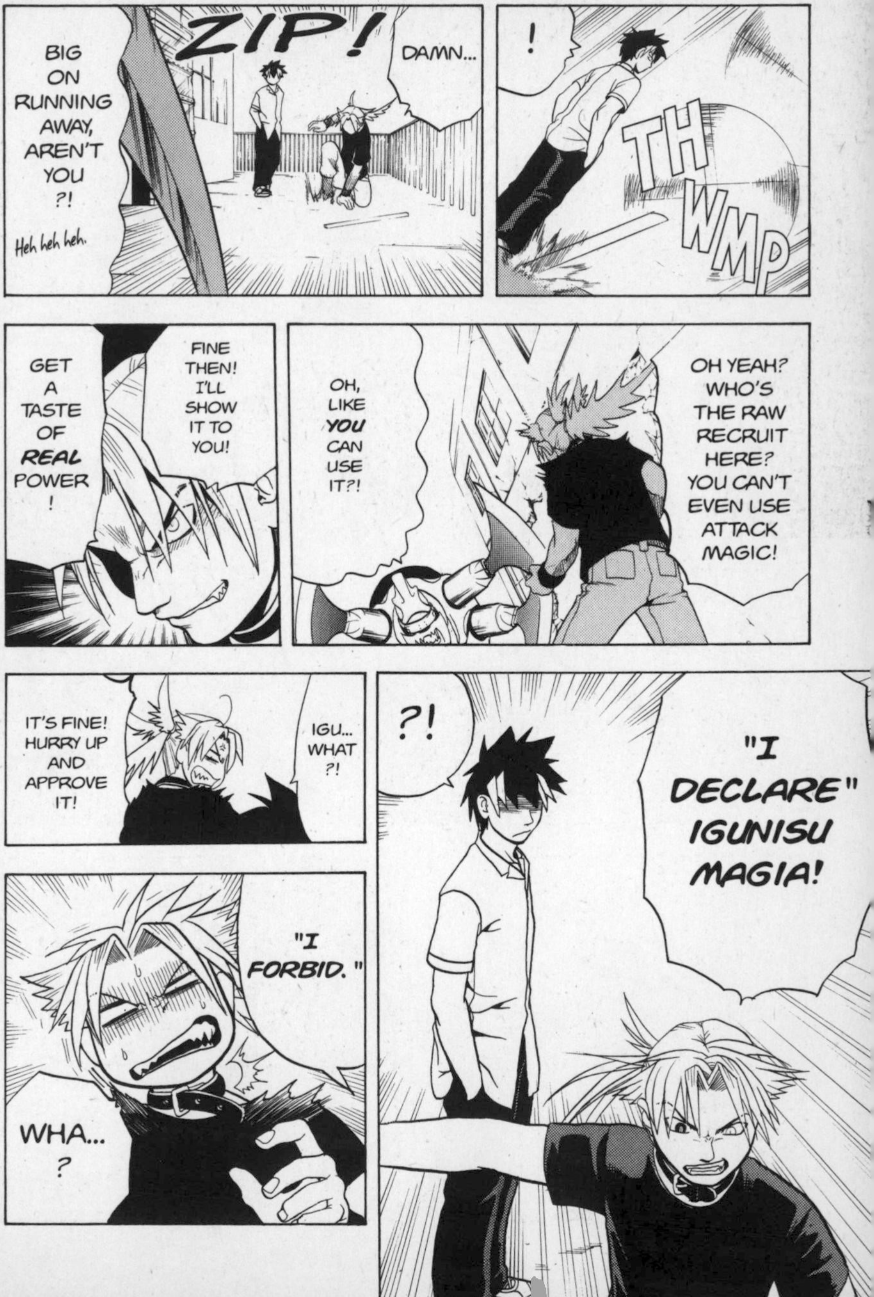
!
THWMP
DAMN...
ZIP!
BIG ON RUNNING AWAY, AREN'T YOU ?!
Heh heh heh.
OH YEAH? WHO'S THE RAW RECRUIT HERE? YOU CAN'T EVEN USE ATTACK MAGIC!
OH, LIKE ***YOU*** CAN USE IT?!
FINE THEN! I'LL SHOW IT TO YOU!
GET A TASTE OF ***REAL*** POWER!
"I DECLARE" IGUNISU MAGIA!
?!
IGU... WHAT ?!
IT'S FINE! HURRY UP AND APPROVE IT!
"I FORBID."
WHA... ?

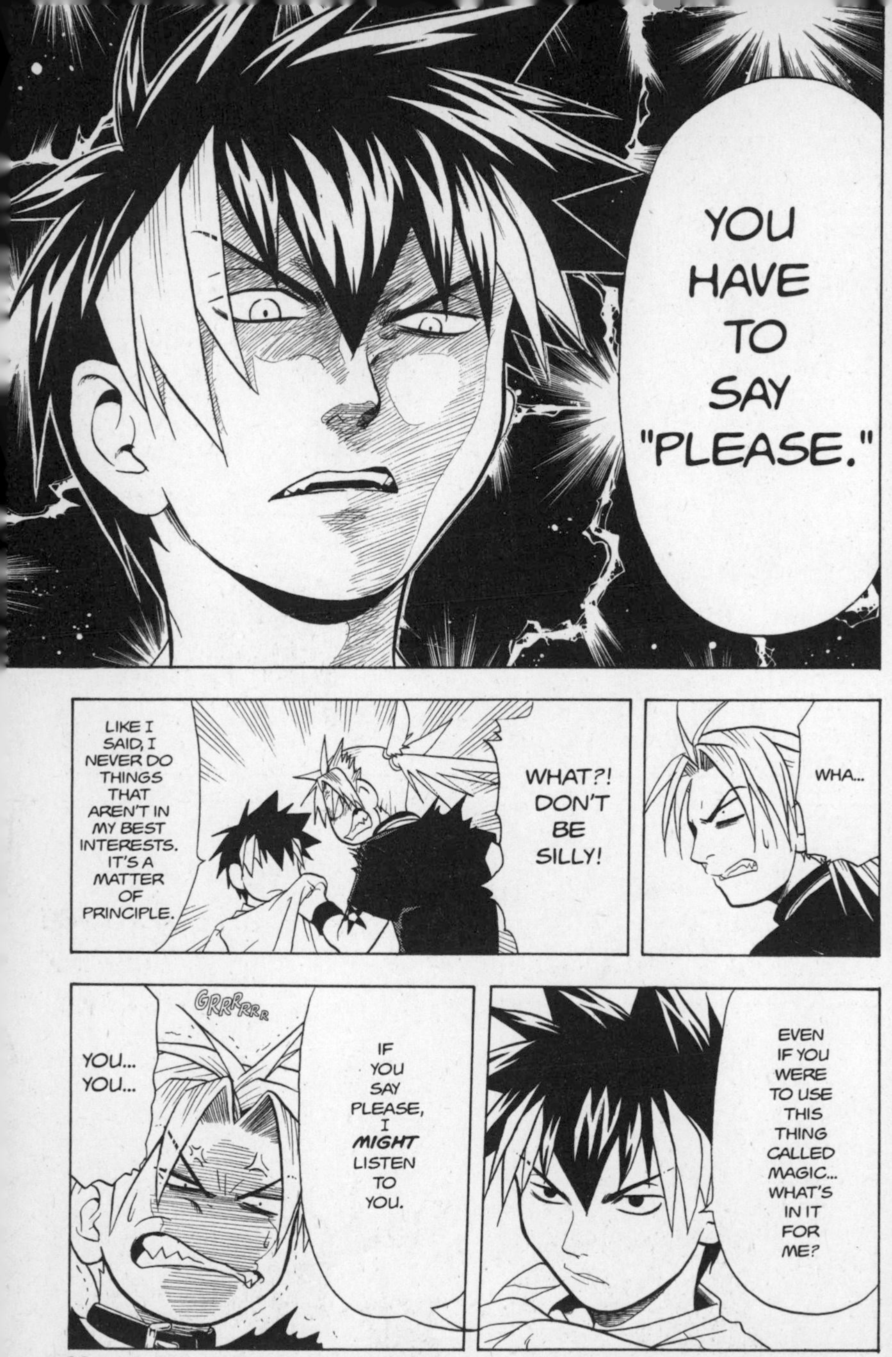
YOU HAVE TO SAY "PLEASE."
WHA...
WHAT?! DON'T BE SILLY!
LIKE I SAID, I NEVER DO THINGS THAT AREN'T IN MY BEST INTERESTS. IT'S A MATTER OF PRINCIPLE.
EVEN IF YOU WERE TO USE THIS THING CALLED MAGIC... WHAT'S IN IT FOR ME?
IF YOU SAY PLEASE, I **MIGHT** LISTEN TO YOU.
GRRRRRR
YOU... YOU...

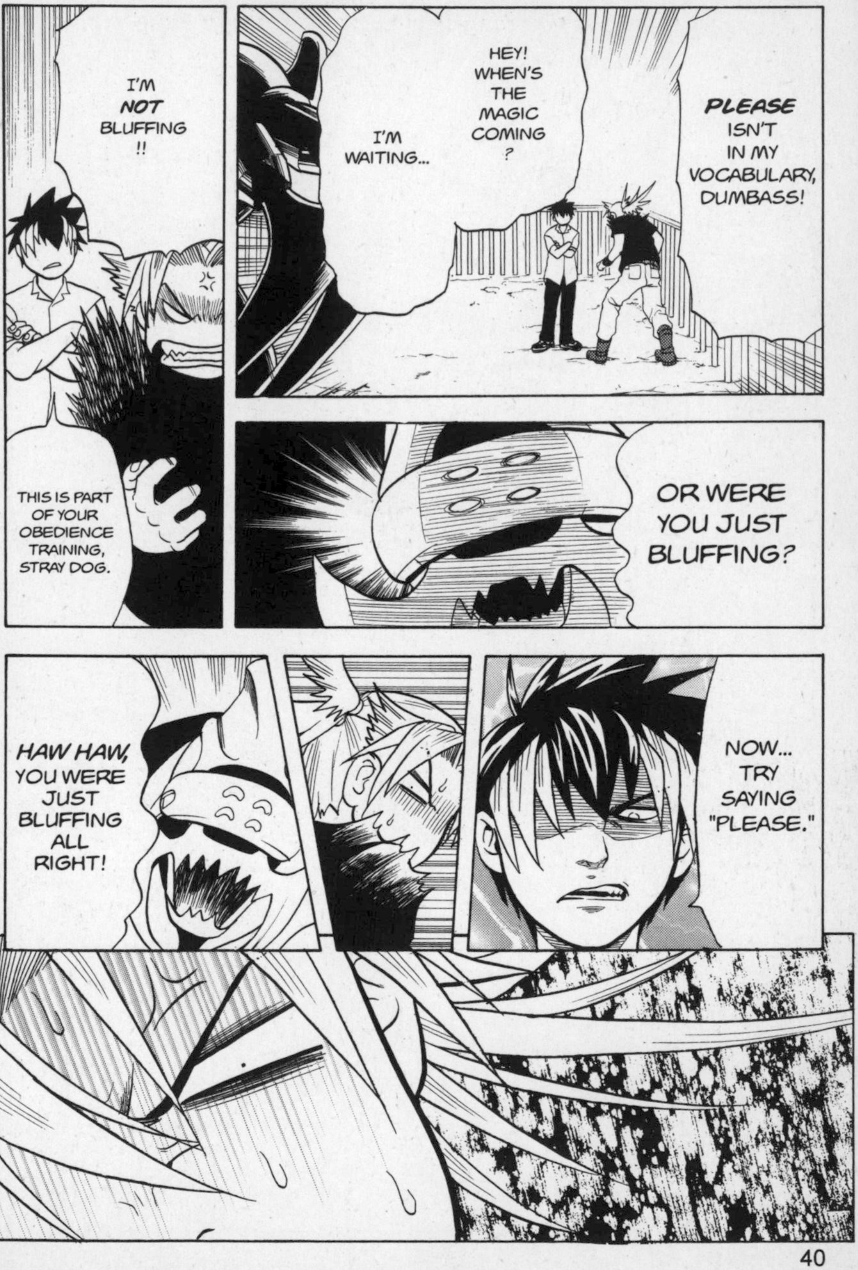
PLEASE ISN'T IN MY VOCABULARY, DUMBASS!
HEY! WHEN'S THE MAGIC COMING ?
I'M WAITING...
OR WERE YOU JUST BLUFFING?
I'M *NOT* BLUFFING !!
THIS IS PART OF YOUR OBEDIENCE TRAINING, STRAY DOG.
NOW... TRY SAYING "PLEASE."
HAW HAW, YOU WERE JUST BLUFFING ALL RIGHT!

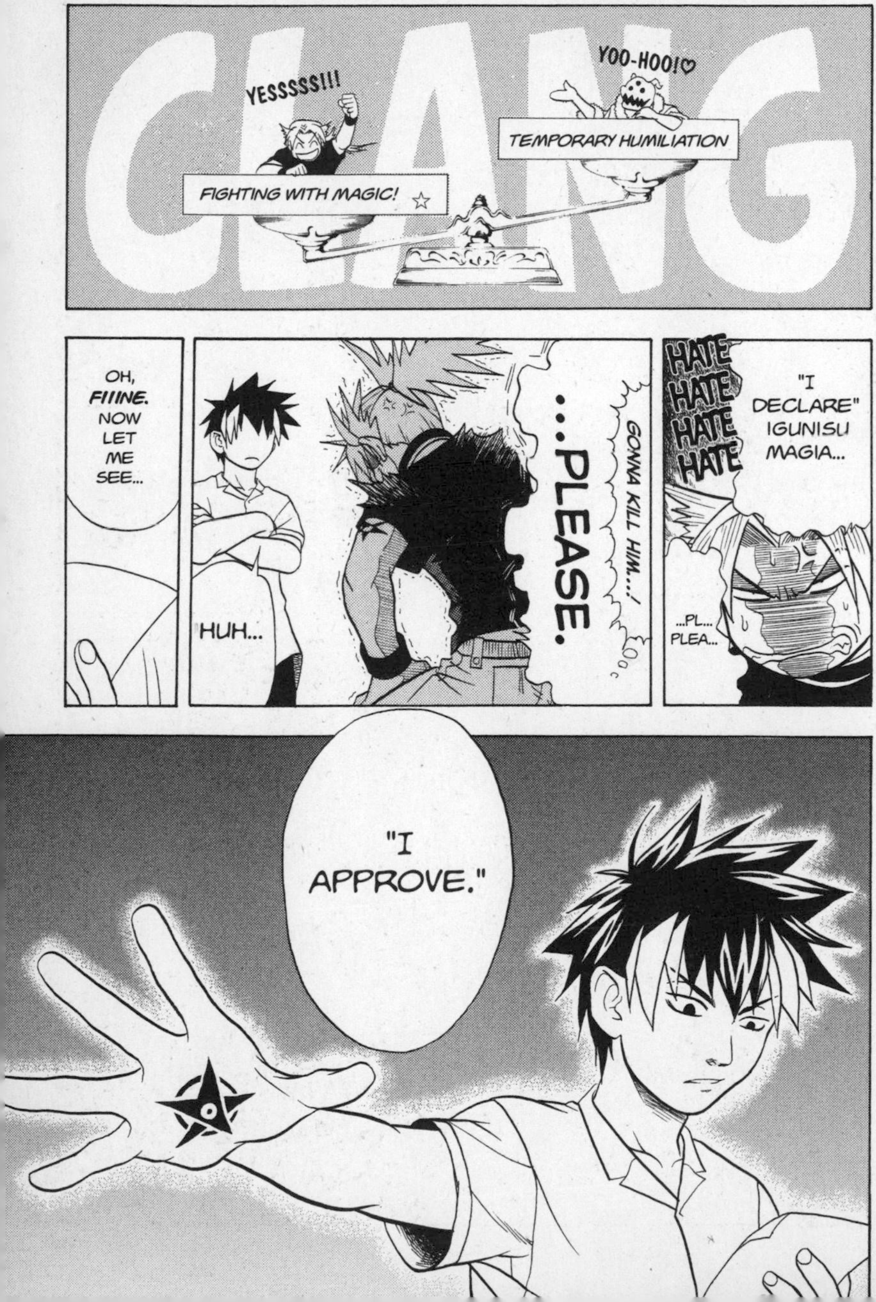
CLANG
YOO-HOO!♡
TEMPORARY HUMILIATION
YESSSSS!!!
FIGHTING WITH MAGIC! ☆
HATE HATE HATE HATE
"I DECLARE" IGUNISU MAGIA...
...PL... PLEA...
GONNA KILL HIM...!
...PLEASE.
HUH...
OH, FIIINE. NOW LET ME SEE...
"I APPROVE."

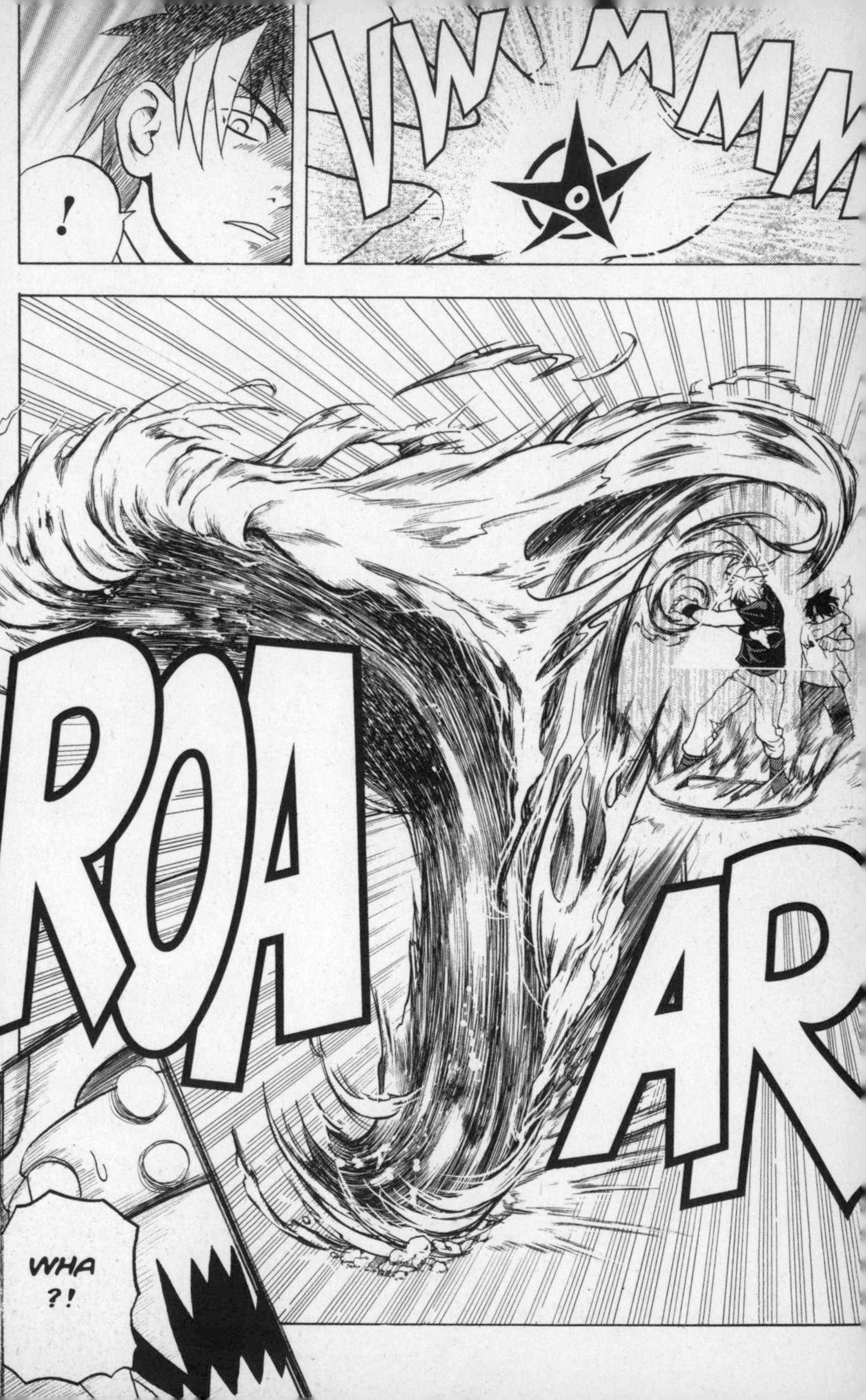
VWMMM
!
ROAAR
WHA ?!

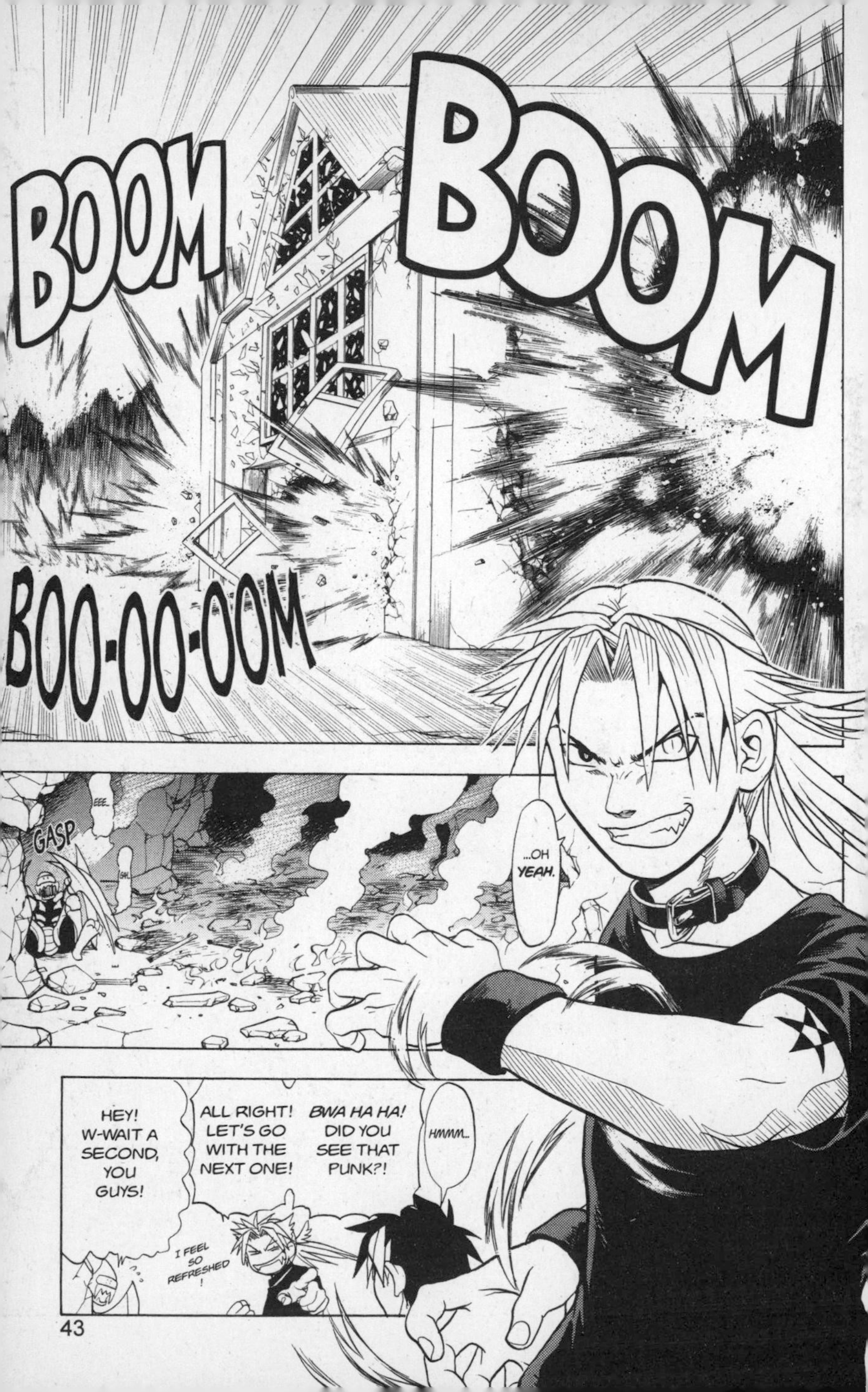
BOOM
BOOM
BOO-OO-OOM
...OH YEAH.
EEE...
GASP
GAH...
HMMM..
BWA HA HA! DID YOU SEE THAT PUNK?!
ALL RIGHT! LET'S GO WITH THE NEXT ONE!
HEY! W-WAIT A SECOND, YOU GUYS!
I FEEL SO REFRESHED!

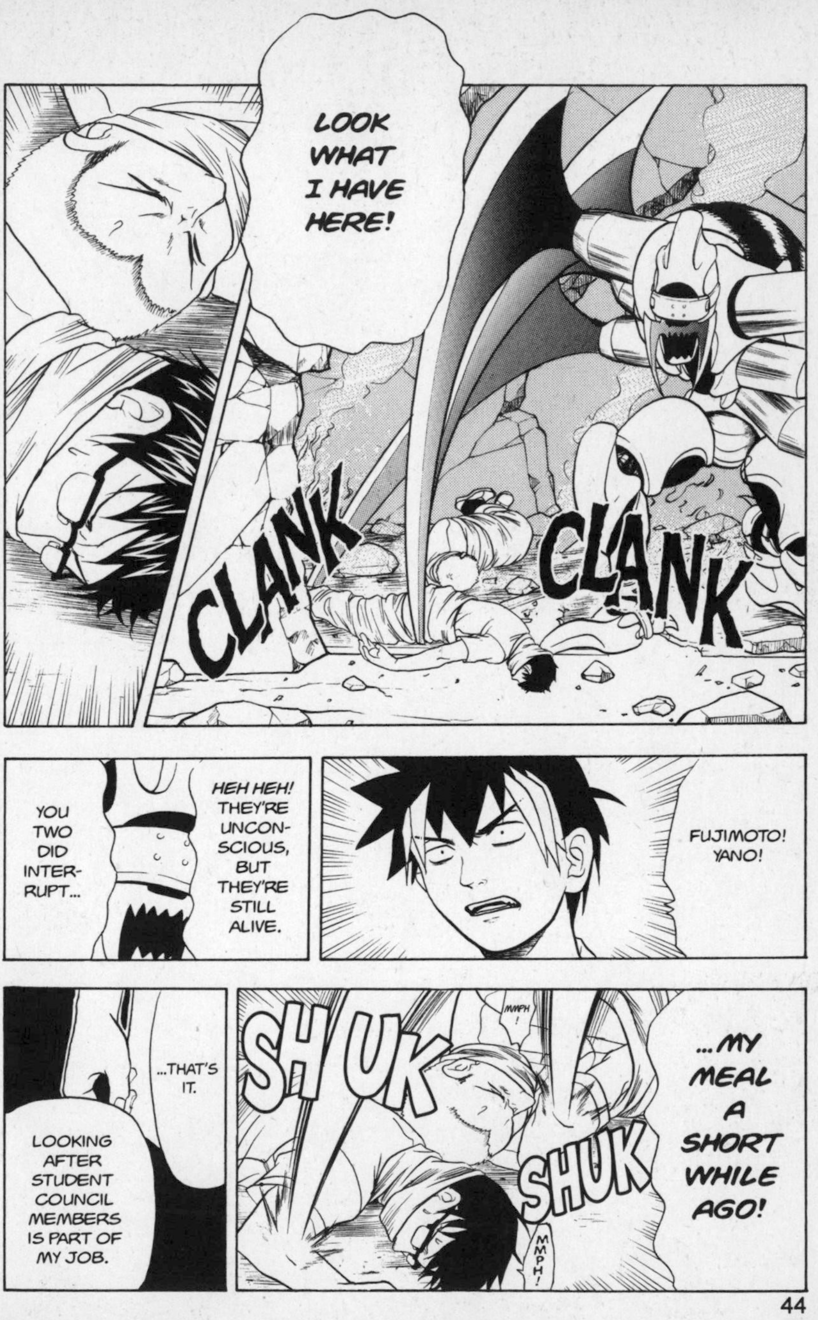
LOOK WHAT I HAVE HERE!
CLANK
CLANK
FUJIMOTO! YANO!
HEH HEH! THEY'RE UNCONSCIOUS, BUT THEY'RE STILL ALIVE.
YOU TWO DID INTERRUPT...
...MY MEAL A SHORT WHILE AGO!
MMPH!
SHUK
SHUK
MMPH!
...THAT'S IT.
LOOKING AFTER STUDENT COUNCIL MEMBERS IS PART OF MY JOB.

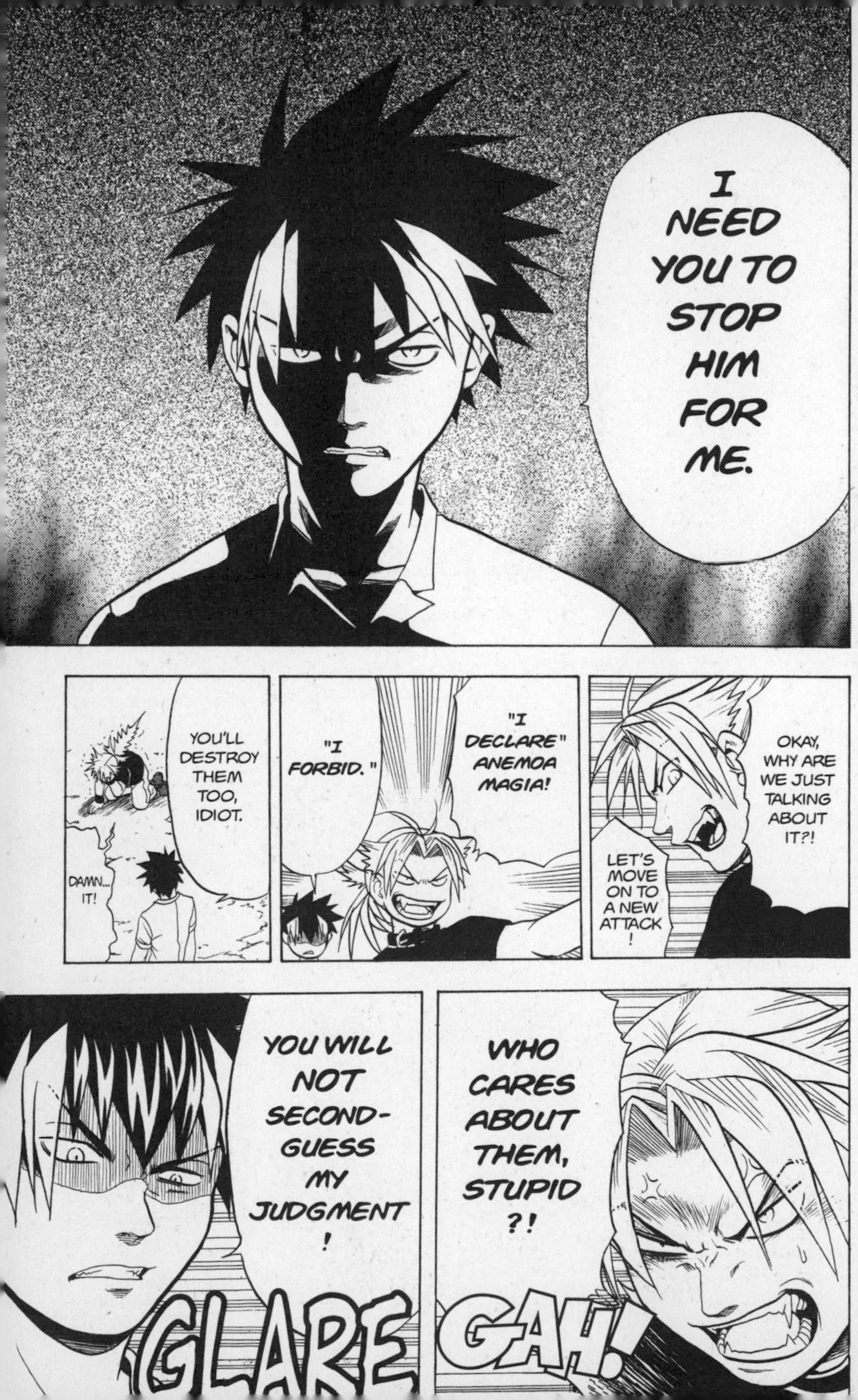
I NEED YOU TO STOP HIM FOR ME.
OKAY, WHY ARE WE JUST TALKING ABOUT IT?!
LET'S MOVE ON TO A NEW ATTACK!
"I DECLARE" ANEMOA MAGIA!
"I FORBID."
YOU'LL DESTROY THEM TOO, IDIOT.
DAMN... IT!
WHO CARES ABOUT THEM, STUPID?!
GAH!
YOU WILL NOT SECOND-GUESS MY JUDGMENT!
GLARE

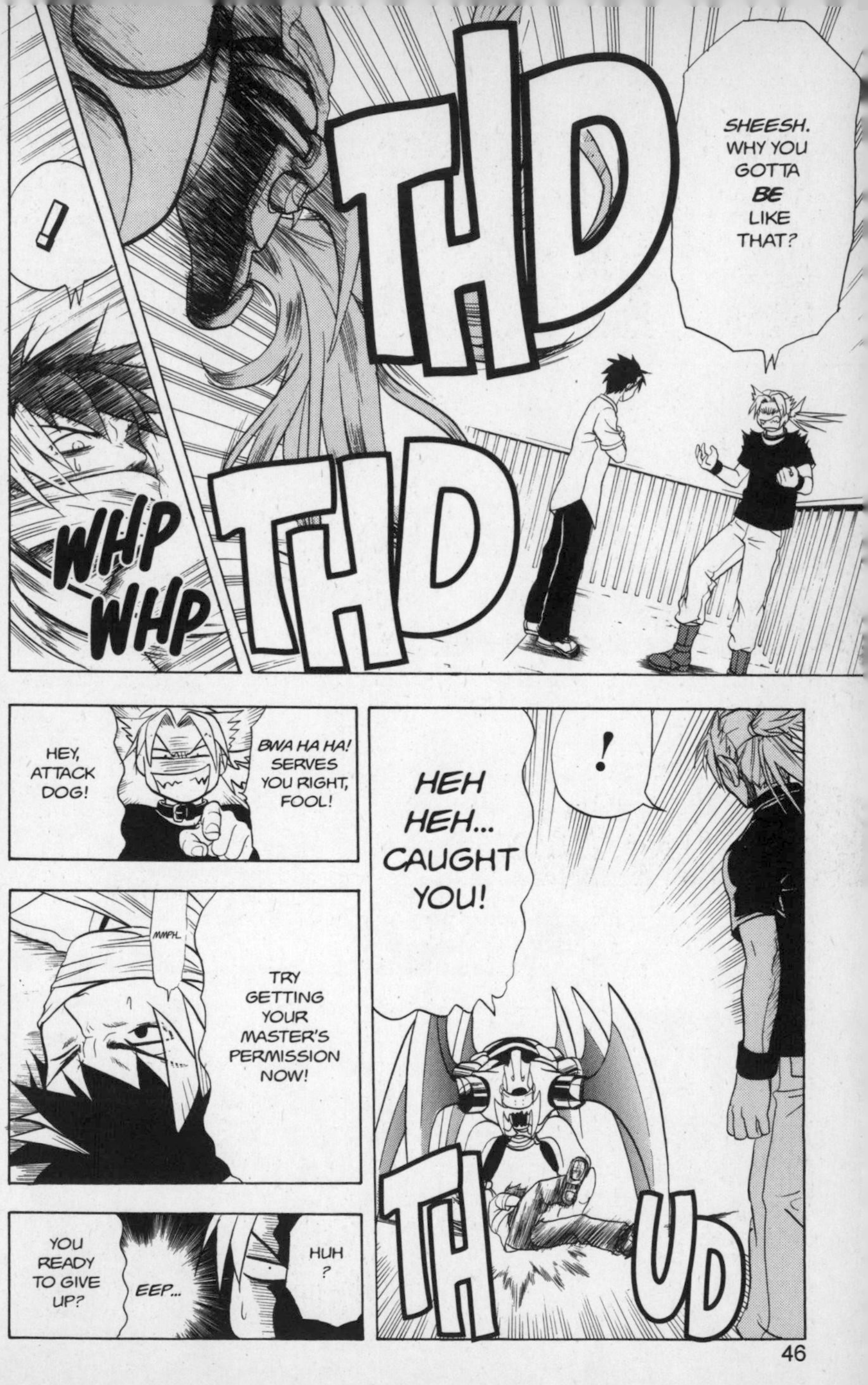
SHEESH. WHY YOU GOTTA BE LIKE THAT?
THD
!
THD
WHP WHP
!
HEH HEH... CAUGHT YOU!
THUD
BWA HA HA! SERVES YOU RIGHT, FOOL!
HEY, ATTACK DOG!
MMPH.
TRY GETTING YOUR MASTER'S PERMISSION NOW!
HUH ?
EEP...
YOU READY TO GIVE UP?

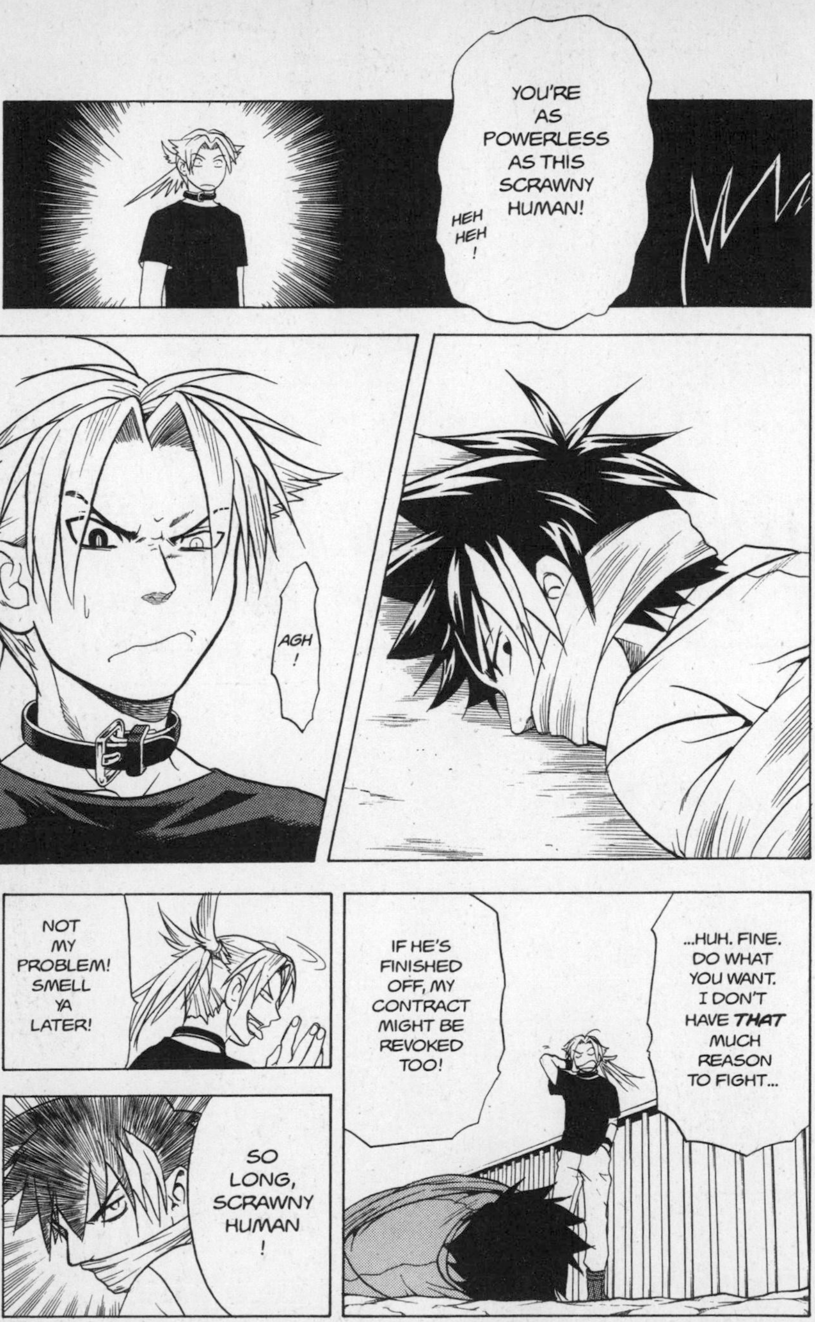
YOU'RE AS POWERLESS AS THIS SCRAWNY HUMAN!
HEH HEH!
AGH!
...HUH. FINE. DO WHAT YOU WANT. I DON'T HAVE *THAT* MUCH REASON TO FIGHT...
IF HE'S FINISHED OFF, MY CONTRACT MIGHT BE REVOKED TOO!
NOT MY PROBLEM! SMELL YA LATER!
SO LONG, SCRAWNY HUMAN!

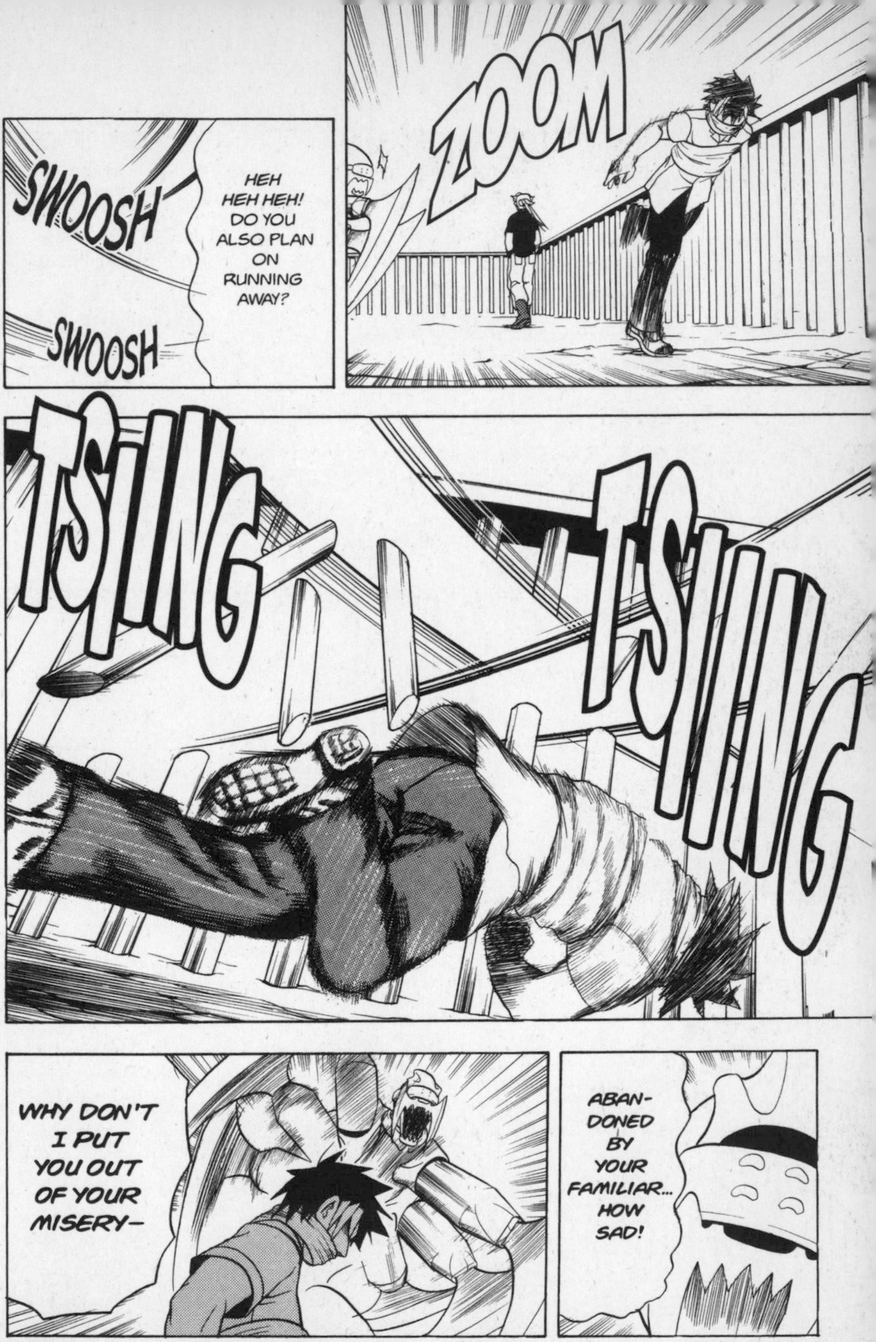
ZOOM
SWOOSH
SWOOSH
HEH HEH HEH! DO YOU ALSO PLAN ON RUNNING AWAY?
TSING
TSING
ABAN-DONED BY YOUR FAMILIAR... HOW SAD!
WHY DON'T I PUT YOU OUT OF YOUR MISERY—

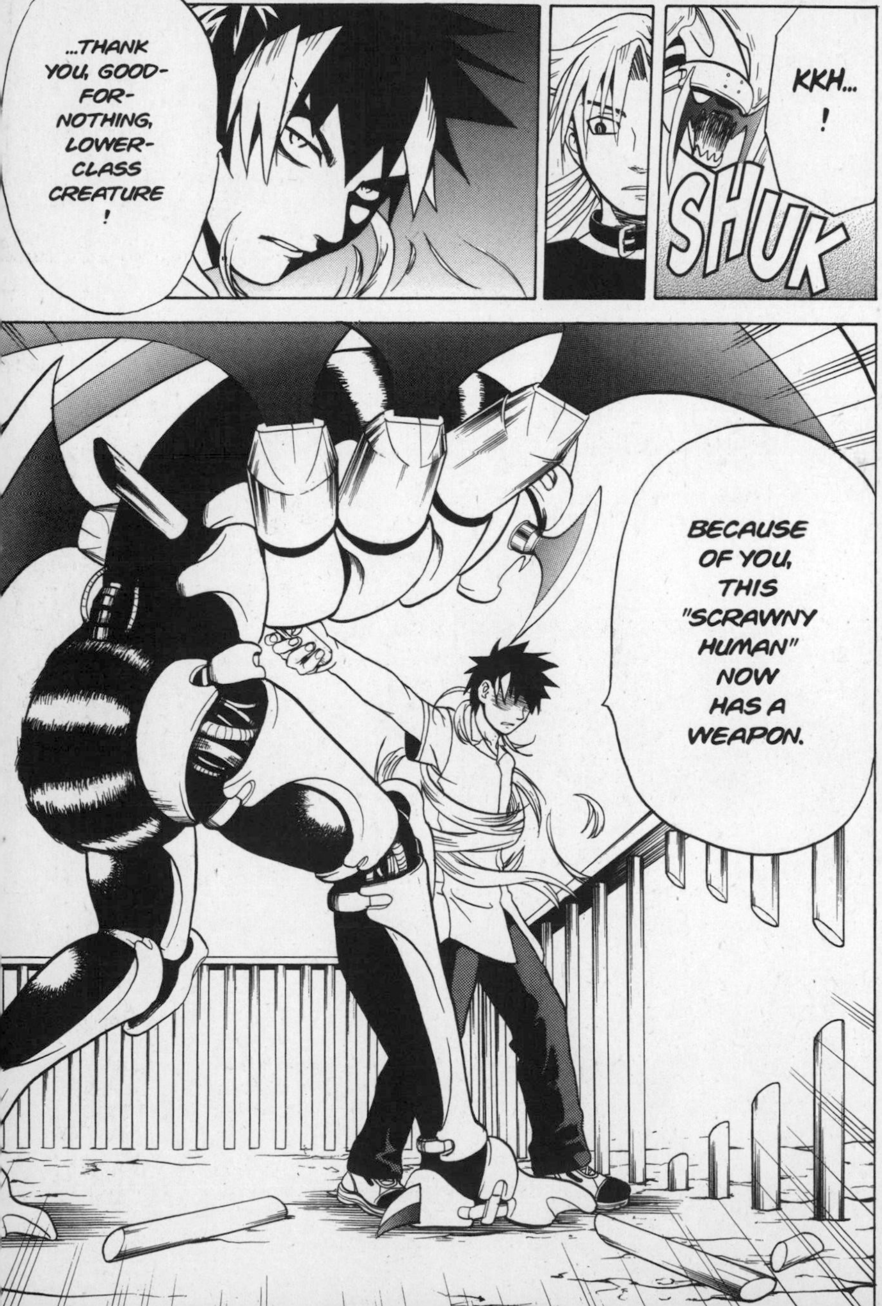
KKH... !
SHUK
...THANK YOU, GOOD-FOR-NOTHING, LOWER-CLASS CREATURE !
BECAUSE OF YOU, THIS "SCRAWNY HUMAN" NOW HAS A WEAPON.

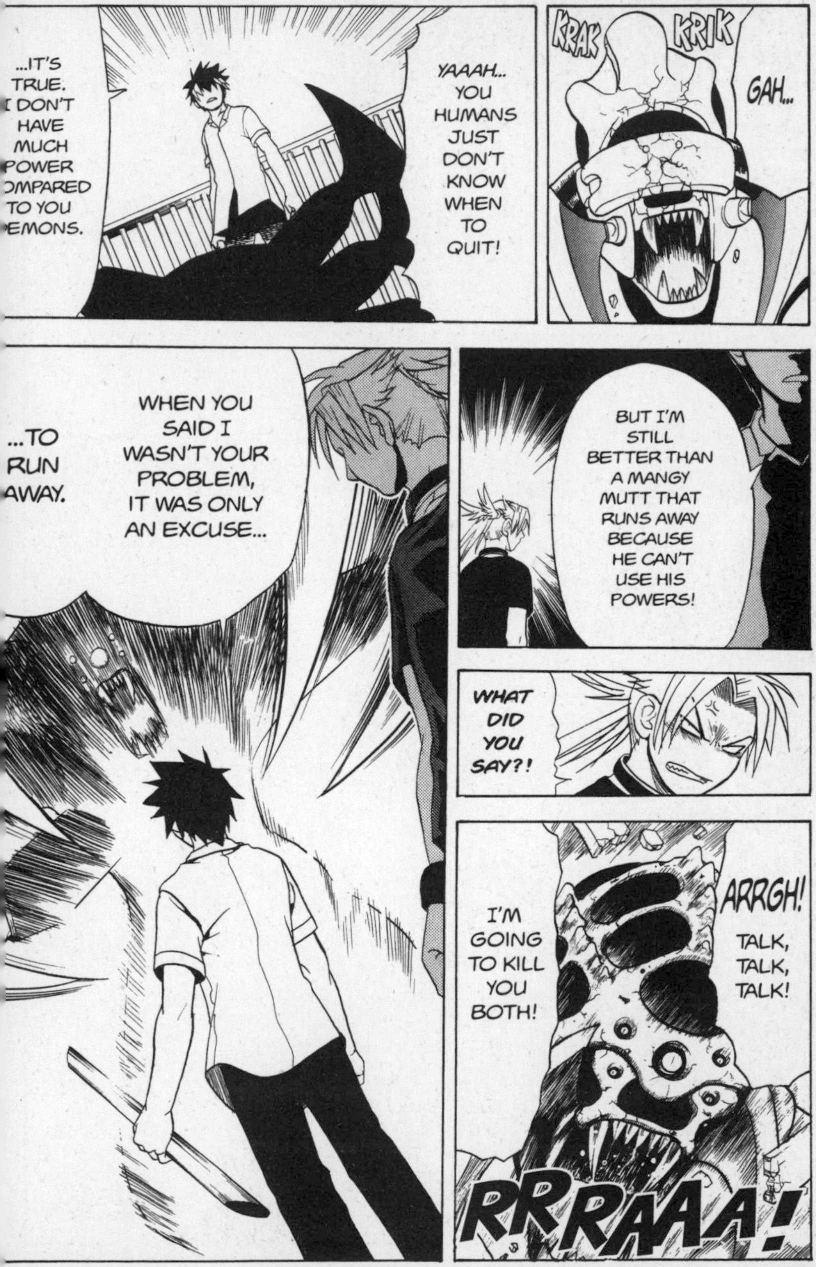
KRAK
KRIK
GAH...
YAAAH... YOU HUMANS JUST DON'T KNOW WHEN TO QUIT!
...IT'S TRUE. I DON'T HAVE MUCH POWER OMPARED TO YOU EMONS.
BUT I'M STILL BETTER THAN A MANGY MUTT THAT RUNS AWAY BECAUSE HE CAN'T USE HIS POWERS!
WHAT DID YOU SAY?!
ARRGH!
TALK, TALK, TALK!
I'M GOING TO KILL YOU BOTH!
RRRAAA!
WHEN YOU SAID I WASN'T YOUR PROBLEM, IT WAS ONLY AN EXCUSE...
...TO RUN AWAY.

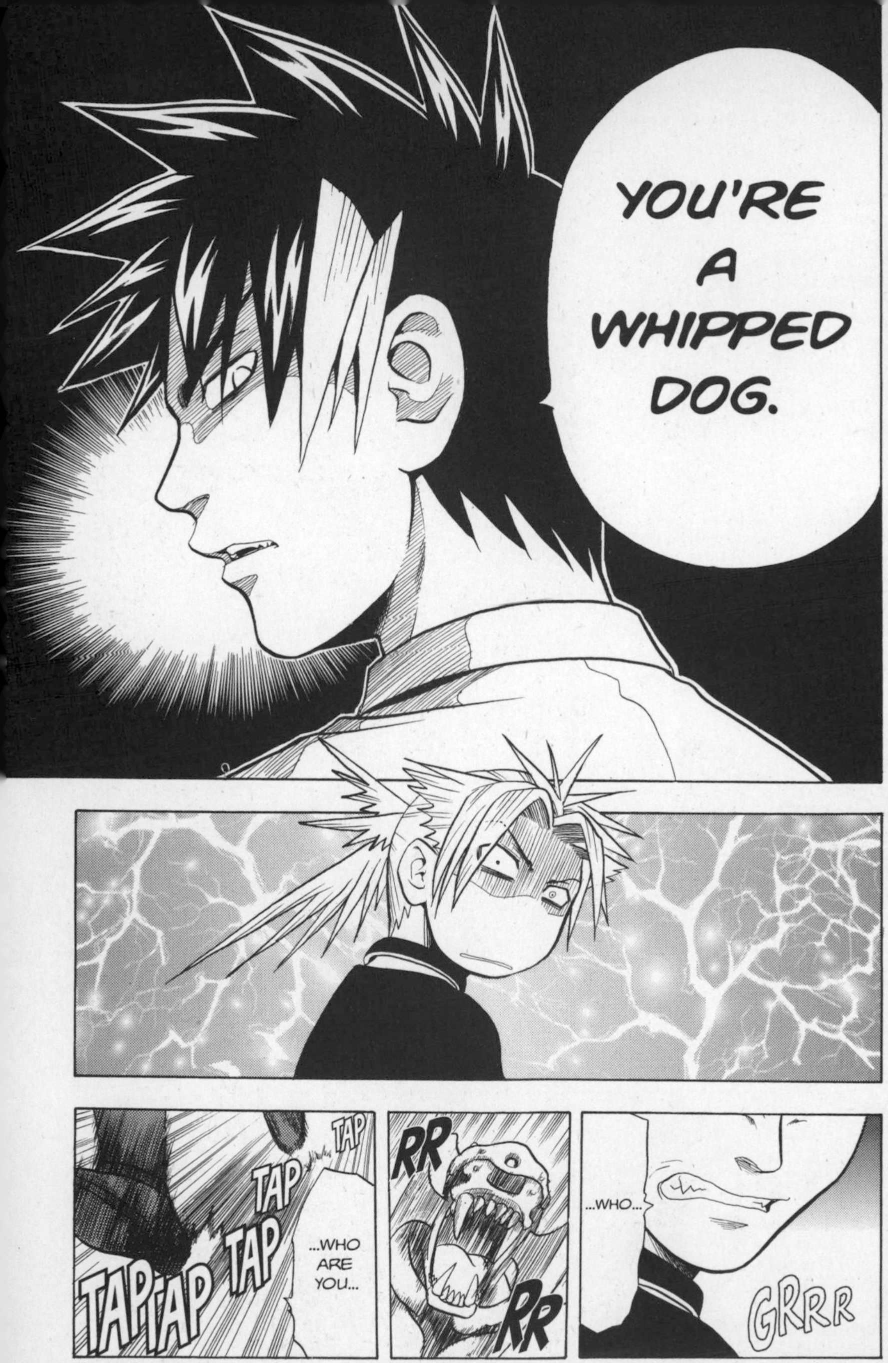
YOU'RE A WHIPPED DOG.
...WHO...
GRRR
RR
RR
TAP
TAP
TAP TAP TAP
...WHO ARE YOU...

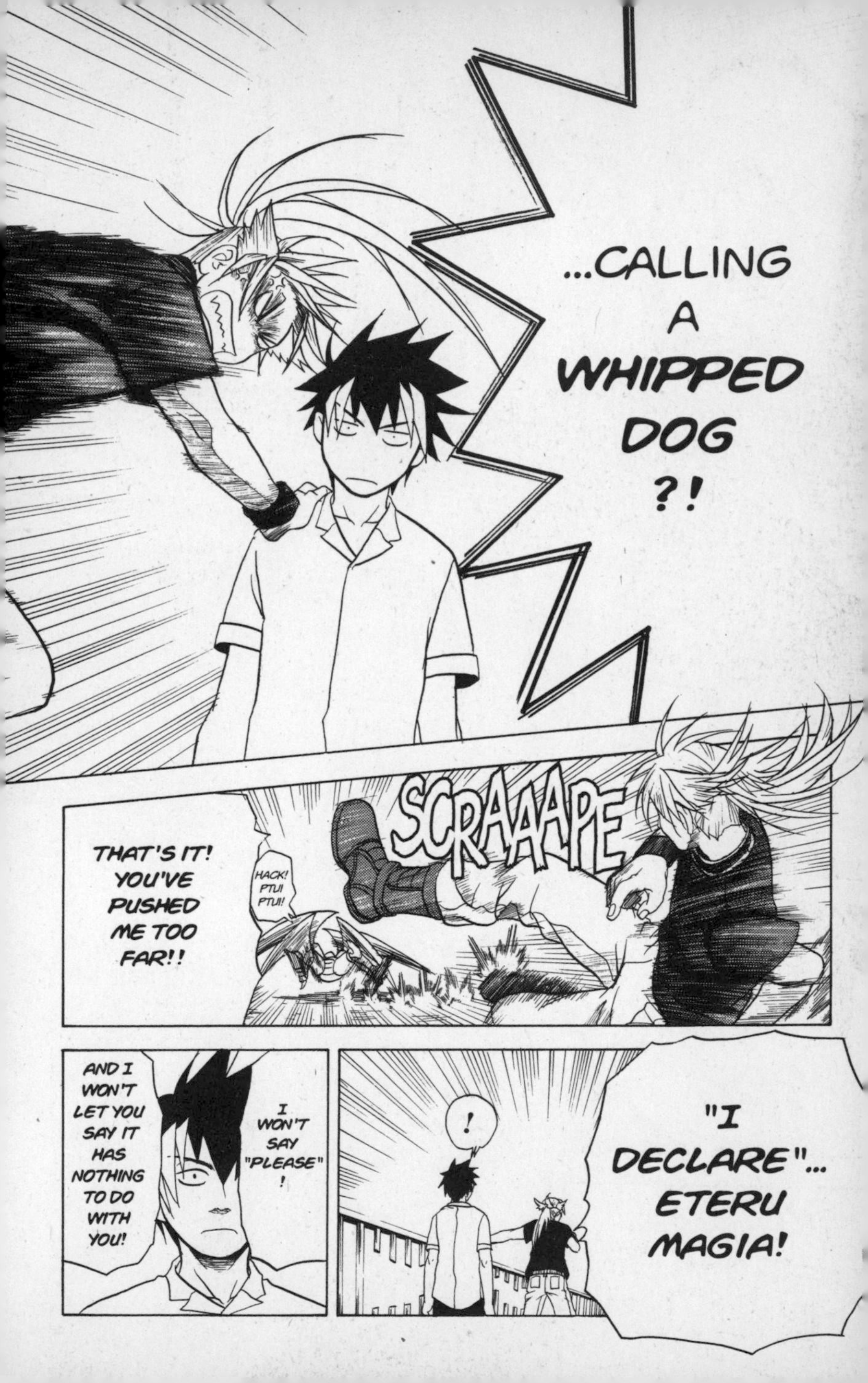
...CALLING A WHIPPED DOG ?!
SCRAAAPE
HACK! PTUI PTUI!
THAT'S IT! YOU'VE PUSHED ME TOO FAR!!
"I DECLARE"... ETERU MAGIA!
!
I WON'T SAY "PLEASE"!
AND I WON'T LET YOU SAY IT HAS NOTHING TO DO WITH YOU!

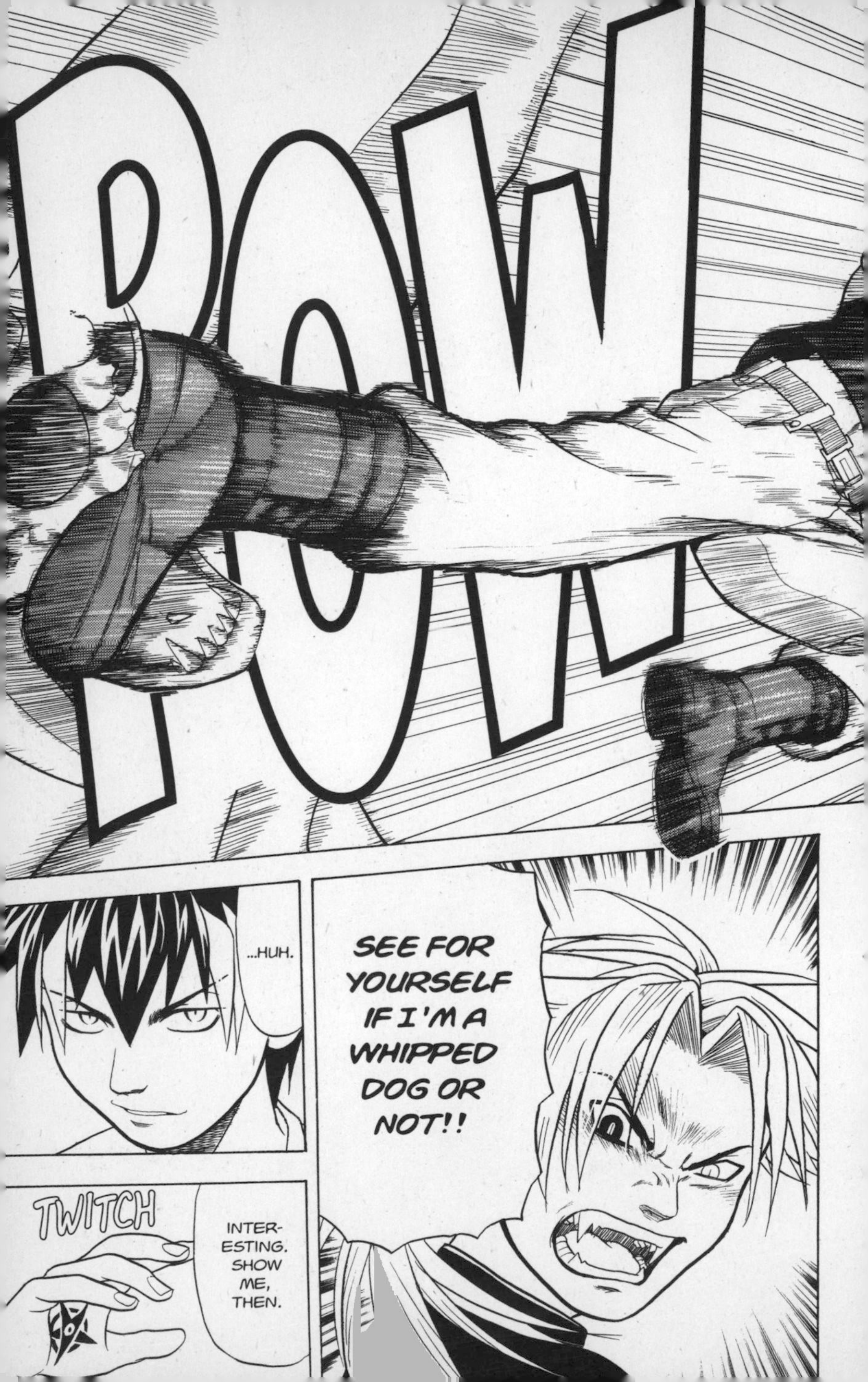
POW
SEE FOR YOURSELF IF I'M A WHIPPED DOG OR NOT!!
...HUH.
TWITCH
INTER-ESTING. SHOW ME, THEN.

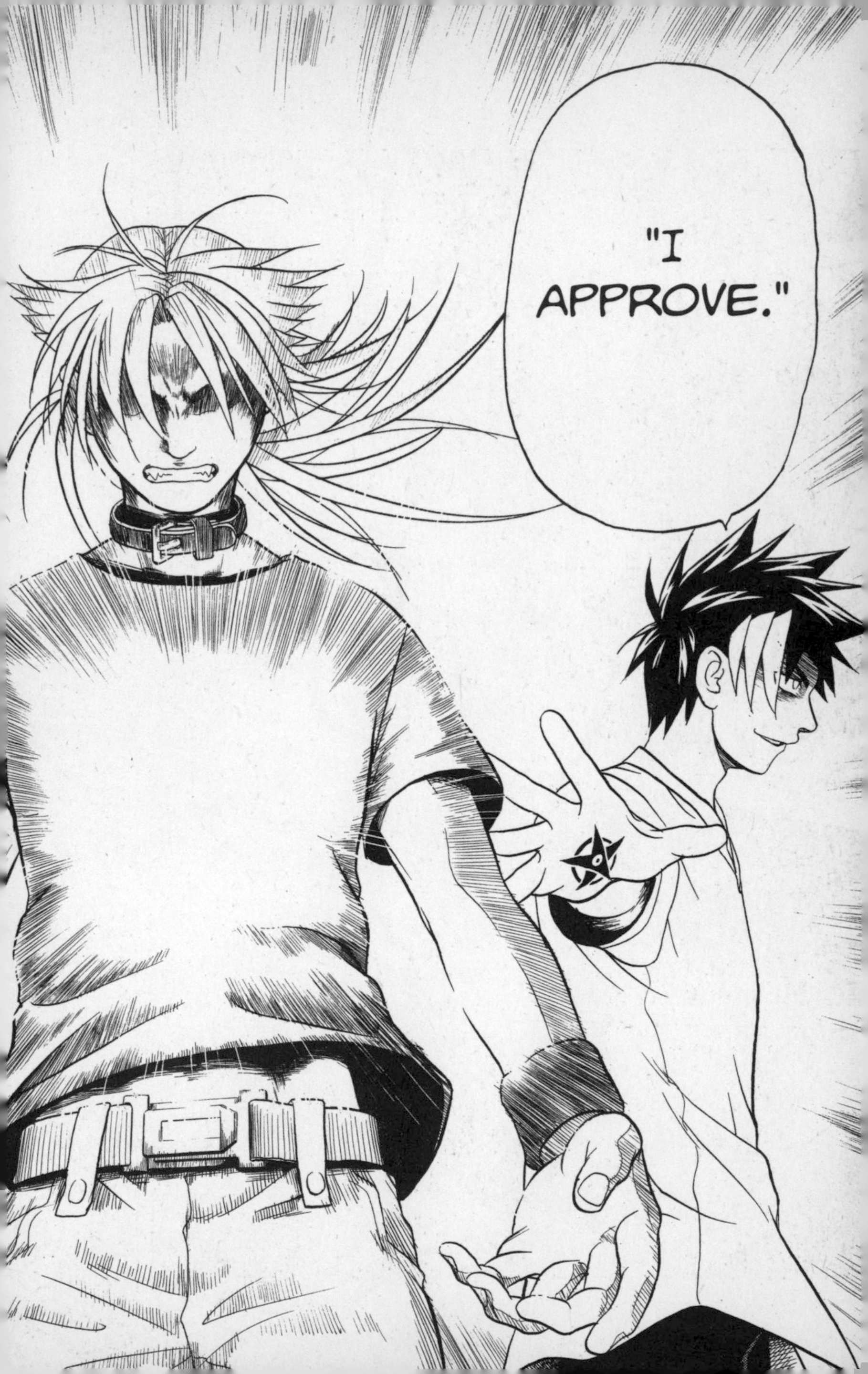
"I APPROVE."

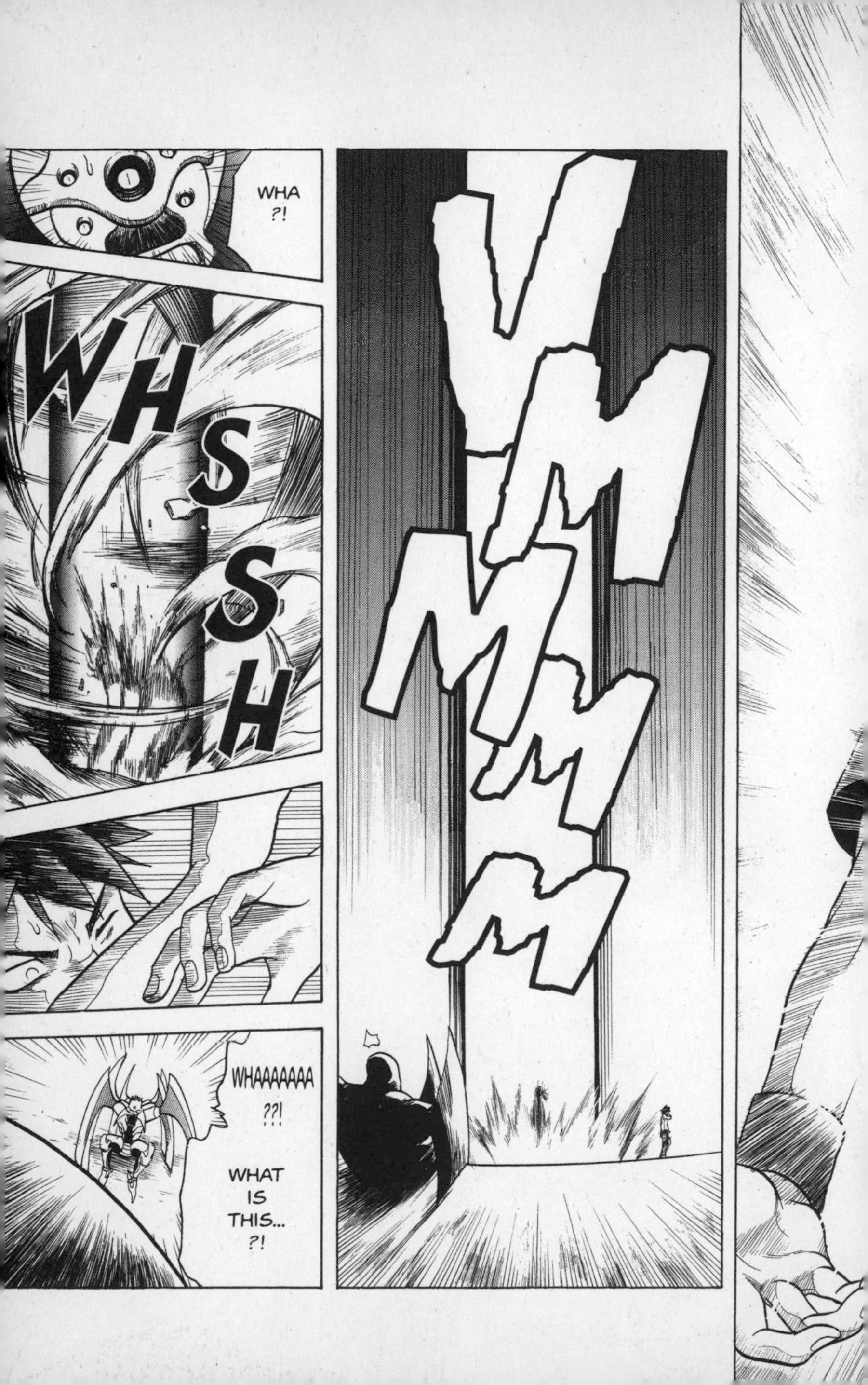
VMMMM
WHA ?!
WHSSH
WHAAAAAAA ??!
WHAT IS THIS... ?!

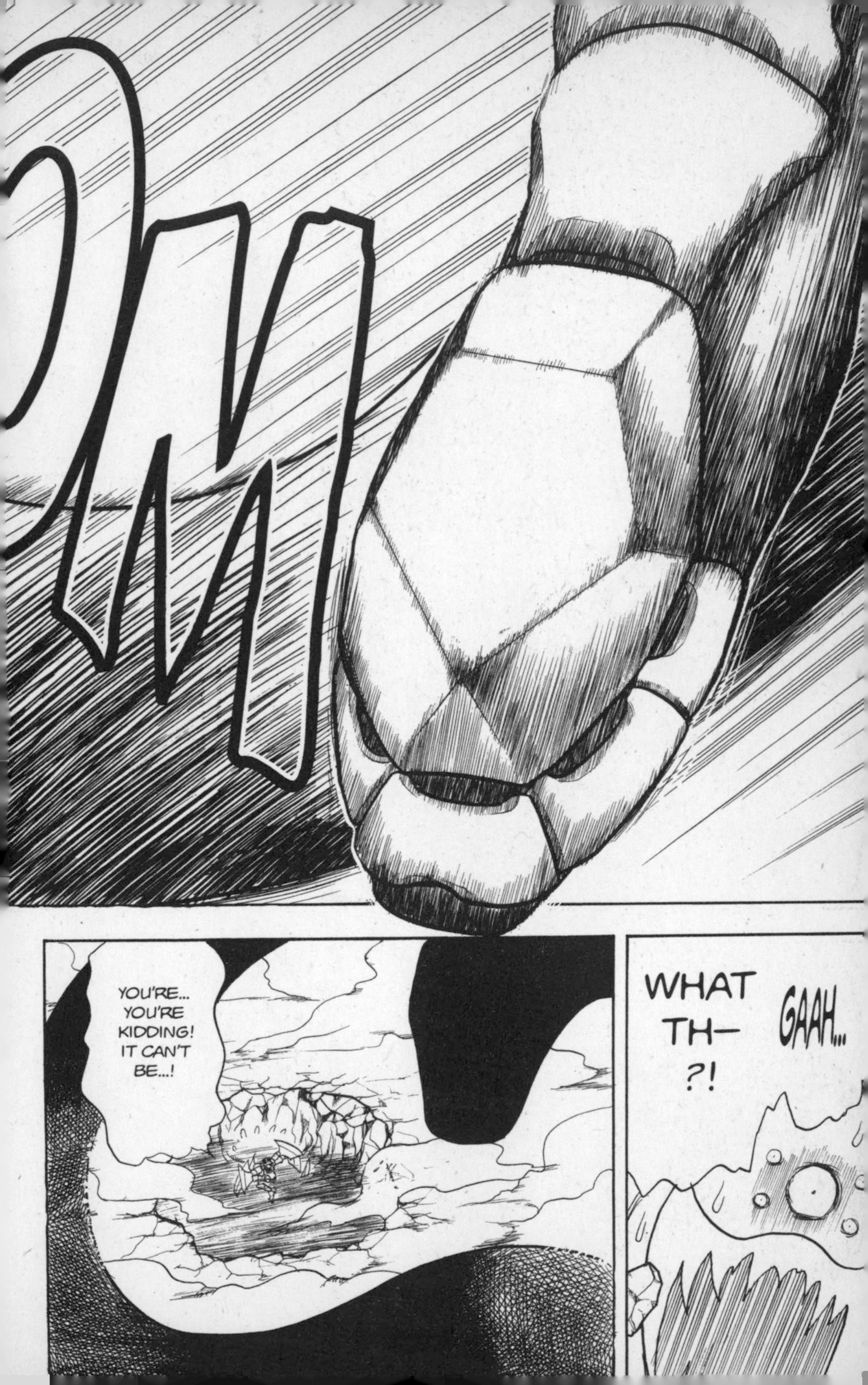
GAAH...
WHAT TH— ?!
YOU'RE... YOU'RE KIDDING! IT CAN'T BE...!

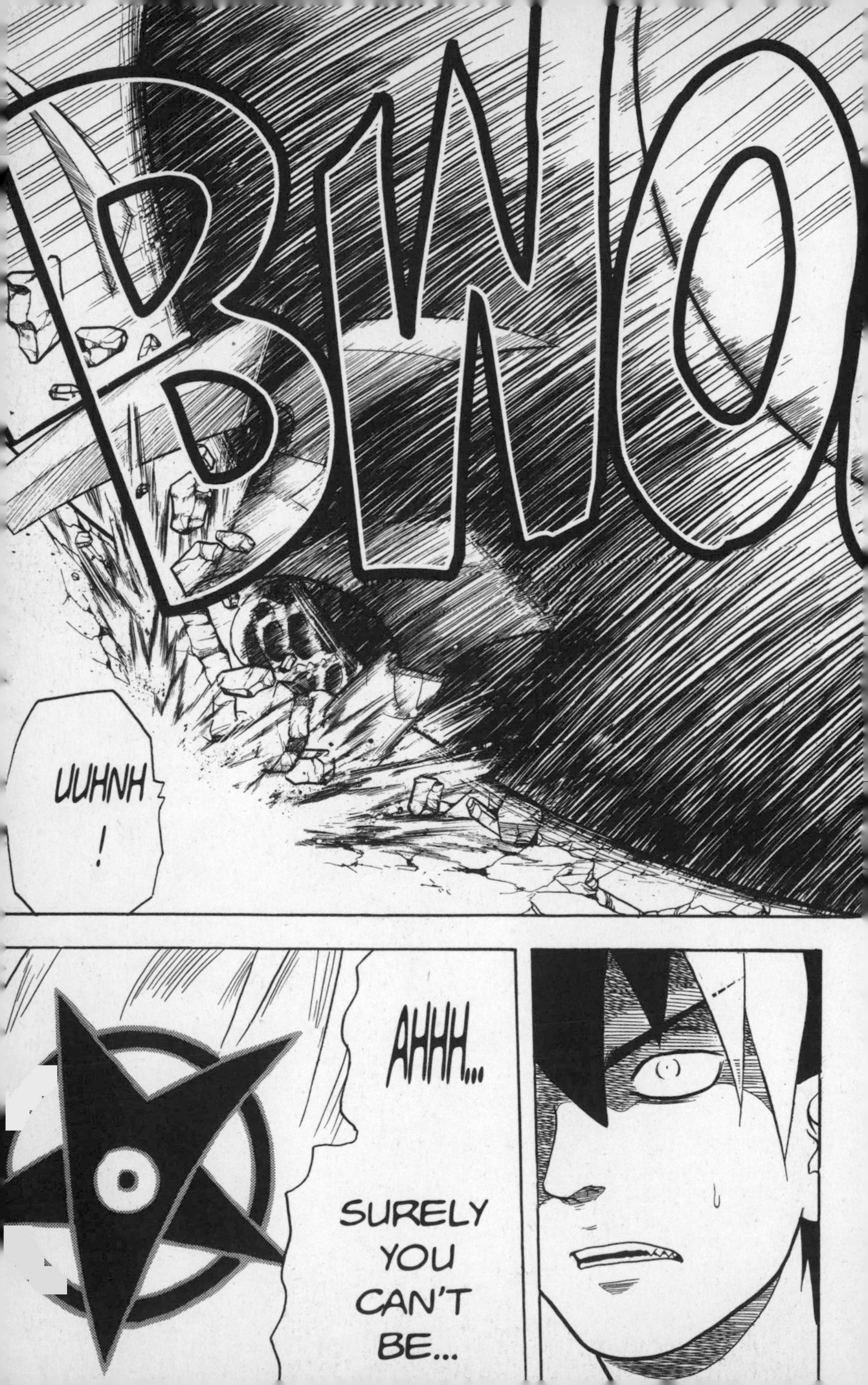
BWO
UUHNH!
AHHH...
SURELY YOU CAN'T BE...

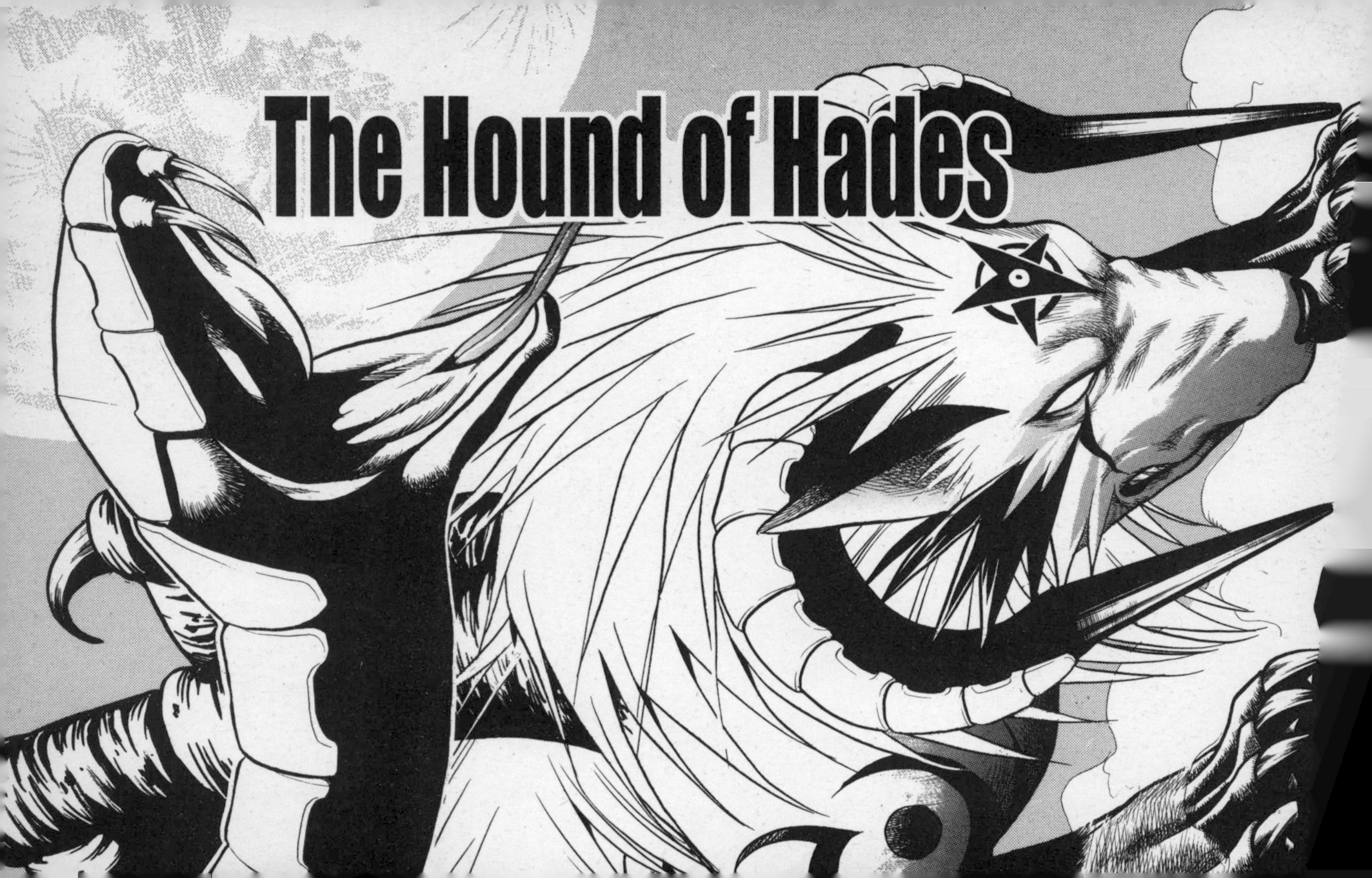
The Hound of Hades

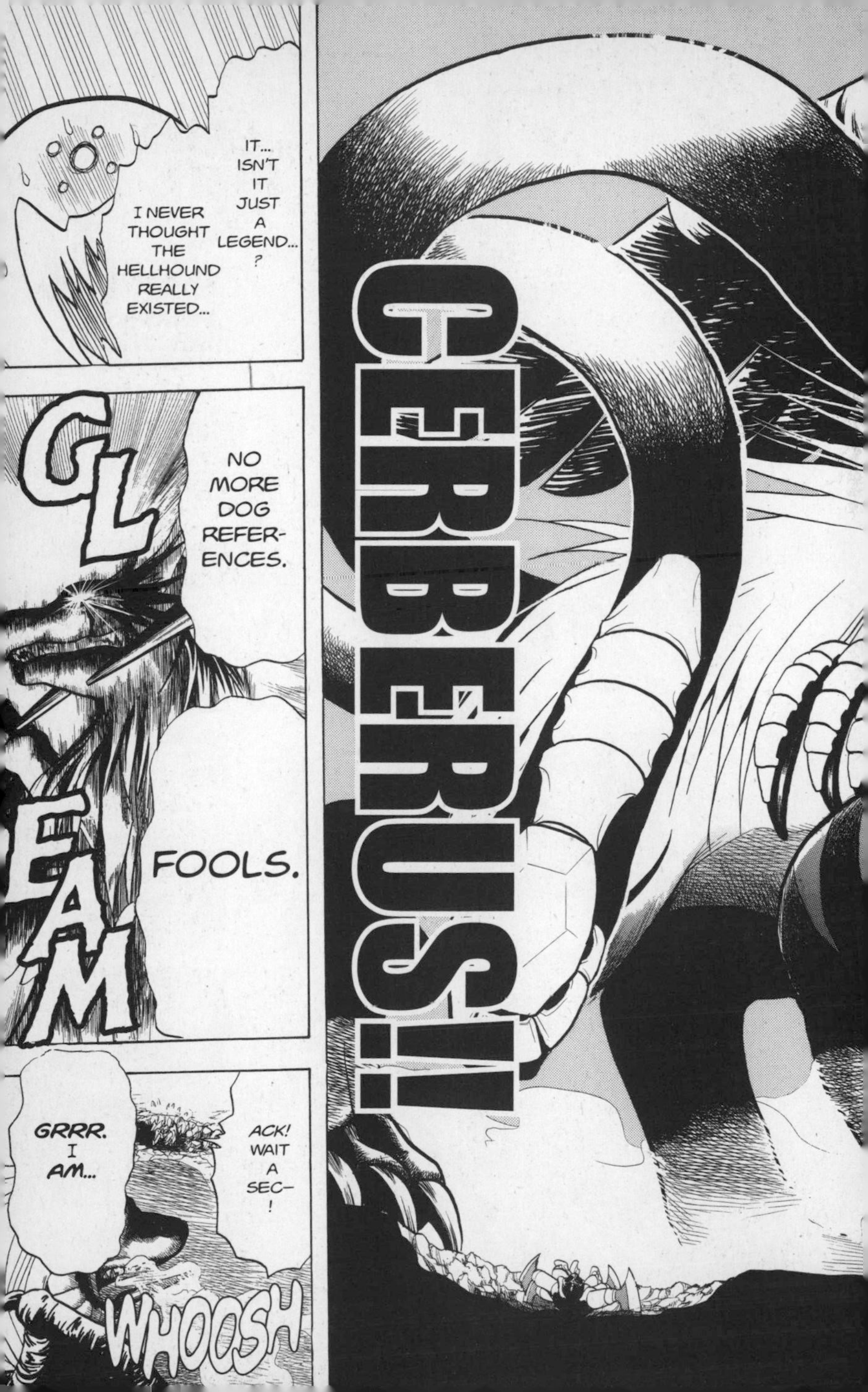
CERBERUS!!
IT... ISN'T IT JUST A LEGEND...?
I NEVER THOUGHT THE HELLHOUND REALLY EXISTED...
NO MORE DOG REFER-ENCES.
GLEAM
FOOLS.
ACK! WAIT A SEC-!
GRRR. I AM...
WHOOSH

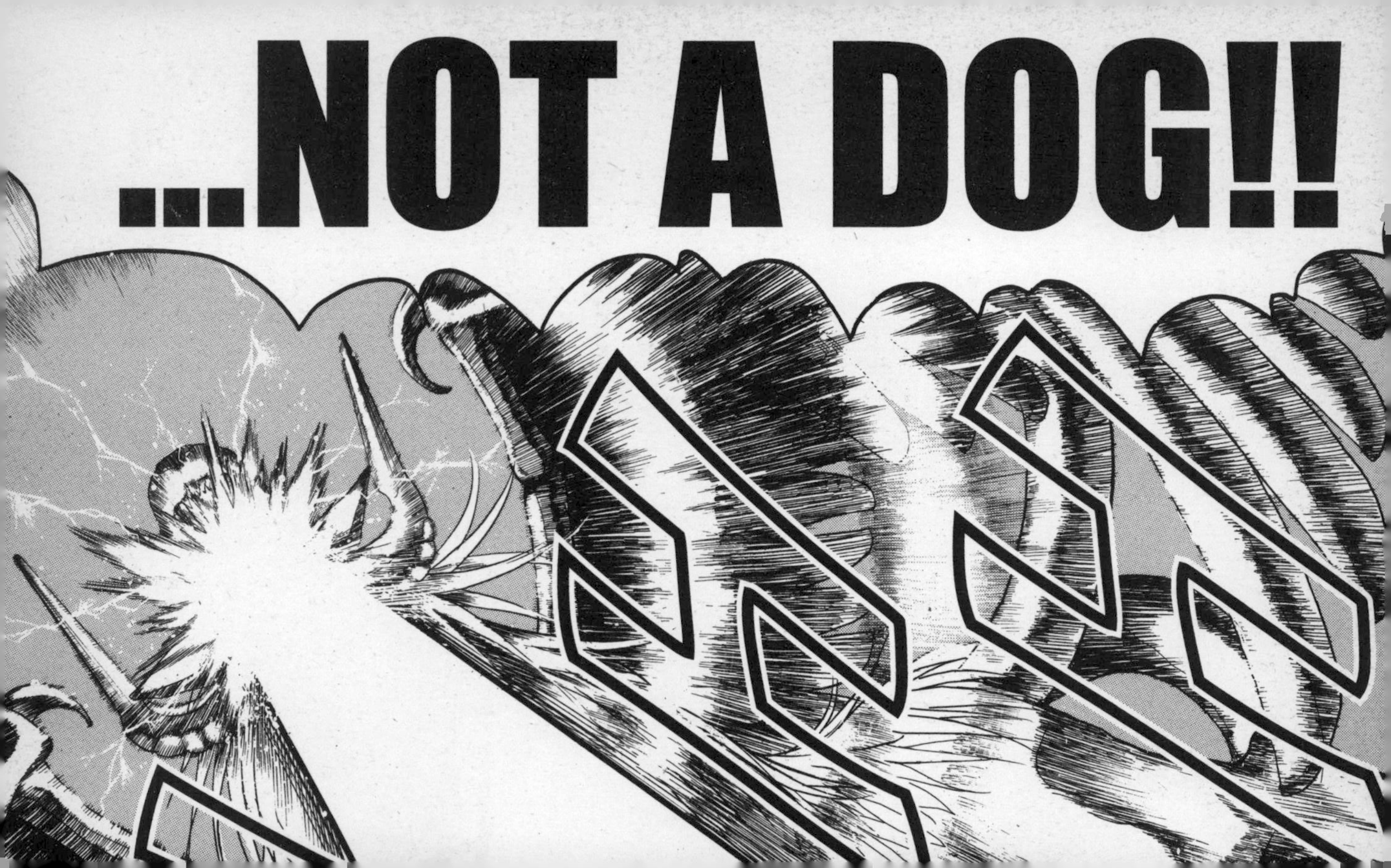
...NOT A DOG!!

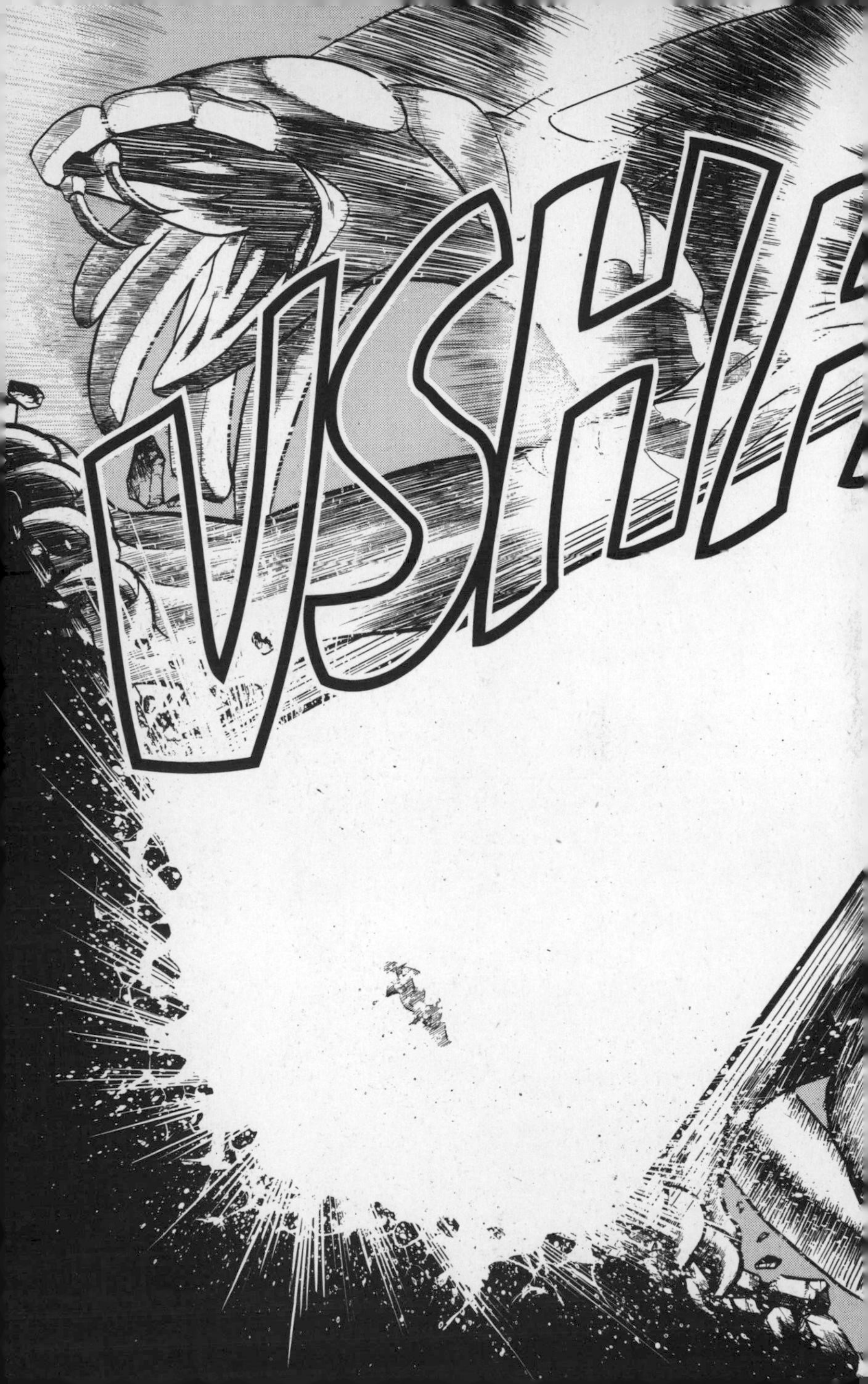
VSHH

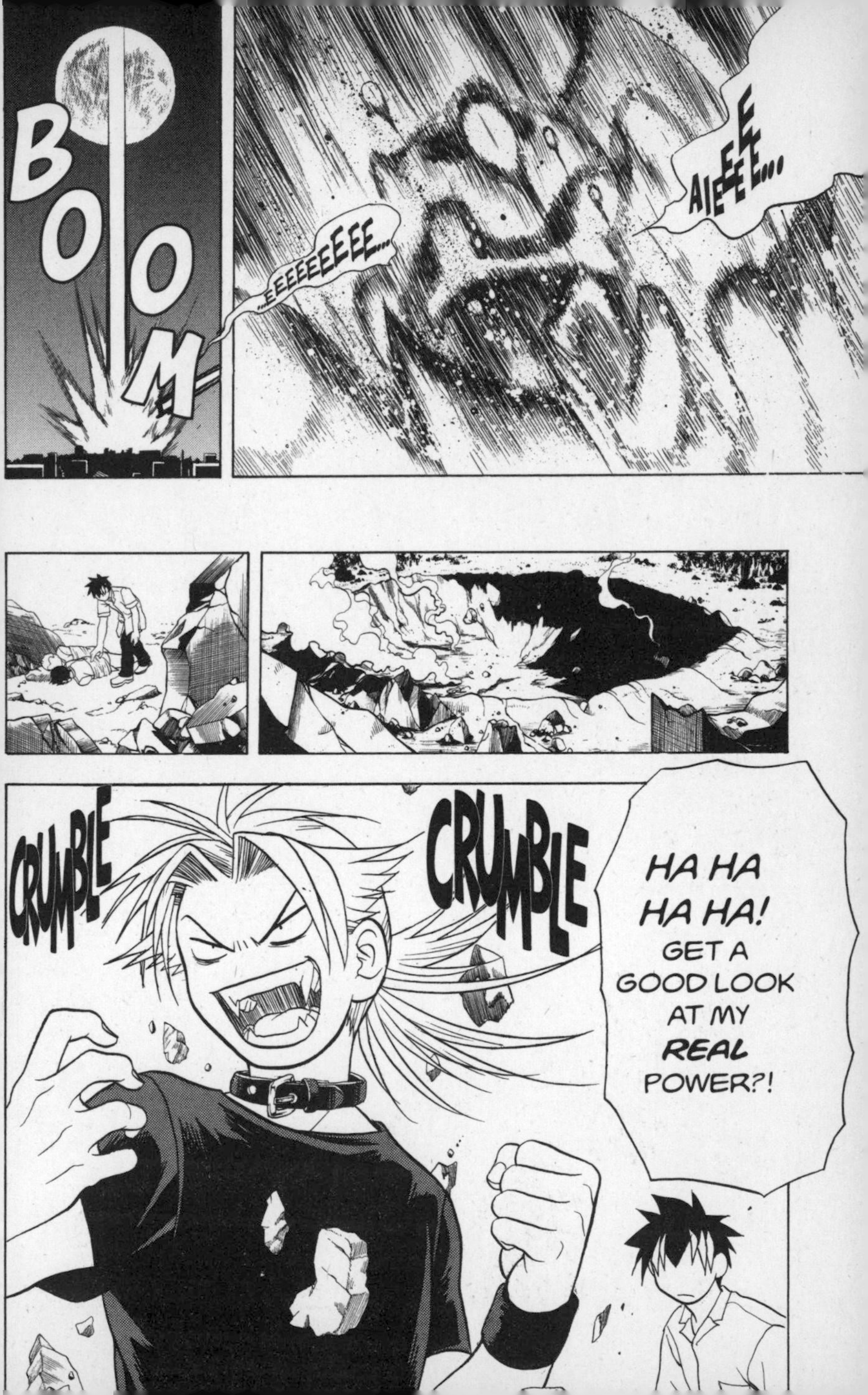
AIEEEEE...
...EEEEEEEEEE...
BOOM
CRUMBLE
CRUMBLE
HA HA HA HA! GET A GOOD LOOK AT MY *REAL* POWER?!

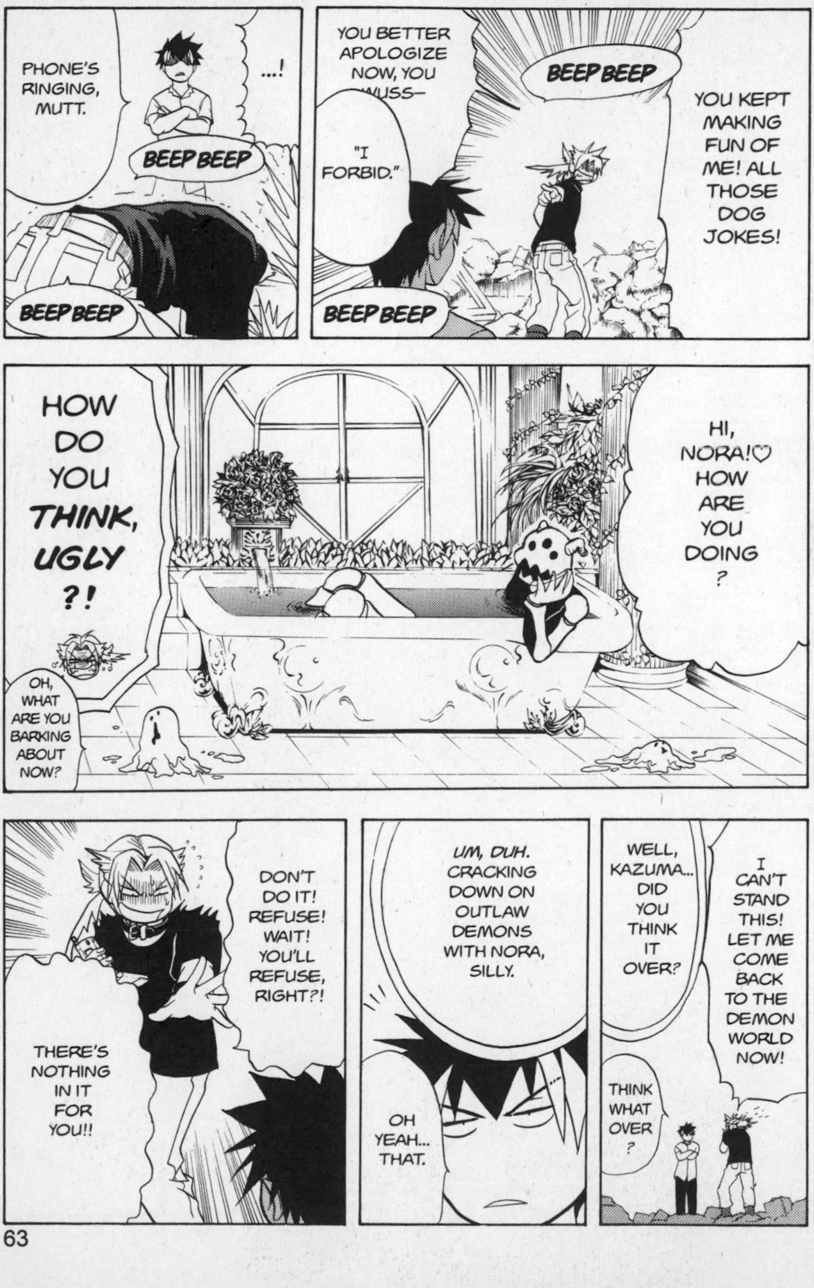
YOU KEPT MAKING FUN OF ME! ALL THOSE DOG JOKES!
BEEP BEEP
YOU BETTER APOLOGIZE NOW, YOU WUSS—
"I FORBID."
BEEP BEEP
...!
PHONE'S RINGING, MUTT.
BEEP BEEP
BEEP BEEP
HI, NORA!♡ HOW ARE YOU DOING?
HOW DO YOU THINK, UGLY?!
OH, WHAT ARE YOU BARKING ABOUT NOW?
I CAN'T STAND THIS! LET ME COME BACK TO THE DEMON WORLD NOW!
WELL, KAZUMA... DID YOU THINK IT OVER?
THINK WHAT OVER?
UM, DUH. CRACKING DOWN ON OUTLAW DEMONS WITH NORA, SILLY.
OH YEAH... THAT.
DON'T DO IT! REFUSE! WAIT! YOU'LL REFUSE, RIGHT?!
THERE'S NOTHING IN IT FOR YOU!!

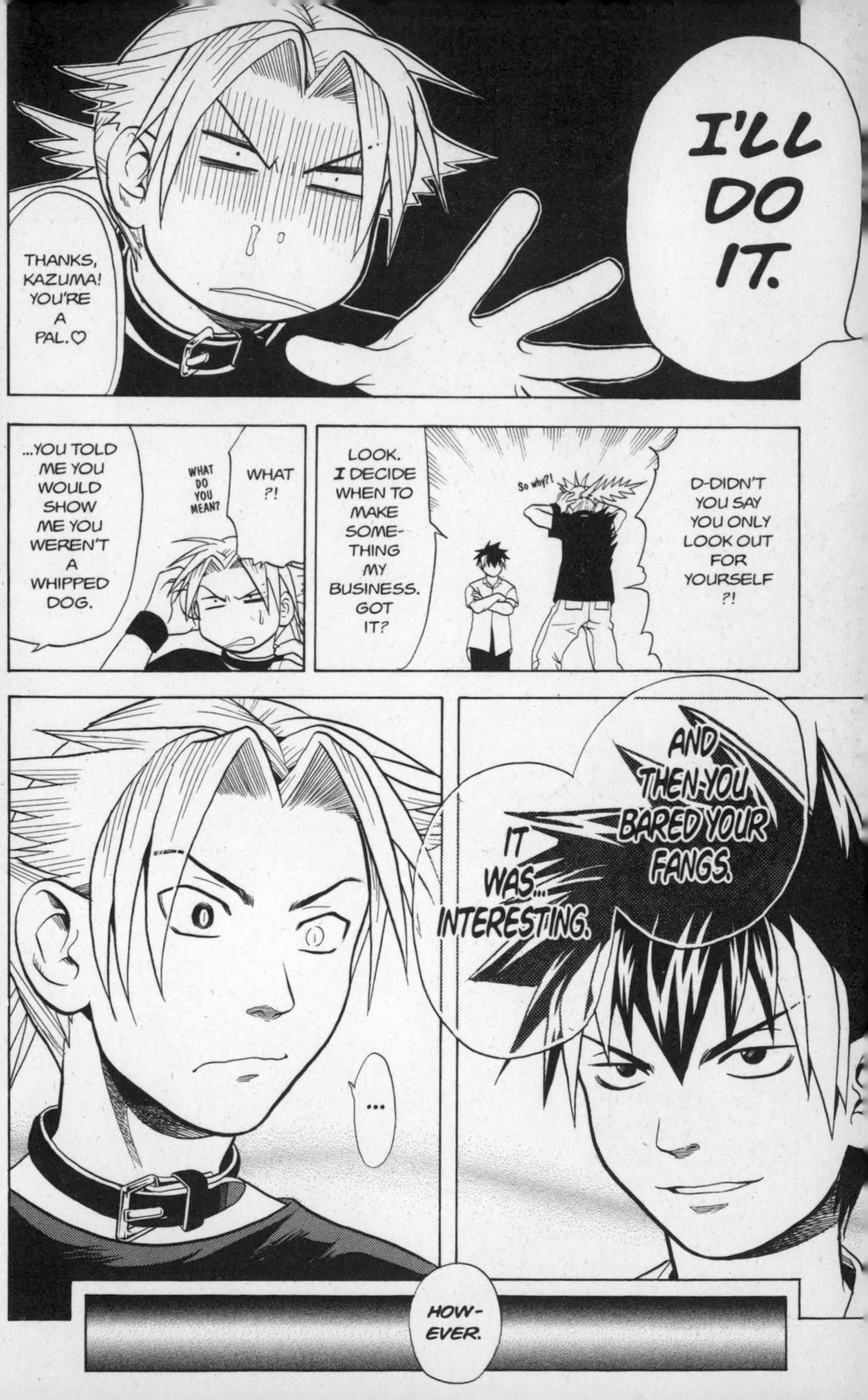
I'LL DO IT.
THANKS, KAZUMA! YOU'RE A PAL.♡
D-DIDN'T YOU SAY YOU ONLY LOOK OUT FOR YOURSELF ?!
So why?!
LOOK. I DECIDE WHEN TO MAKE SOME-THING MY BUSINESS. GOT IT?
WHAT ?!
WHAT DO YOU MEAN?
...YOU TOLD ME YOU WOULD SHOW ME YOU WEREN'T A WHIPPED DOG.
AND THEN YOU BARED YOUR FANGS.
IT WAS... INTERESTING.
...
HOW-EVER.

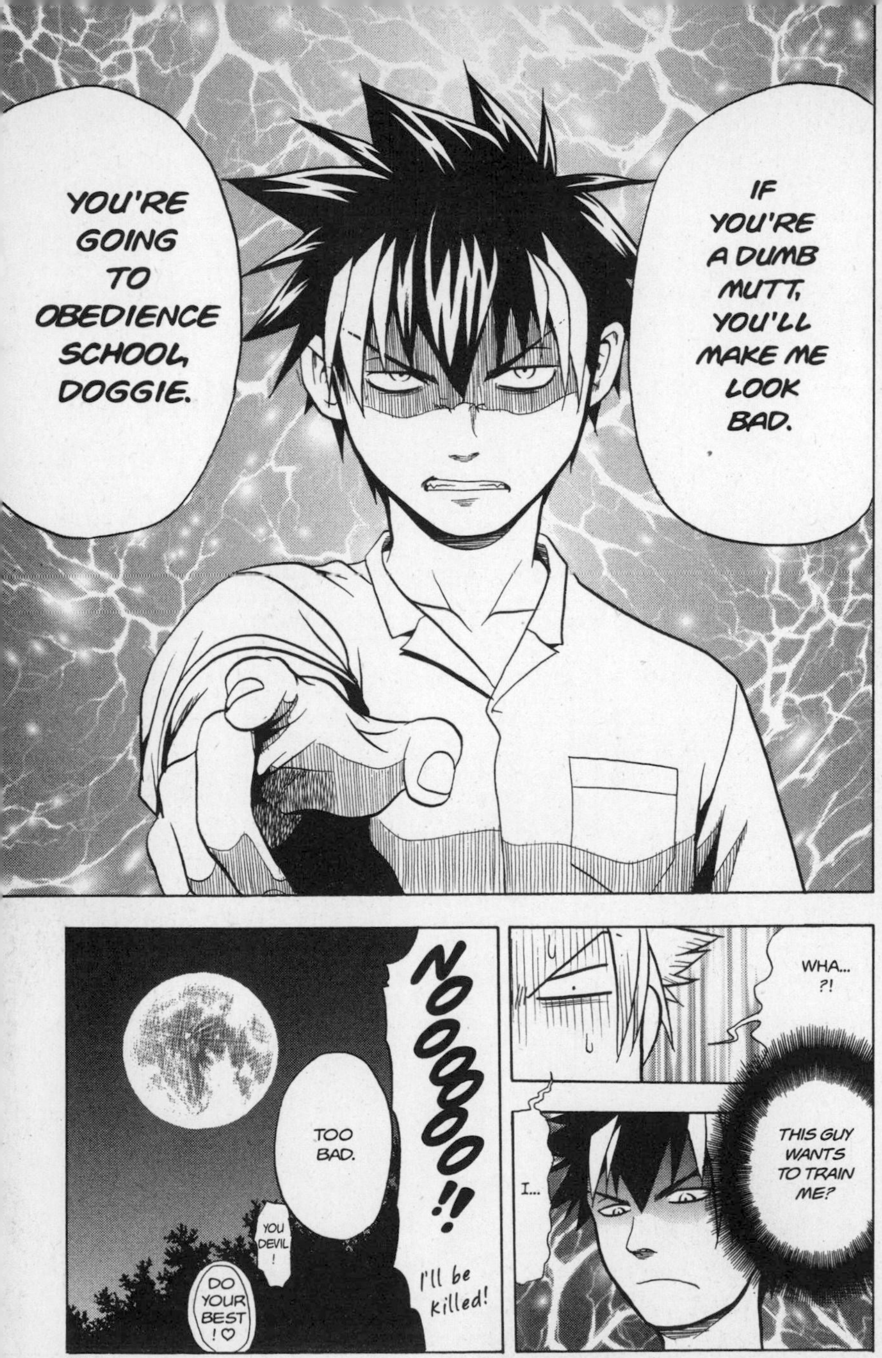
IF YOU'RE A DUMB MUTT, YOU'LL MAKE ME LOOK BAD.
YOU'RE GOING TO OBEDIENCE SCHOOL, DOGGIE.
WHA... ?!
THIS GUY WANTS TO TRAIN ME?
I...
NOOOOOO!!
I'll be killed!
TOO BAD.
YOU DEVIL!
DO YOUR BEST! ♡

Dearest Nora,

IT'S ME, THE DARK LIEGE! ♡ MY, HOW TIME FLIES. HOW'S EVERY LITTLE THING? WAIT...YOU DIDN'T FORGET ABOUT ME—! OH, YOU'RE A BAD DOG! ALWAYS TOYING WITH MY AFFECTIONS! OGRE! DEVIL! OH, BY THE WAY, THAT REMINDS ME...THE **LAST CHRONICLE OF DEVILDOM** IS ABOUT TO BEGIN! AND IF YOU DON'T READ EVERY LAST PAGE OF IT, YOU'LL REGRET IT! LOTS! ☆ SO DON'T DISAPPOINT MOOKSIE NOW! I'M COUNTING ON YOU! ♡

KISSES!

THIS WAS SUPPOSED TO BE A PREVIEW PAGE IN THE ISSUE BEFORE THE FIRST SERIALIZED CHAPTER OF NORA. BUT IT MUST HAVE BEEN TOO CUTE, BECAUSE IT WAS REJECTED. DAMMIT.

Story 2: Give and Take

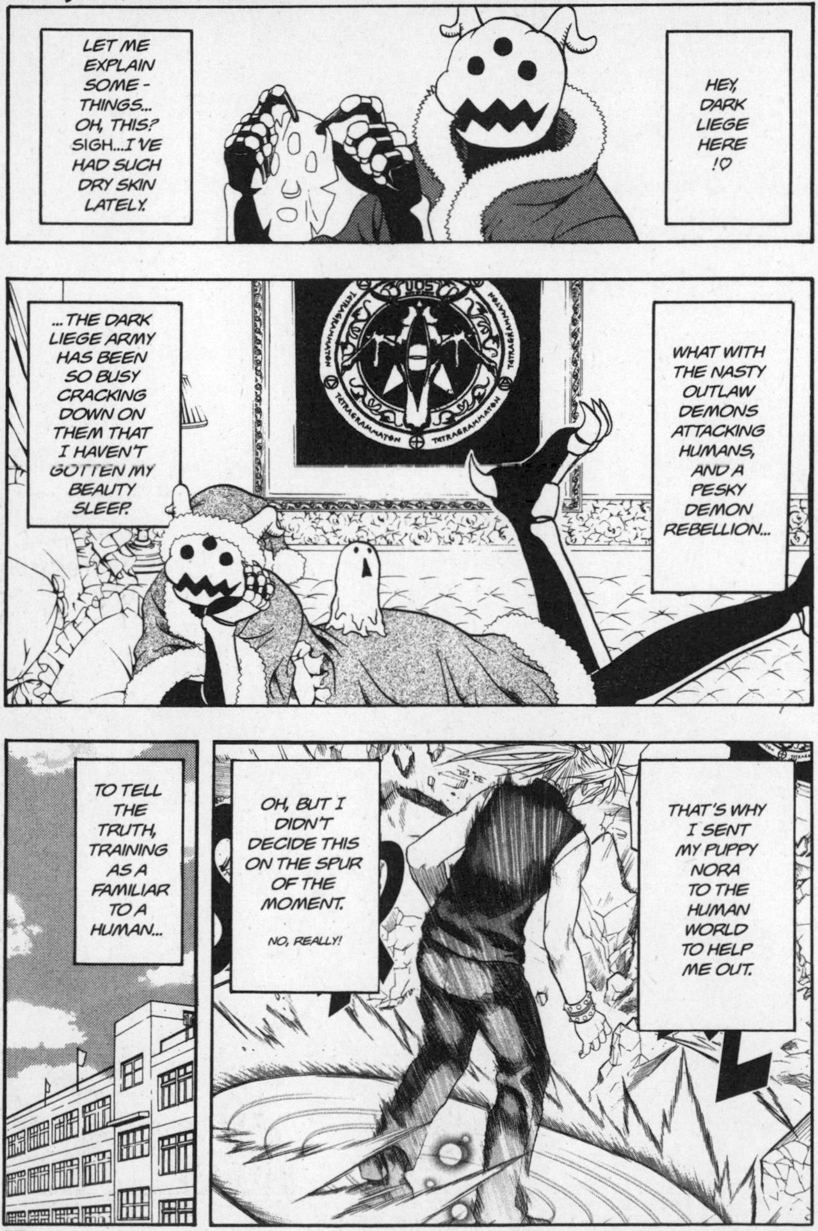
HEY, DARK LIEGE HERE! ♡
LET ME EXPLAIN SOME - THINGS... OH, THIS? SIGH...I'VE HAD SUCH DRY SKIN LATELY.
WHAT WITH THE NASTY OUTLAW DEMONS ATTACKING HUMANS, AND A PESKY DEMON REBELLION...
...THE DARK LIEGE ARMY HAS BEEN SO BUSY CRACKING DOWN ON THEM THAT I HAVEN'T GOTTEN MY BEAUTY SLEEP.
THAT'S WHY I SENT MY PUPPY NORA TO THE HUMAN WORLD TO HELP ME OUT.
OH, BUT I DIDN'T DECIDE THIS ON THE SPUR OF THE MOMENT.
NO, REALLY!
TO TELL THE TRUTH, TRAINING AS A FAMILIAR TO A HUMAN...

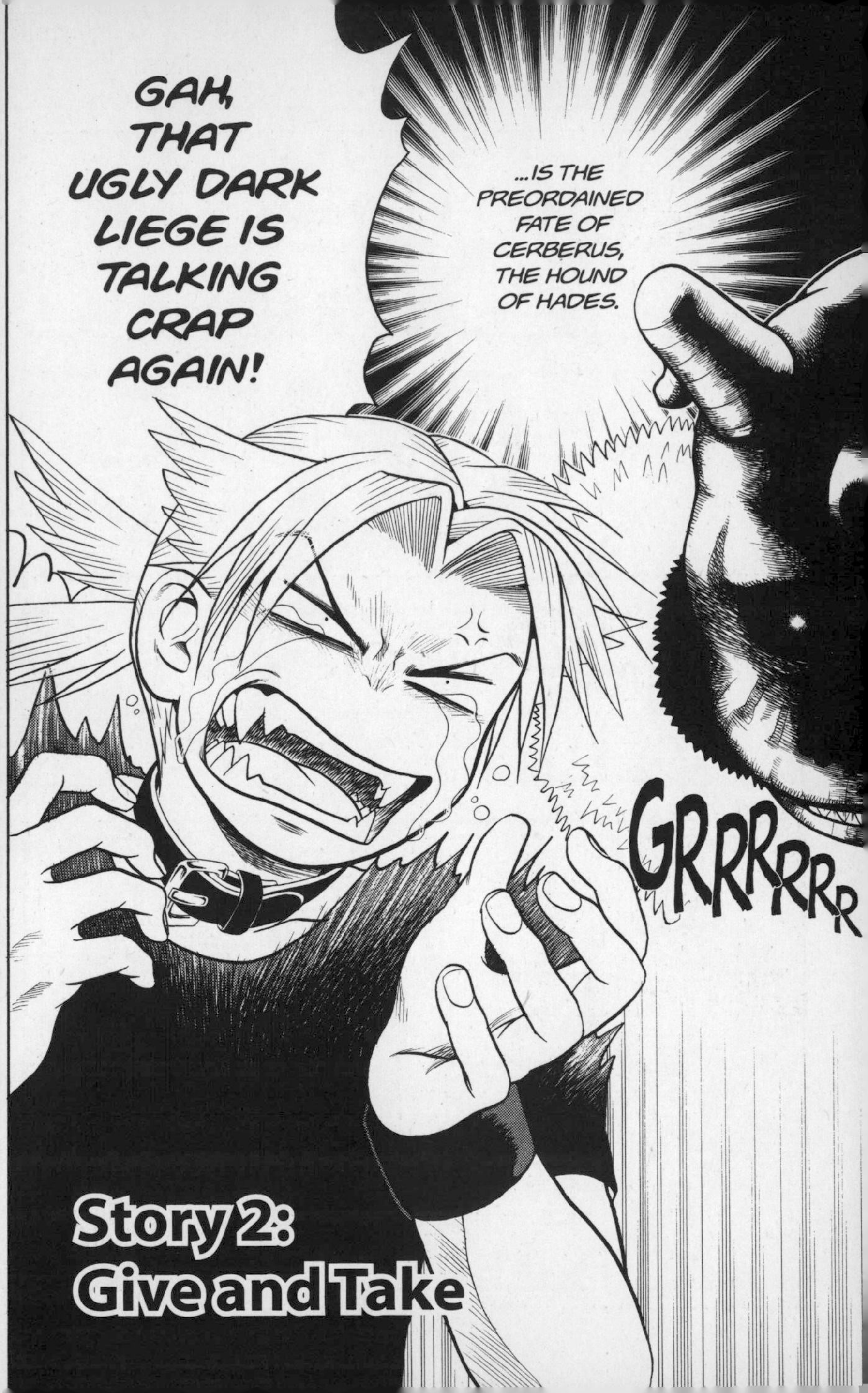
...IS THE PREORDAINED FATE OF CERBERUS, THE HOUND OF HADES.
GAH, THAT UGLY DARK LIEGE IS TALKING CRAP AGAIN!
GRRRRRR
Story 2:
Give and Take

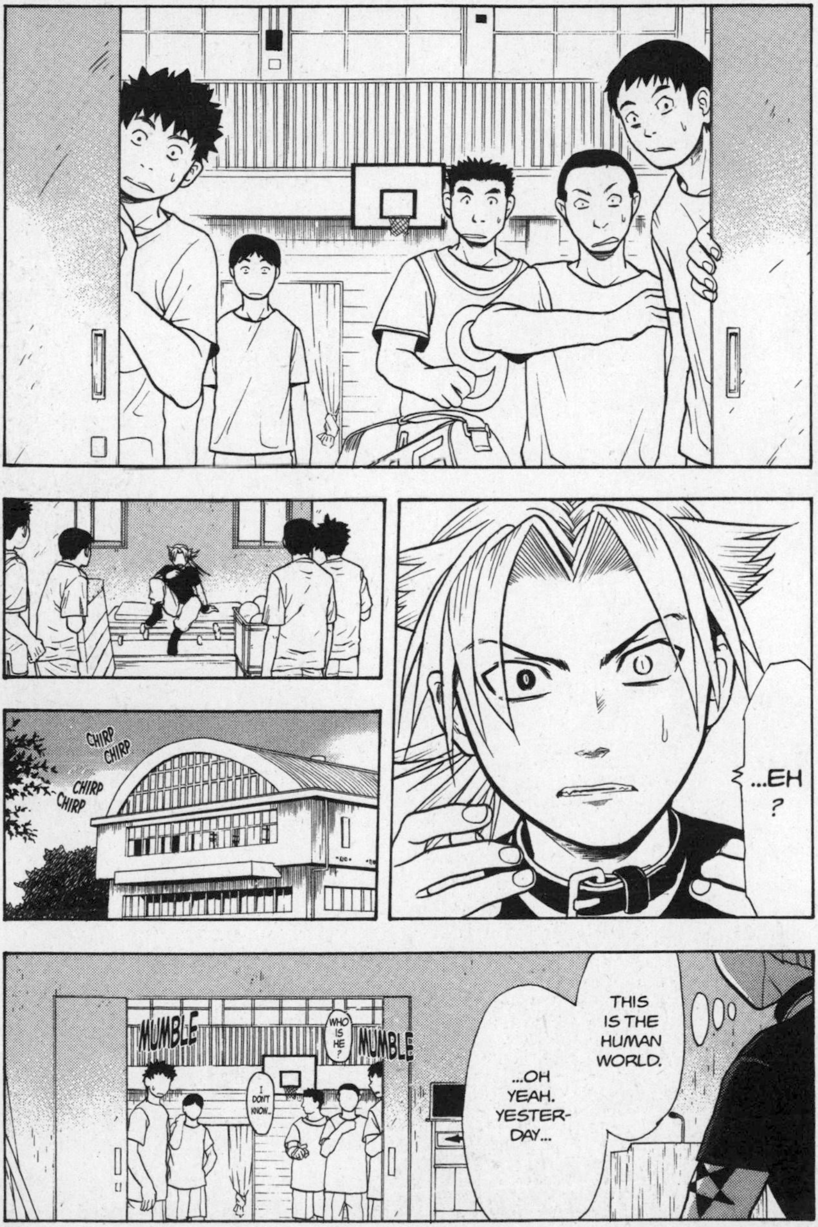
...EH ?
CHIRP CHIRP
CHIRP CHIRP
THIS IS THE HUMAN WORLD.
...OH YEAH. YESTER-DAY...
MUMBLE
WHO IS HE?
MUMBLE
I DON'T KNOW...

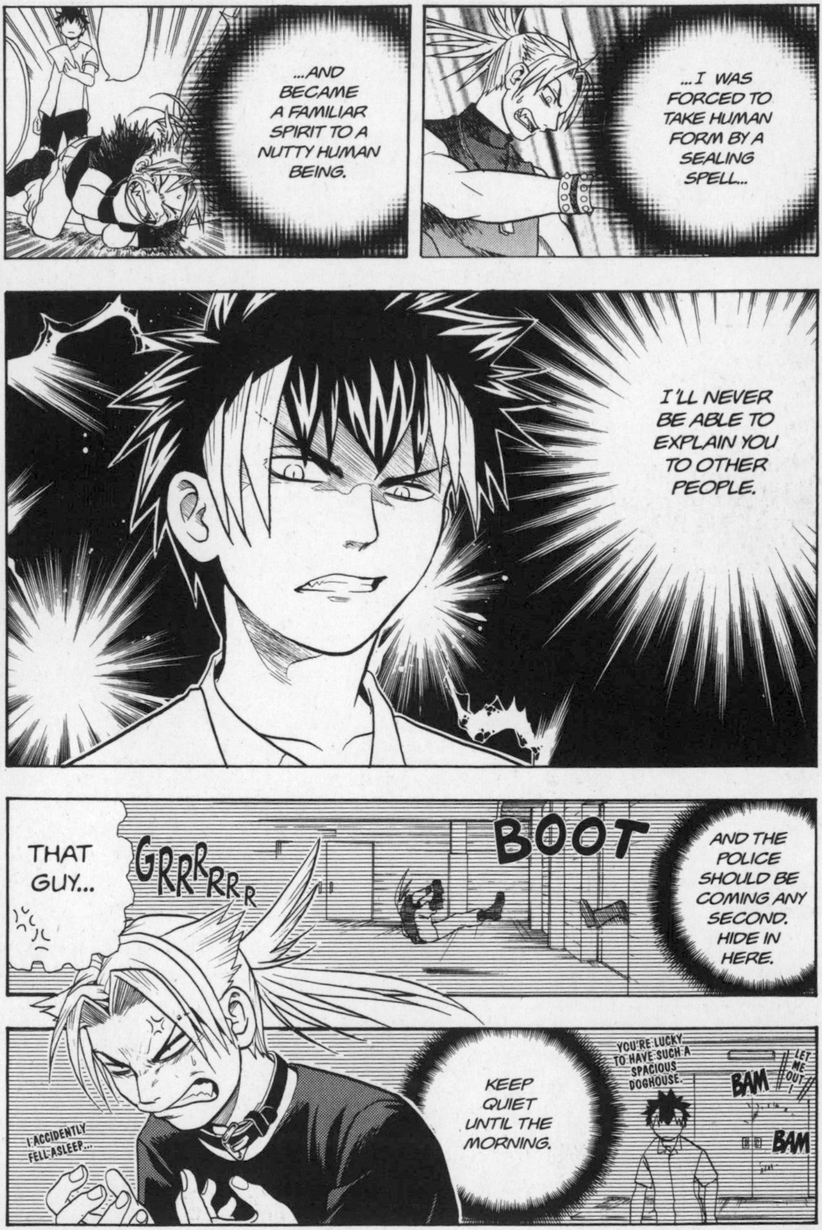
...I WAS FORCED TO TAKE HUMAN FORM BY A SEALING SPELL...
...AND BECAME A FAMILIAR SPIRIT TO A NUTTY HUMAN BEING.
I'LL NEVER BE ABLE TO EXPLAIN YOU TO OTHER PEOPLE.
AND THE POLICE SHOULD BE COMING ANY SECOND. HIDE IN HERE.
BOOT
GRRRRRR
THAT GUY...
LET ME OUT!
BAM
BAM
YOU'RE LUCKY TO HAVE SUCH A SPACIOUS DOGHOUSE.
KEEP QUIET UNTIL THE MORNING.
I ACCIDENTLY FELL ASLEEP...

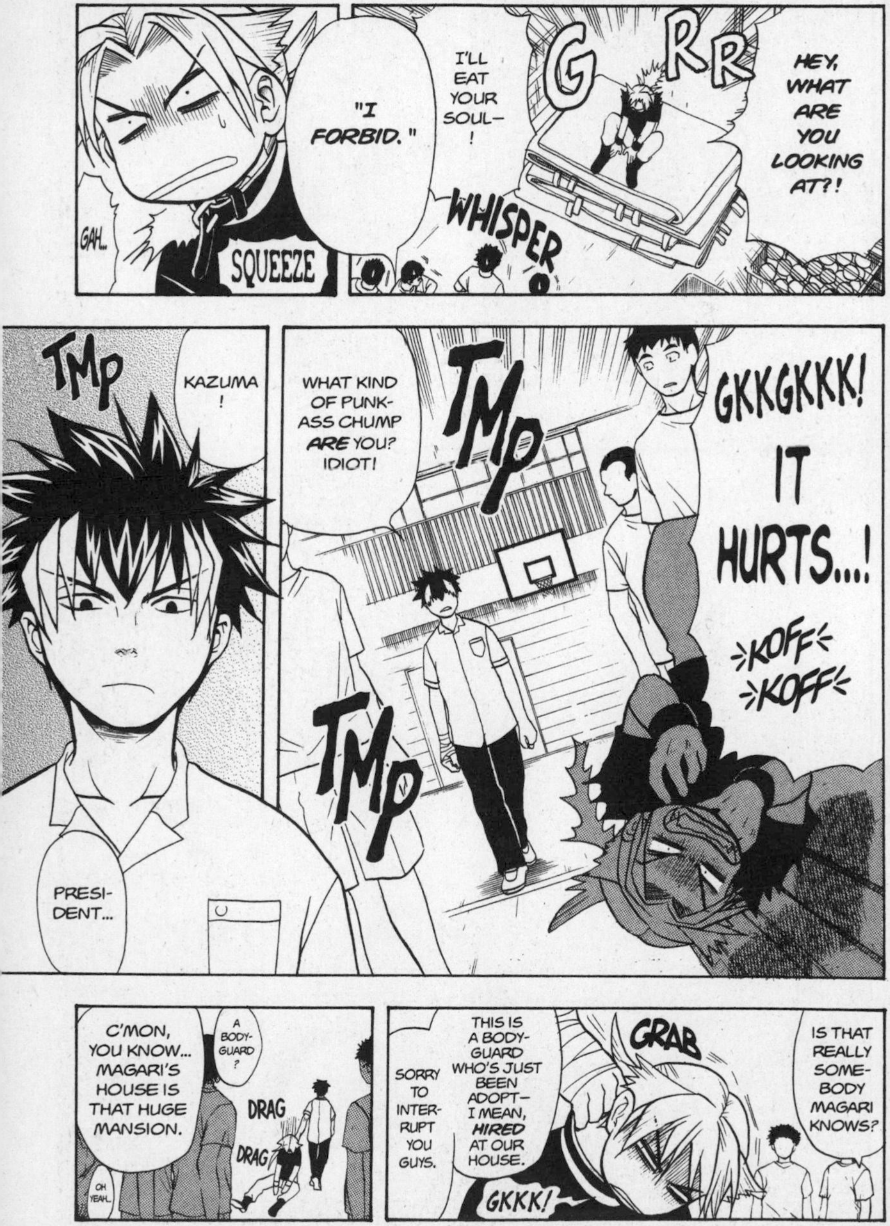
HEY, WHAT ARE YOU LOOKING AT?!
GRR
I'LL EAT YOUR SOUL—!
WHISPER
"I FORBID."
GAH...
SQUEEZE
GKKGKKK! IT HURTS...!
KOFF KOFF
TMP
WHAT KIND OF PUNK-ASS CHUMP ARE YOU? IDIOT!
TMP
TMP
KAZUMA!
PRESI-DENT...
IS THAT REALLY SOME-BODY MAGARI KNOWS?
GRAB
THIS IS A BODY-GUARD WHO'S JUST BEEN ADOPT— I MEAN, HIRED AT OUR HOUSE.
SORRY TO INTER-RUPT YOU GUYS.
GKKK!
A BODY-GUARD?
C'MON, YOU KNOW... MAGARI'S HOUSE IS THAT HUGE MANSION.
DRAG
DRAG
OH YEAH...

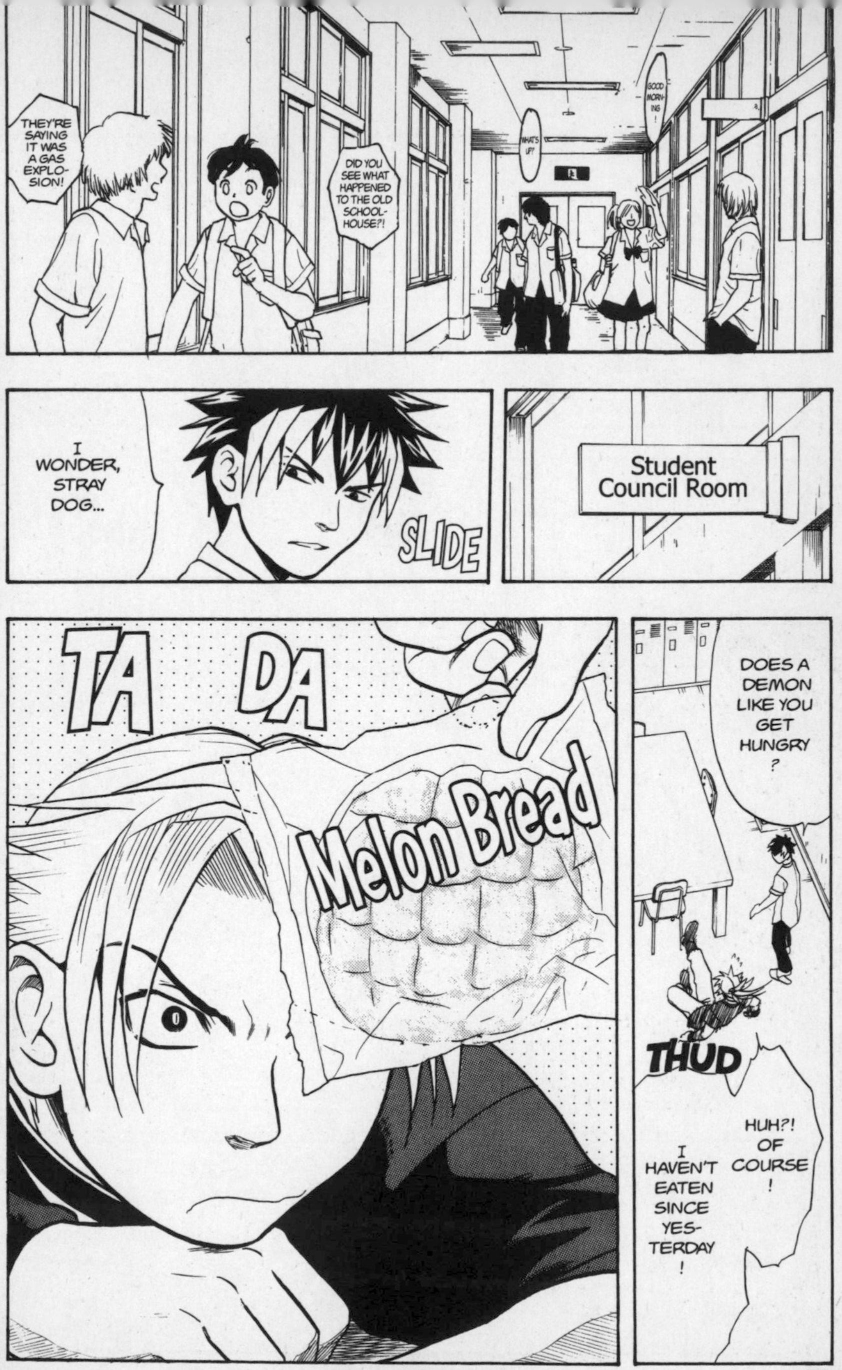
GOOD MORNING!
WHAT'S UP?
DID YOU SEE WHAT HAPPENED TO THE OLD SCHOOLHOUSE?!
THEY'RE SAYING IT WAS A GAS EXPLOSION!
Student Council Room
SLIDE
I WONDER, STRAY DOG...
DOES A DEMON LIKE YOU GET HUNGRY?
THUD
HUH?! OF COURSE!
I HAVEN'T EATEN SINCE YESTERDAY!
TA DA
Melon Bread

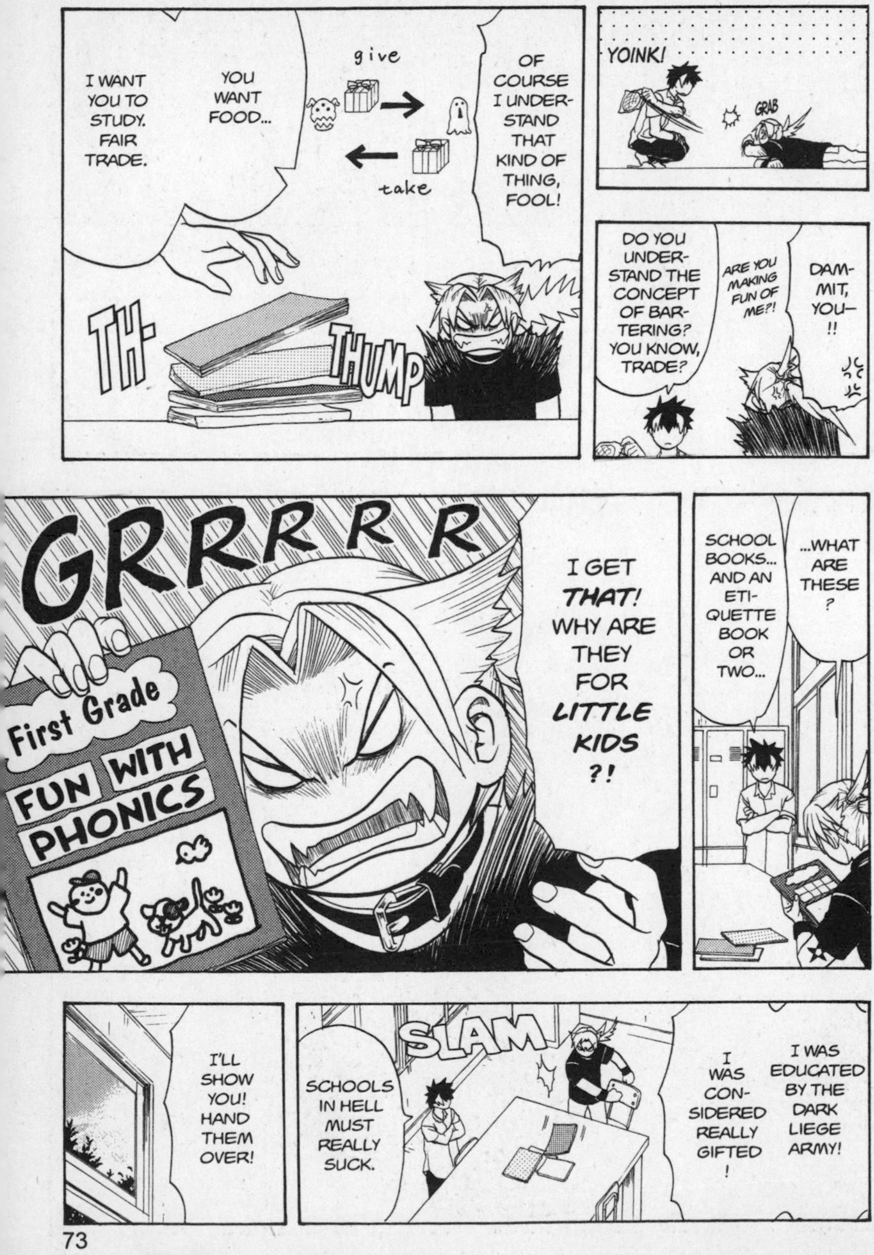

YOINK!
GRAB
DO YOU UNDERSTAND THE CONCEPT OF BARTERING? YOU KNOW, TRADE?
ARE YOU MAKING FUN OF ME?!
DAMMIT, YOU—!!
OF COURSE I UNDERSTAND THAT KIND OF THING, FOOL!
give
take
YOU WANT FOOD...
I WANT YOU TO STUDY. FAIR TRADE.
TH-THUMP
...WHAT ARE THESE?
SCHOOL BOOKS... AND AN ETIQUETTE BOOK OR TWO...
GRRRRR
I GET *THAT*! WHY ARE THEY FOR *LITTLE KIDS*?!
First Grade
FUN WITH PHONICS
I WAS EDUCATED BY THE DARK LIEGE ARMY!
I WAS CONSIDERED REALLY GIFTED!
SLAM
SCHOOLS IN HELL MUST REALLY SUCK.
I'LL SHOW YOU! HAND THEM OVER!

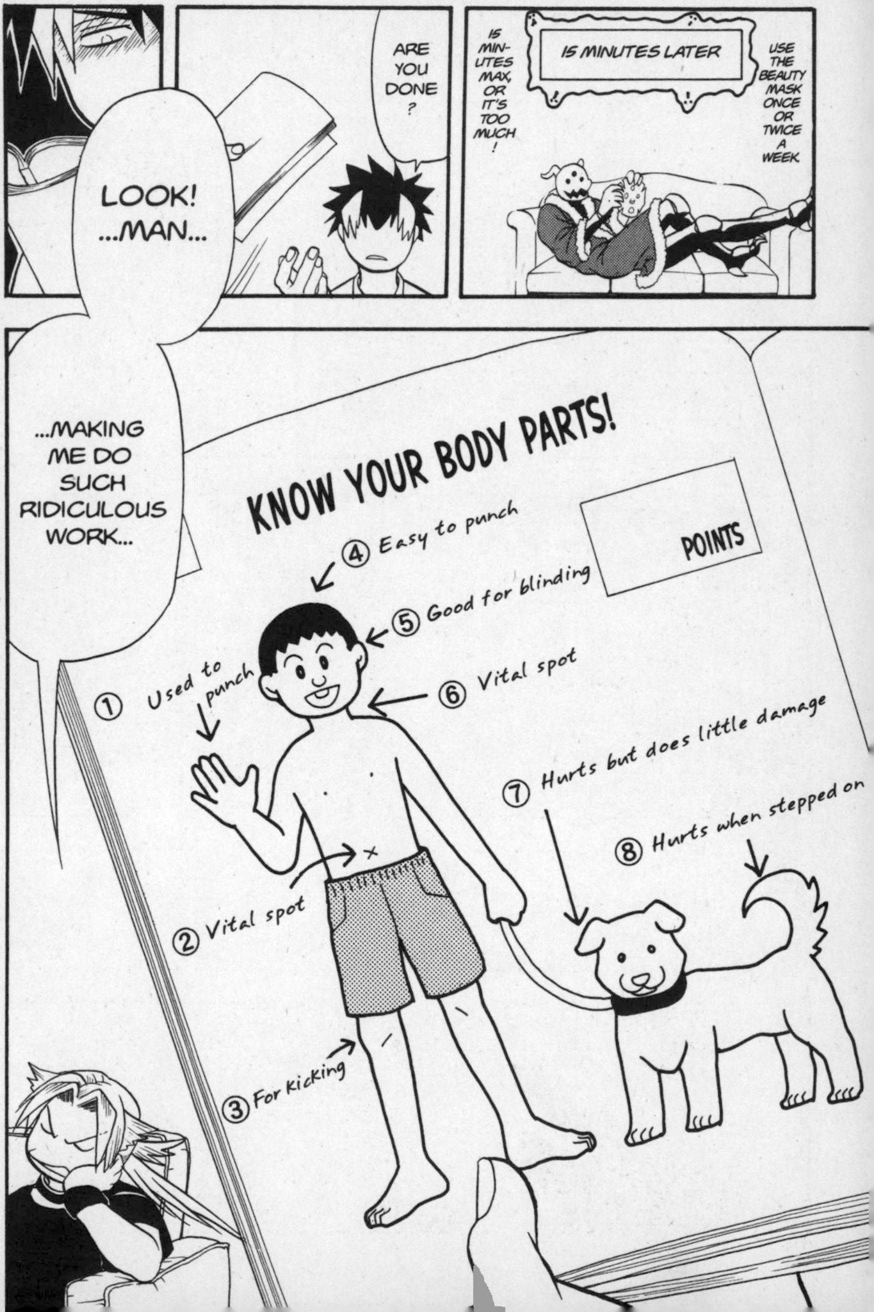
USE THE BEAUTY MASK ONCE OR TWICE A WEEK
15 MINUTES LATER
15 MIN-UTES MAX, OR IT'S TOO MUCH!
ARE YOU DONE?
LOOK! ...MAN...
...MAKING ME DO SUCH RIDICULOUS WORK...
KNOW YOUR BODY PARTS!
POINTS
④ Easy to punch
⑤ Good for blinding
⑥ Vital spot
① Used to punch
⑦ Hurts but does little damage
⑧ Hurts when stepped on
② Vital spot
③ For kicking

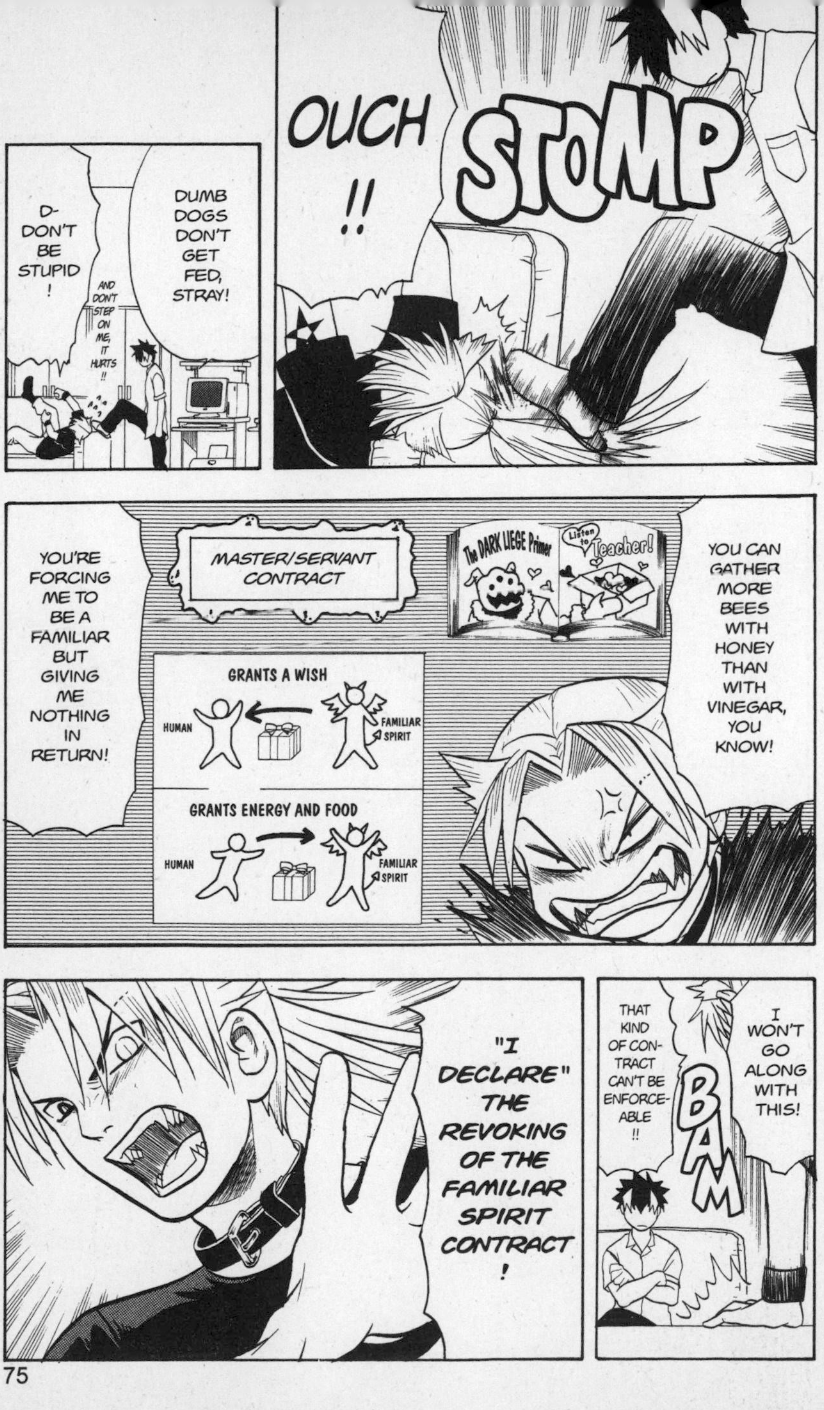

STOMP
OUCH!!
DUMB DOGS DON'T GET FED, STRAY!
D-DON'T BE STUPID!
AND DON'T STEP ON ME, IT HURTS!!
YOU CAN GATHER MORE BEES WITH HONEY THAN WITH VINEGAR, YOU KNOW!
The DARK LIEGE Primer
Listen to Teacher!
MASTER/SERVANT CONTRACT
GRANTS A WISH
HUMAN
FAMILIAR SPIRIT
GRANTS ENERGY AND FOOD
HUMAN
FAMILIAR SPIRIT
YOU'RE FORCING ME TO BE A FAMILIAR BUT GIVING ME NOTHING IN RETURN!
I WON'T GO ALONG WITH THIS!
BAM
THAT KIND OF CONTRACT CAN'T BE ENFORCEABLE!!
"I DECLARE" THE REVOKING OF THE FAMILIAR SPIRIT CONTRACT!

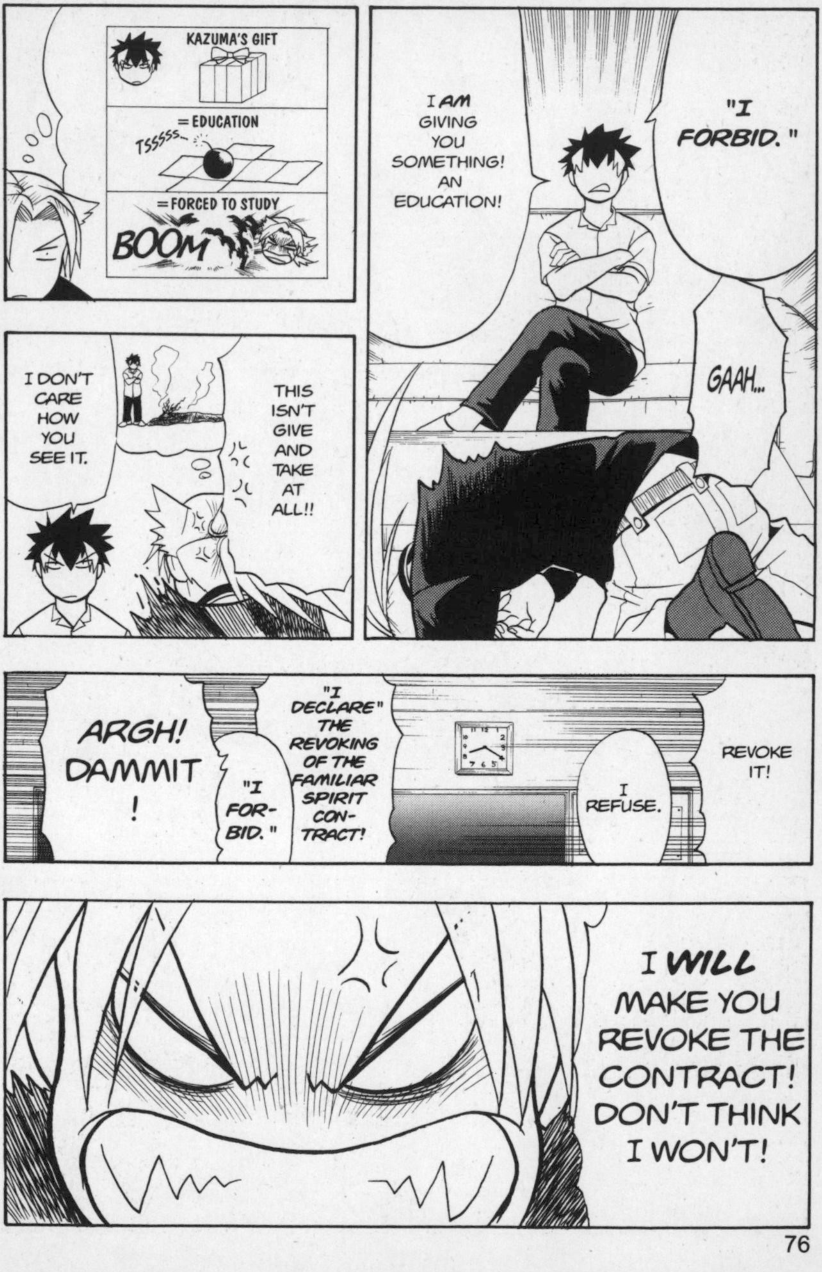
"I FORBID."
I AM GIVING YOU SOMETHING! AN EDUCATION!
GAAH...
KAZUMA'S GIFT
= EDUCATION
TSSSSS...
= FORCED TO STUDY
BOOM
THIS ISN'T GIVE AND TAKE AT ALL!!
I DON'T CARE HOW YOU SEE IT.
REVOKE IT!
I REFUSE.
"I DECLARE" THE REVOKING OF THE FAMILIAR SPIRIT CONTRACT!
"I FORBID."
ARGH! DAMMIT!
I WILL MAKE YOU REVOKE THE CONTRACT! DON'T THINK I WON'T!

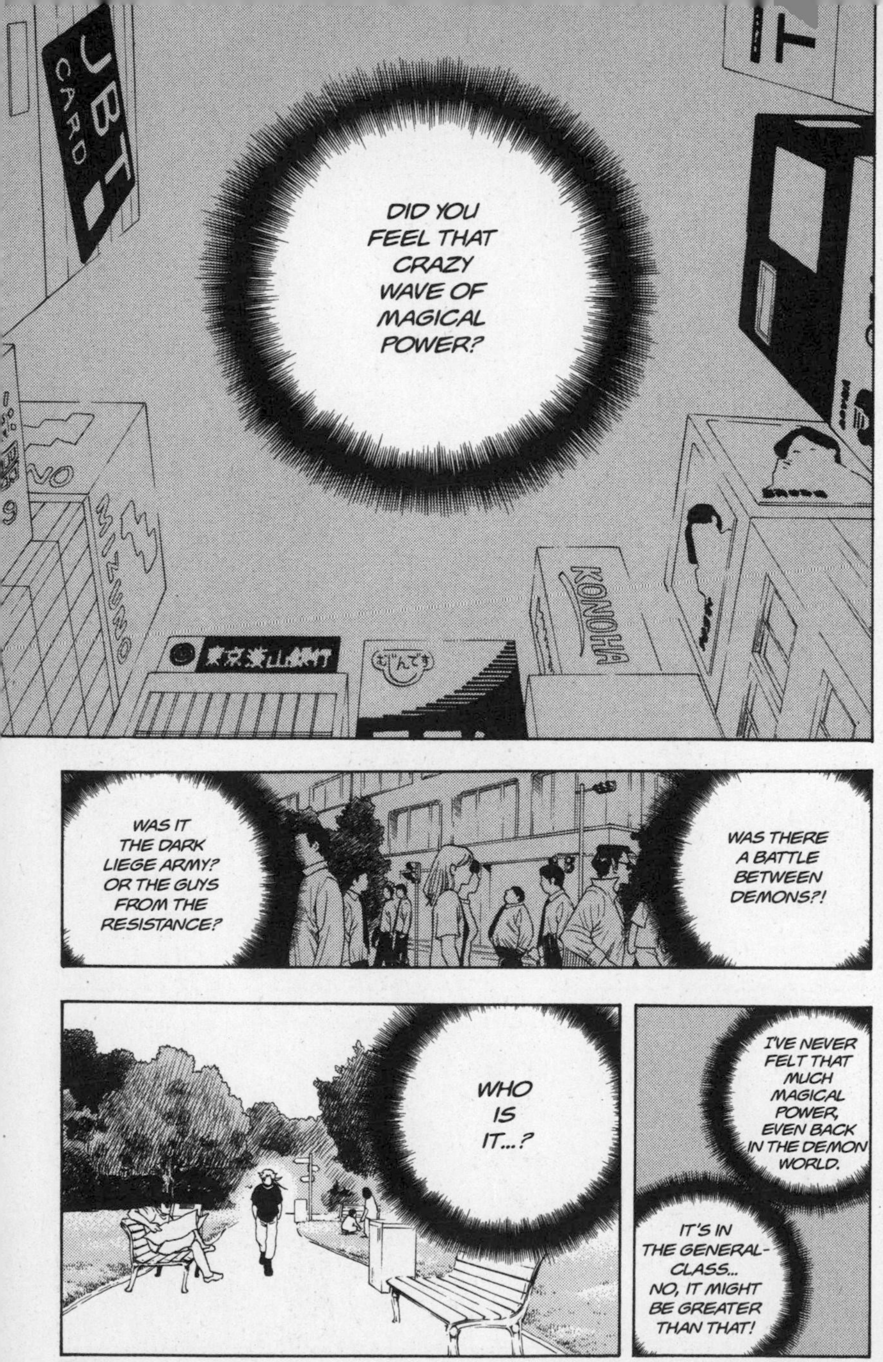
JBT CARD
MIZUNO
KONOHA
DID YOU FEEL THAT CRAZY WAVE OF MAGICAL POWER?
WAS THERE A BATTLE BETWEEN DEMONS?!
WAS IT THE DARK LIEGE ARMY? OR THE GUYS FROM THE RESISTANCE?
I'VE NEVER FELT THAT MUCH MAGICAL POWER, EVEN BACK IN THE DEMON WORLD.
IT'S IN THE GENERAL-CLASS... NO, IT MIGHT BE GREATER THAN THAT!
WHO IS IT...?

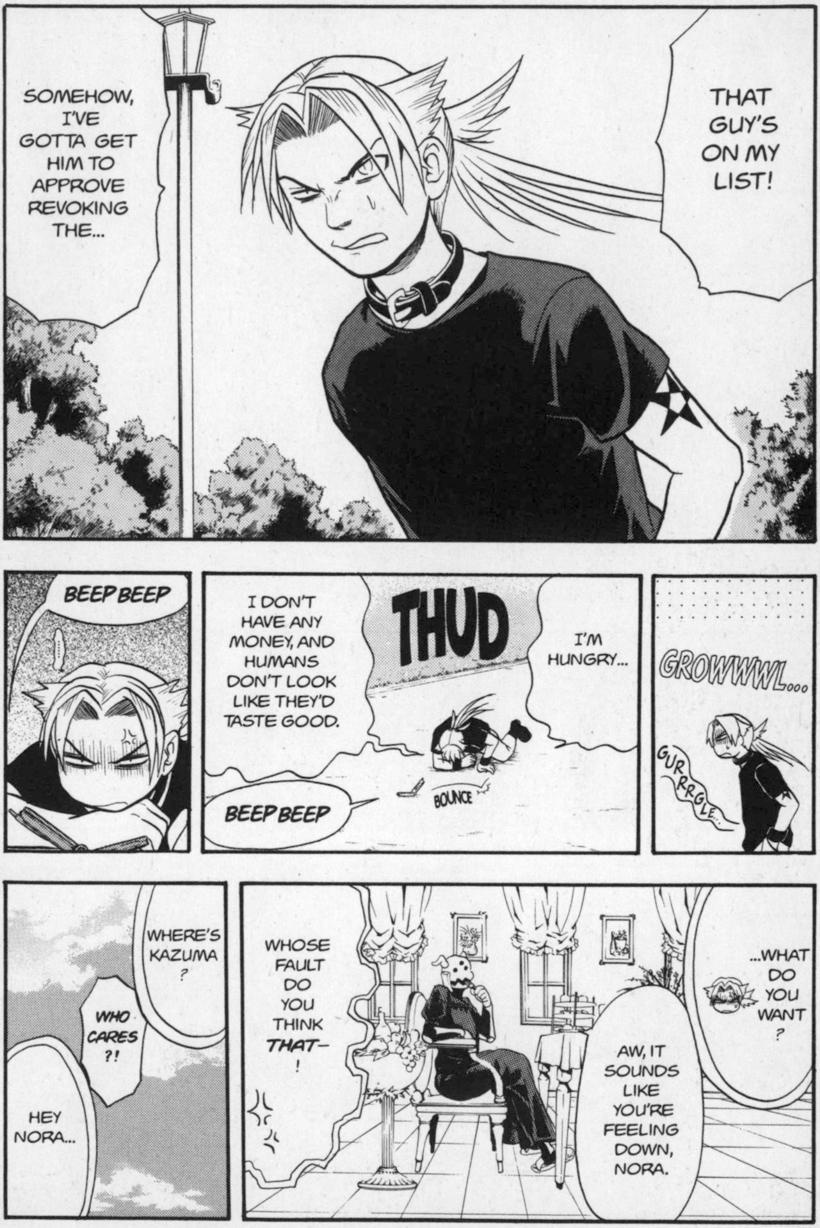
THAT GUY'S ON MY LIST!
SOMEHOW, I'VE GOTTA GET HIM TO APPROVE REVOKING THE...
GROWWWL...
GURRRGLE...
I'M HUNGRY...
THUD
I DON'T HAVE ANY MONEY, AND HUMANS DON'T LOOK LIKE THEY'D TASTE GOOD.
BOUNCE
BEEP BEEP
BEEP BEEP
...WHAT DO YOU WANT?
AW, IT SOUNDS LIKE YOU'RE FEELING DOWN, NORA.
WHOSE FAULT DO YOU THINK ***THAT***-!
WHERE'S KAZUMA?
WHO CARES?!
HEY NORA...

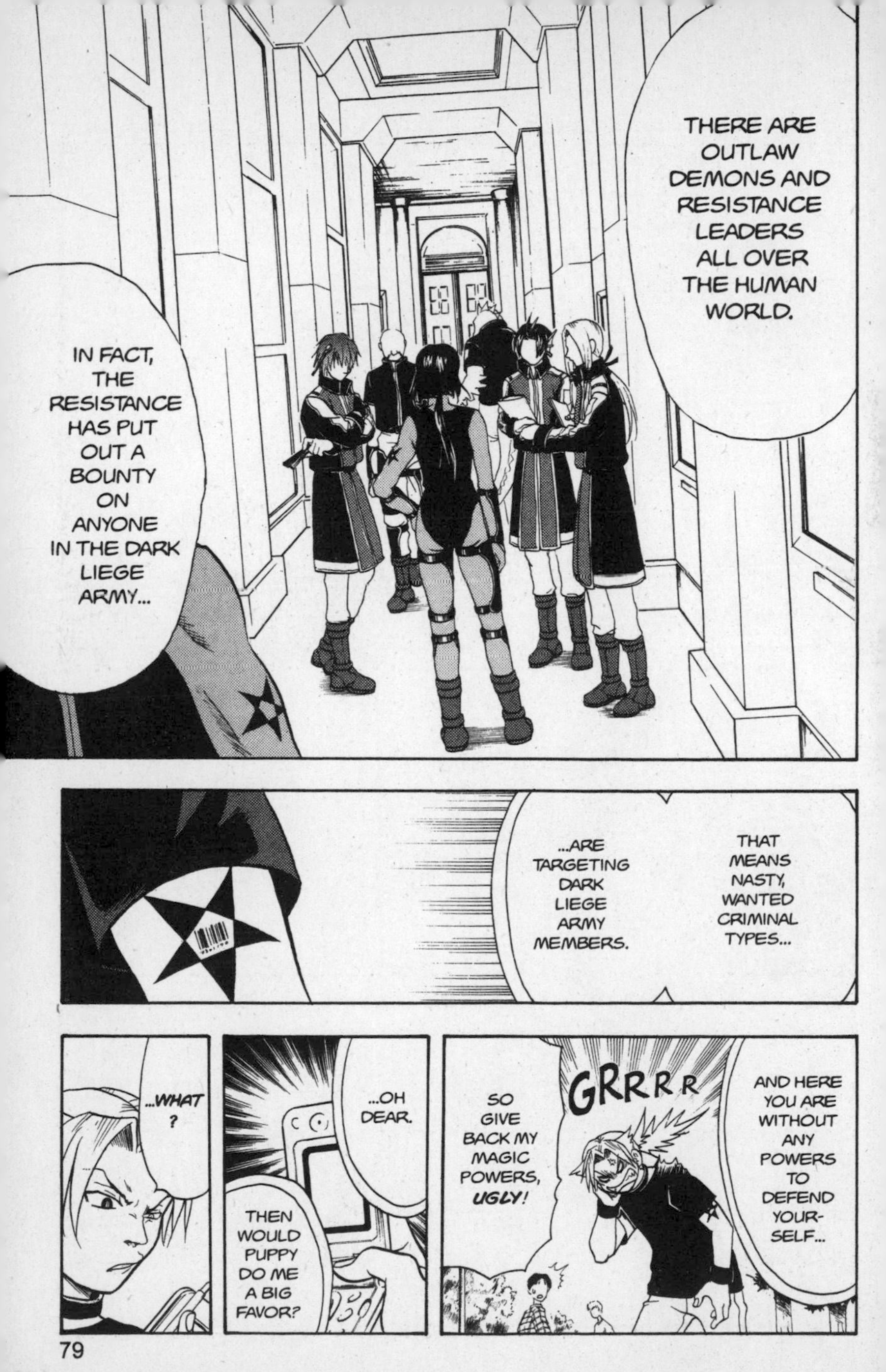
THERE ARE OUTLAW DEMONS AND RESISTANCE LEADERS ALL OVER THE HUMAN WORLD.
IN FACT, THE RESISTANCE HAS PUT OUT A BOUNTY ON ANYONE IN THE DARK LIEGE ARMY...
THAT MEANS NASTY, WANTED CRIMINAL TYPES...
...ARE TARGETING DARK LIEGE ARMY MEMBERS.
AND HERE YOU ARE WITHOUT ANY POWERS TO DEFEND YOURSELF...
GRRRR
SO GIVE BACK MY MAGIC POWERS, ***UGLY!***
...OH DEAR.
THEN WOULD PUPPY DO ME A BIG FAVOR?
...WHAT?

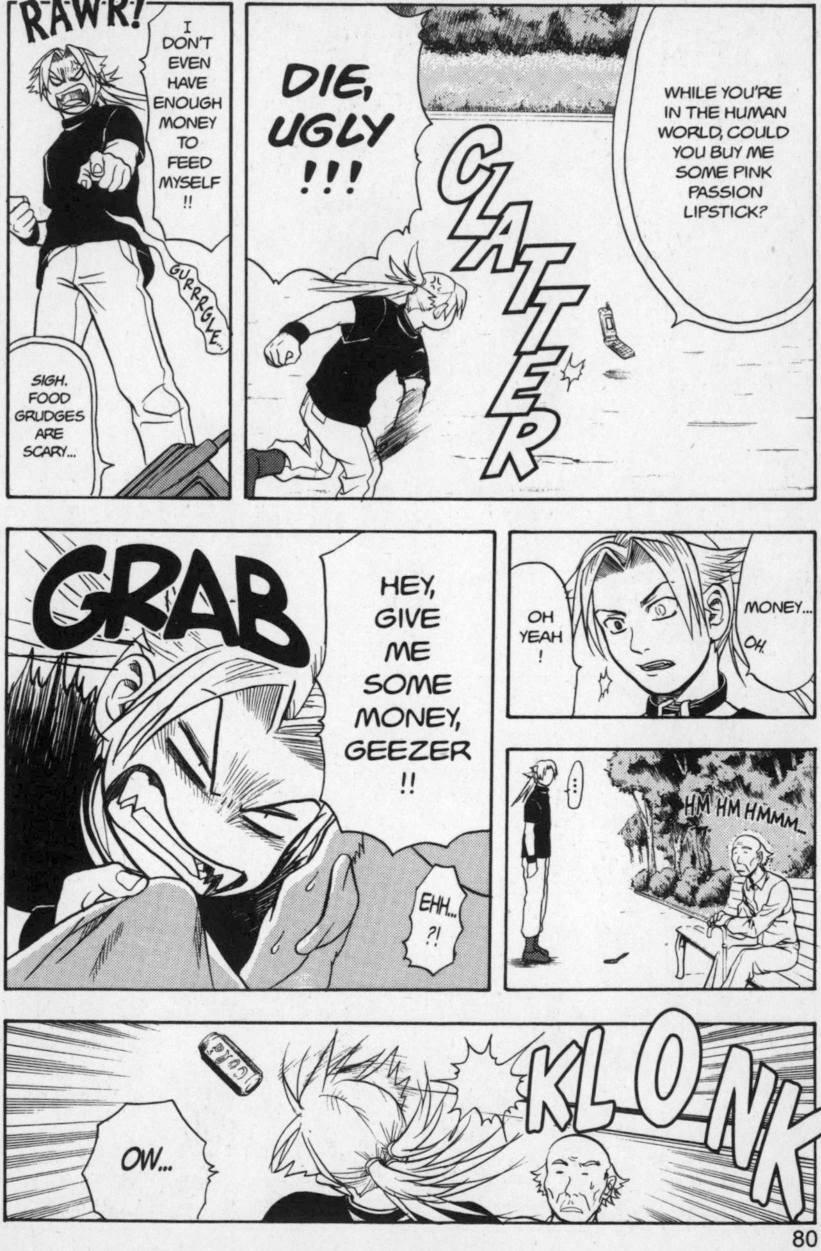
WHILE YOU'RE IN THE HUMAN WORLD, COULD YOU BUY ME SOME PINK PASSION LIPSTICK?
CLATTER
DIE, UGLY !!!
RAWR!
I DON'T EVEN HAVE ENOUGH MONEY TO FEED MYSELF !!
GURRRGLE...
SIGH. FOOD GRUDGES ARE SCARY...
MONEY...
OH.
OH YEAH !
...
HM HM HMMM...
GRAB
HEY, GIVE ME SOME MONEY, GEEZER !!
EHH... ?!
KLONK
OW...

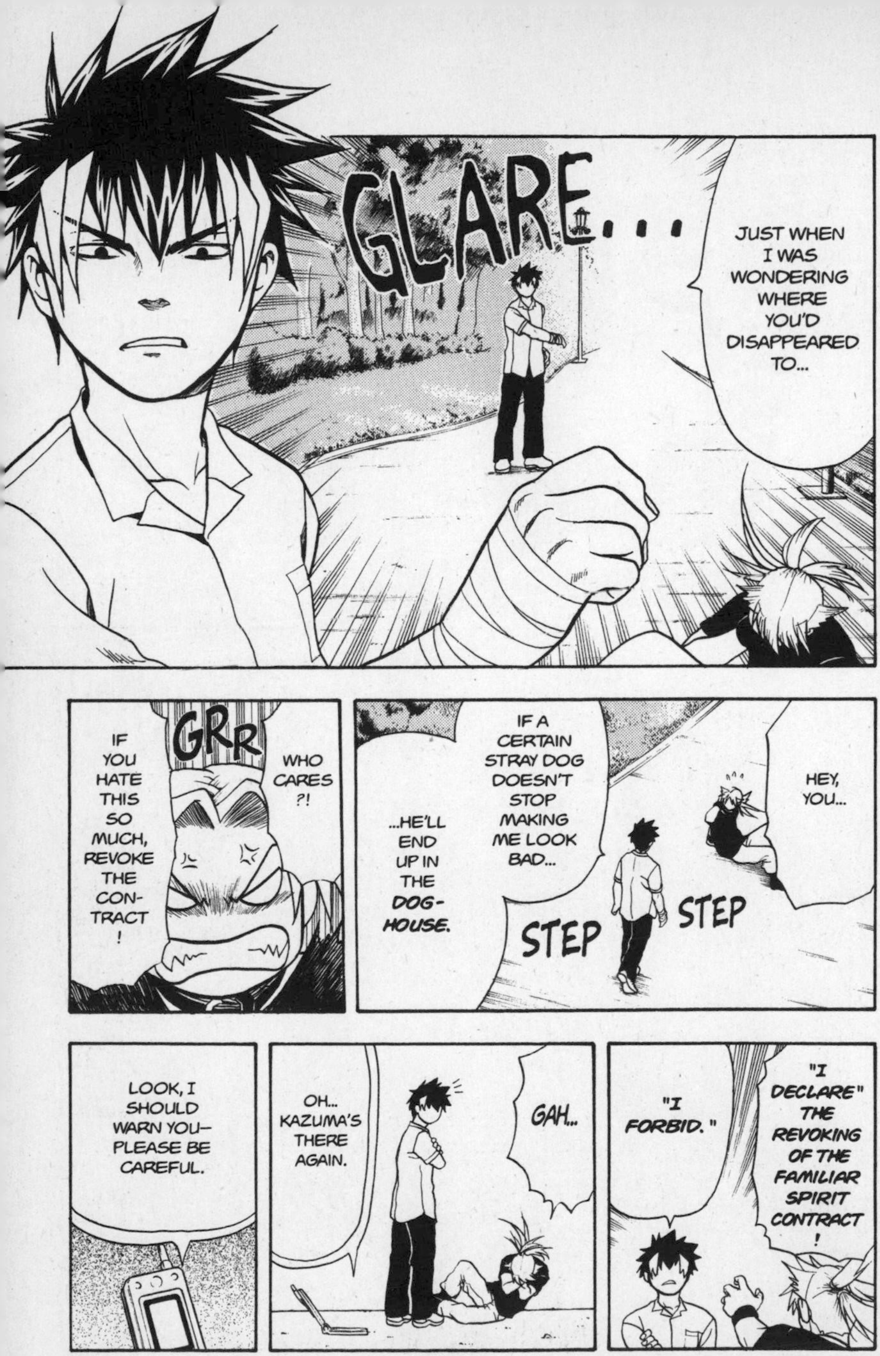
JUST WHEN I WAS WONDERING WHERE YOU'D DISAPPEARED TO...
GLARE...
HEY, YOU...
IF A CERTAIN STRAY DOG DOESN'T STOP MAKING ME LOOK BAD...
...HE'LL END UP IN THE *DOG-HOUSE.*
STEP
STEP
WHO CARES ?!
GRR
IF YOU HATE THIS SO MUCH, REVOKE THE CONTRACT !
"I DECLARE" THE REVOKING OF THE FAMILIAR SPIRIT CONTRACT !
"I FORBID."
GAH...
OH... KAZUMA'S THERE AGAIN.
LOOK, I SHOULD WARN YOU—PLEASE BE CAREFUL.

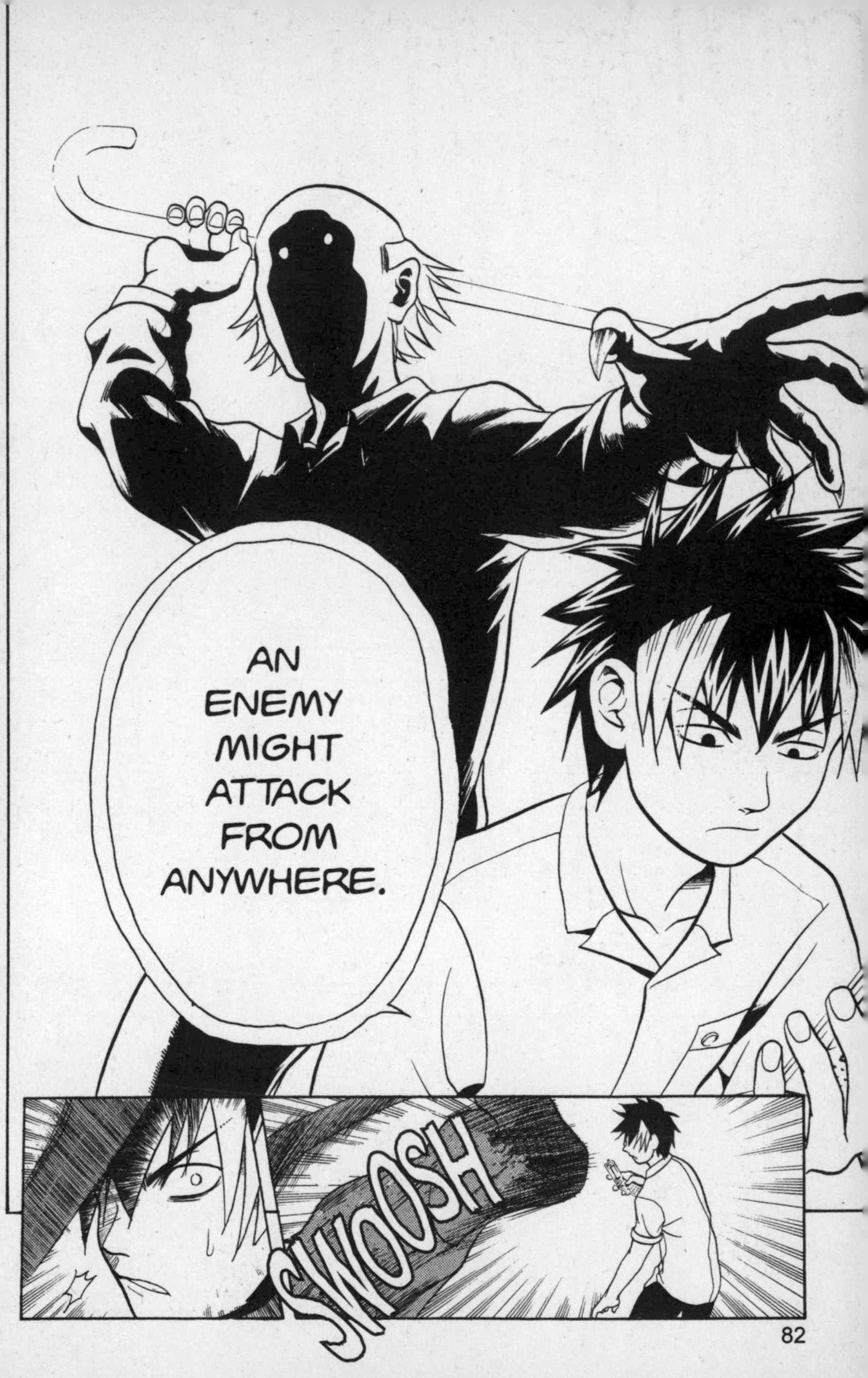
AN ENEMY MIGHT ATTACK FROM ANYWHERE.
SWOOSH

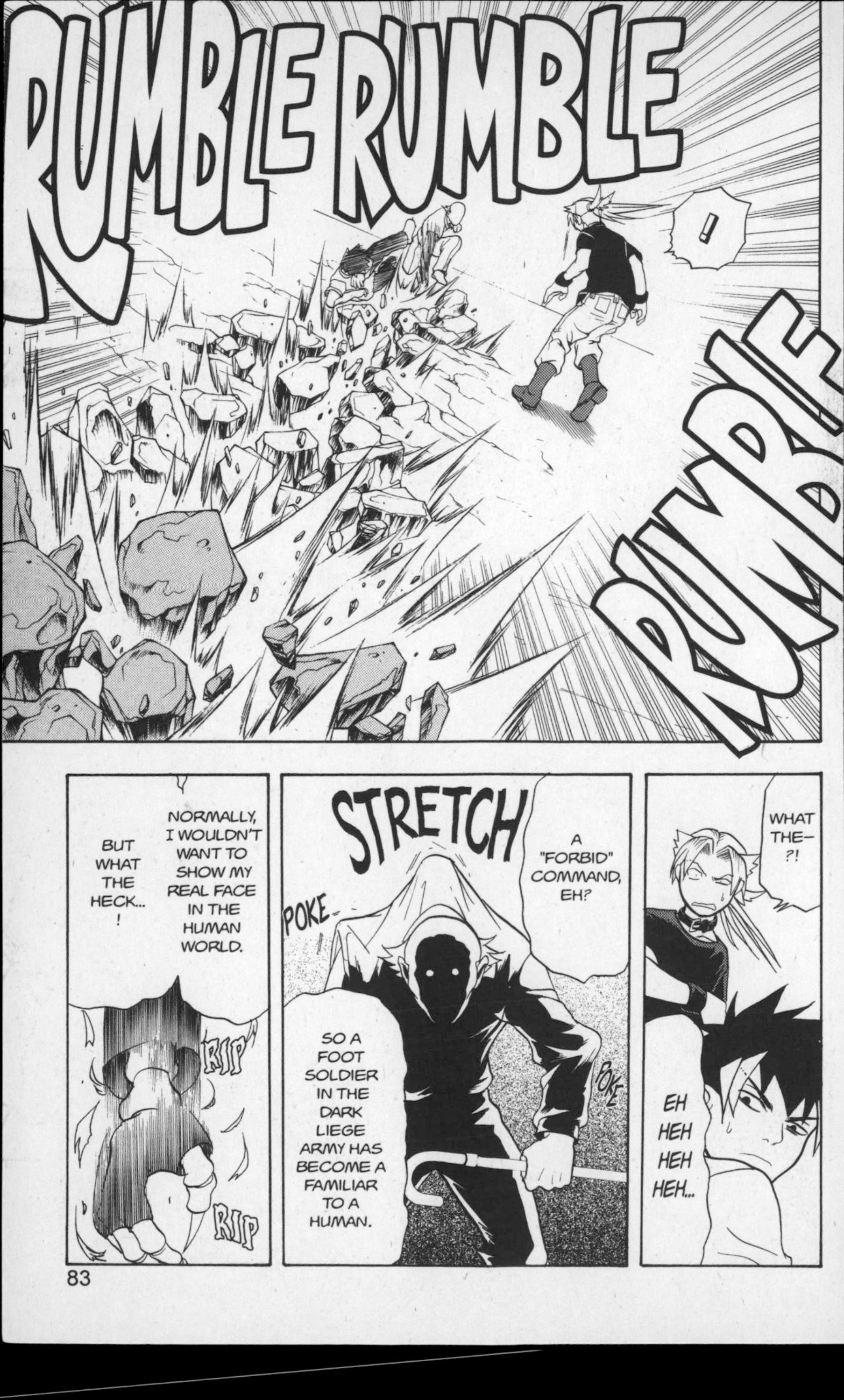
RUMBLE RUMBLE
!
RUMBLE
WHAT THE—?!
EH HEH HEH HEH...
A "FORBID" COMMAND, EH?
STRETCH
POKE
POKE
SO A FOOT SOLDIER IN THE DARK LIEGE ARMY HAS BECOME A FAMILIAR TO A HUMAN.
NORMALLY, I WOULDN'T WANT TO SHOW MY REAL FACE IN THE HUMAN WORLD.
BUT WHAT THE HECK...!
RIP
RIP

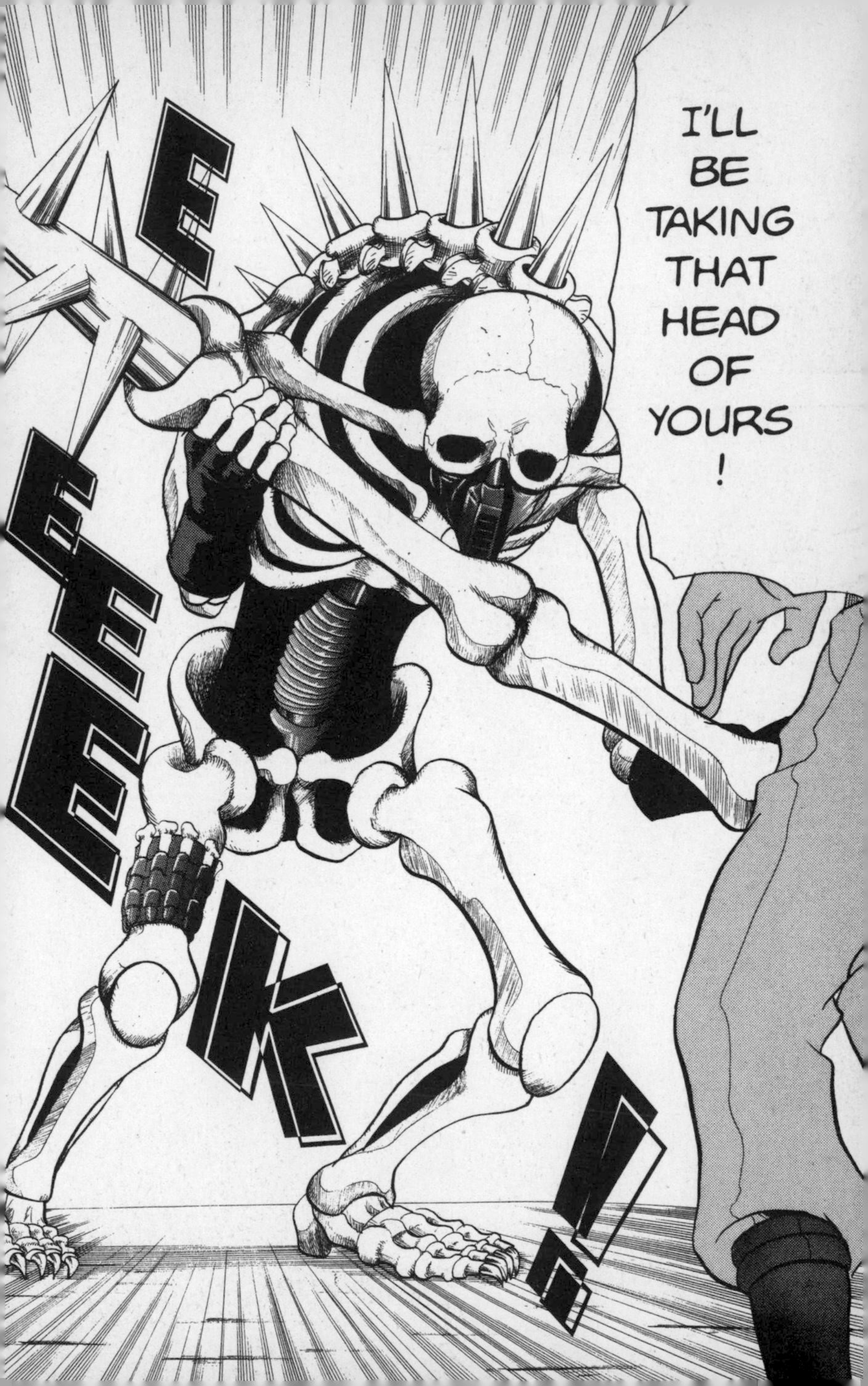
I'LL BE TAKING THAT HEAD OF YOURS!
EEEEEK!!

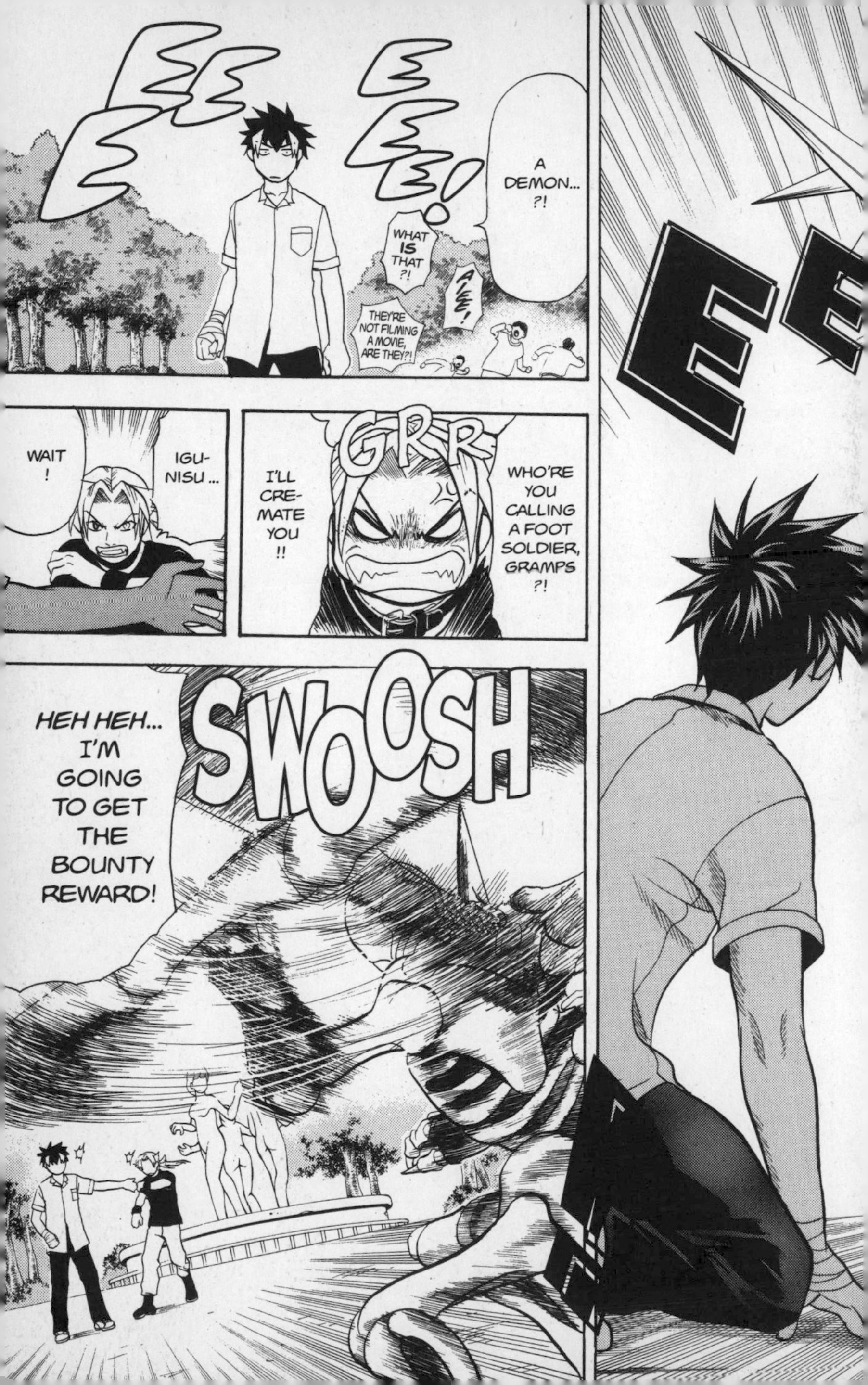
EEE
A DEMON...?!
EEEEEEEE!
WHAT IS THAT?!
AIEE!
THEY'RE NOT FILMING A MOVIE, ARE THEY?!
WHO'RE YOU CALLING A FOOT SOLDIER, GRAMPS?!
GRR
I'LL CREMATE YOU!!
IGUNISU...
WAIT!
SWOOSH
HEH HEH... I'M GOING TO GET THE BOUNTY REWARD!

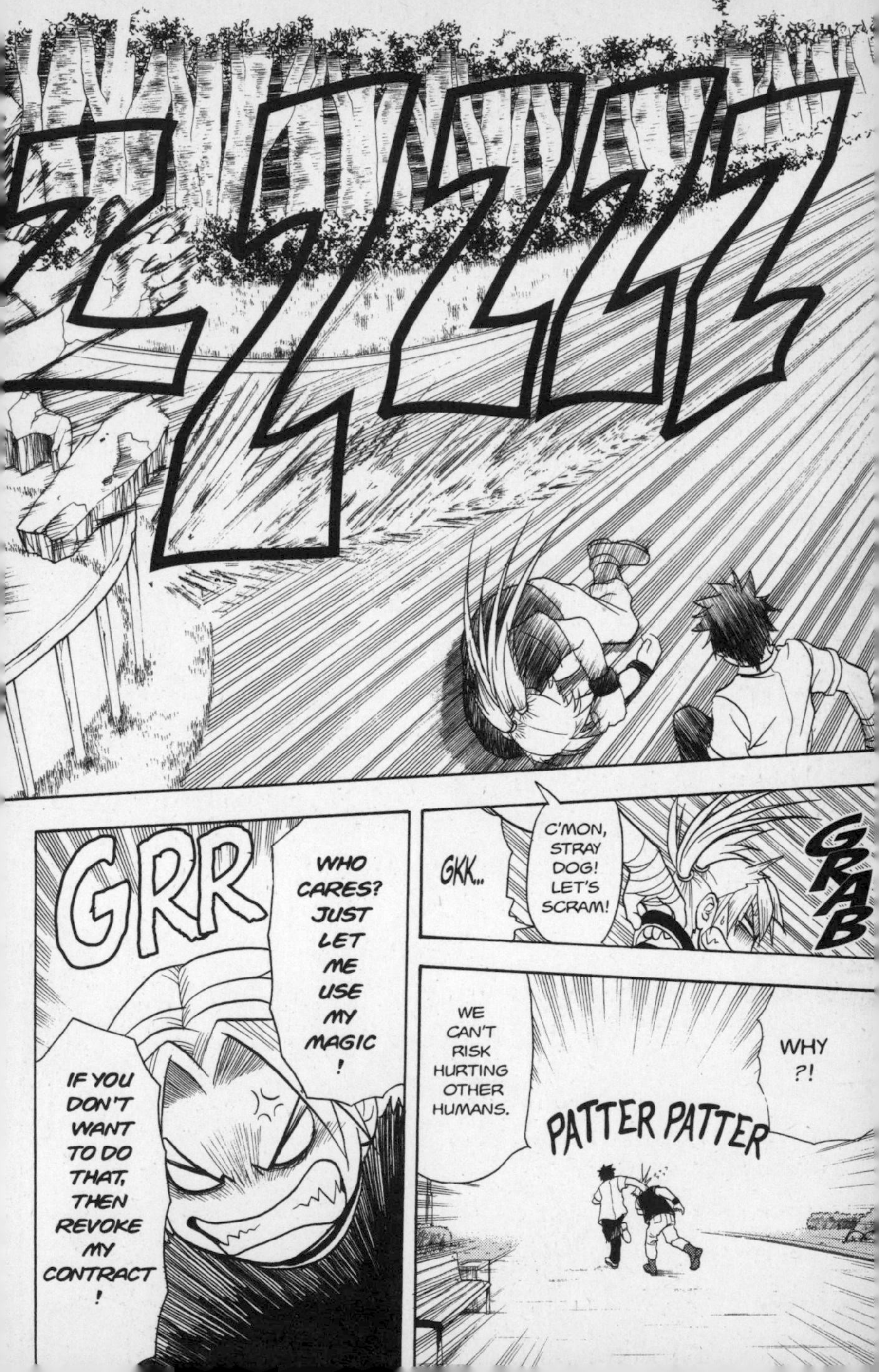
GRAB
C'MON, STRAY DOG! LET'S SCRAM!
GKK...
WHY?!
WE CAN'T RISK HURTING OTHER HUMANS.
PATTER PATTER
GRR
WHO CARES? JUST LET ME USE MY MAGIC!
IF YOU DON'T WANT TO DO THAT, THEN REVOKE MY CONTRACT!

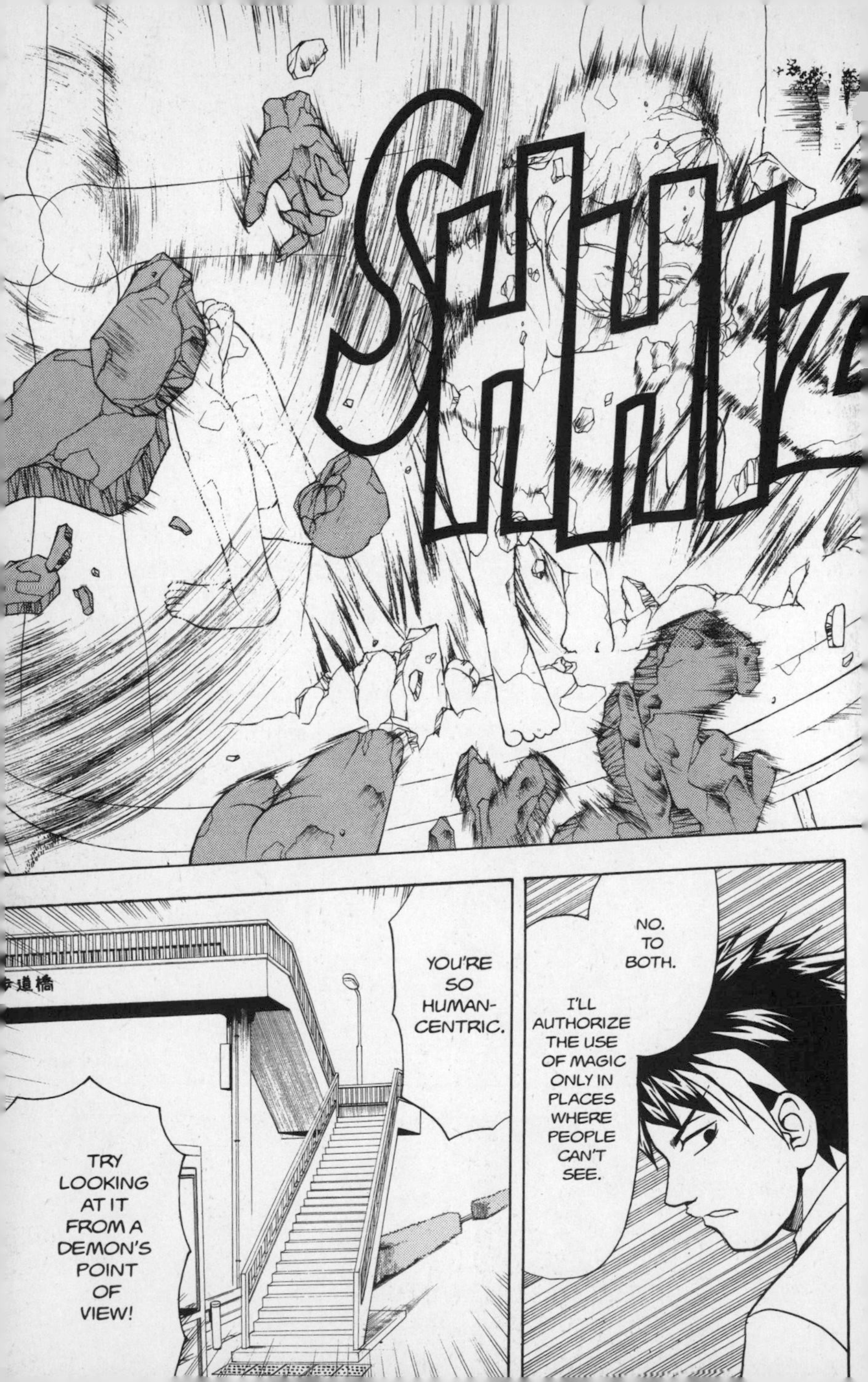
NO. TO BOTH.
I'LL AUTHORIZE THE USE OF MAGIC ONLY IN PLACES WHERE PEOPLE CAN'T SEE.
YOU'RE SO HUMAN-CENTRIC.
TRY LOOKING AT IT FROM A DEMON'S POINT OF VIEW!

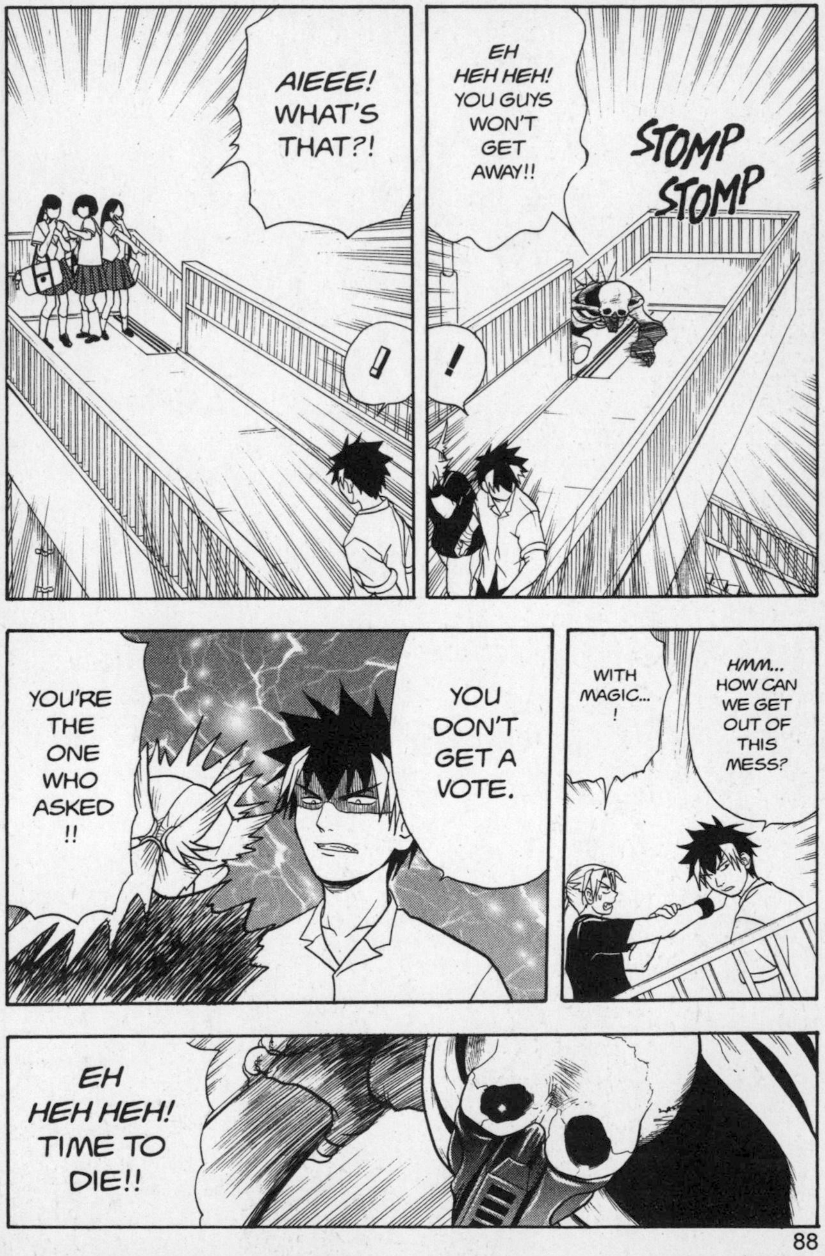
EH HEH HEH! YOU GUYS WON'T GET AWAY!!
STOMP
STOMP
!
AIEEE! WHAT'S THAT?!
!
HMM... HOW CAN WE GET OUT OF THIS MESS?
WITH MAGIC... !
YOU DON'T GET A VOTE.
YOU'RE THE ONE WHO ASKED !!
EH HEH HEH! TIME TO DIE!!

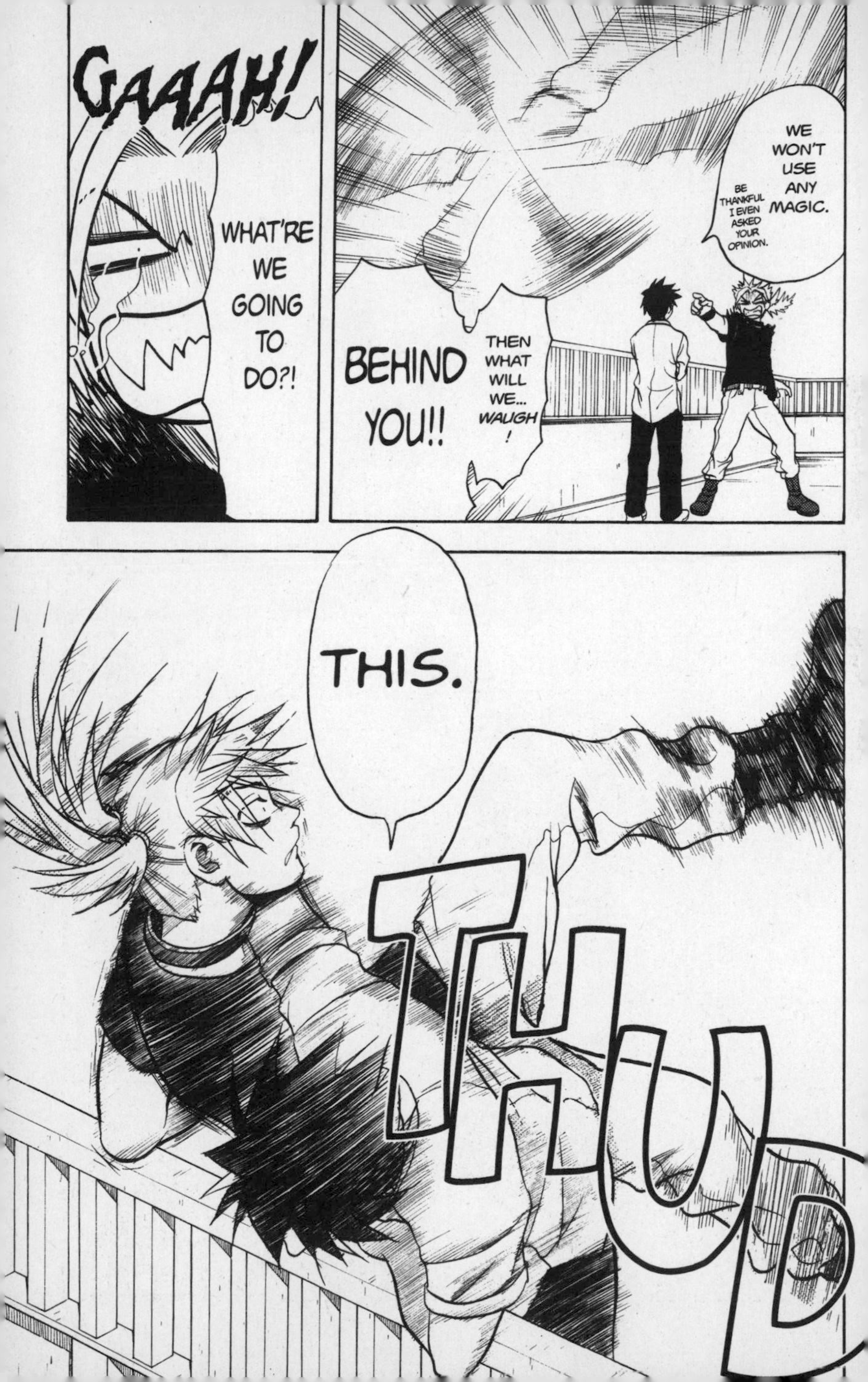
WE WON'T USE ANY MAGIC.
BE THANKFUL I EVEN ASKED YOUR OPINION.
THEN WHAT WILL WE... WAUGH!
BEHIND YOU!!
GAAAH!
WHAT'RE WE GOING TO DO?!
THIS.
THUD

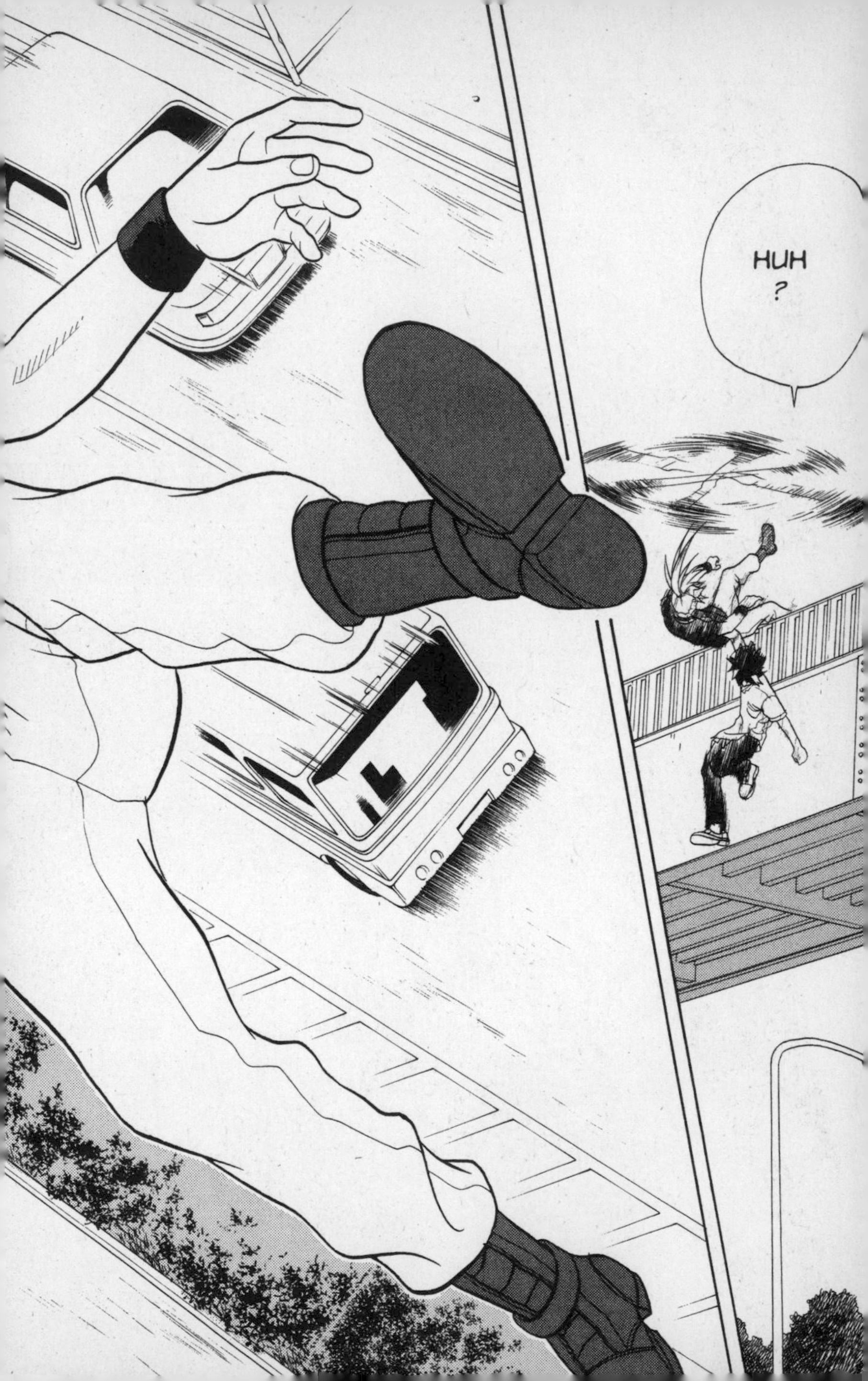
HUH
?

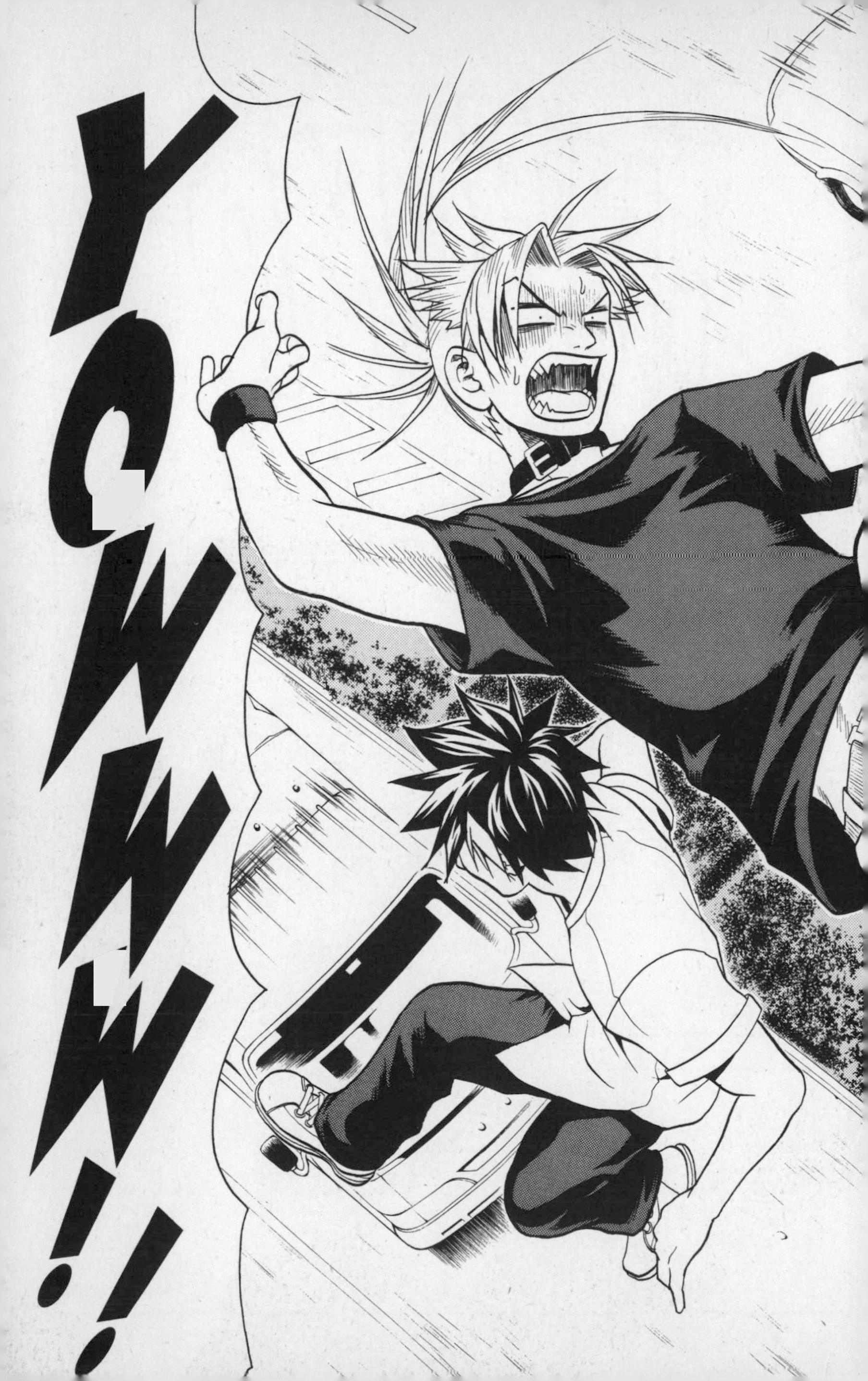
YOWWW!!

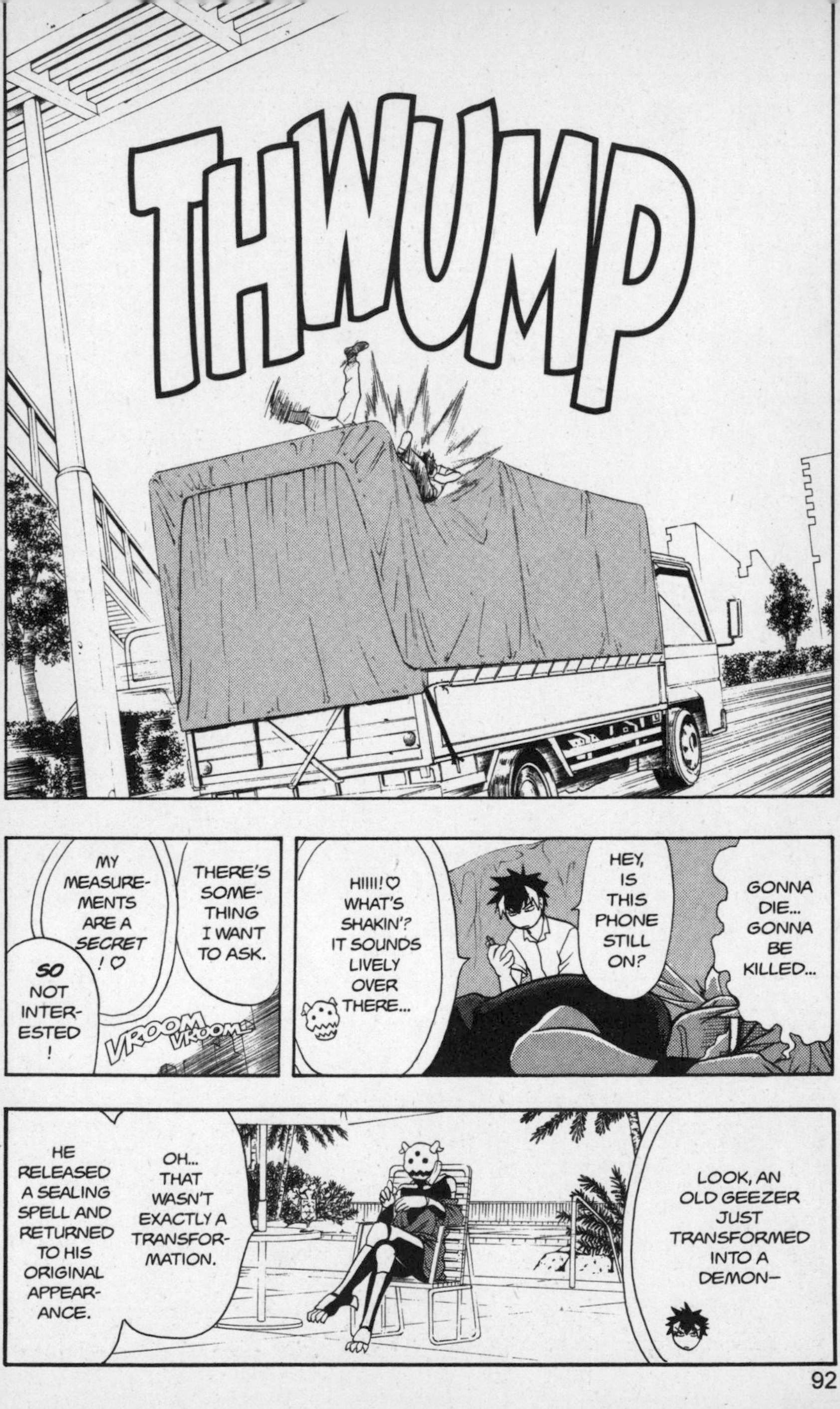
THWUMP
GONNA DIE... GONNA BE KILLED...
HEY, IS THIS PHONE STILL ON?
HIIII! ♡ WHAT'S SHAKIN'? IT SOUNDS LIVELY OVER THERE...
THERE'S SOMETHING I WANT TO ASK.
MY MEASUREMENTS ARE A SECRET! ♡
SO NOT INTERESTED!
VROOM VROOM
LOOK, AN OLD GEEZER JUST TRANSFORMED INTO A DEMON—
OH... THAT WASN'T EXACTLY A TRANSFORMATION.
HE RELEASED A SEALING SPELL AND RETURNED TO HIS ORIGINAL APPEARANCE.

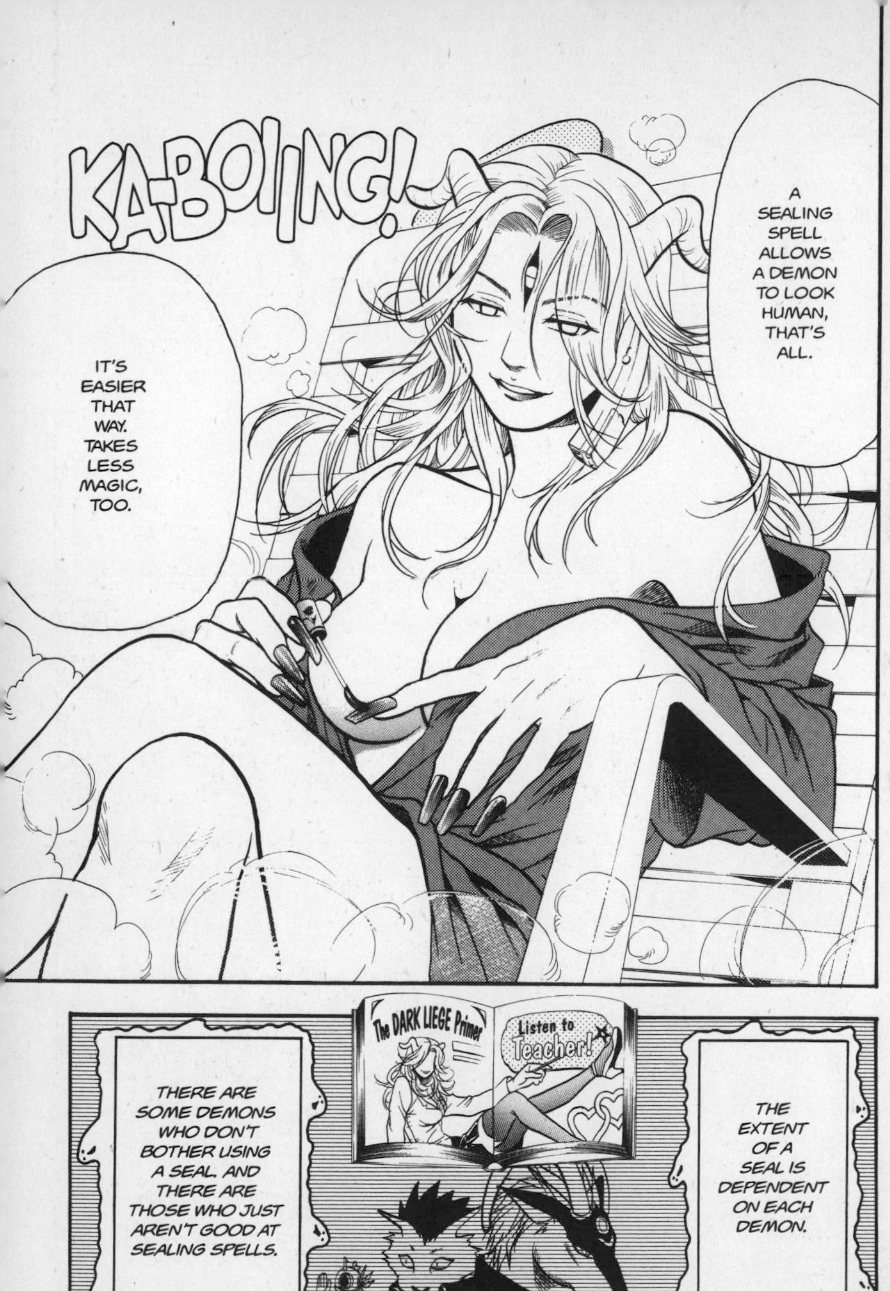
A SEALING SPELL ALLOWS A DEMON TO LOOK HUMAN, THAT'S ALL.
KA-BOING!
IT'S EASIER THAT WAY. TAKES LESS MAGIC, TOO.
The DARK LIEGE Primer
Listen to Teacher!
THE EXTENT OF A SEAL IS DEPENDENT ON EACH DEMON.
THERE ARE SOME DEMONS WHO DON'T BOTHER USING A SEAL. AND THERE ARE THOSE WHO JUST AREN'T GOOD AT SEALING SPELLS.

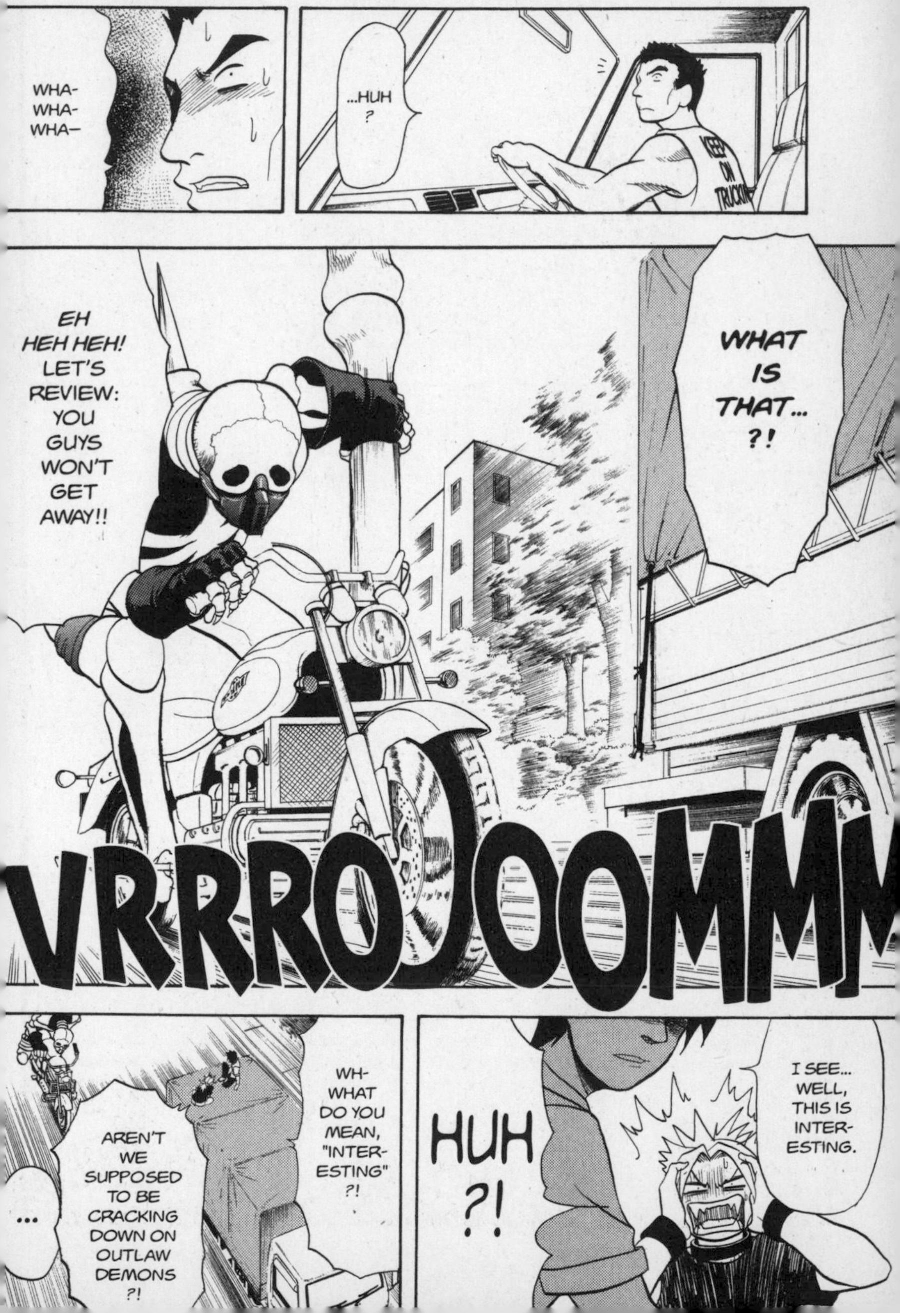
...HUH ?
WHA-WHA-WHA-
WHAT IS THAT...?!
EH HEH HEH! LET'S REVIEW: YOU GUYS WON'T GET AWAY!!
VRRROOOMMM
I SEE... WELL, THIS IS INTER-ESTING.
HUH ?!
WH-WHAT DO YOU MEAN, "INTER-ESTING" ?!
AREN'T WE SUPPOSED TO BE CRACKING DOWN ON OUTLAW DEMONS ?!
...

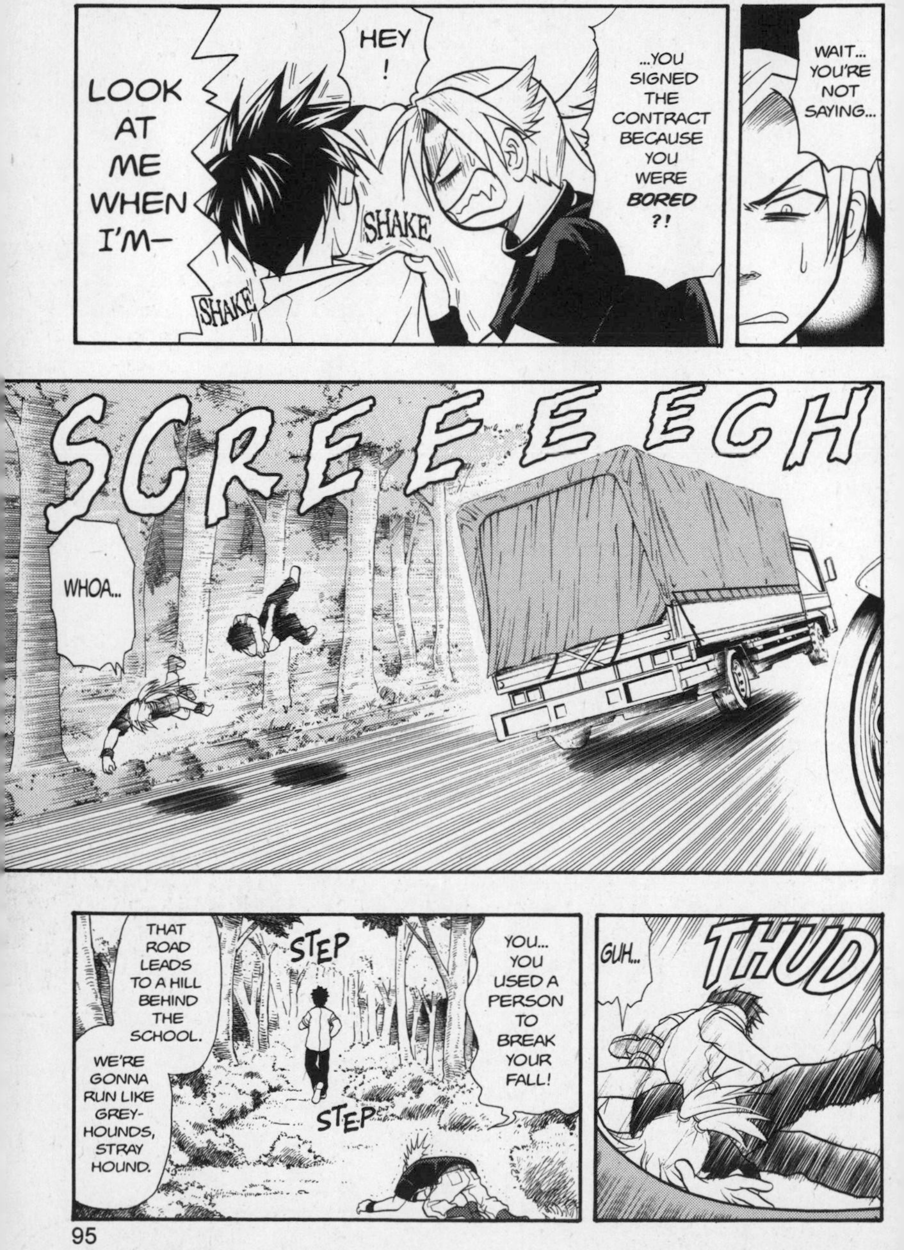
WAIT... YOU'RE NOT SAYING...
...YOU SIGNED THE CONTRACT BECAUSE YOU WERE *BORED* ?!
HEY !
SHAKE
LOOK AT ME WHEN I'M—
SHAKE
SCREEECH
WHOA...
THUD
GUH...
YOU... YOU USED A PERSON TO BREAK YOUR FALL!
STEP
THAT ROAD LEADS TO A HILL BEHIND THE SCHOOL.
WE'RE GONNA RUN LIKE GREY-HOUNDS, STRAY HOUND.
STEP

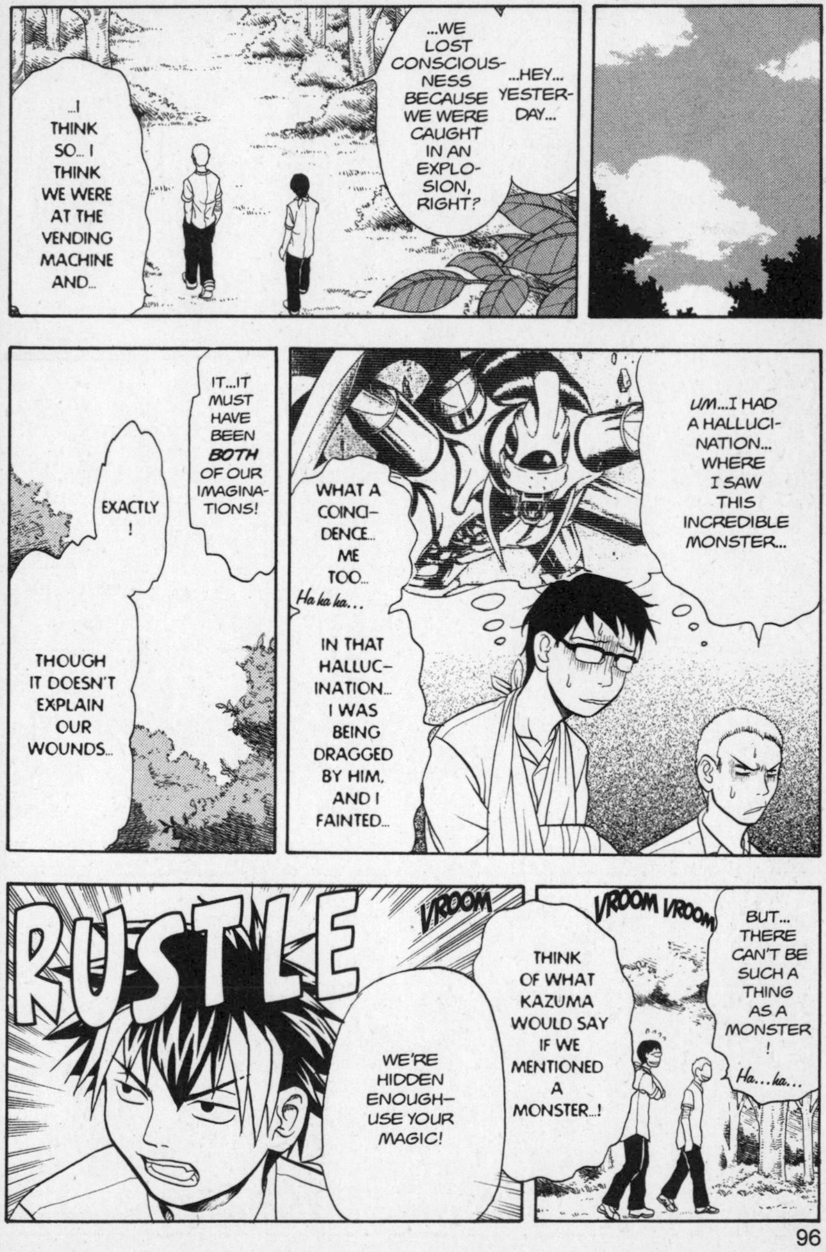
...HEY... YESTERDAY...
...WE LOST CONSCIOUSNESS BECAUSE WE WERE CAUGHT IN AN EXPLOSION, RIGHT?
...I THINK SO... I THINK WE WERE AT THE VENDING MACHINE AND...
UM...I HAD A HALLUCINATION... WHERE I SAW THIS INCREDIBLE MONSTER...
WHAT A COINCIDENCE... ME TOO...
Ha ka ka...
IN THAT HALLUCINATION... I WAS BEING DRAGGED BY HIM, AND I FAINTED...
IT...IT MUST HAVE BEEN *BOTH* OF OUR IMAGINATIONS!
EXACTLY!
THOUGH IT DOESN'T EXPLAIN OUR WOUNDS...
VROOM VROOM
BUT... THERE CAN'T BE SUCH A THING AS A MONSTER!
Ha...ka...
THINK OF WHAT KAZUMA WOULD SAY IF WE MENTIONED A MONSTER...!
VROOM
RUSTLE
WE'RE HIDDEN ENOUGH— USE YOUR MAGIC!

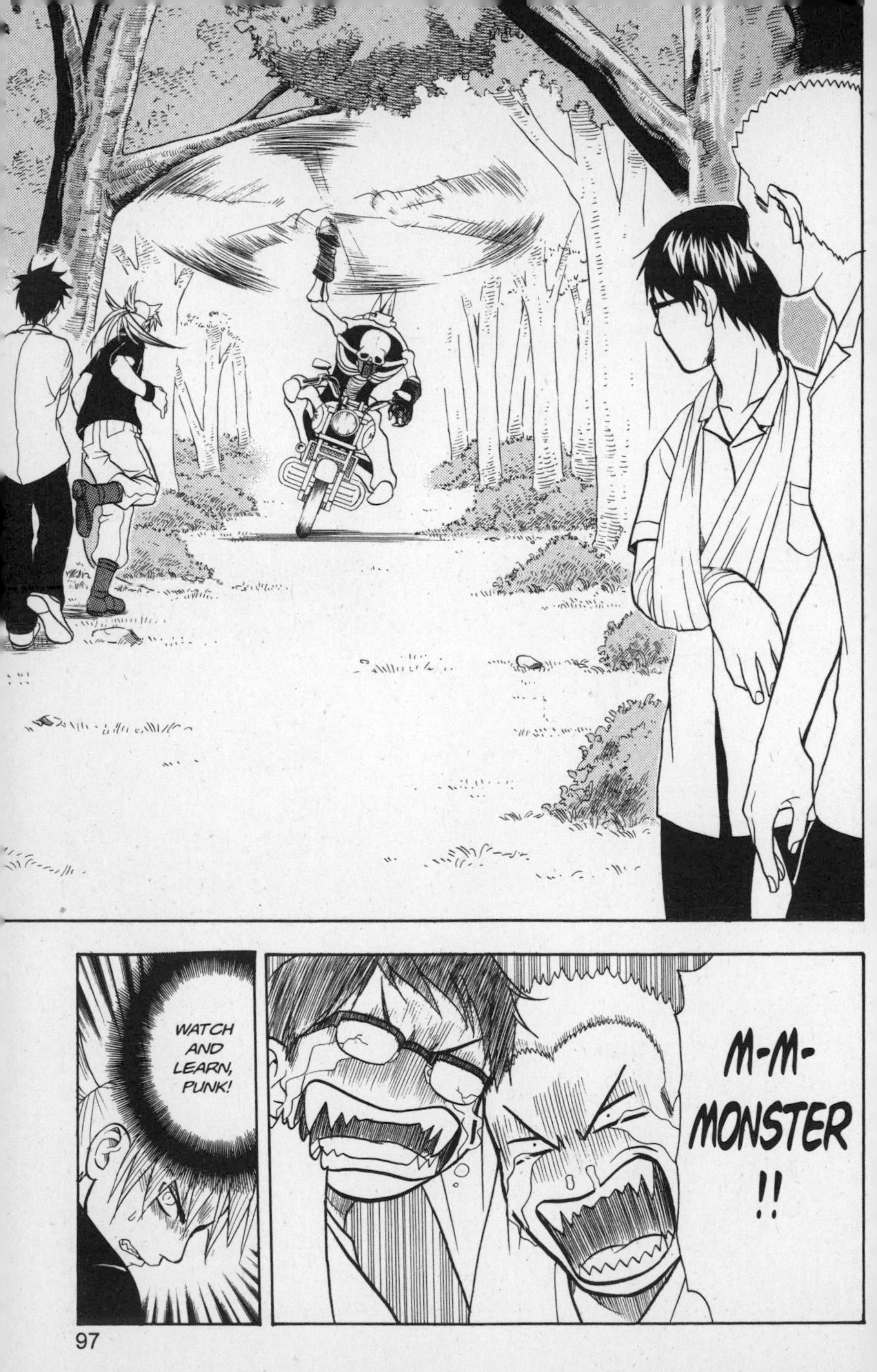
M-M-MONSTER!!
WATCH AND LEARN, PUNK!

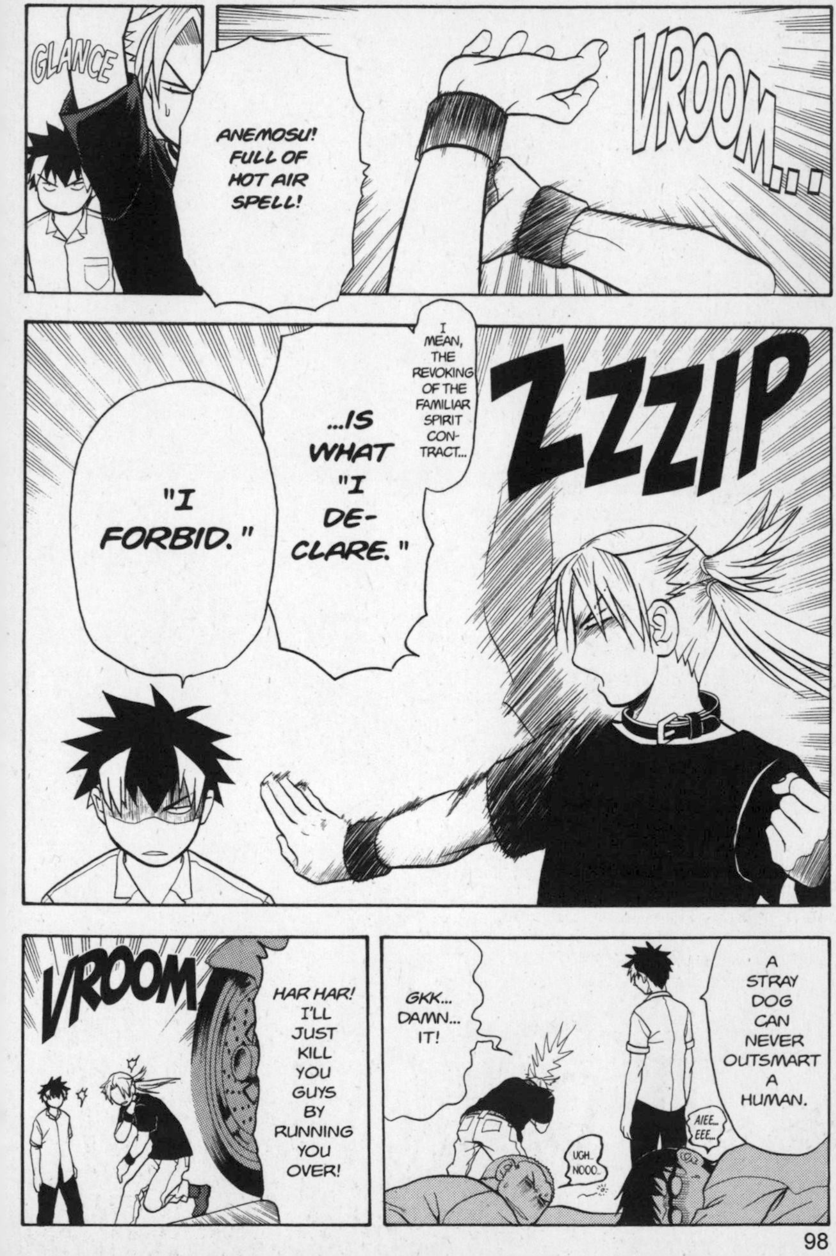
VROOM...
GLANCE
ANEMOSU! FULL OF HOT AIR SPELL!
ZZZIP
I MEAN, THE REVOKING OF THE FAMILIAR SPIRIT CONTRACT...
...IS WHAT "I DECLARE."
"I FORBID."
A STRAY DOG CAN NEVER OUTSMART A HUMAN.
AIEE... EEE...
GKK... DAMN... IT!
UGH... NOOO...
HAR HAR! I'LL JUST KILL YOU GUYS BY RUNNING YOU OVER!
VROOM

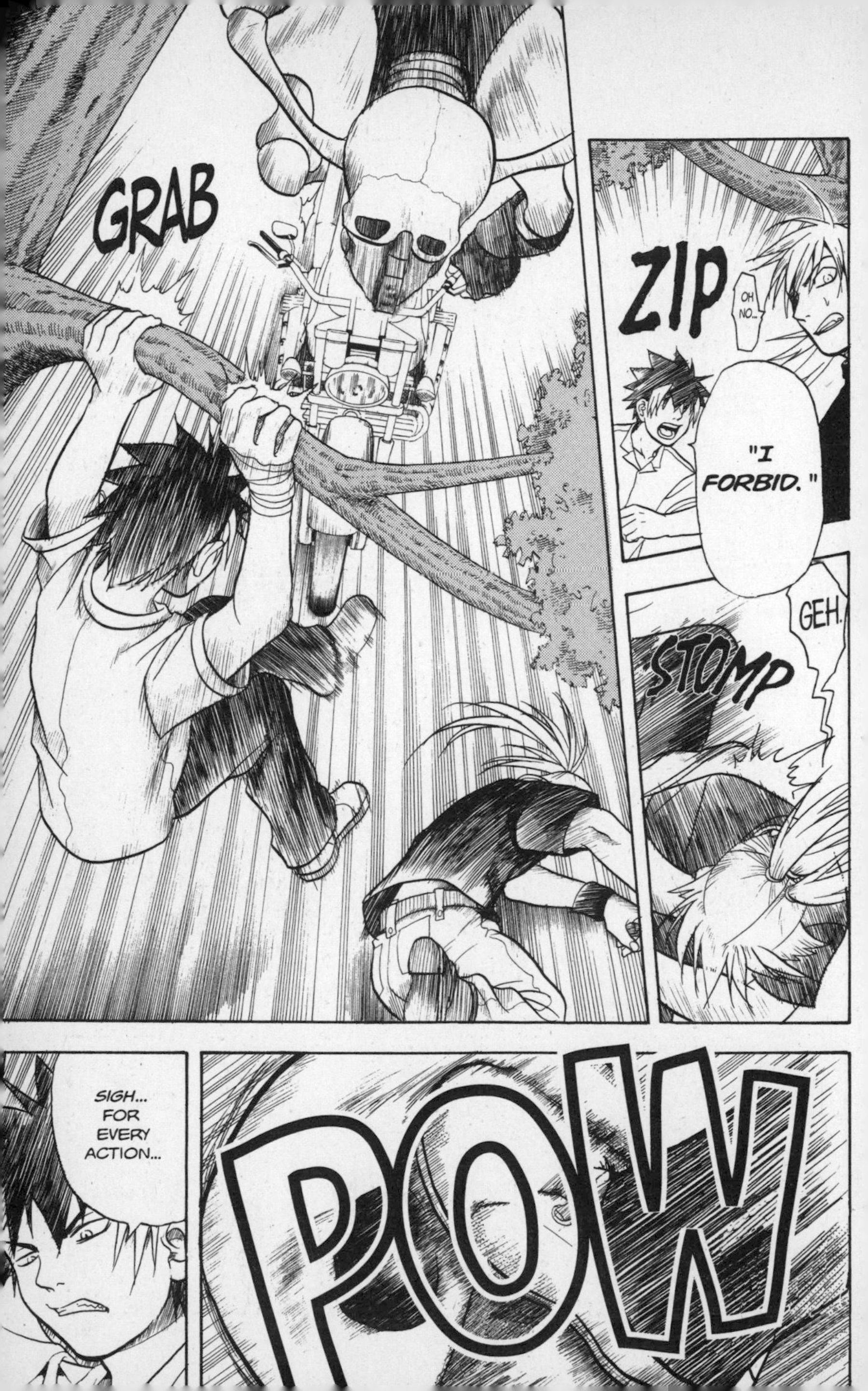
ZIP
OH NO...
"I FORBID."
STOMP
GEH.
GRAB
POW
SIGH... FOR EVERY ACTION...

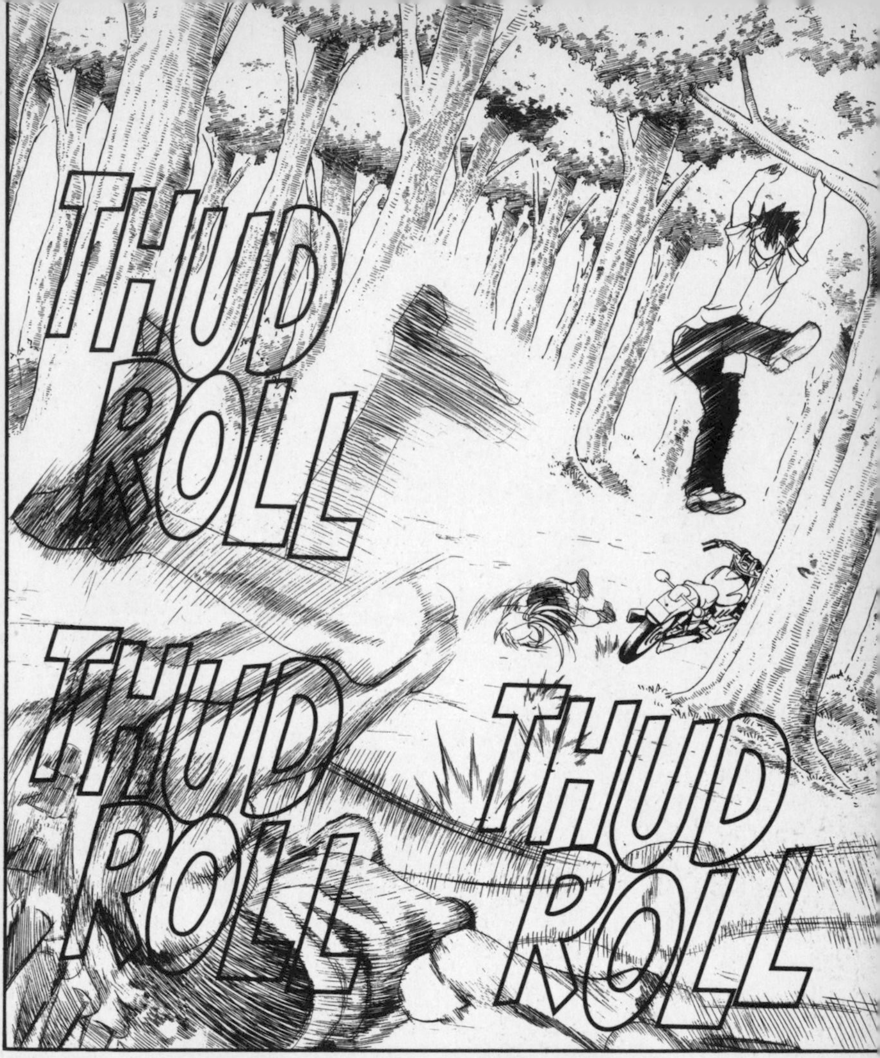
THUD
ROLL
THUD
ROLL
THUD
ROLL

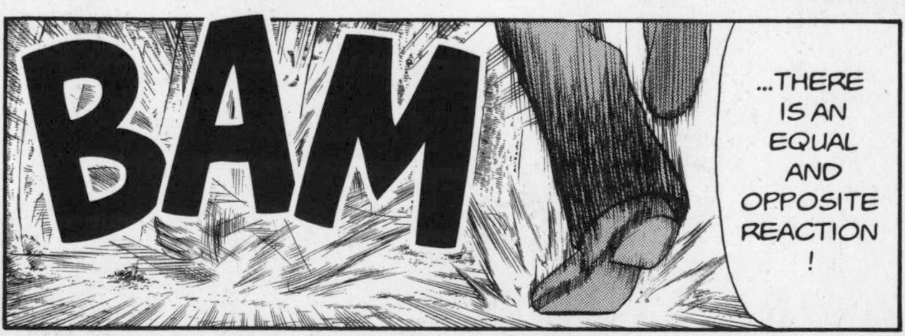
...THERE IS AN EQUAL AND OPPOSITE REACTION !
BAM

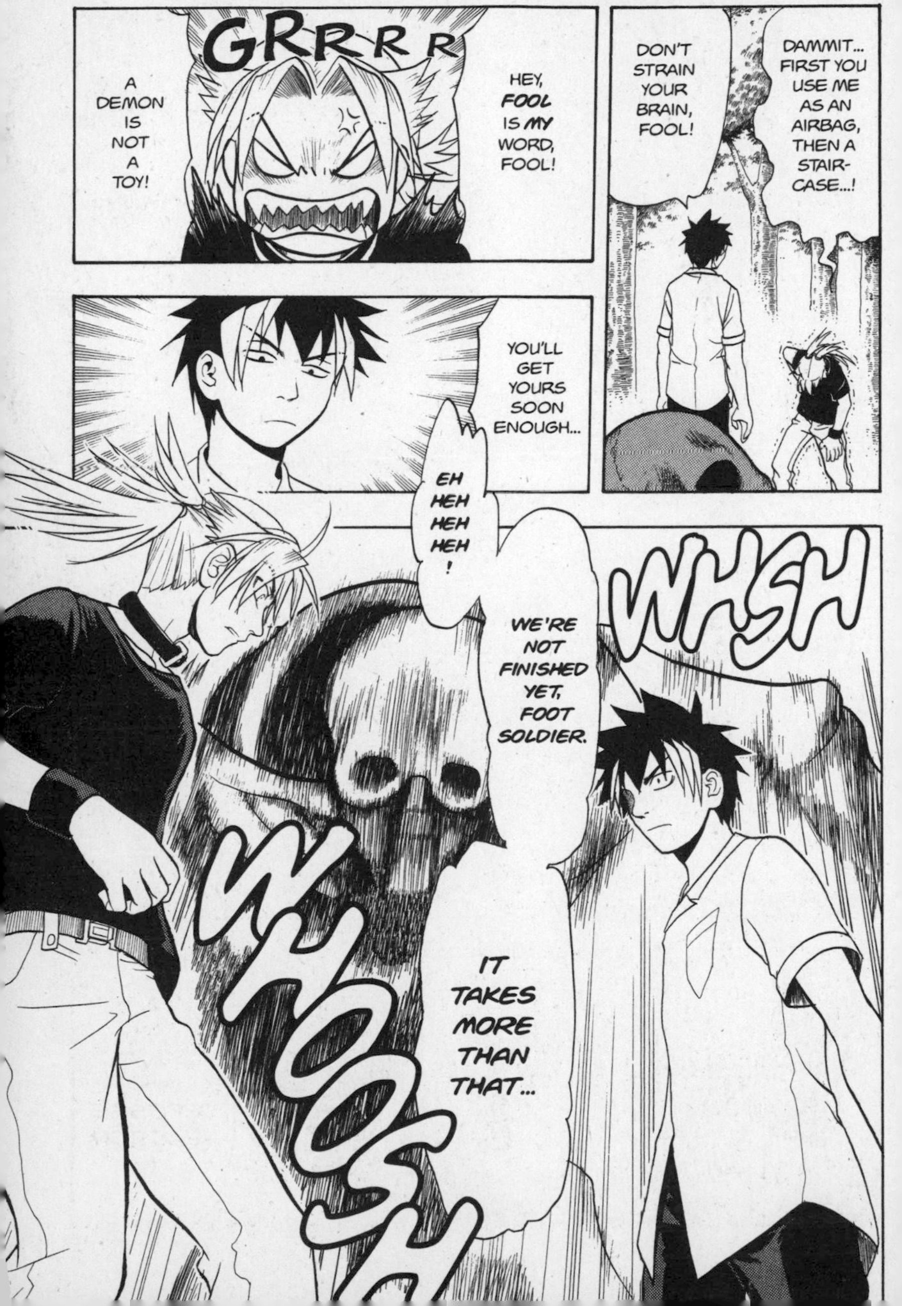
DAMMIT... FIRST YOU USE ME AS AN AIRBAG, THEN A STAIRCASE...!
DON'T STRAIN YOUR BRAIN, FOOL!
HEY, FOOL IS MY WORD, FOOL!
GRRRRR
A DEMON IS NOT A TOY!
YOU'LL GET YOURS SOON ENOUGH...
EH HEH HEH HEH!
WHSH
WE'RE NOT FINISHED YET, FOOT SOLDIER.
IT TAKES MORE THAN THAT...
WHOOOSH

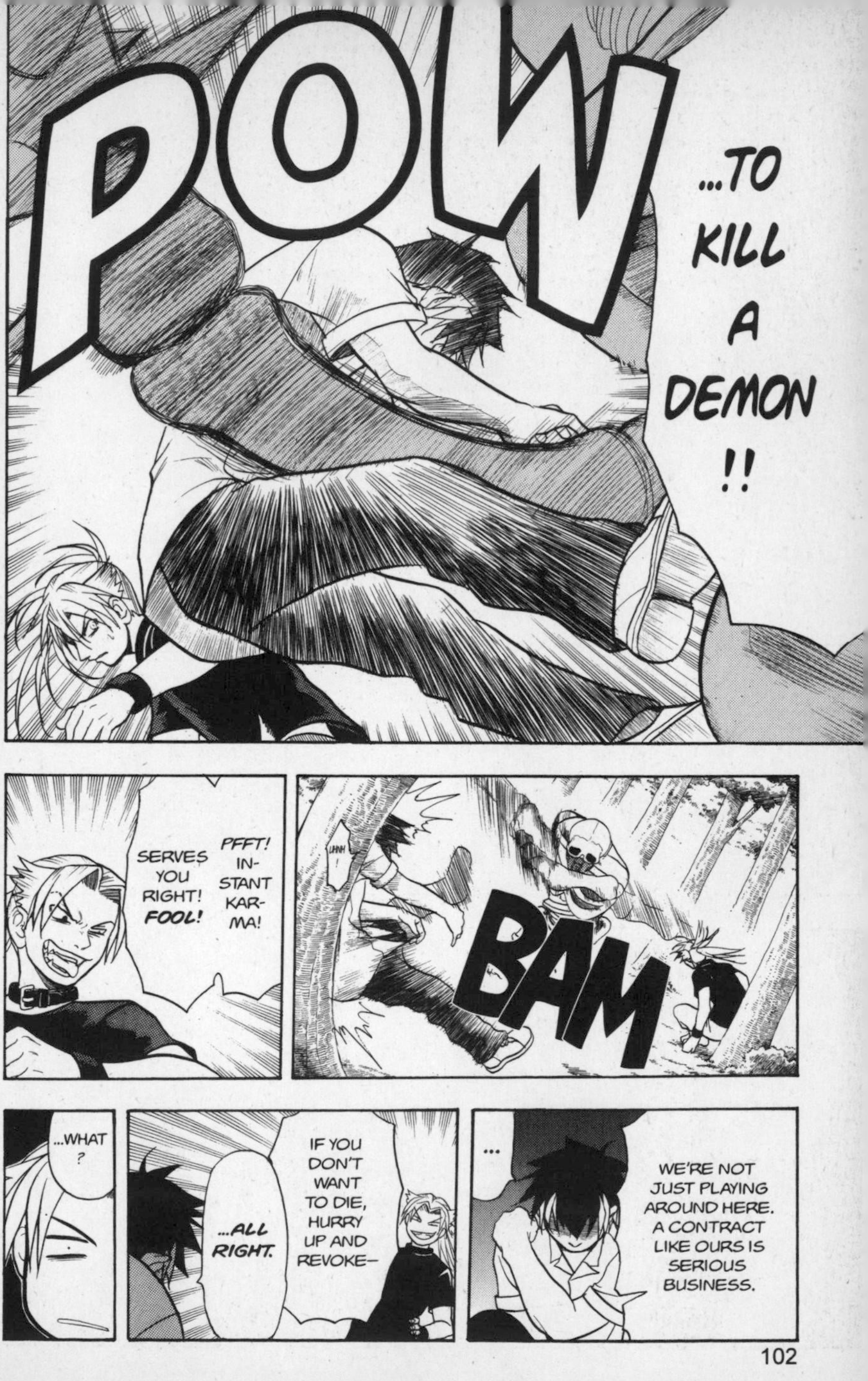
POW
...TO KILL A DEMON!!
UHNH!
BAM
PFFT! IN-STANT KAR-MA!
SERVES YOU RIGHT! **FOOL!**
...
WE'RE NOT JUST PLAYING AROUND HERE. A CONTRACT LIKE OURS IS SERIOUS BUSINESS.
IF YOU DON'T WANT TO DIE, HURRY UP AND REVOKE—
...ALL RIGHT.
...WHAT?

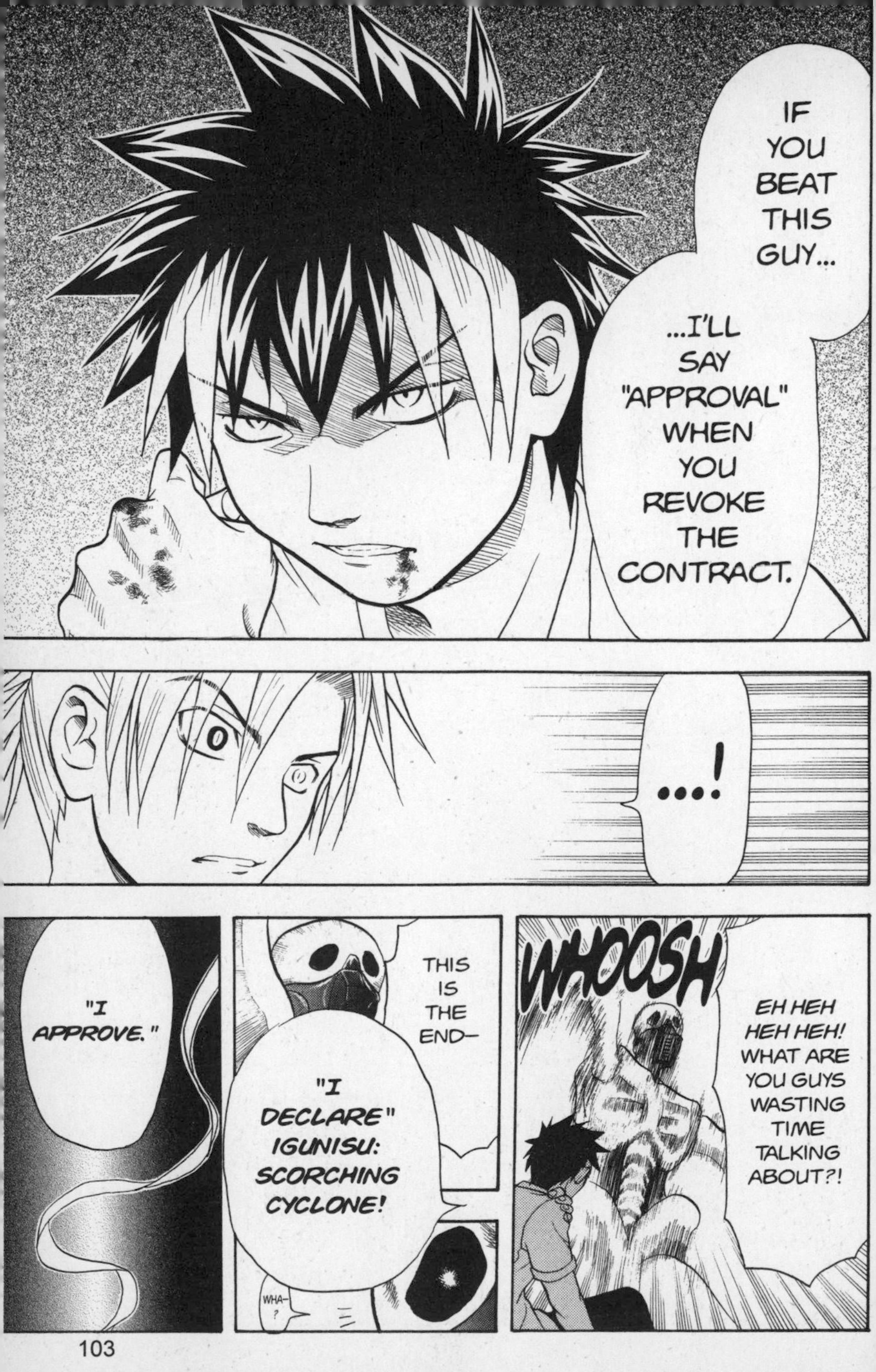
IF YOU BEAT THIS GUY...
...I'LL SAY "APPROVAL" WHEN YOU REVOKE THE CONTRACT.
...!
WHOOSH
EH HEH HEH HEH! WHAT ARE YOU GUYS WASTING TIME TALKING ABOUT?!
THIS IS THE END—
"I DECLARE" IGUNISU: SCORCHING CYCLONE!
WHA-?
"I APPROVE."

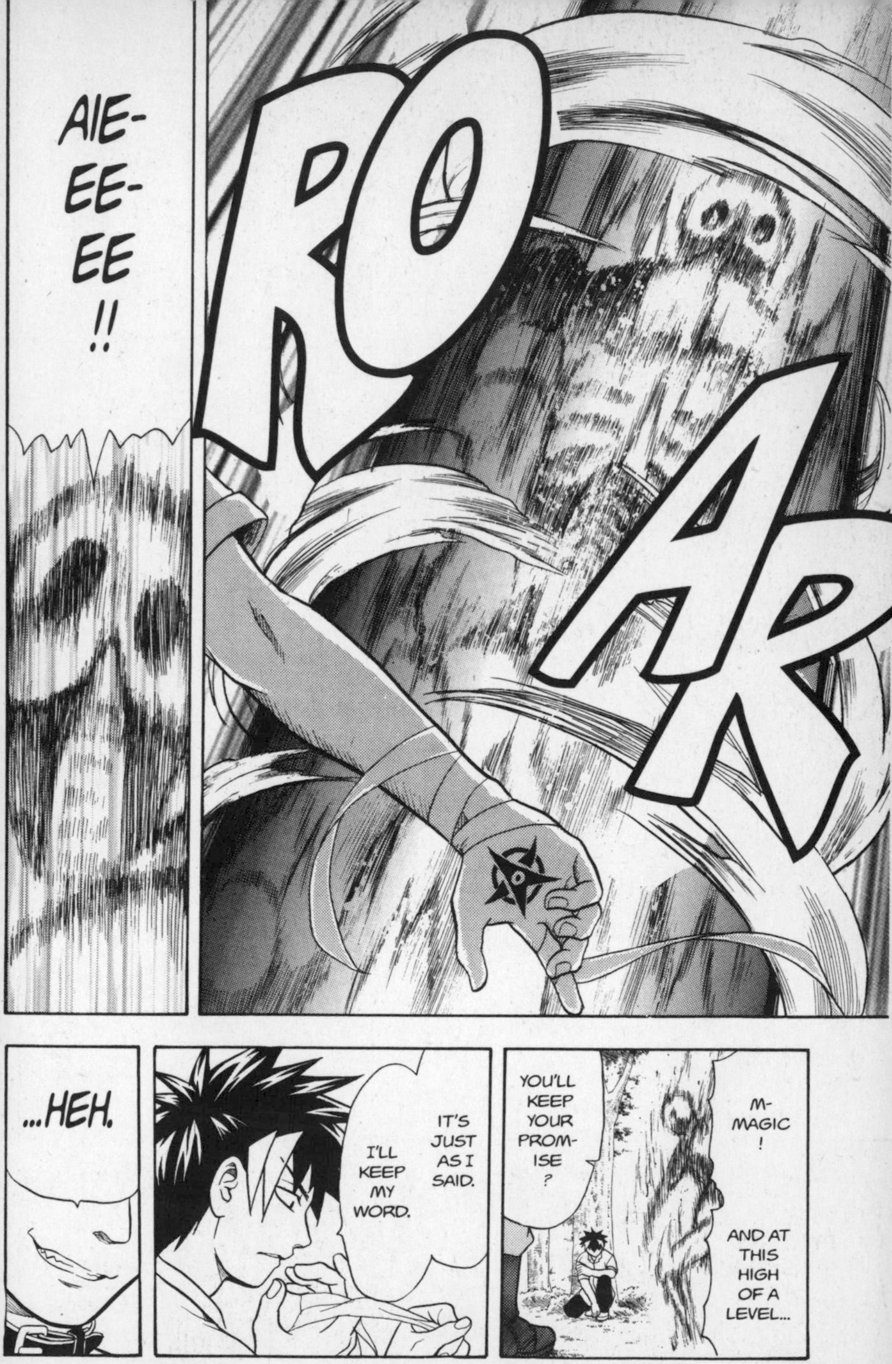
ROAR
AIE-EE-EE!!
M-MAGIC!
AND AT THIS HIGH OF A LEVEL...
YOU'LL KEEP YOUR PROMISE?
IT'S JUST AS I SAID.
I'LL KEEP MY WORD.
...HEH.

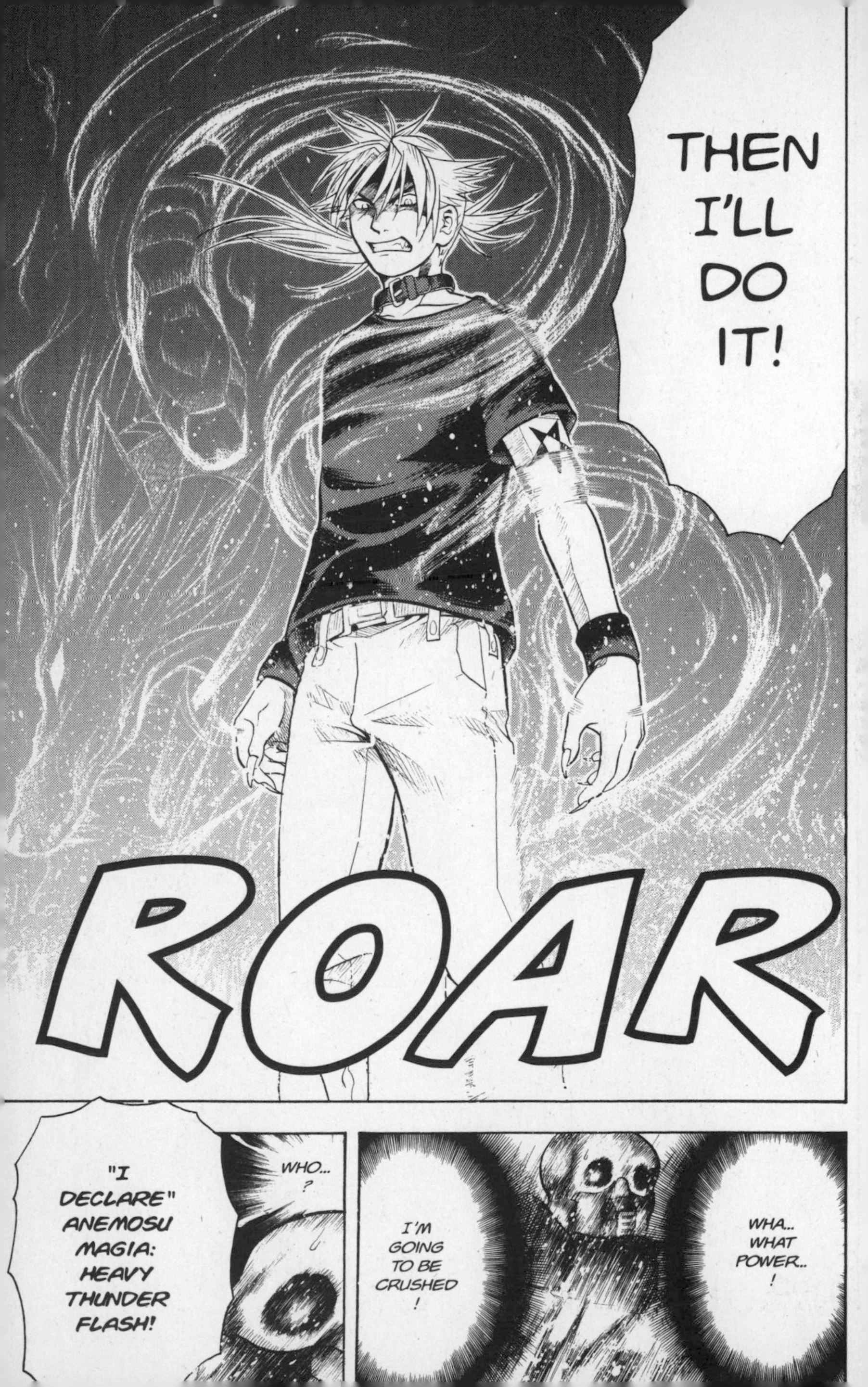
THEN I'LL DO IT!
ROAR
WHA.. WHAT POWER.. !
I'M GOING TO BE CRUSHED !
WHO... ?
"I DECLARE" ANEMOSU MAGIA: HEAVY THUNDER FLASH!

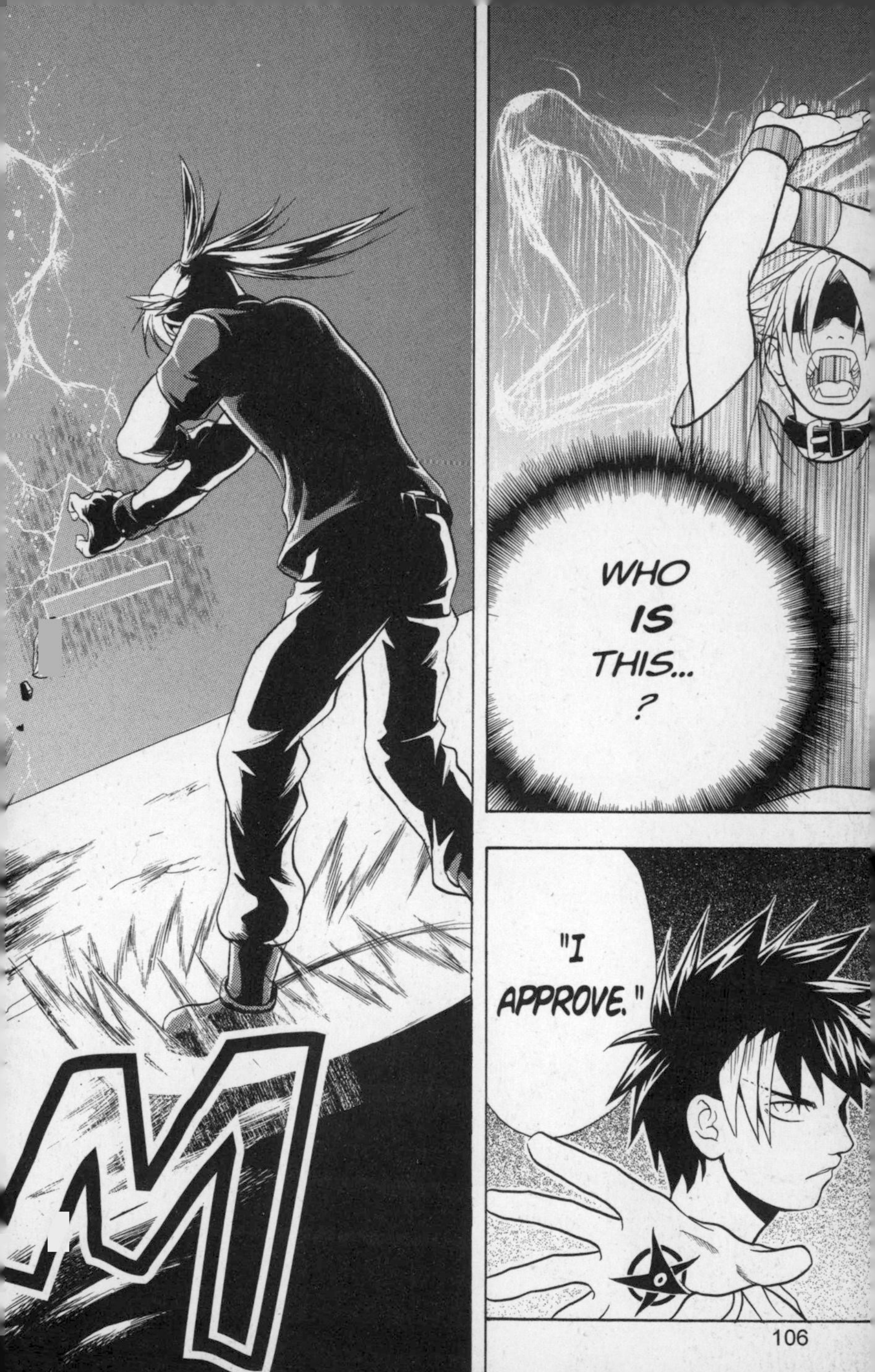
WHO IS THIS... ?
"I APPROVE."
M

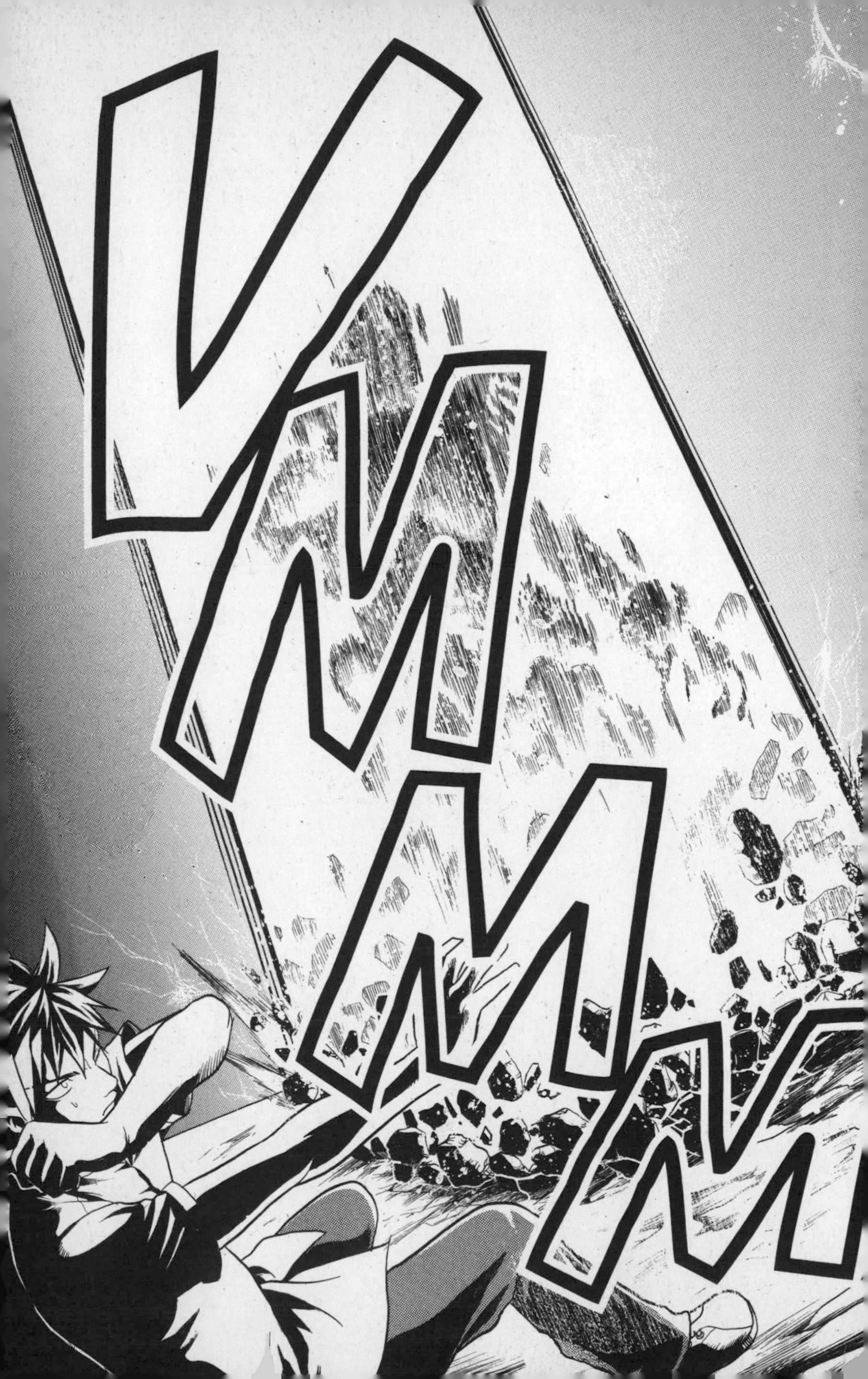
VMMM

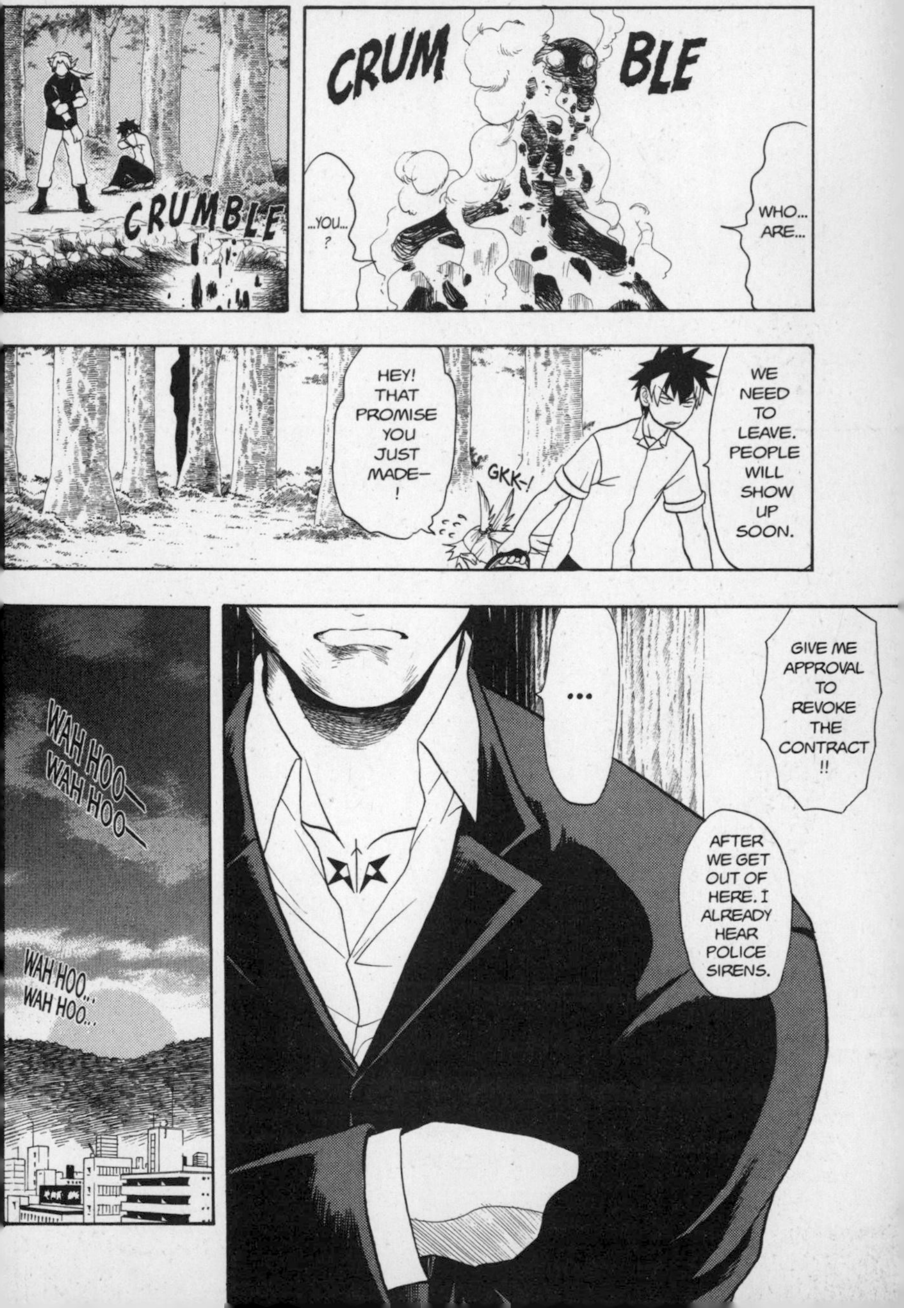
CRUM BLE
WHO... ARE...
...YOU... ?
CRUMBLE
WE NEED TO LEAVE. PEOPLE WILL SHOW UP SOON.
HEY! THAT PROMISE YOU JUST MADE—!
GKK-!
GIVE ME APPROVAL TO REVOKE THE CONTRACT!!
...
AFTER WE GET OUT OF HERE. I ALREADY HEAR POLICE SIRENS.
WAH HOO— WAH HOO—
WAH HOO... WAH HOO...

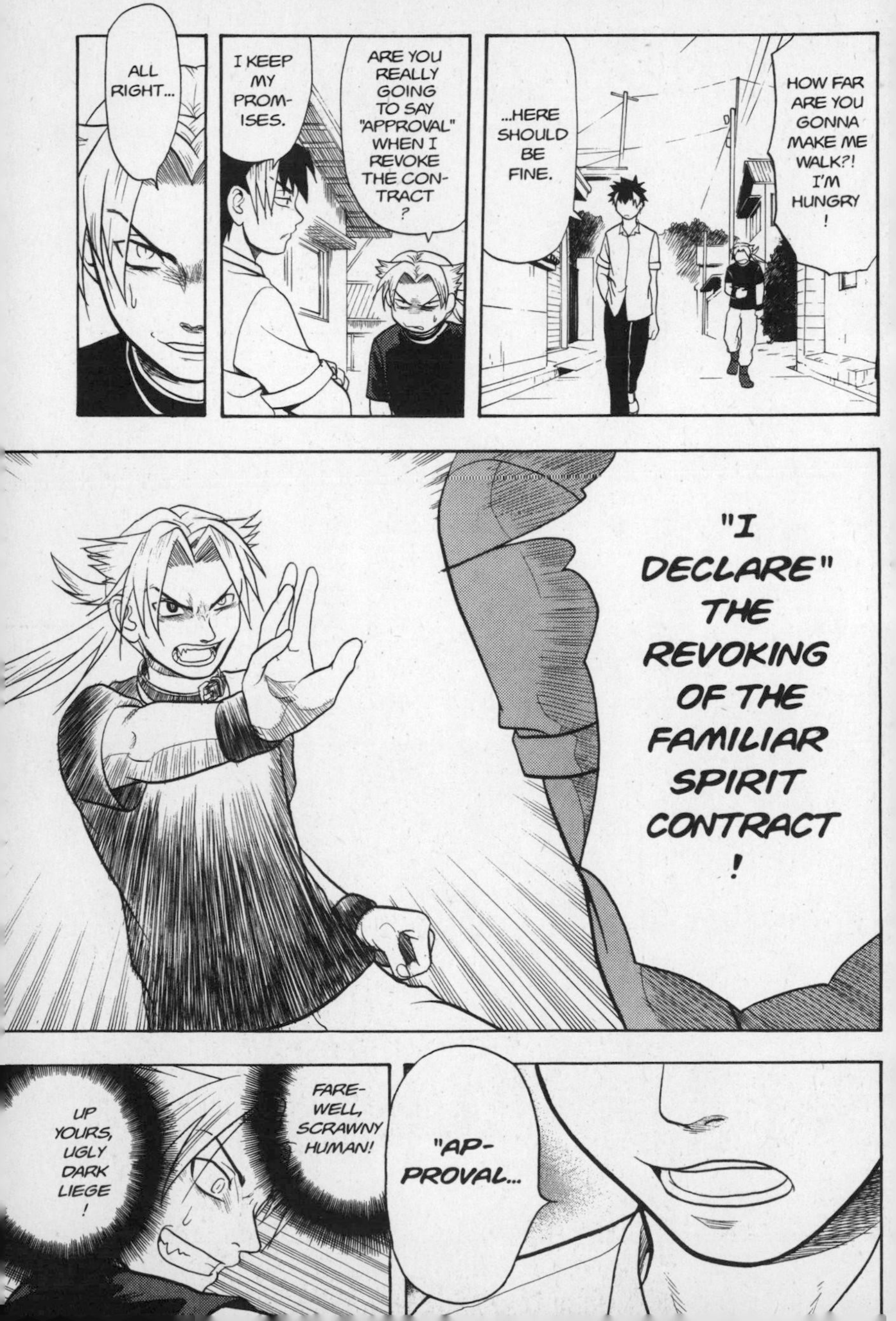
HOW FAR ARE YOU GONNA MAKE ME WALK?! I'M HUNGRY!
...HERE SHOULD BE FINE.
ARE YOU REALLY GOING TO SAY "APPROVAL" WHEN I REVOKE THE CONTRACT?
I KEEP MY PROMISES.
ALL RIGHT...
"I DECLARE" THE REVOKING OF THE FAMILIAR SPIRIT CONTRACT!
"APPROVAL...
FAREWELL, SCRAWNY HUMAN!
UP YOURS, UGLY DARK LIEGE!

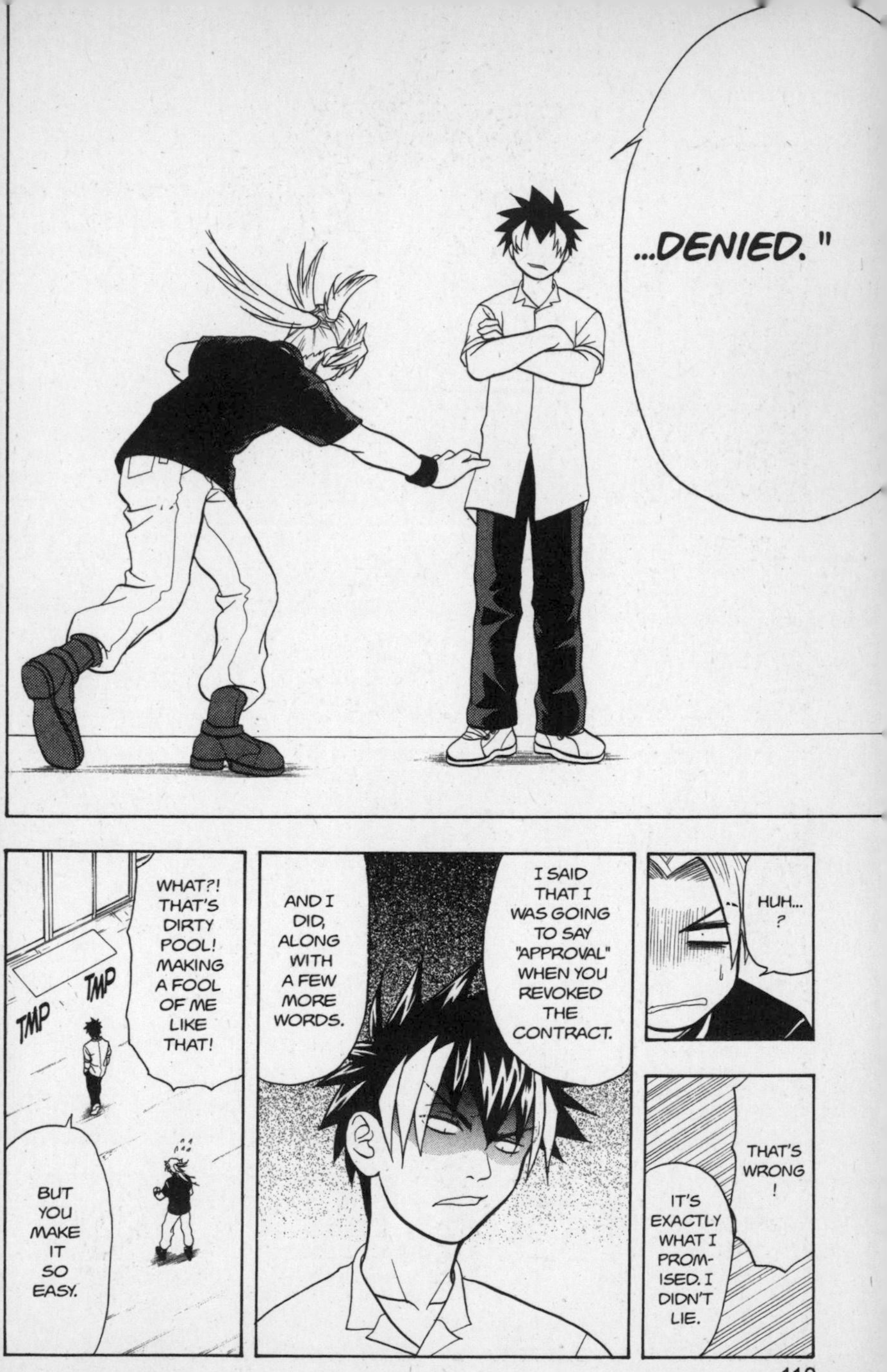
...DENIED."
HUH...?
THAT'S WRONG!
IT'S EXACTLY WHAT I PROMISED. I DIDN'T LIE.
I SAID THAT I WAS GOING TO SAY "APPROVAL" WHEN YOU REVOKED THE CONTRACT.
AND I DID, ALONG WITH A FEW MORE WORDS.
WHAT?! THAT'S DIRTY POOL! MAKING A FOOL OF ME LIKE THAT!
TMP
TMP
BUT YOU MAKE IT SO EASY.

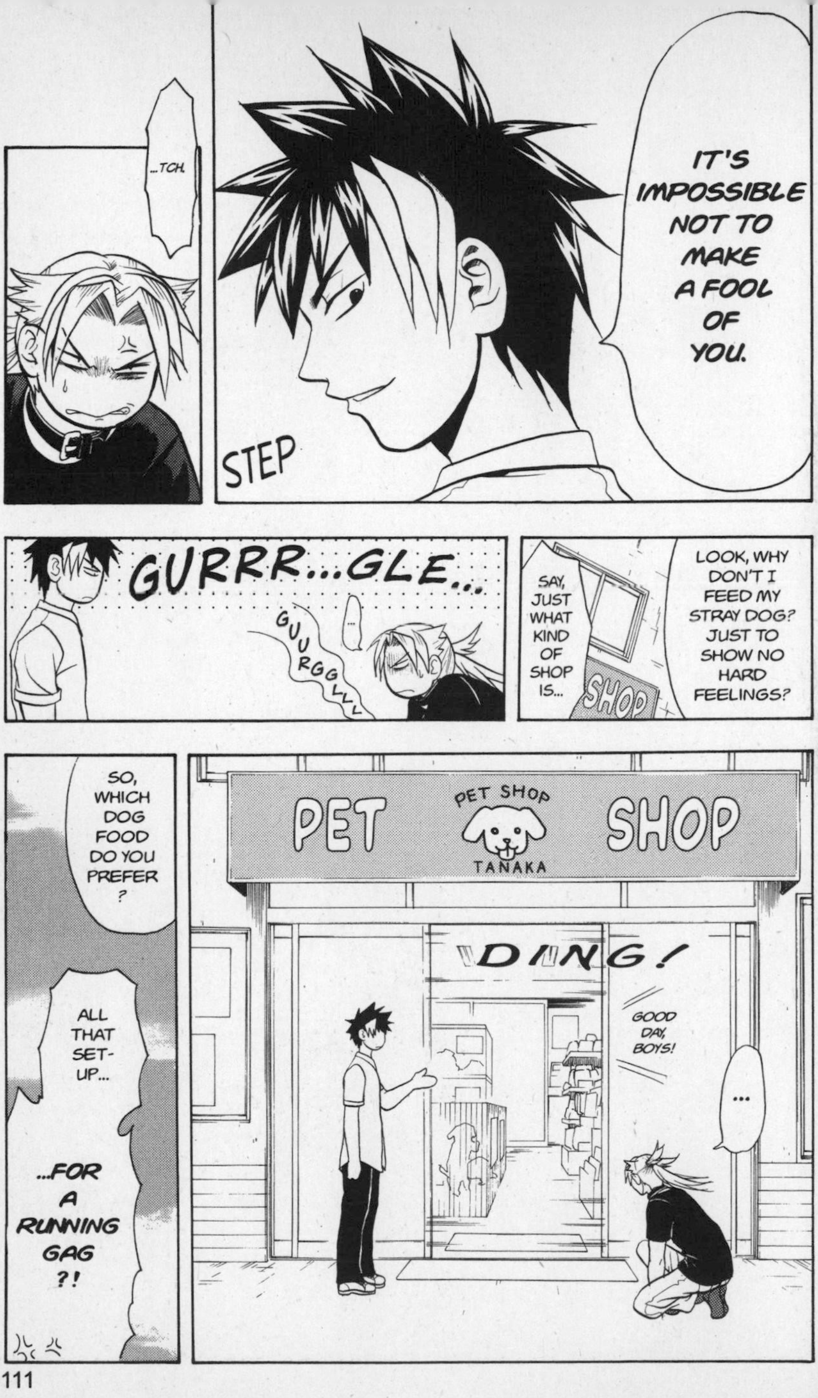
IT'S IMPOSSIBLE NOT TO MAKE A FOOL OF YOU.
STEP
...TCH.
LOOK, WHY DON'T I FEED MY STRAY DOG? JUST TO SHOW NO HARD FEELINGS?
SAY, JUST WHAT KIND OF SHOP IS...
SHOP
GURRR...GLE...
GUURGGLLL
...
PET SHOP
PET SHOP
TANAKA
DING!
GOOD DAY, BOYS!
...
SO, WHICH DOG FOOD DO YOU PREFER?
ALL THAT SET-UP...
...FOR A RUNNING GAG?!

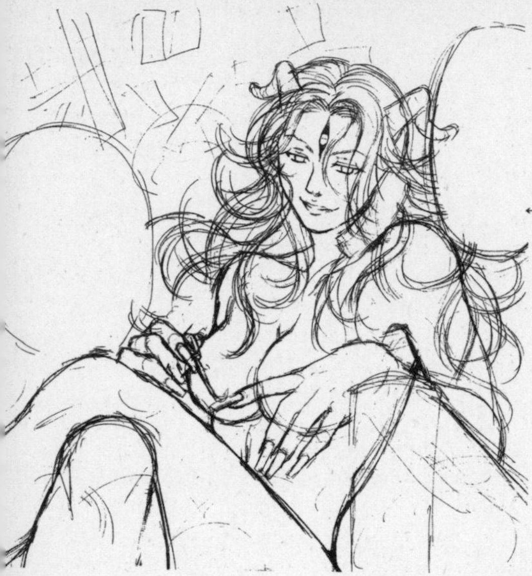

←IN THE ROUGH CONCEPT STAGE, THE DARK LIEGE WAS IN HER BIRTHDAY SUIT. IN THE END I PUT CLOTHING ON HER, BUT IT HONESTLY DIDN'T CHANGE THAT MUCH.

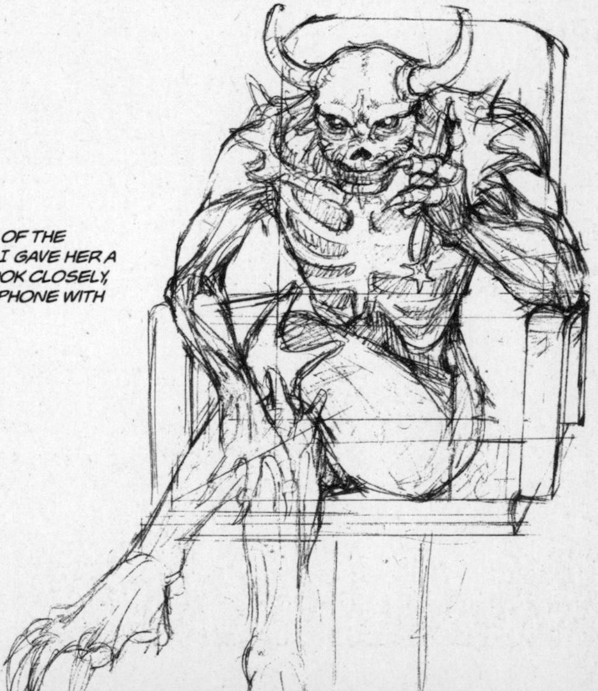

MY ORIGINAL SKETCH OF THE DARK LIEGE BEFORE I GAVE HER A MAKEOVER. IF YOU LOOK CLOSELY, YOU CAN SEE A CELL PHONE WITH A CHARM STRAP! →

Story 3: The Watcher

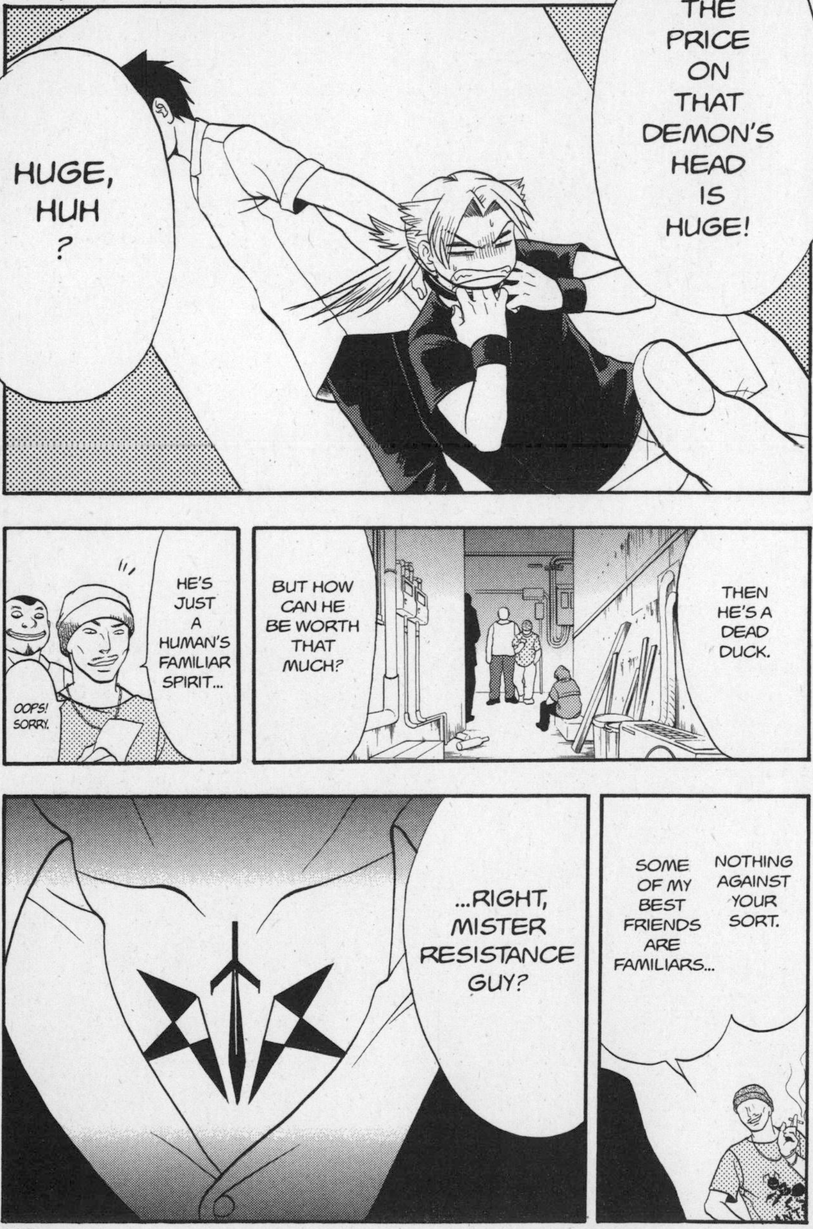
THE PRICE ON THAT DEMON'S HEAD IS HUGE!
HUGE, HUH?
THEN HE'S A DEAD DUCK.
BUT HOW CAN HE BE WORTH THAT MUCH?
HE'S JUST A HUMAN'S FAMILIAR SPIRIT...
OOPS! SORRY.
NOTHING AGAINST YOUR SORT.
SOME OF MY BEST FRIENDS ARE FAMILIARS...
...RIGHT, MISTER RESISTANCE GUY?

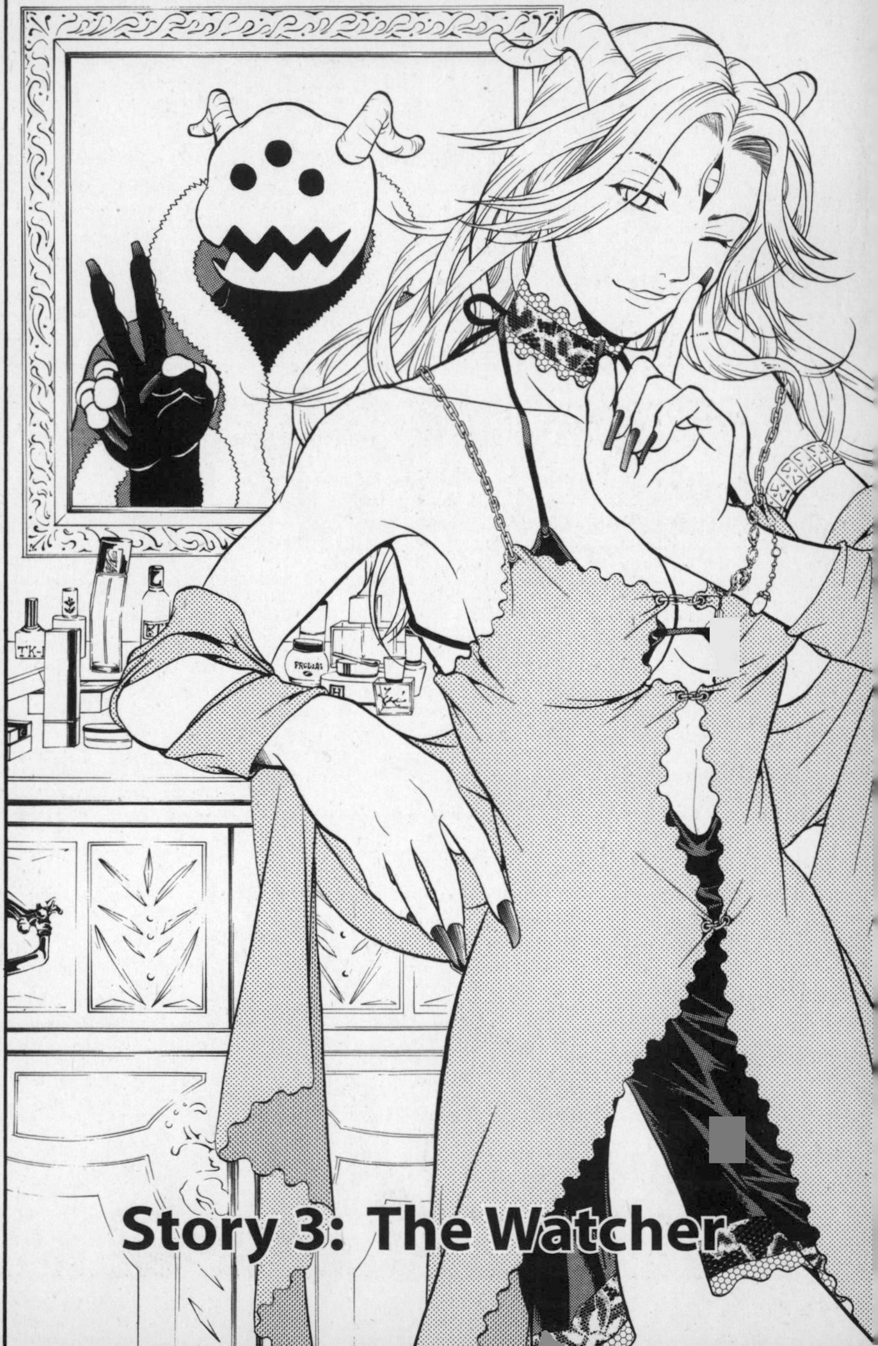

Story 3: The Watcher

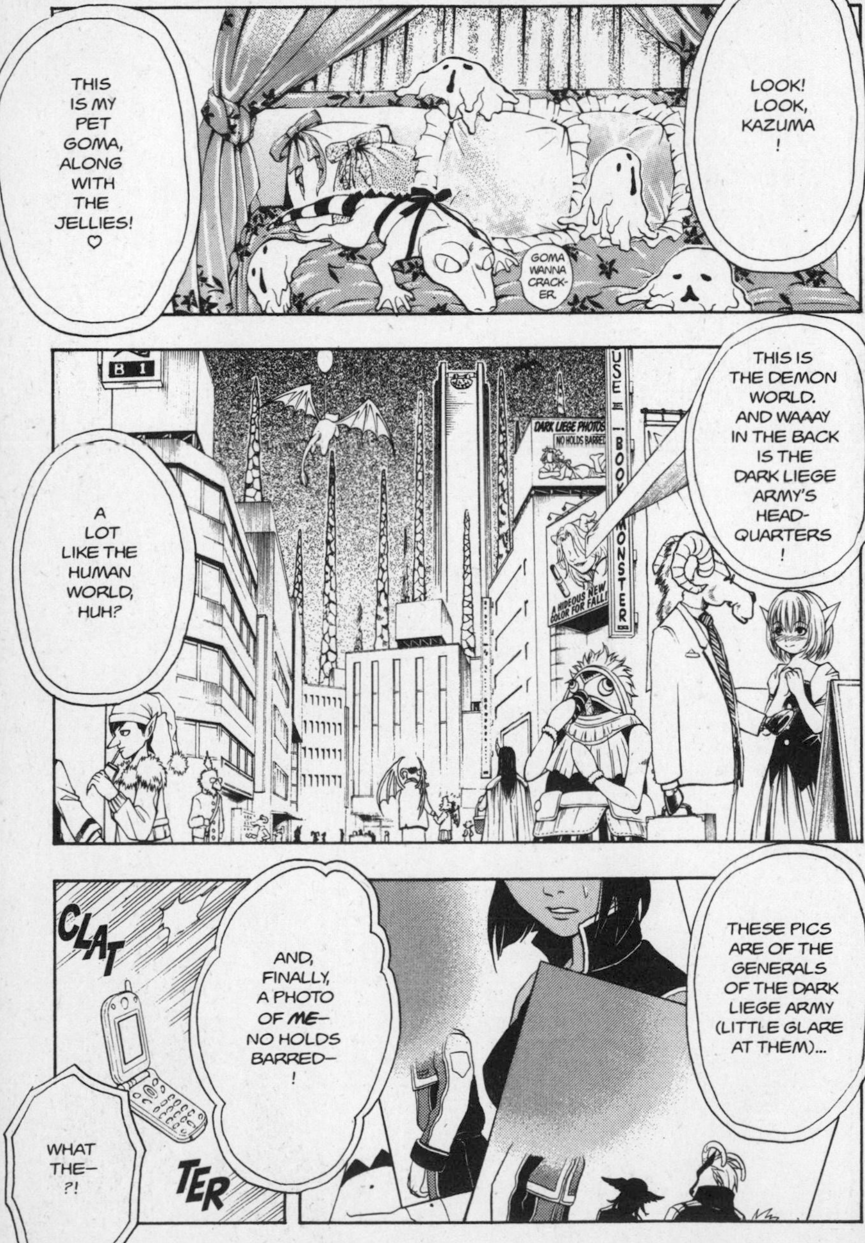
LOOK! LOOK, KAZUMA!
THIS IS MY PET GOMA, ALONG WITH THE JELLIES! ♡
GOMA WANNA CRACKER.
THIS IS THE DEMON WORLD. AND WAAAY IN THE BACK IS THE DARK LIEGE ARMY'S HEADQUARTERS!
DARK LIEGE PHOTOS
NO HOLDS BARRED
BOOK MONSTER
A HIDEOUS NEW COLOR FOR FALL!
B1
A LOT LIKE THE HUMAN WORLD, HUH?
THESE PICS ARE OF THE GENERALS OF THE DARK LIEGE ARMY (LITTLE GLARE AT THEM)...
AND, FINALLY, A PHOTO OF *ME*— NO HOLDS BARRED—!
CLAT
TER
WHAT THE—?!

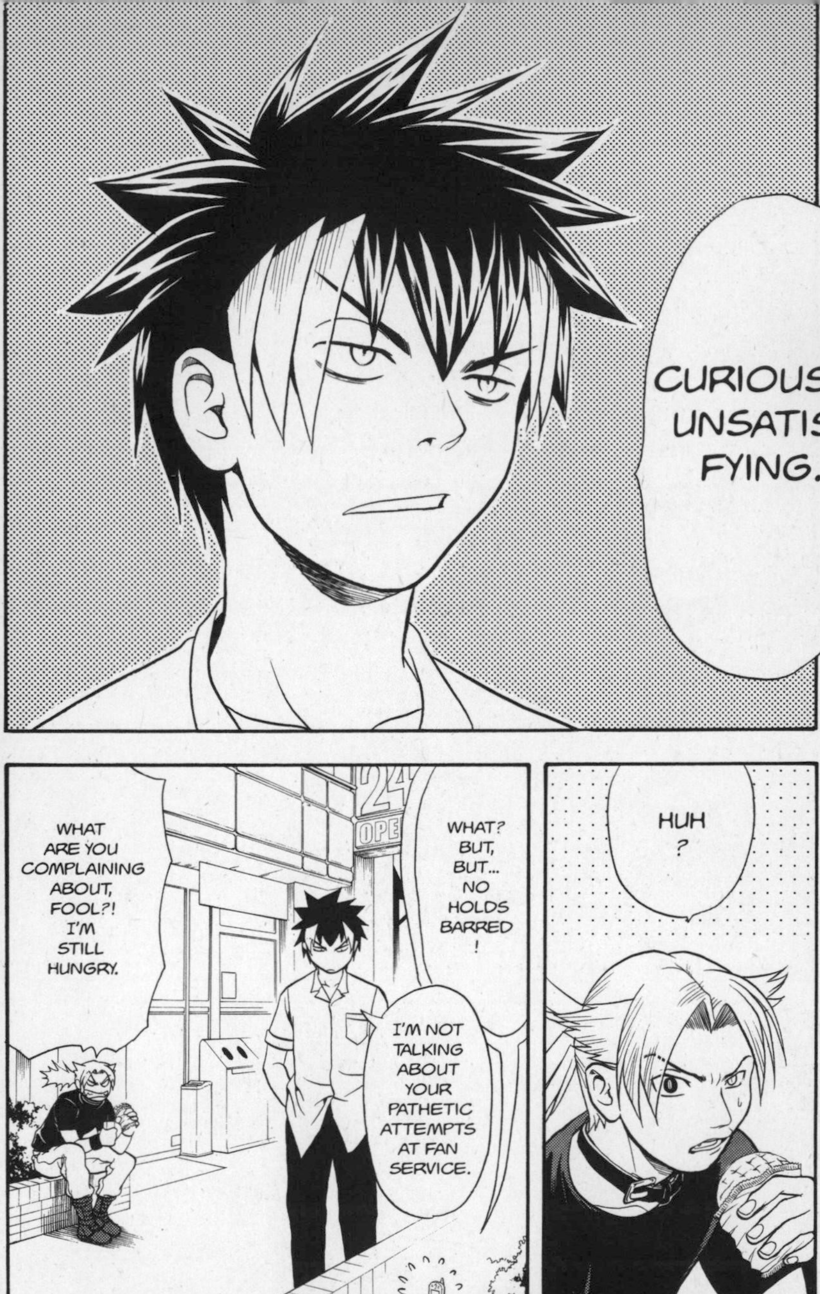
CURIOUSLY UNSATIS-FYING.
HUH ?
WHAT? BUT, BUT... NO HOLDS BARRED !
WHAT ARE YOU COMPLAINING ABOUT, FOOL?! I'M STILL HUNGRY.
I'M NOT TALKING ABOUT YOUR PATHETIC ATTEMPTS AT FAN SERVICE.

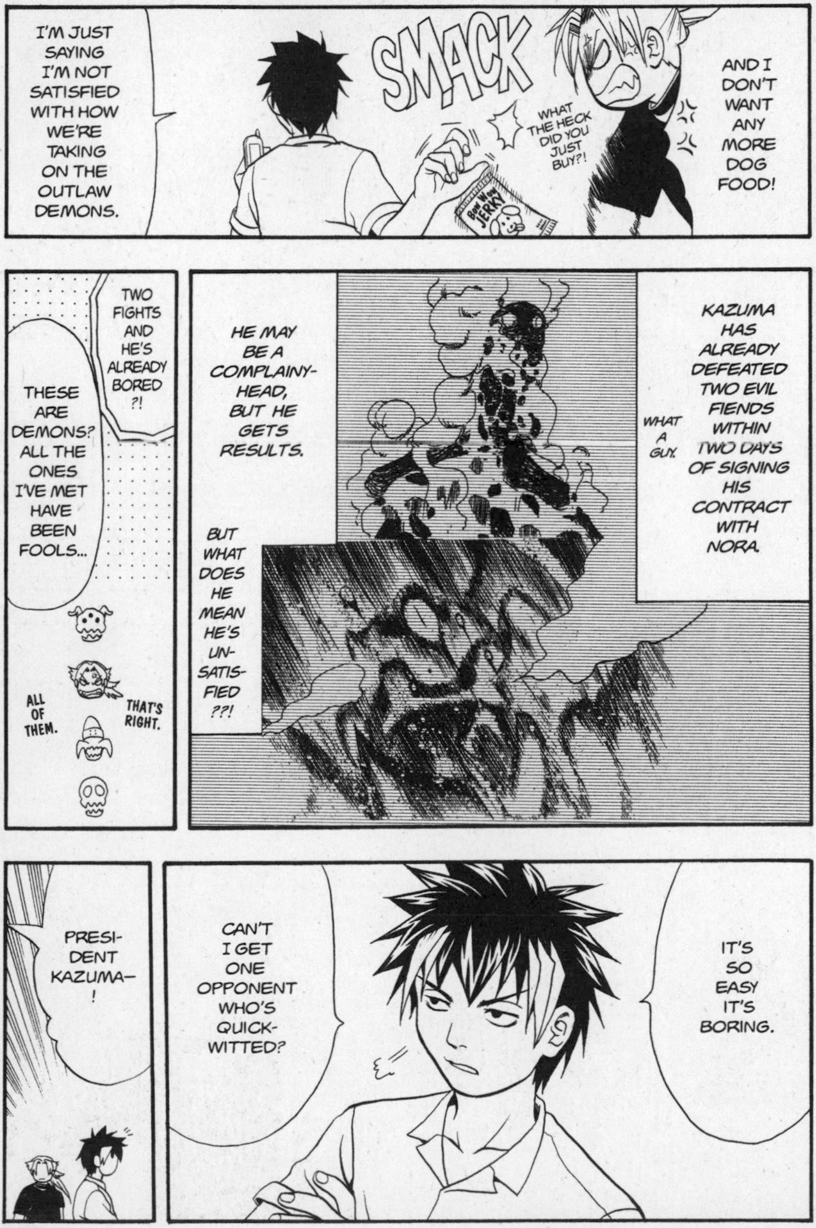
AND I DON'T WANT ANY MORE DOG FOOD!
SMACK
WHAT THE HECK DID YOU JUST BUY?!
Bow Wow JERKY
I'M JUST SAYING I'M NOT SATISFIED WITH HOW WE'RE TAKING ON THE OUTLAW DEMONS.
KAZUMA HAS ALREADY DEFEATED TWO EVIL FIENDS WITHIN TWO DAYS OF SIGNING HIS CONTRACT WITH NORA.
WHAT A GUY.
HE MAY BE A COMPLAINY-HEAD, BUT HE GETS RESULTS.
BUT WHAT DOES HE MEAN HE'S UN-SATIS-FIED ??!
TWO FIGHTS AND HE'S ALREADY BORED ?!
THESE ARE DEMONS? ALL THE ONES I'VE MET HAVE BEEN FOOLS...
THAT'S RIGHT.
ALL OF THEM.
IT'S SO EASY IT'S BORING.
CAN'T I GET ONE OPPONENT WHO'S QUICK-WITTED?
PRESI-DENT KAZUMA—!

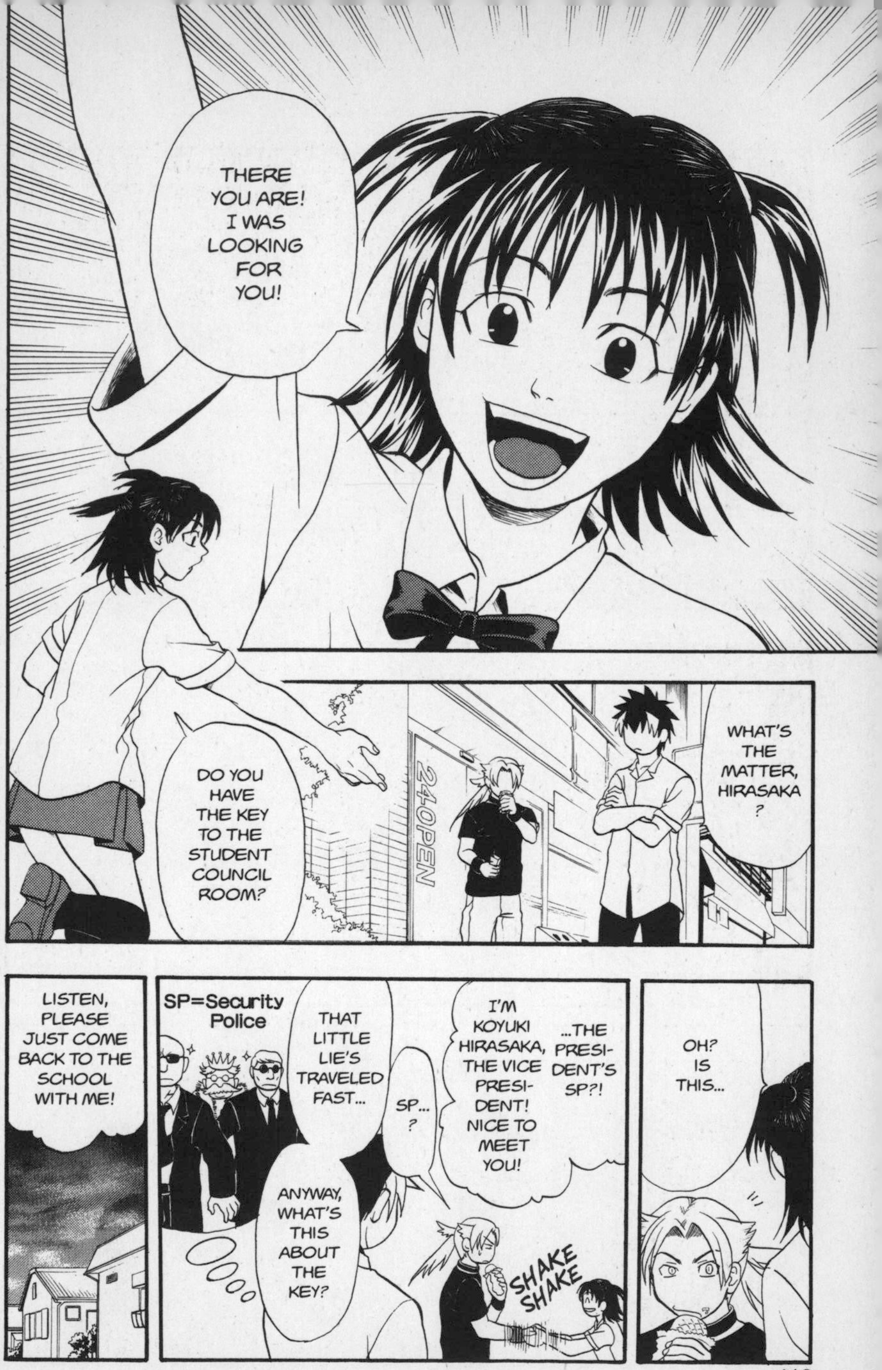
THERE YOU ARE! I WAS LOOKING FOR YOU!
WHAT'S THE MATTER, HIRASAKA?
DO YOU HAVE THE KEY TO THE STUDENT COUNCIL ROOM?
OH? IS THIS...
...THE PRESI-DENT'S SP?!
I'M KOYUKI HIRASAKA, THE VICE PRESI-DENT! NICE TO MEET YOU!
SHAKE SHAKE
SP...?
THAT LITTLE LIE'S TRAVELED FAST...
SP=Security Police
ANYWAY, WHAT'S THIS ABOUT THE KEY?
LISTEN, PLEASE JUST COME BACK TO THE SCHOOL WITH ME!

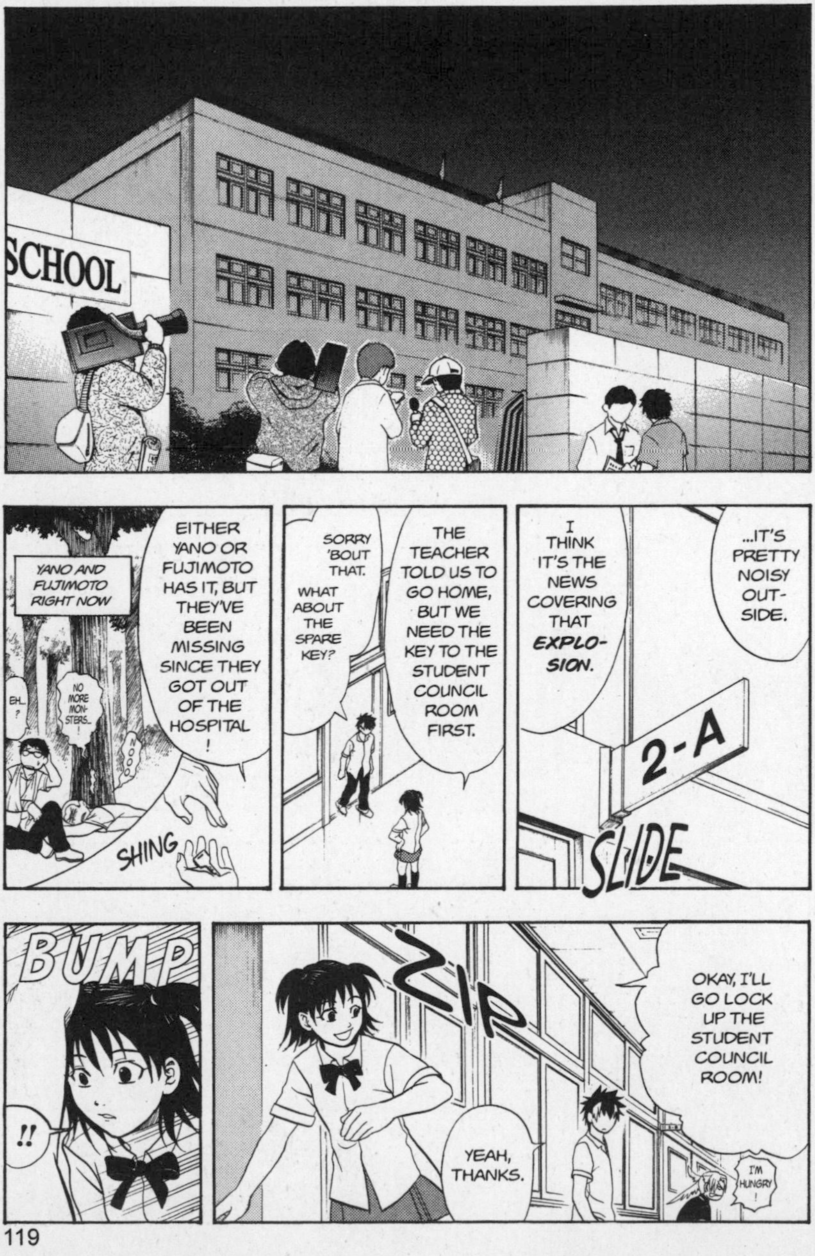
SCHOOL
...IT'S PRETTY NOISY OUTSIDE.
I THINK IT'S THE NEWS COVERING THAT EXPLOSION.
2-A
SLIDE
THE TEACHER TOLD US TO GO HOME, BUT WE NEED THE KEY TO THE STUDENT COUNCIL ROOM FIRST.
SORRY 'BOUT THAT.
WHAT ABOUT THE SPARE KEY?
EITHER YANO OR FUJIMOTO HAS IT, BUT THEY'VE BEEN MISSING SINCE THEY GOT OUT OF THE HOSPITAL!
YANO AND FUJIMOTO RIGHT NOW
NO MORE MONSTERS...!
NOOO
EH...?
SHING
OKAY, I'LL GO LOCK UP THE STUDENT COUNCIL ROOM!
ZIP
YEAH, THANKS.
I'M HUNGRY!
BUMP
!!

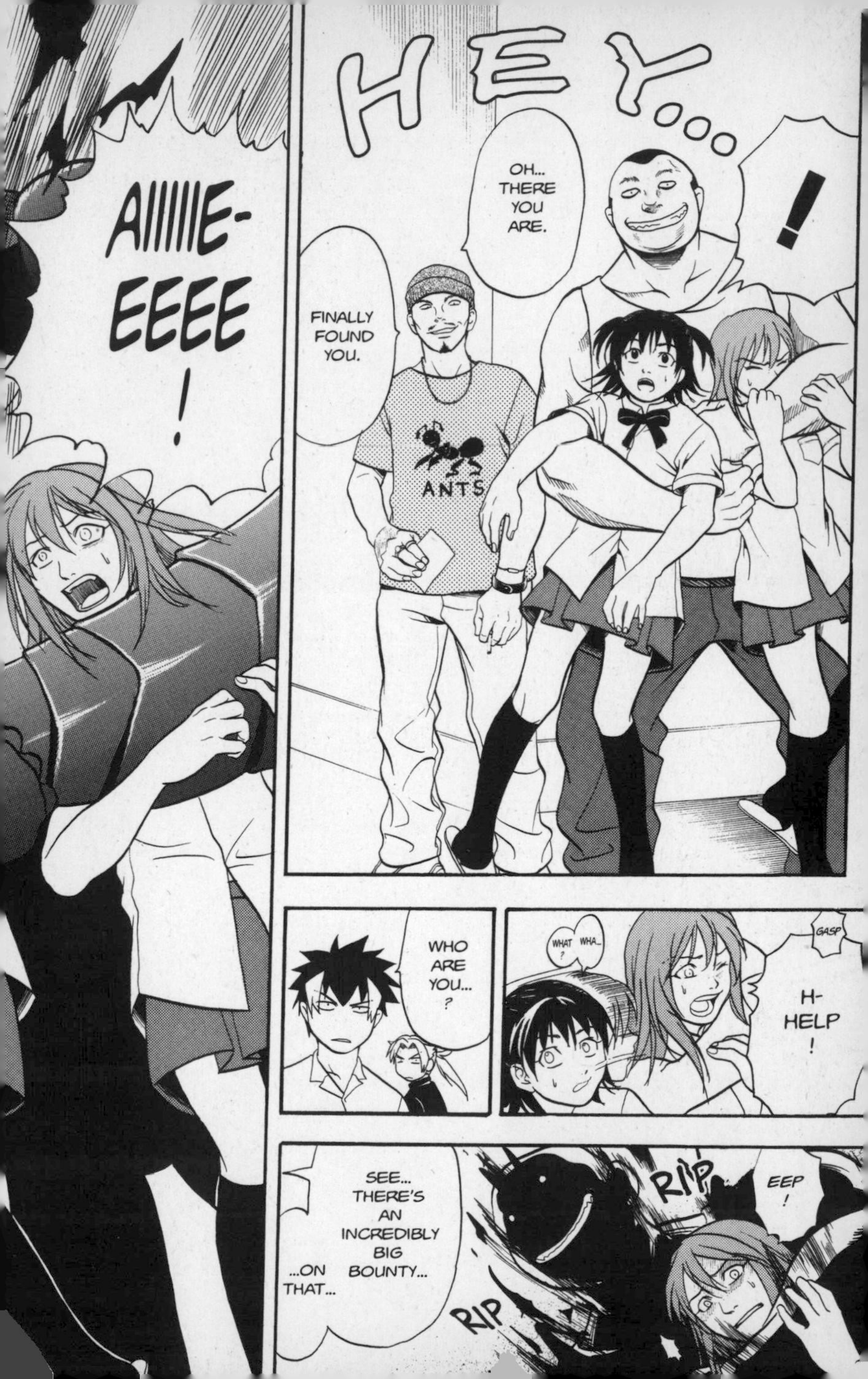
HEY...
!
OH... THERE YOU ARE.
FINALLY FOUND YOU.
GASP
H-HELP!
WHAT? WHA...
WHO ARE YOU...?
EEP!
RIP
SEE... THERE'S AN INCREDIBLY BIG BOUNTY...
...ON THAT...
RIP
AIIIIE-EEEEE!

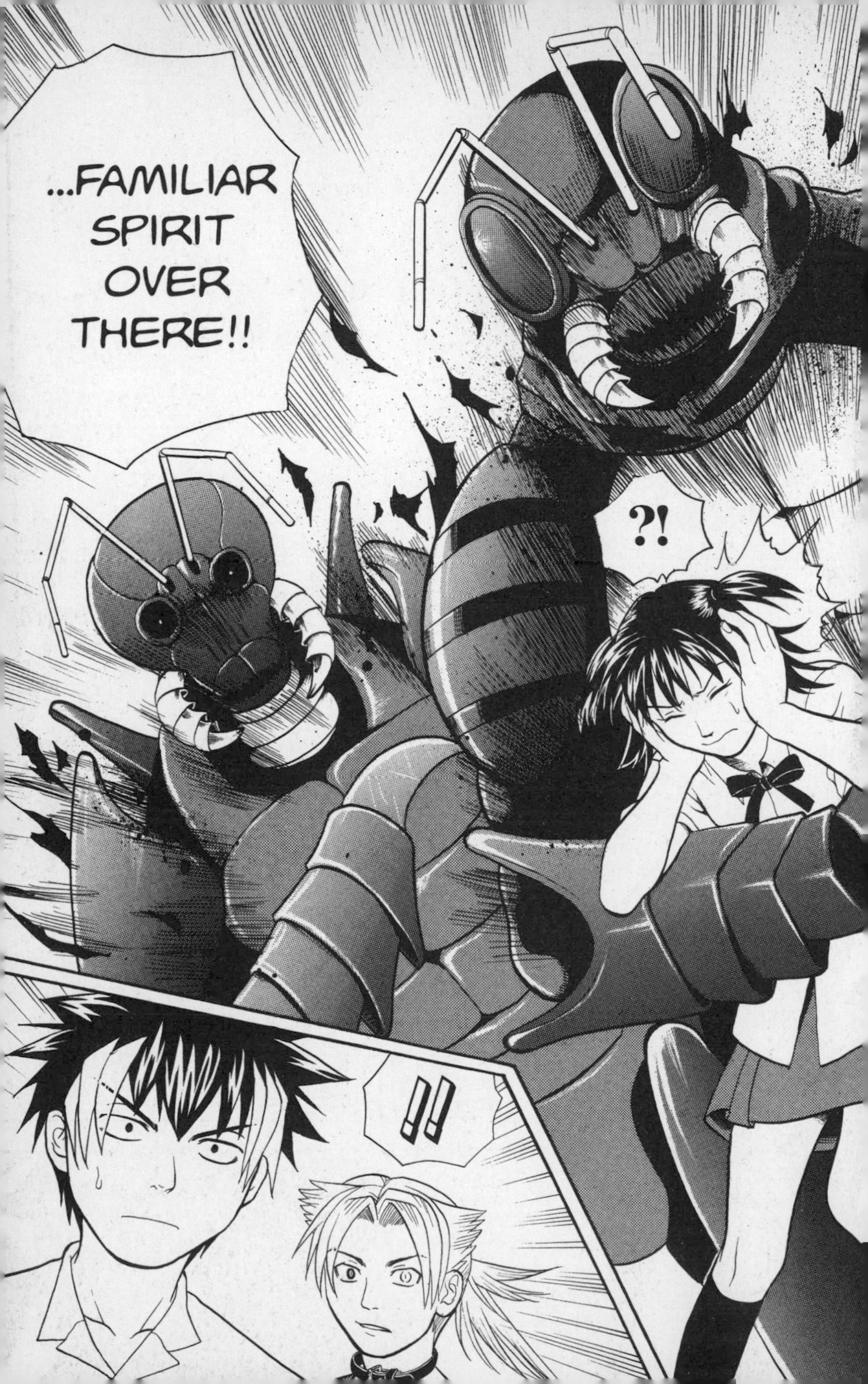
...FAMILIAR SPIRIT OVER THERE!!
?!
!!

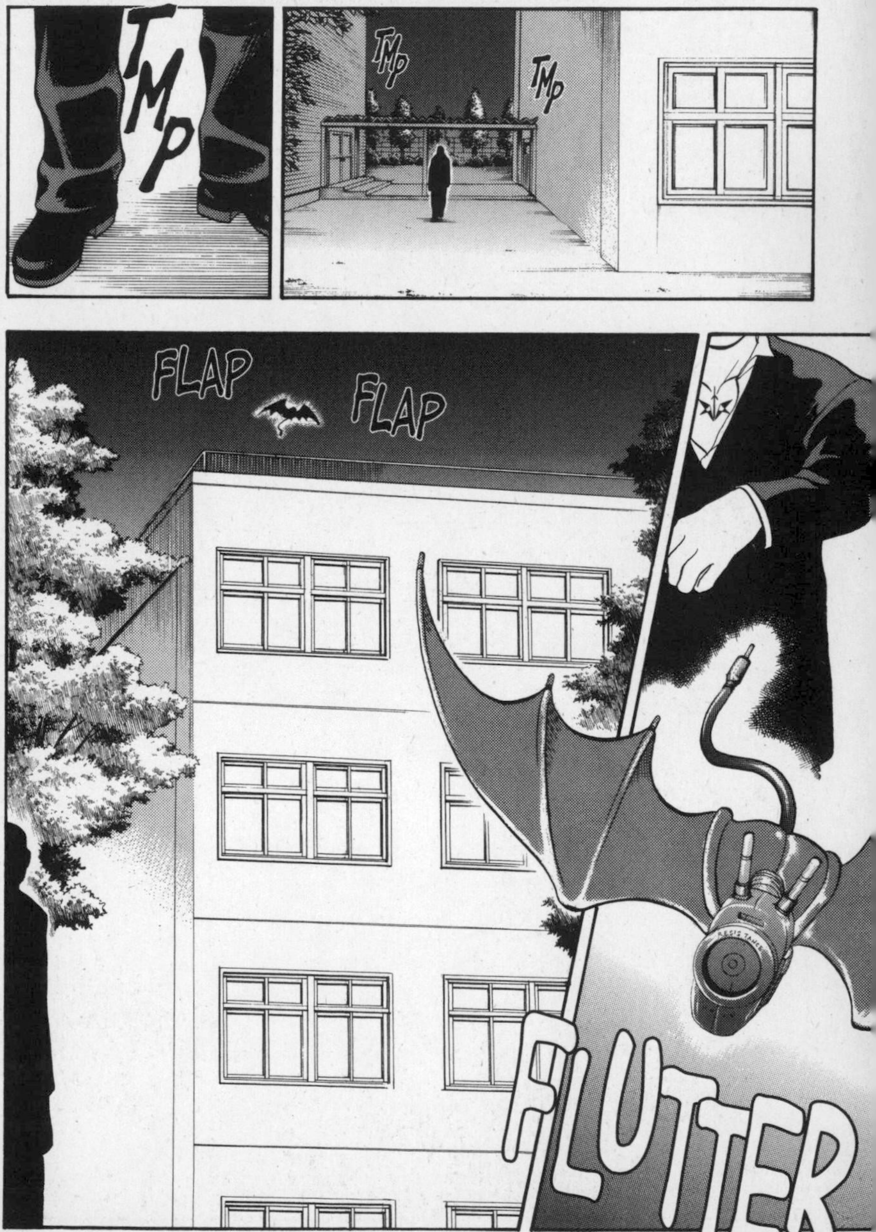
TMP
TMP
TMP
FLUTTER
FLAP
FLAP

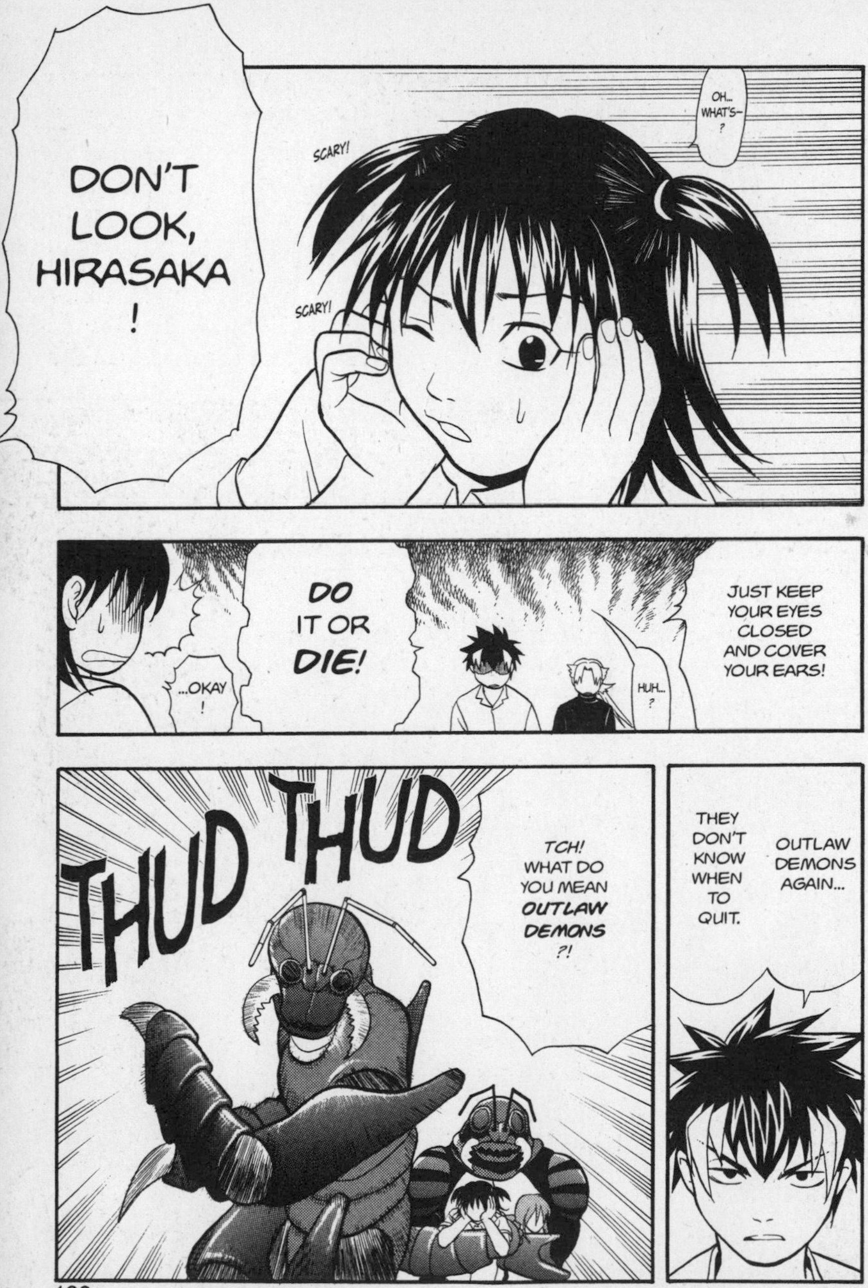
OH... WHAT'S—?
SCARY!
SCARY!
DON'T LOOK, HIRASAKA!
JUST KEEP YOUR EYES CLOSED AND COVER YOUR EARS!
HUH...?
DO IT OR DIE!
...OKAY!
OUTLAW DEMONS AGAIN...
THEY DON'T KNOW WHEN TO QUIT.
TCH! WHAT DO YOU MEAN OUTLAW DEMONS?!
THUD THUD

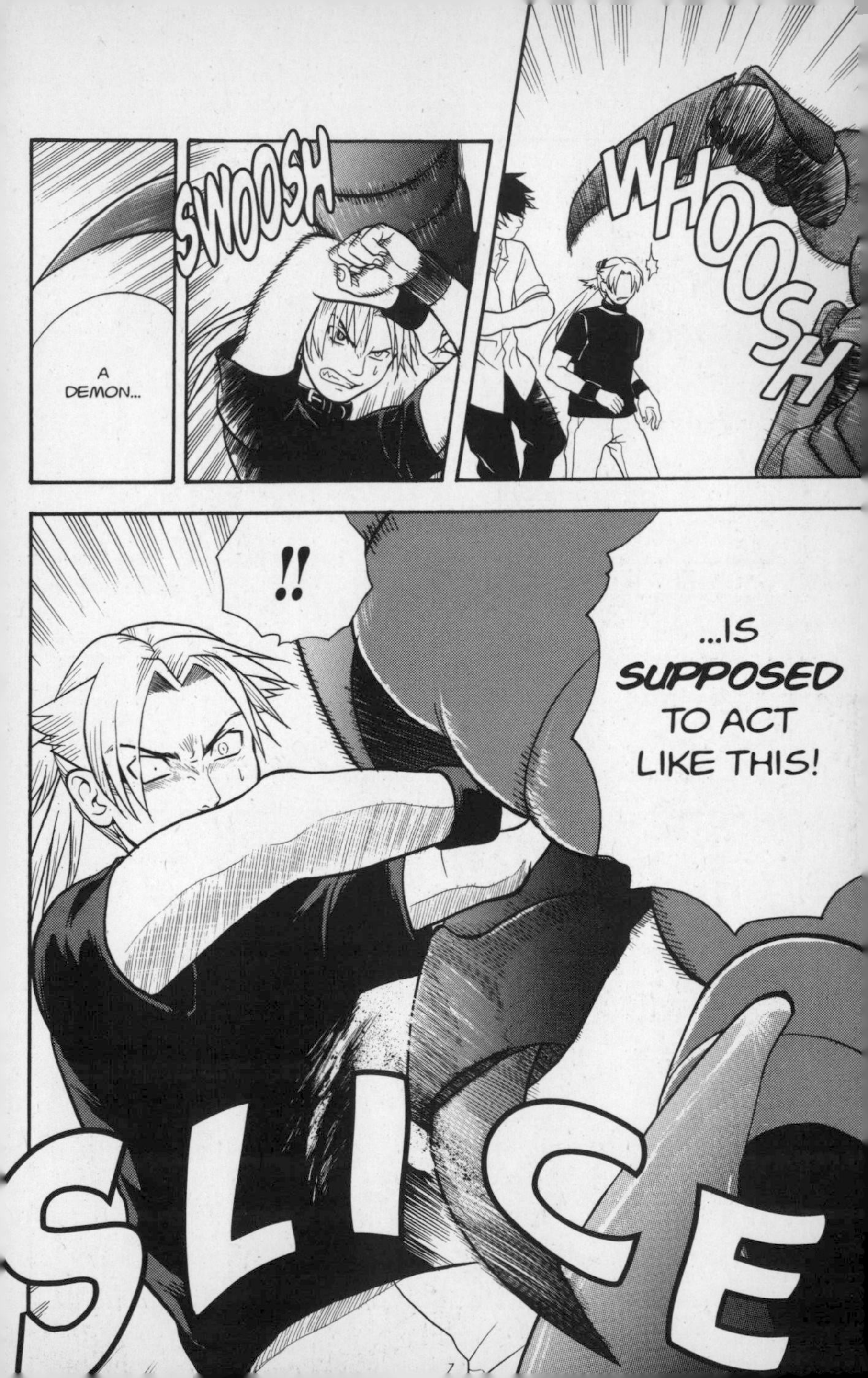
WHOOSH
SWOOSH
A DEMON...
!!
...IS SUPPOSED TO ACT LIKE THIS!
SLICE

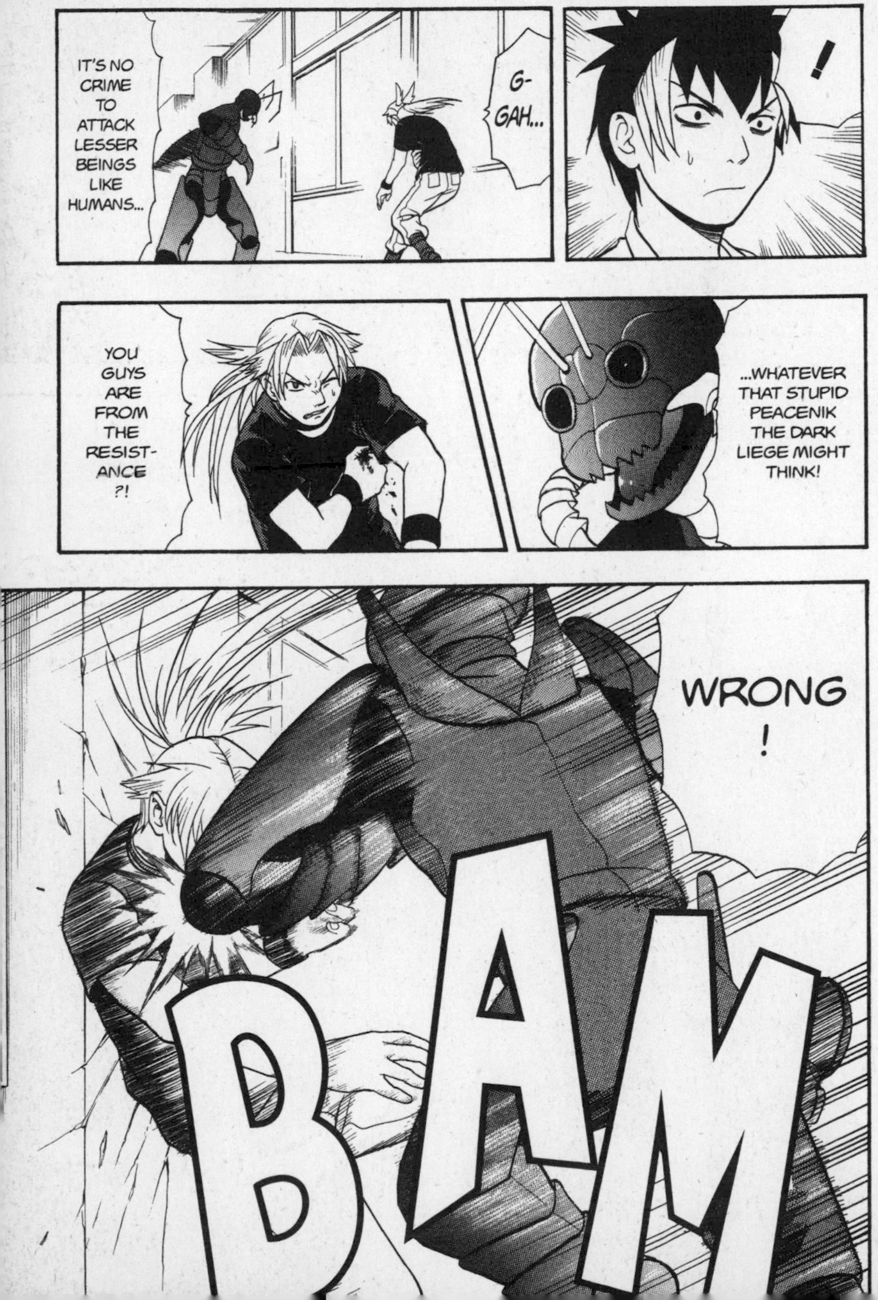
!
G-GAH...
IT'S NO CRIME TO ATTACK LESSER BEINGS LIKE HUMANS...
...WHATEVER THAT STUPID PEACENIK THE DARK LIEGE MIGHT THINK!
YOU GUYS ARE FROM THE RESIST-ANCE?!
WRONG!
BAM

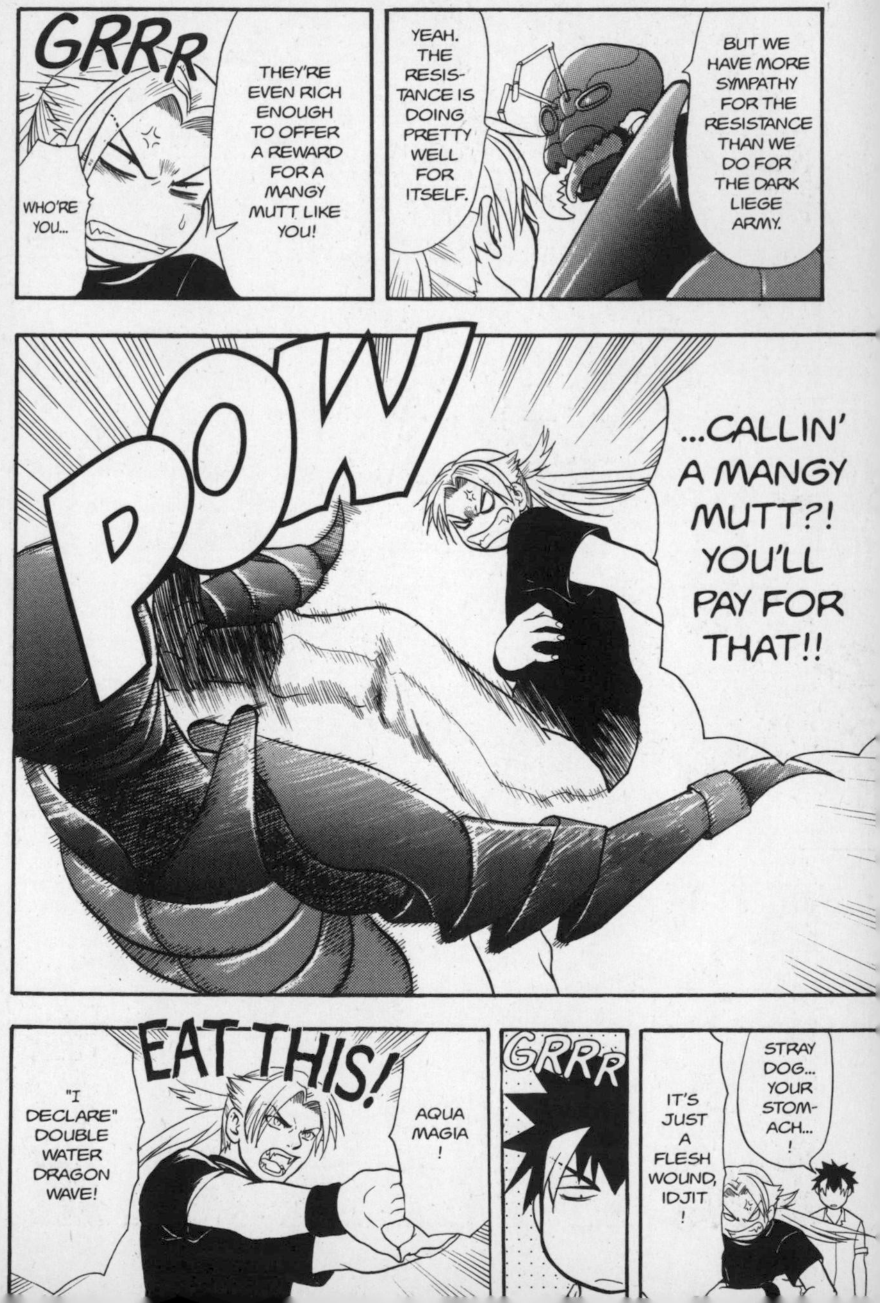
BUT WE HAVE MORE SYMPATHY FOR THE RESISTANCE THAN WE DO FOR THE DARK LIEGE ARMY.
YEAH. THE RESIS-TANCE IS DOING PRETTY WELL FOR ITSELF.
THEY'RE EVEN RICH ENOUGH TO OFFER A REWARD FOR A MANGY MUTT LIKE YOU!
GRRR
WHO'RE YOU...
...CALLIN' A MANGY MUTT?! YOU'LL PAY FOR THAT!!
POW
STRAY DOG... YOUR STOM-ACH... !
IT'S JUST A FLESH WOUND, IDJIT !
GRRR
EAT THIS!
AQUA MAGIA !
"I DECLARE" DOUBLE WATER DRAGON WAVE!

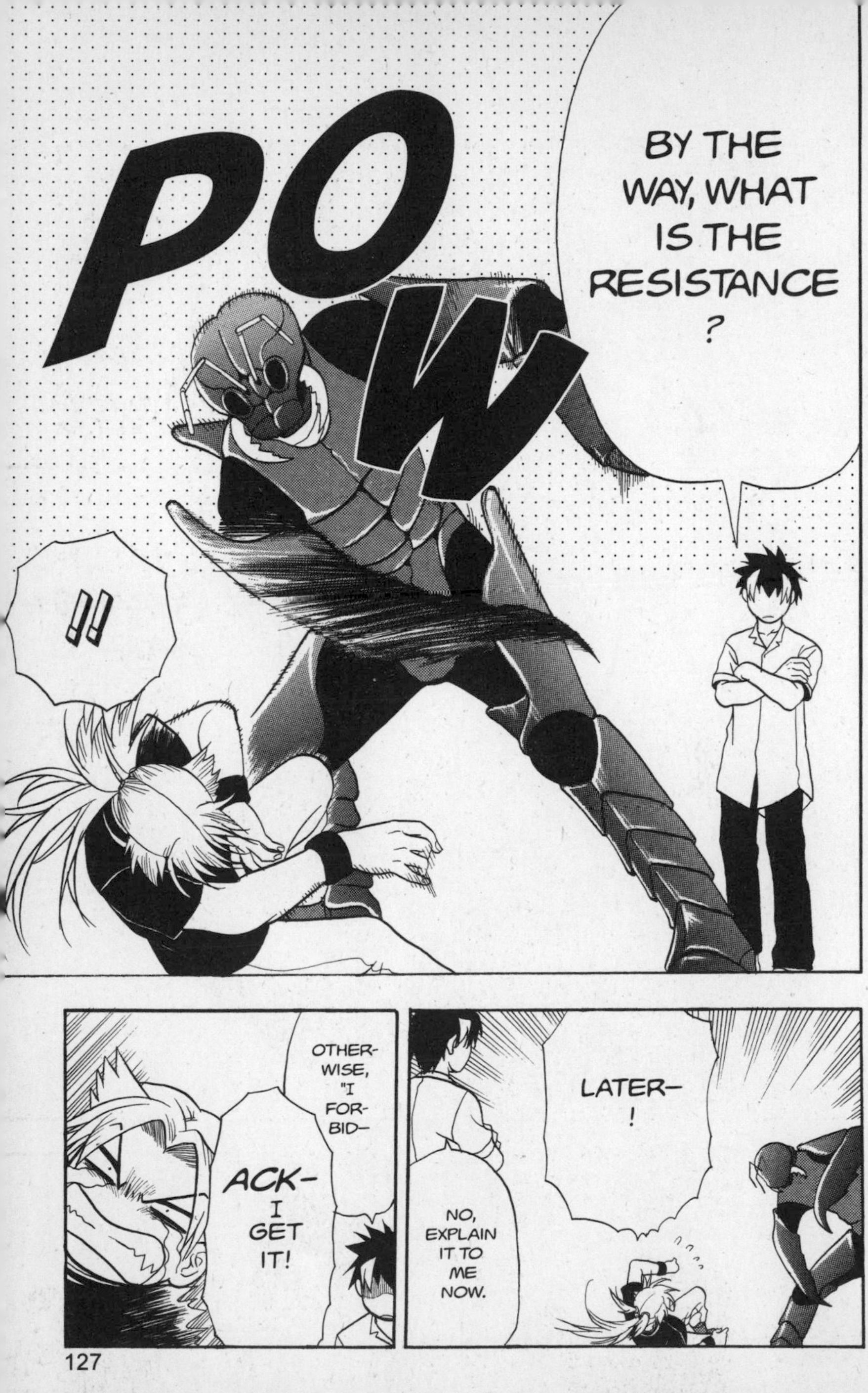
POW
BY THE WAY, WHAT IS THE RESISTANCE?
!!
LATER—!
NO, EXPLAIN IT TO ME NOW.
OTHER-WISE, "I FOR-BID—
ACK— I GET IT!

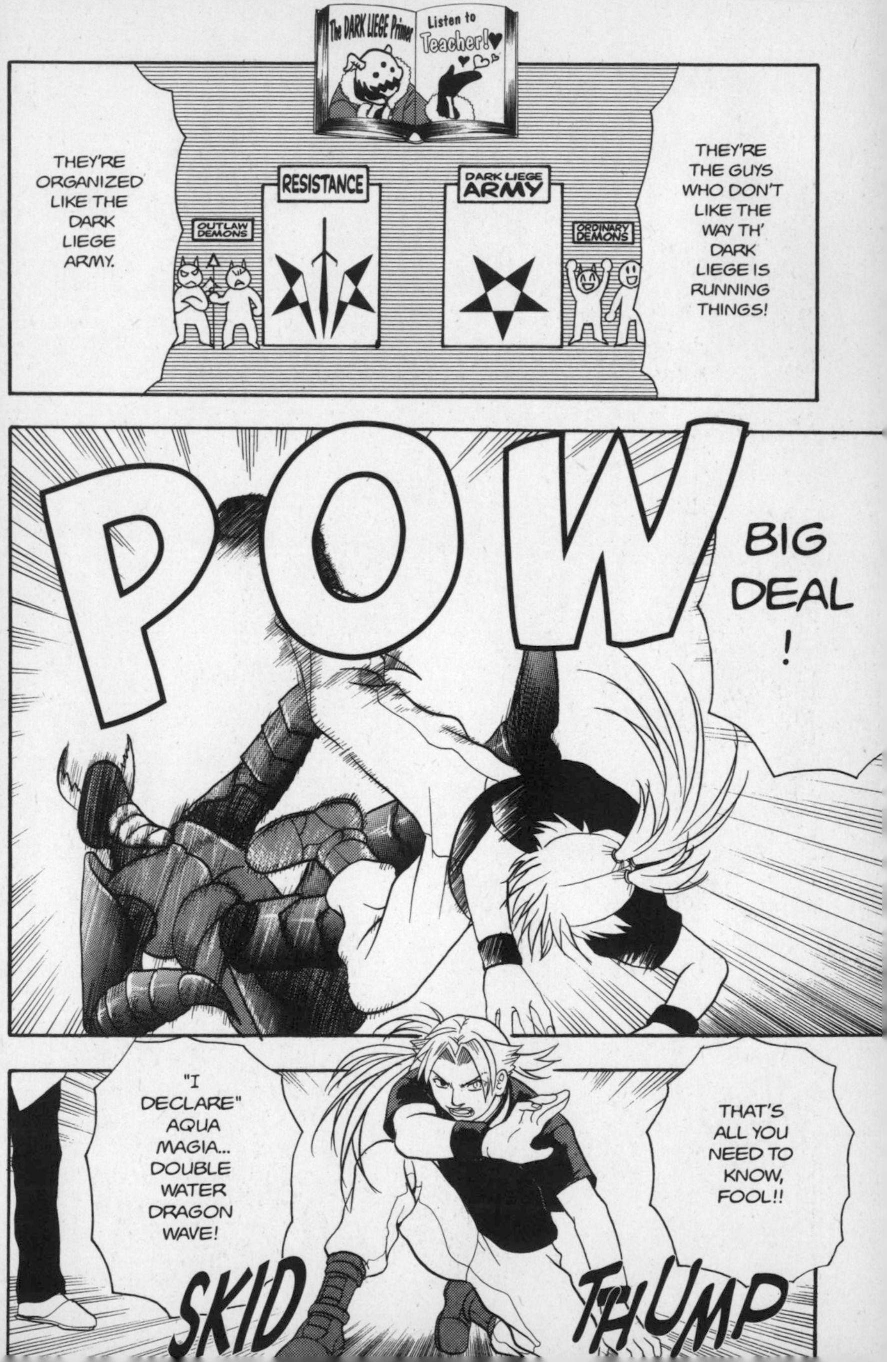

The DARK LIEGE Primer
Listen to Teacher!♥
THEY'RE THE GUYS WHO DON'T LIKE THE WAY TH' DARK LIEGE IS RUNNING THINGS!
ORDINARY DEMONS
DARK LIEGE ARMY
RESISTANCE
OUTLAW DEMONS
THEY'RE ORGANIZED LIKE THE DARK LIEGE ARMY.
BIG DEAL!
POW
THAT'S ALL YOU NEED TO KNOW, FOOL!!
"I DECLARE" AQUA MAGIA... DOUBLE WATER DRAGON WAVE!
THUMP
SKID

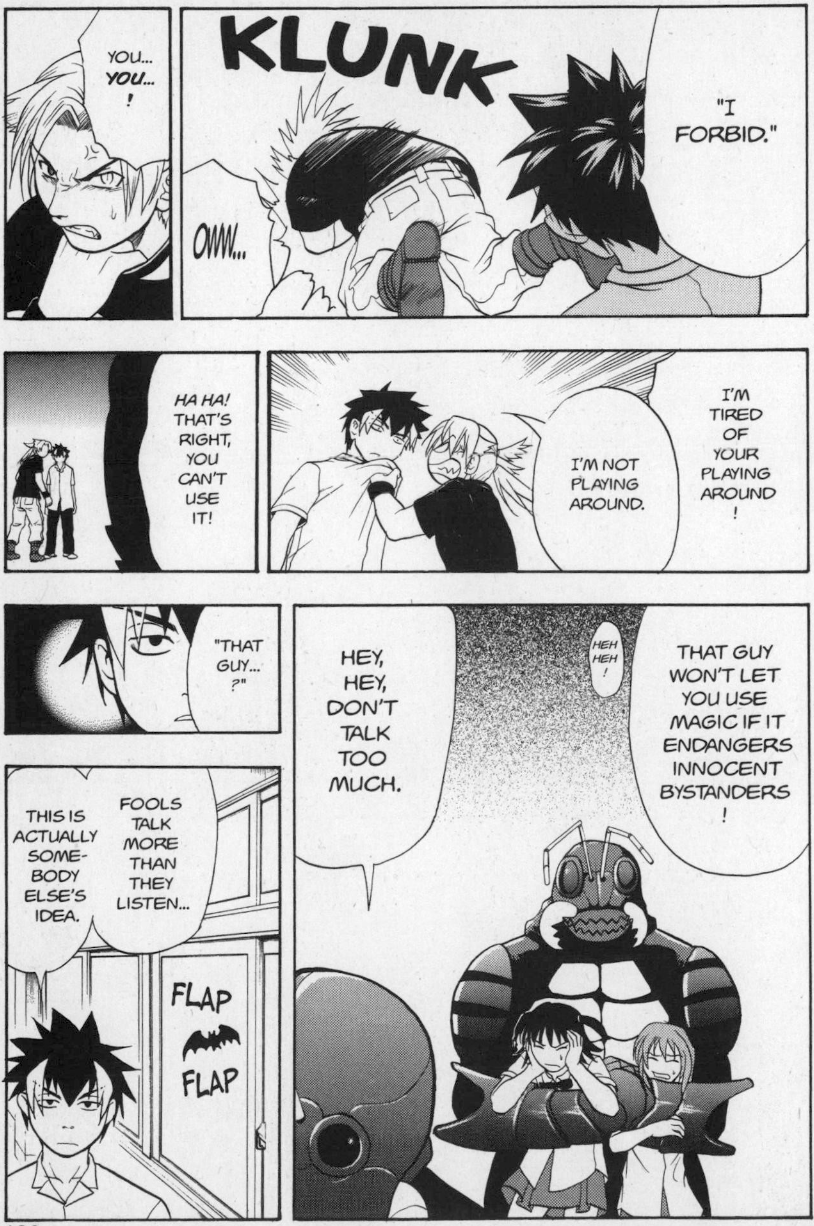
KLUNK
"I FORBID."
OWW...
YOU... YOU...!
I'M TIRED OF YOUR PLAYING AROUND!
I'M NOT PLAYING AROUND.
HA HA! THAT'S RIGHT, YOU CAN'T USE IT!
THAT GUY WON'T LET YOU USE MAGIC IF IT ENDANGERS INNOCENT BYSTANDERS!
HEH HEH!
HEY, HEY, DON'T TALK TOO MUCH.
"THAT GUY...?"
FOOLS TALK MORE THAN THEY LISTEN...
THIS IS ACTUALLY SOMEBODY ELSE'S IDEA.
FLAP
FLAP

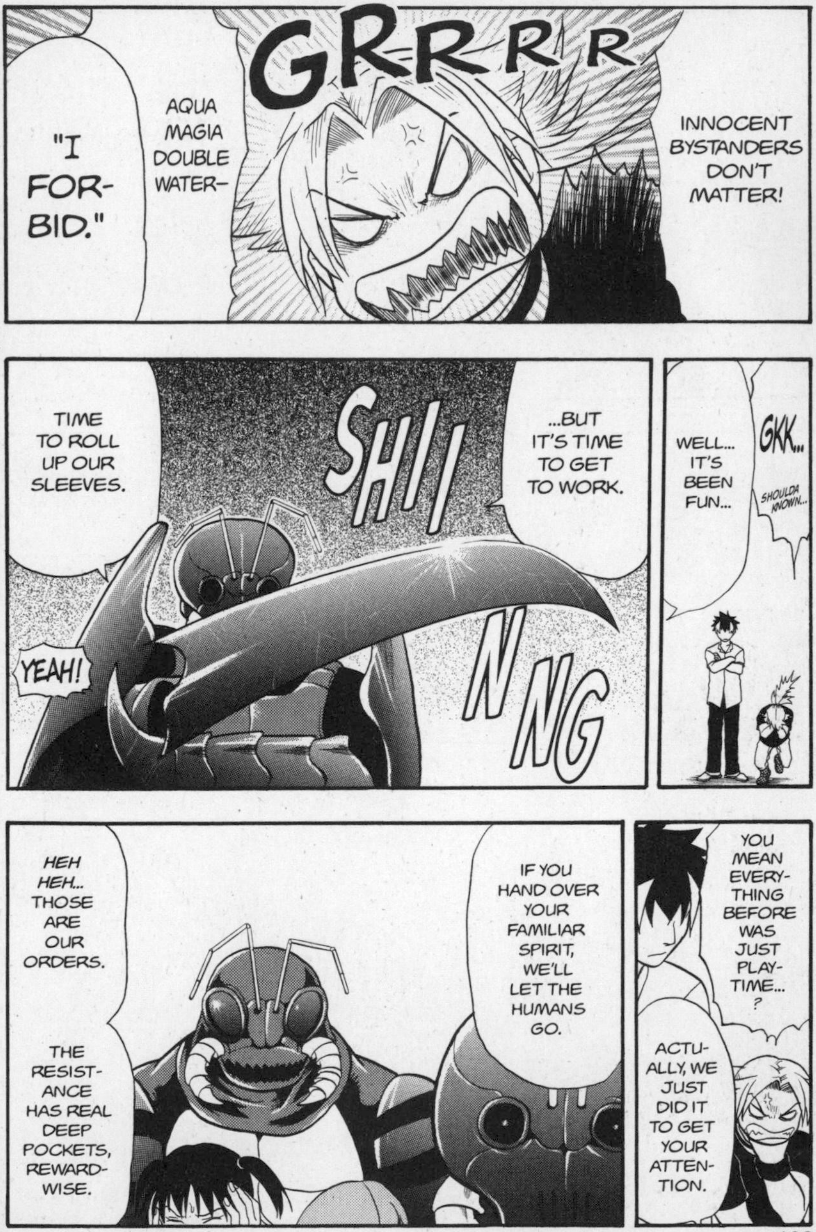

INNOCENT BYSTANDERS DON'T MATTER!
GRRRRR
AQUA MAGIA DOUBLE WATER—
"I FORBID."
GKK...
SHOULDA KNOWN...
WELL... IT'S BEEN FUN...
...BUT IT'S TIME TO GET TO WORK.
SHIINNNG
TIME TO ROLL UP OUR SLEEVES.
YEAH!
YOU MEAN EVERYTHING BEFORE WAS JUST PLAYTIME...?
ACTUALLY, WE JUST DID IT TO GET YOUR ATTENTION.
IF YOU HAND OVER YOUR FAMILIAR SPIRIT, WE'LL LET THE HUMANS GO.
HEH HEH... THOSE ARE OUR ORDERS.
THE RESISTANCE HAS REAL DEEP POCKETS, REWARDWISE.

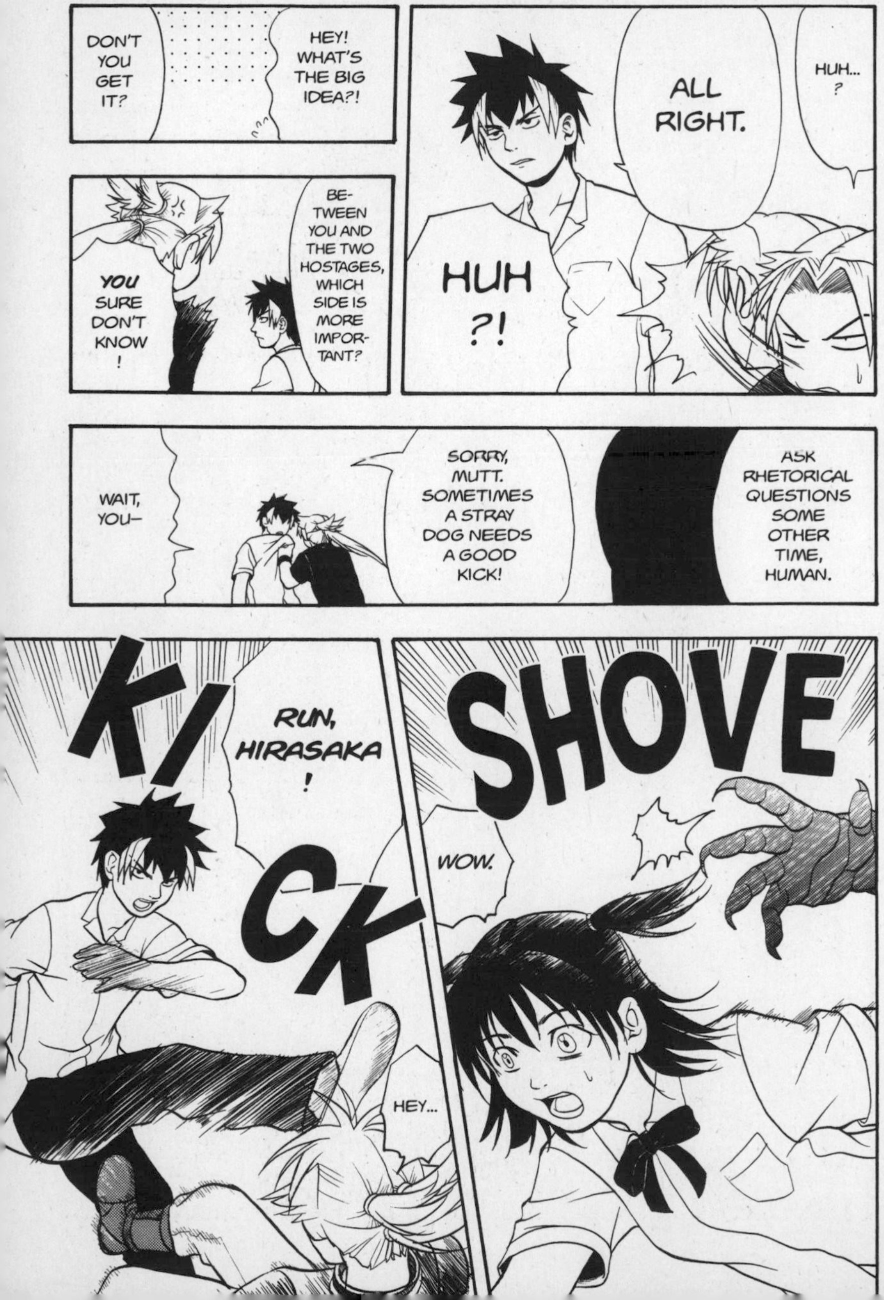
HUH... ?
ALL RIGHT.
HUH ?!
HEY! WHAT'S THE BIG IDEA?!
DON'T YOU GET IT?
BE- TWEEN YOU AND THE TWO HOSTAGES, WHICH SIDE IS MORE IMPOR- TANT?
YOU SURE DON'T KNOW!
ASK RHETORICAL QUESTIONS SOME OTHER TIME, HUMAN.
SORRY, MUTT. SOMETIMES A STRAY DOG NEEDS A GOOD KICK!
WAIT, YOU-
SHOVE
WOW.
KI CK
RUN, HIRASAKA!
HEY...

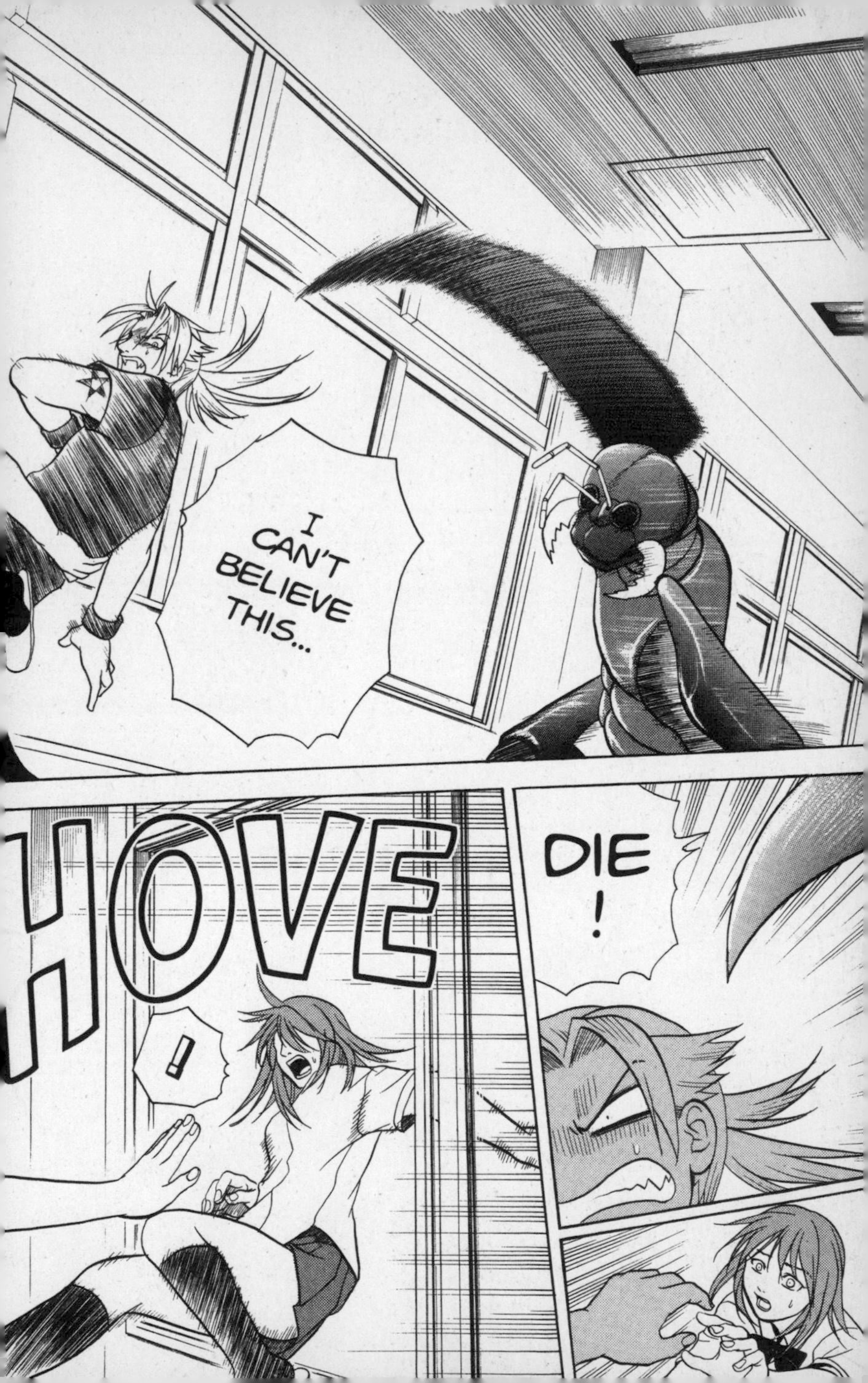
I CAN'T BELIEVE THIS...
DIE !
HOVE
!

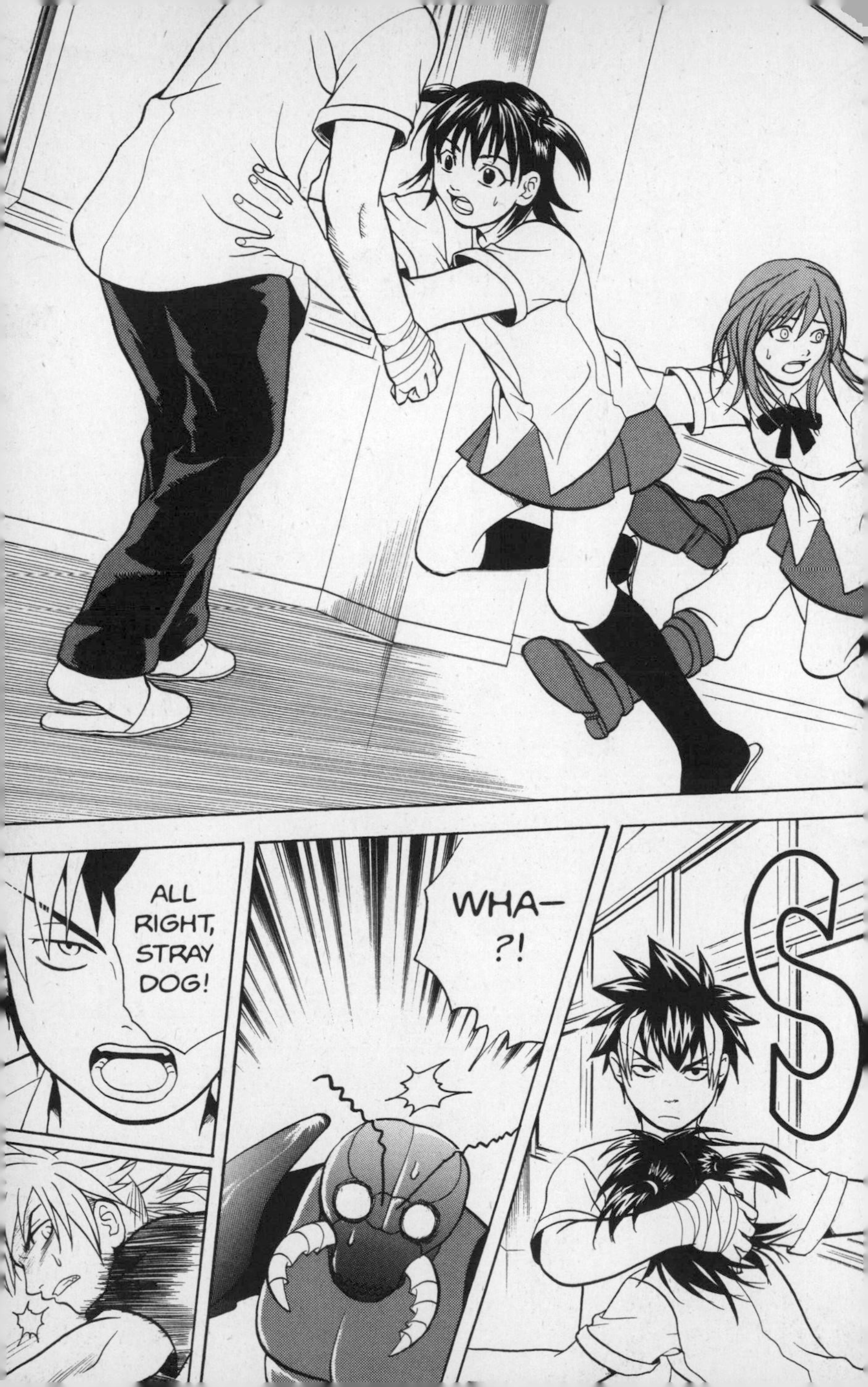
S
WHA-?!
ALL RIGHT, STRAY DOG!

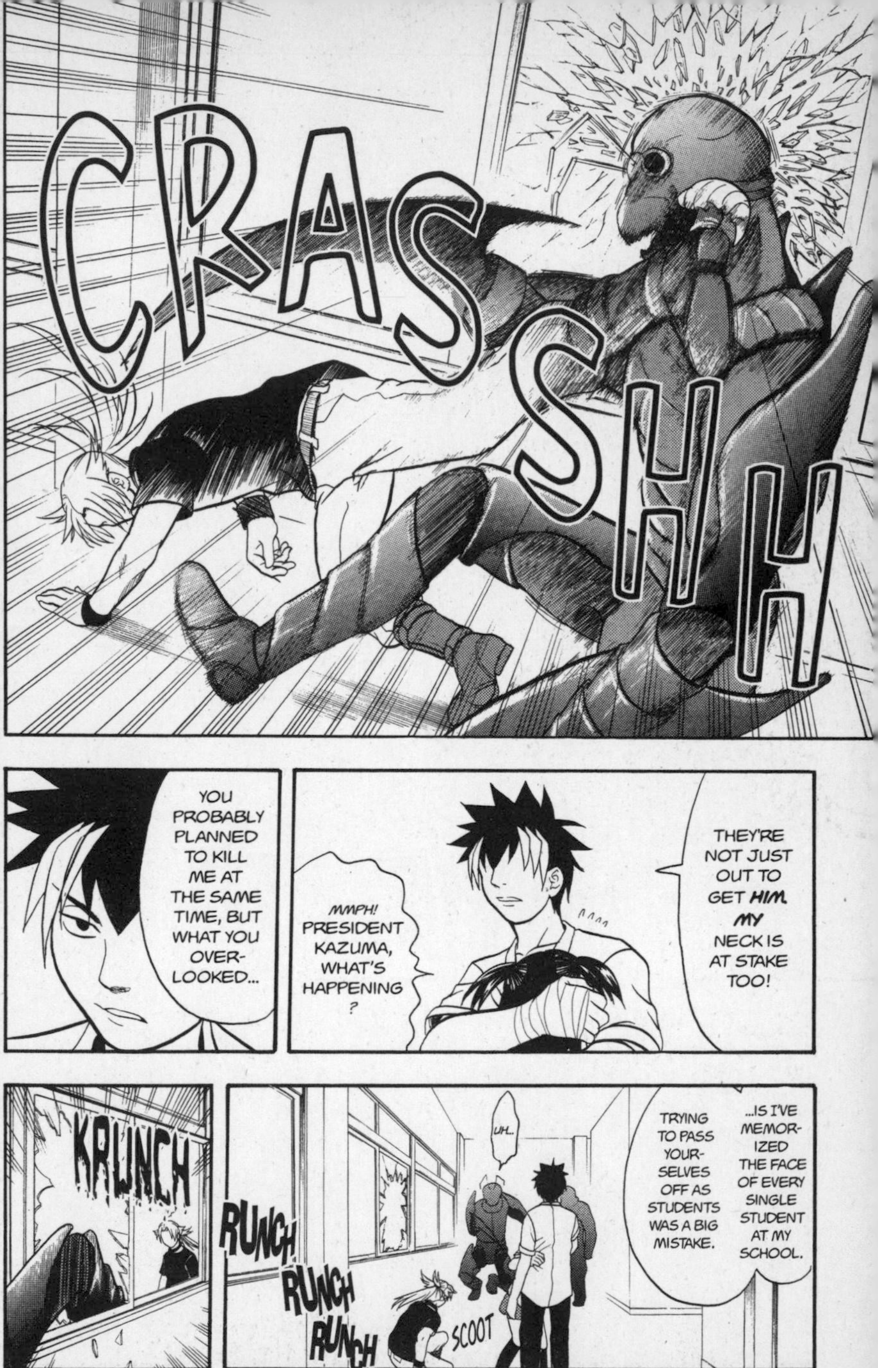
CRASSHH
THEY'RE NOT JUST OUT TO GET HIM, MY NECK IS AT STAKE TOO!
MMPH! PRESIDENT KAZUMA, WHAT'S HAPPENING?
YOU PROBABLY PLANNED TO KILL ME AT THE SAME TIME, BUT WHAT YOU OVER-LOOKED...
...IS I'VE MEMOR-IZED THE FACE OF EVERY SINGLE STUDENT AT MY SCHOOL.
TRYING TO PASS YOUR-SELVES OFF AS STUDENTS WAS A BIG MISTAKE.
UH..
SCOOT
KRUNCH
RUNCH
RUNCH
RUNCH

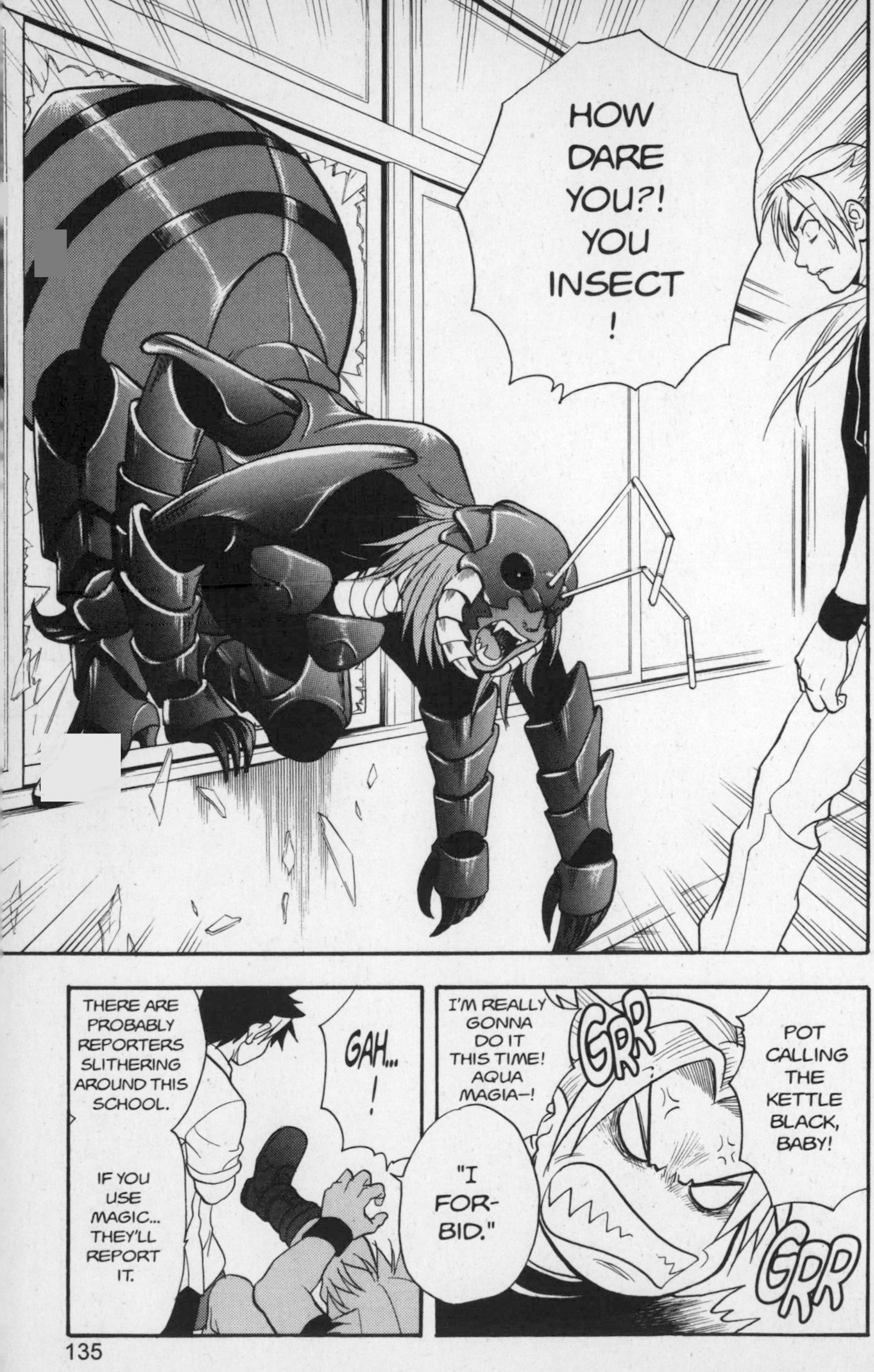
HOW DARE YOU?! YOU INSECT!
POT CALLING THE KETTLE BLACK, BABY!
GRR
I'M REALLY GONNA DO IT THIS TIME! AQUA MAGIA—!
GRR
THERE ARE PROBABLY REPORTERS SLITHERING AROUND THIS SCHOOL.
GAH...!
IF YOU USE MAGIC... THEY'LL REPORT IT.
"I FORBID."

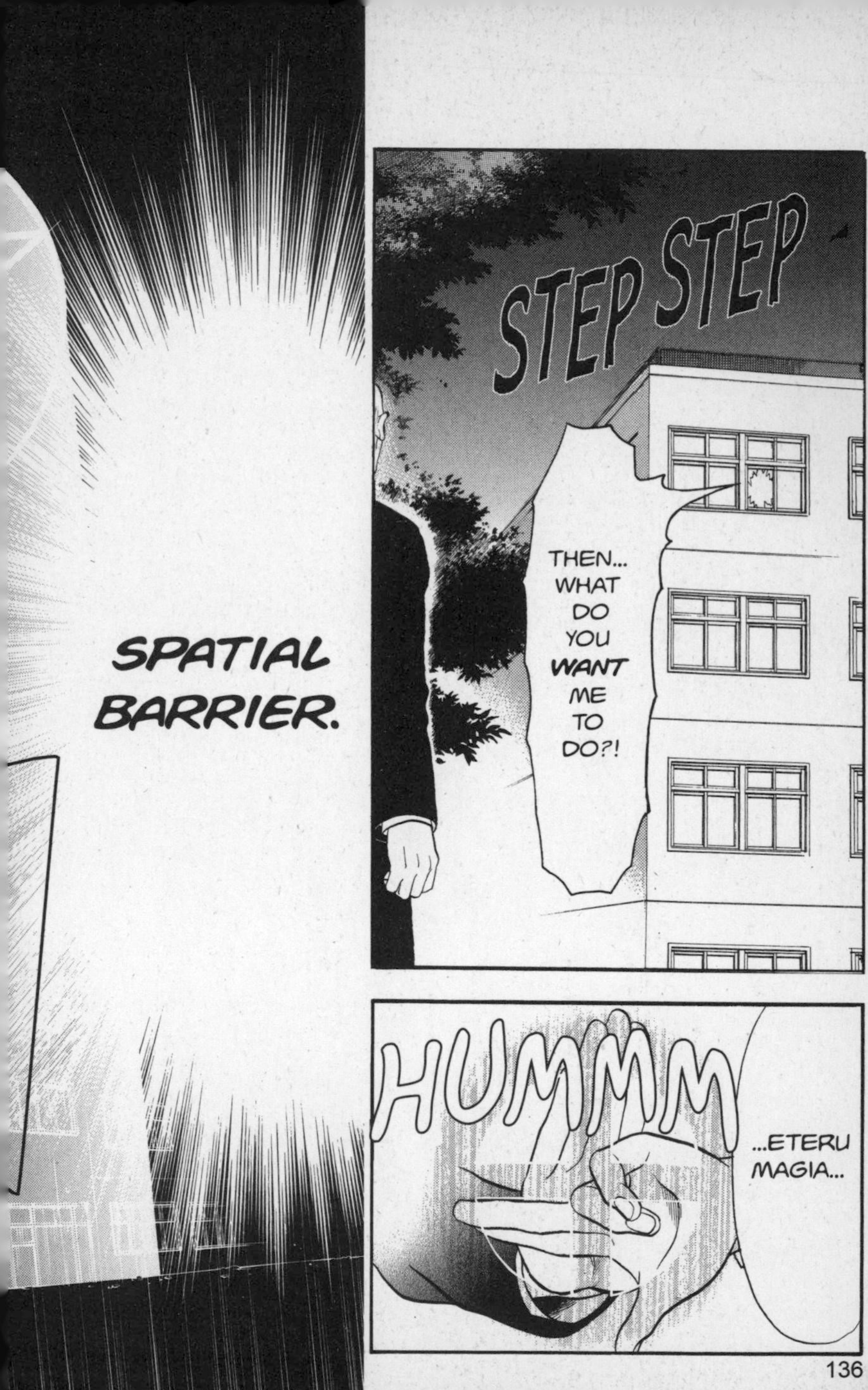
STEP STEP
THEN... WHAT DO YOU WANT ME TO DO?!
HUMMM
...ETERU MAGIA...
SPATIAL BARRIER.

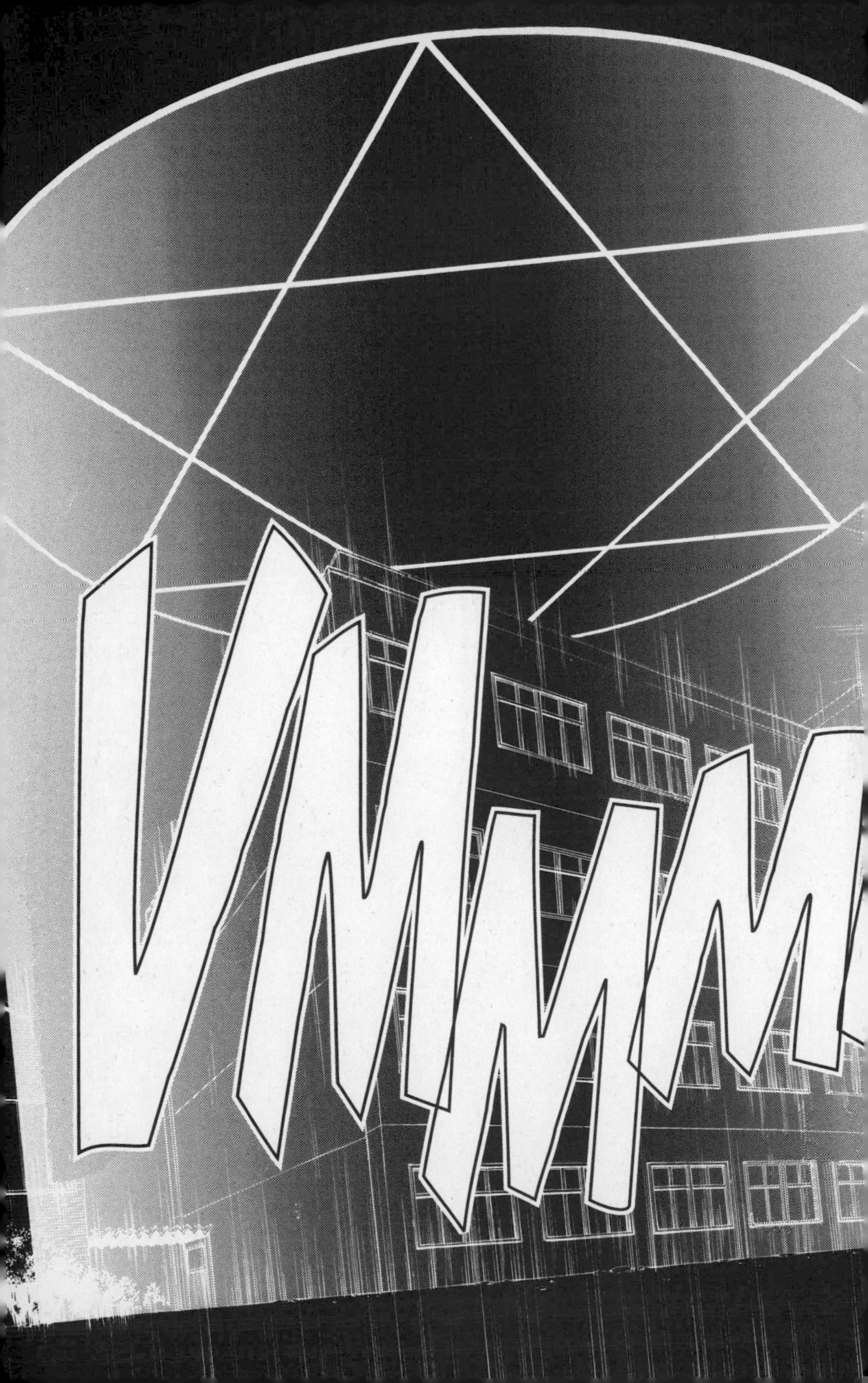
VMMM

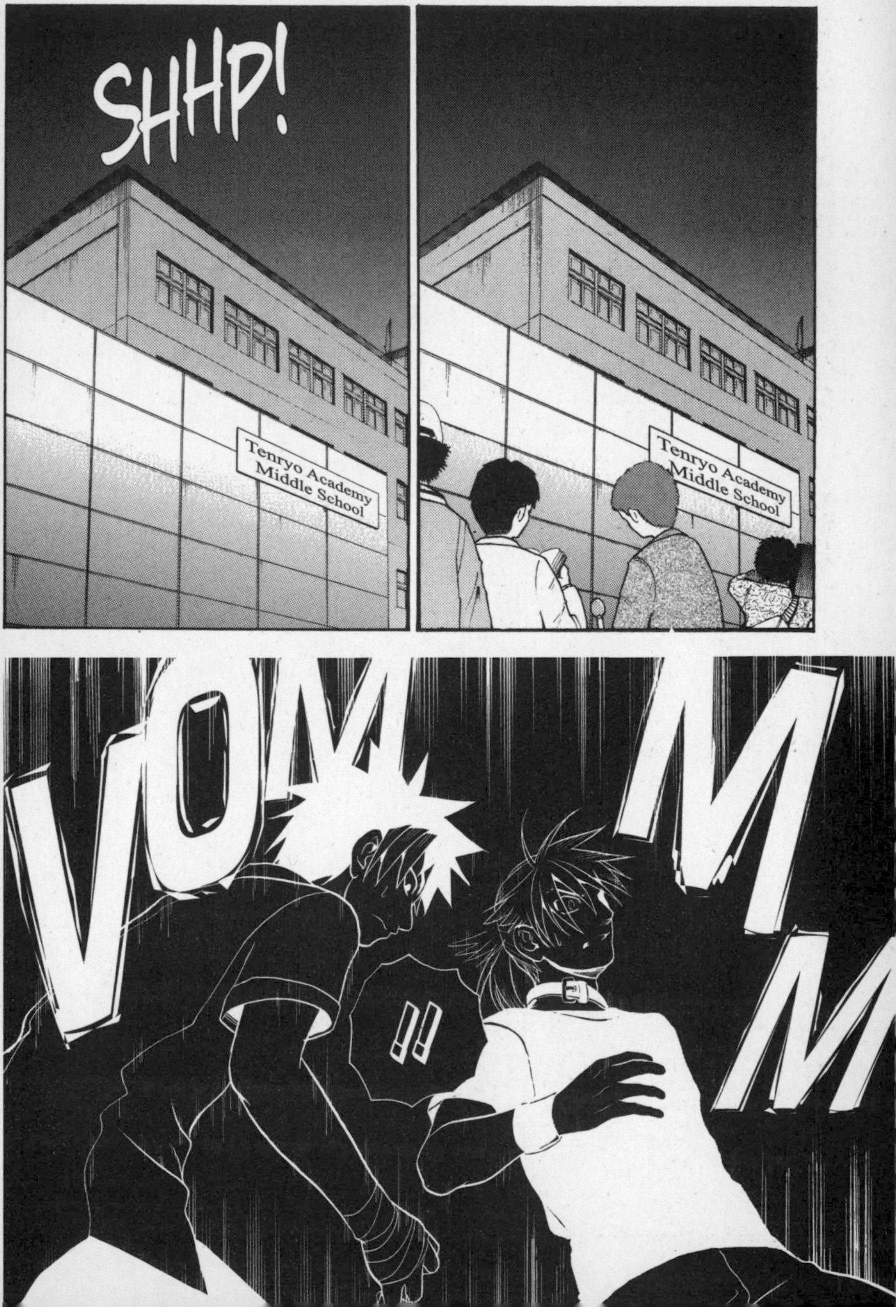

Tenryo Academy Middle School
SHHP!
Tenryo Academy Middle School
VOMMM
!!

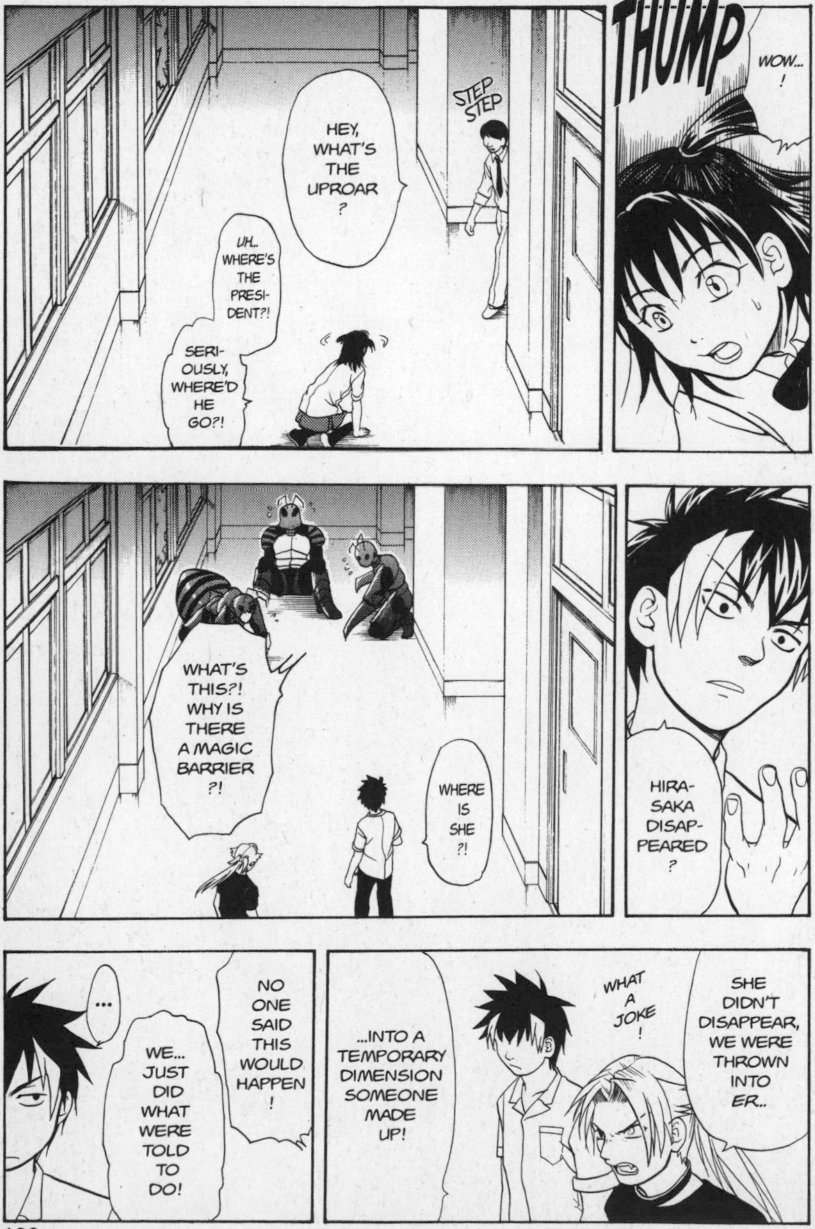
THUMP
WOW... !
STEP STEP
HEY, WHAT'S THE UPROAR ?
UH.. WHERE'S THE PRESI-DENT?!
SERI-OUSLY, WHERE'D HE GO?!
HIRA-SAKA DISAP-PEARED ?
WHERE IS SHE ?!
WHAT'S THIS?! WHY IS THERE A MAGIC BARRIER ?!
SHE DIDN'T DISAPPEAR, WE WERE THROWN INTO ER..
WHAT A JOKE !
...INTO A TEMPORARY DIMENSION SOMEONE MADE UP!
NO ONE SAID THIS WOULD HAPPEN !
...
WE... JUST DID WHAT WERE TOLD TO DO!

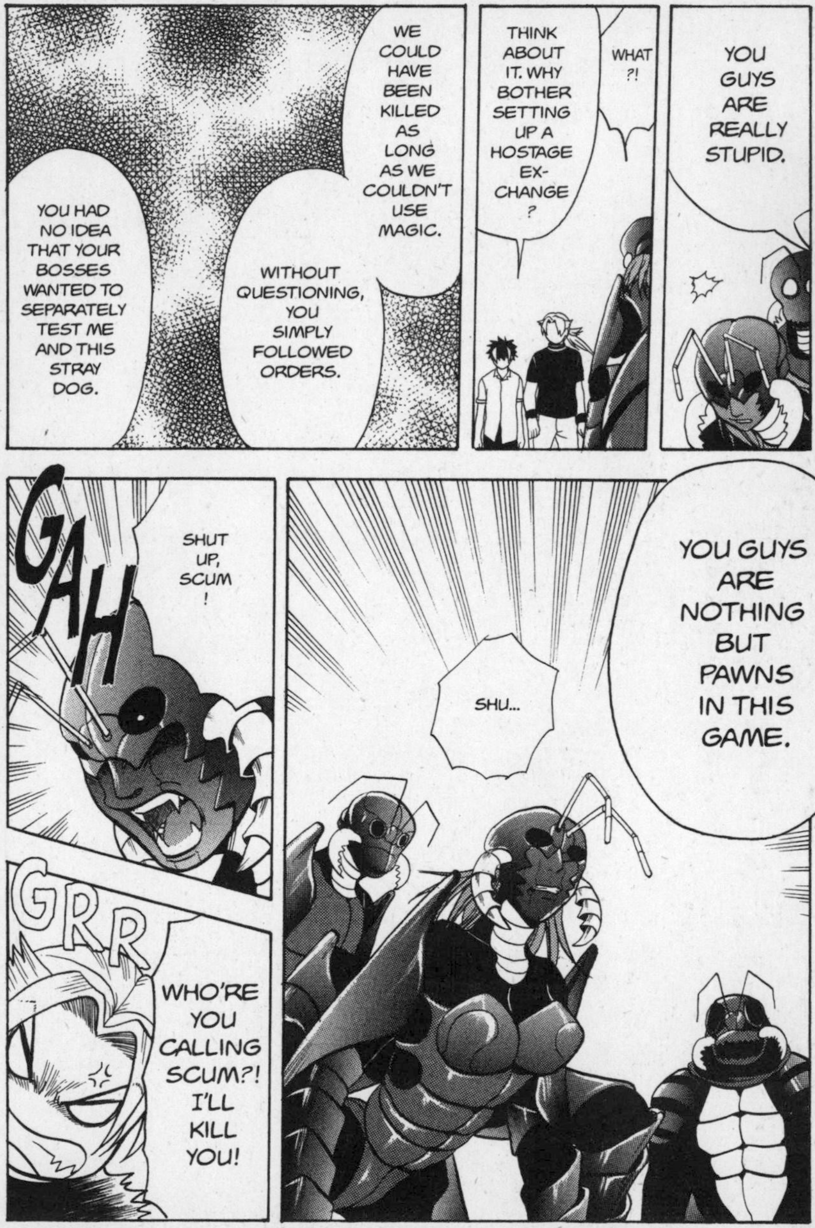
YOU GUYS ARE REALLY STUPID.
WHAT?!
THINK ABOUT IT. WHY BOTHER SETTING UP A HOSTAGE EX-CHANGE?
WE COULD HAVE BEEN KILLED AS LONG AS WE COULDN'T USE MAGIC.
WITHOUT QUESTIONING, YOU SIMPLY FOLLOWED ORDERS.
YOU HAD NO IDEA THAT YOUR BOSSES WANTED TO SEPARATELY TEST ME AND THIS STRAY DOG.
YOU GUYS ARE NOTHING BUT PAWNS IN THIS GAME.
SHU...
GAH
SHUT UP, SCUM!
GRR
WHO'RE YOU CALLING SCUM?! I'LL KILL YOU!

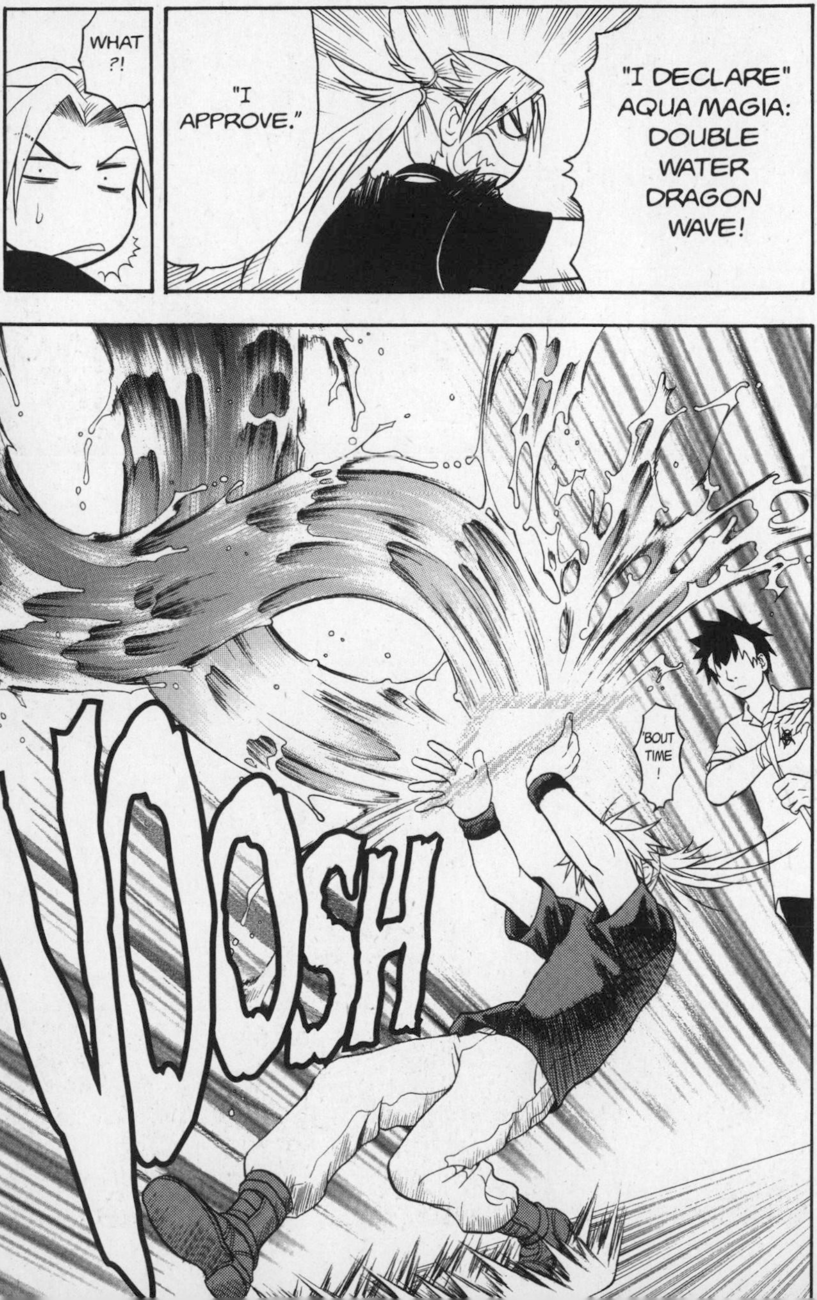
"I DECLARE" AQUA MAGIA: DOUBLE WATER DRAGON WAVE!
"I APPROVE."
WHAT ?!
'BOUT TIME !
VOOSH

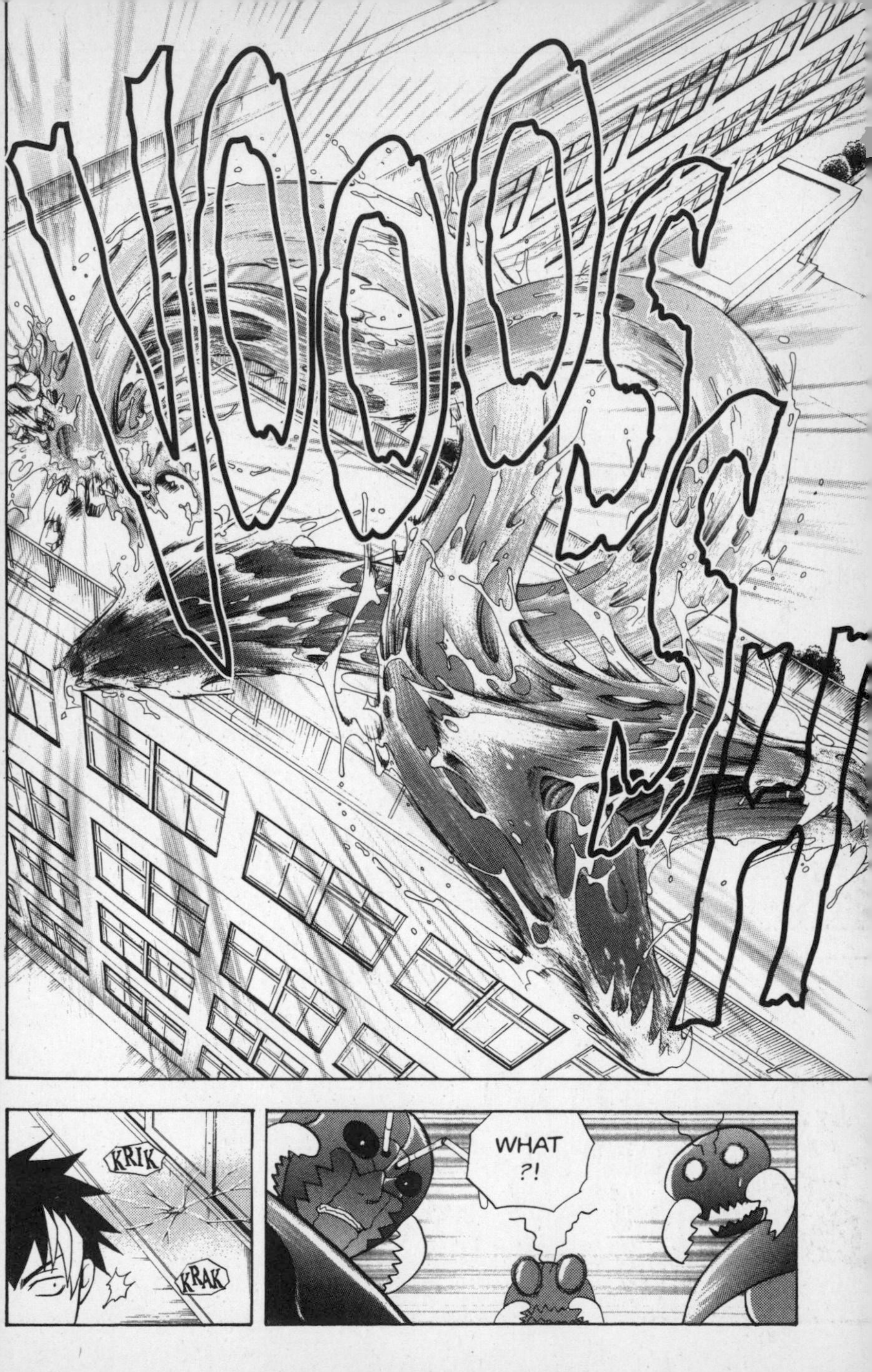
WOOOSSH
WHAT ?!
KRIK
KRAK

READ THIS WAY

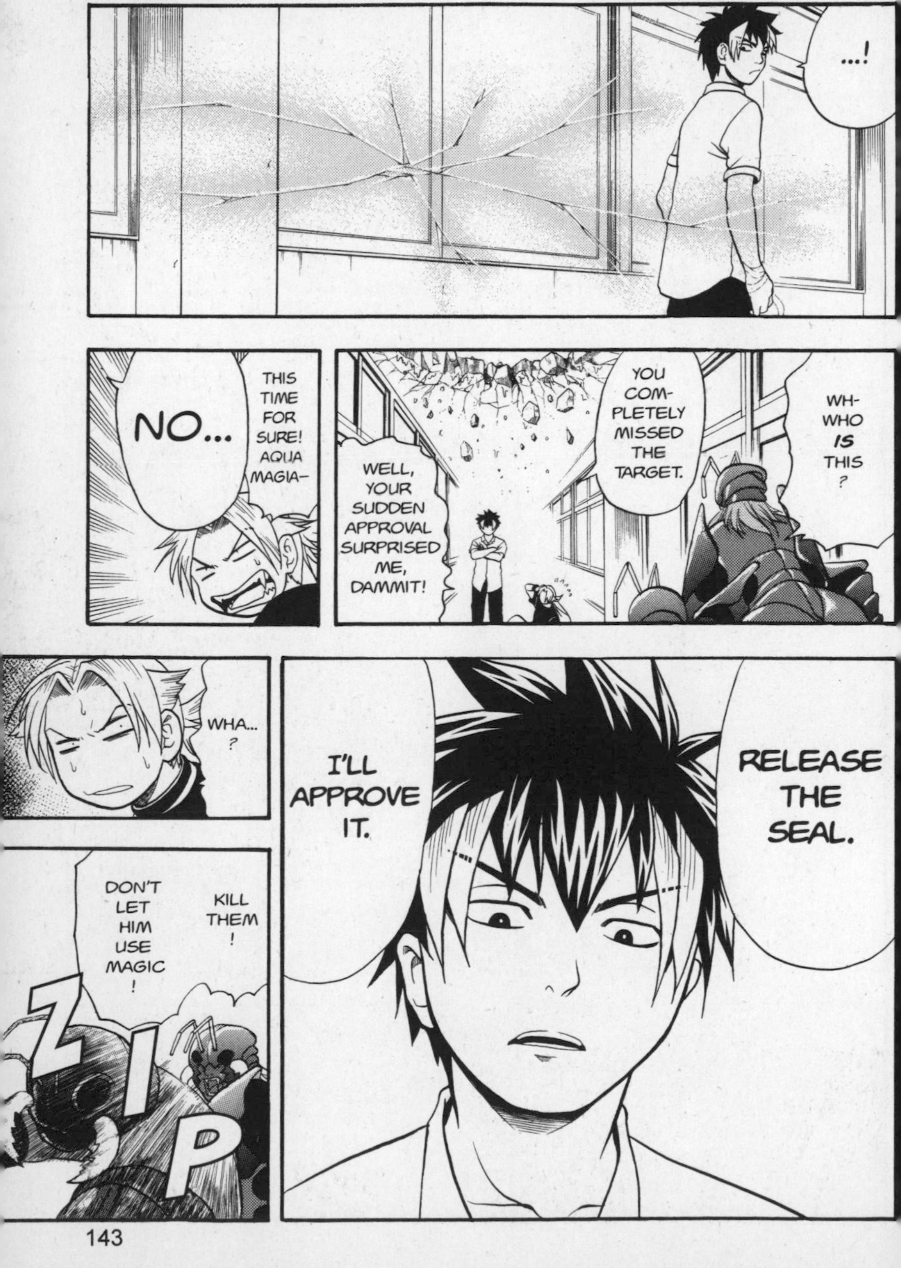
...!
WH-WHO *IS* THIS?
YOU COMPLETELY MISSED THE TARGET.
WELL, YOUR SUDDEN APPROVAL SURPRISED ME, DAMMIT!
THIS TIME FOR SURE! AQUA MAGIA-
NO...
RELEASE THE SEAL.
I'LL APPROVE IT.
WHA...?
KILL THEM!
DON'T LET HIM USE MAGIC!
ZIP

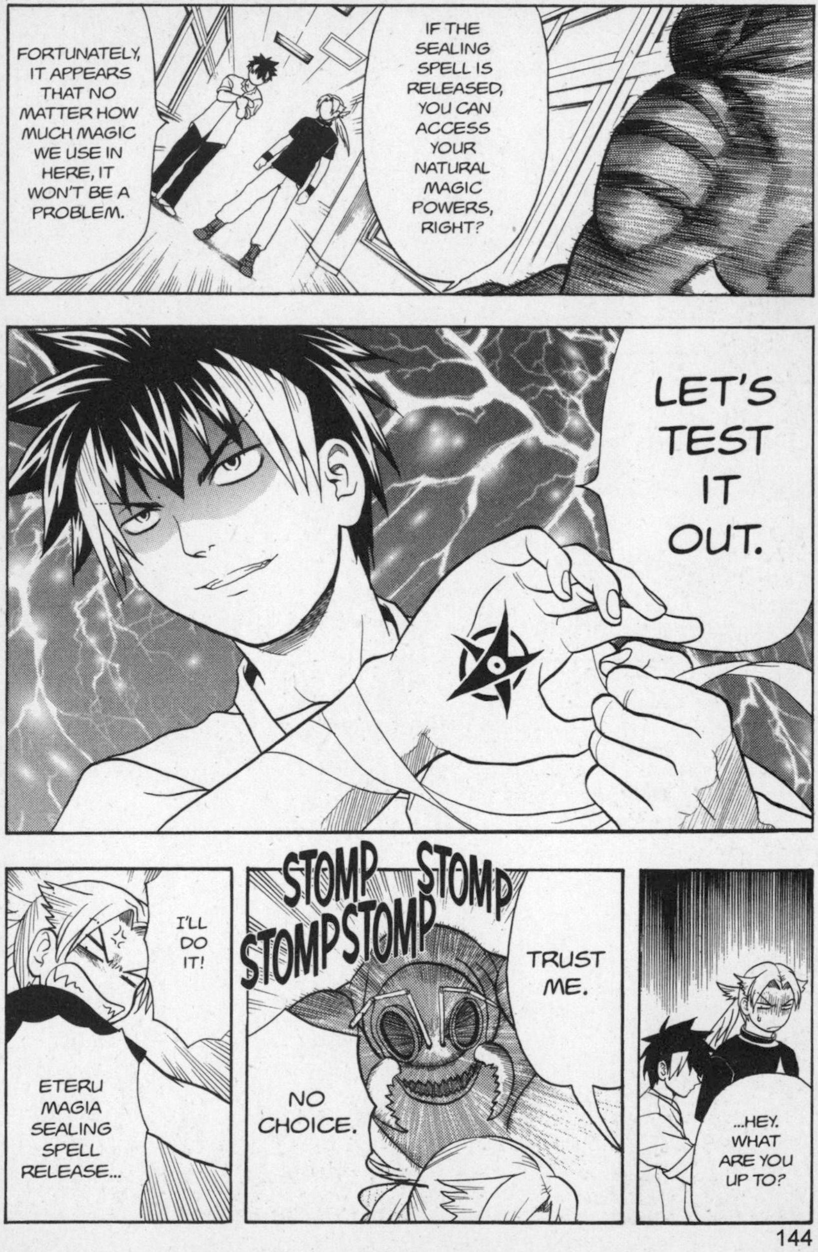

IF THE SEALING SPELL IS RELEASED, YOU CAN ACCESS YOUR NATURAL MAGIC POWERS, RIGHT?
FORTUNATELY, IT APPEARS THAT NO MATTER HOW MUCH MAGIC WE USE IN HERE, IT WON'T BE A PROBLEM.
LET'S TEST IT OUT.
...HEY. WHAT ARE YOU UP TO?
STOMP STOMP
STOMP STOMP
TRUST ME.
NO CHOICE.
I'LL DO IT!
ETERU MAGIA SEALING SPELL RELEASE...

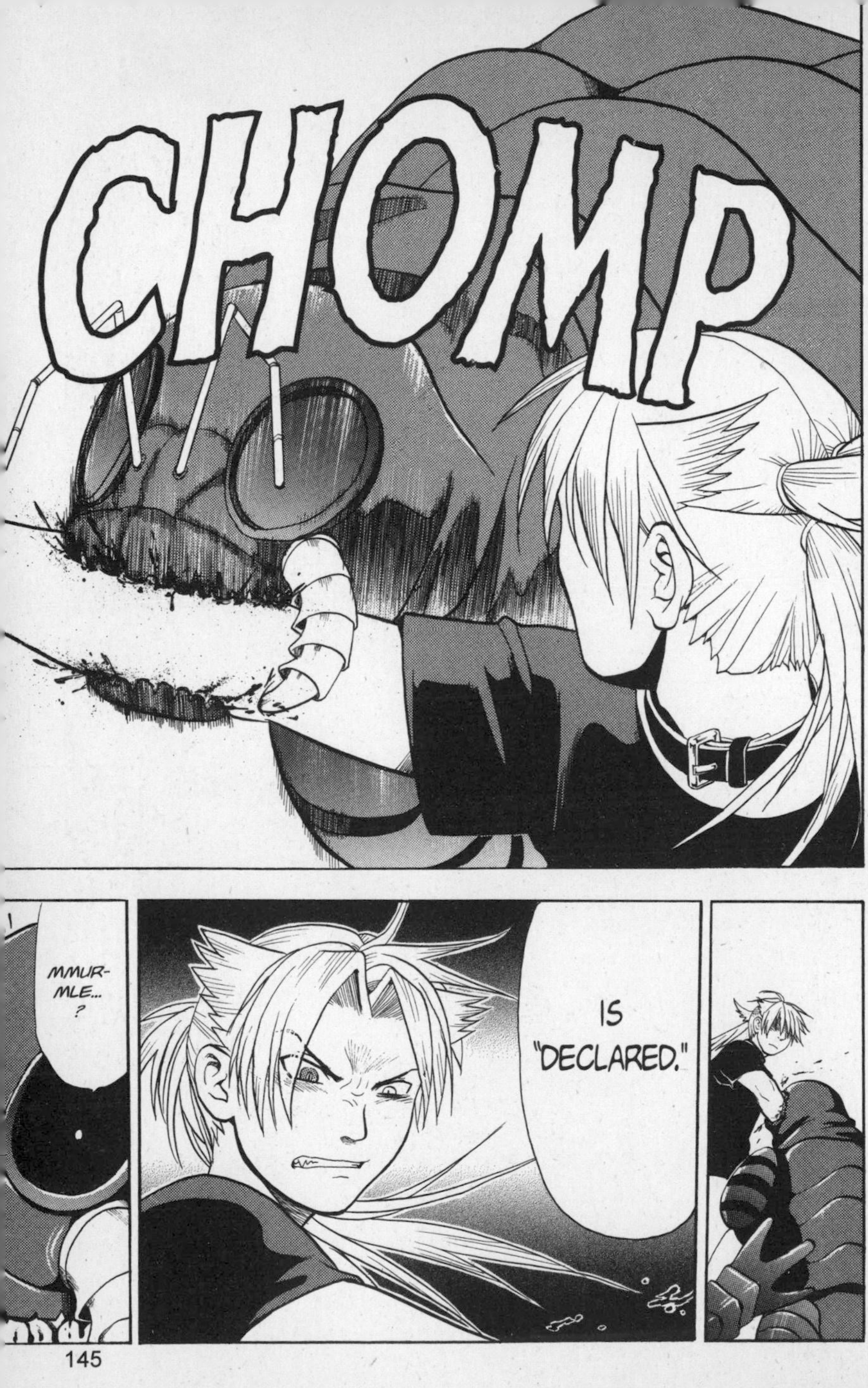
CHOMP
IS "DECLARED."
MMUR-MLE... ?

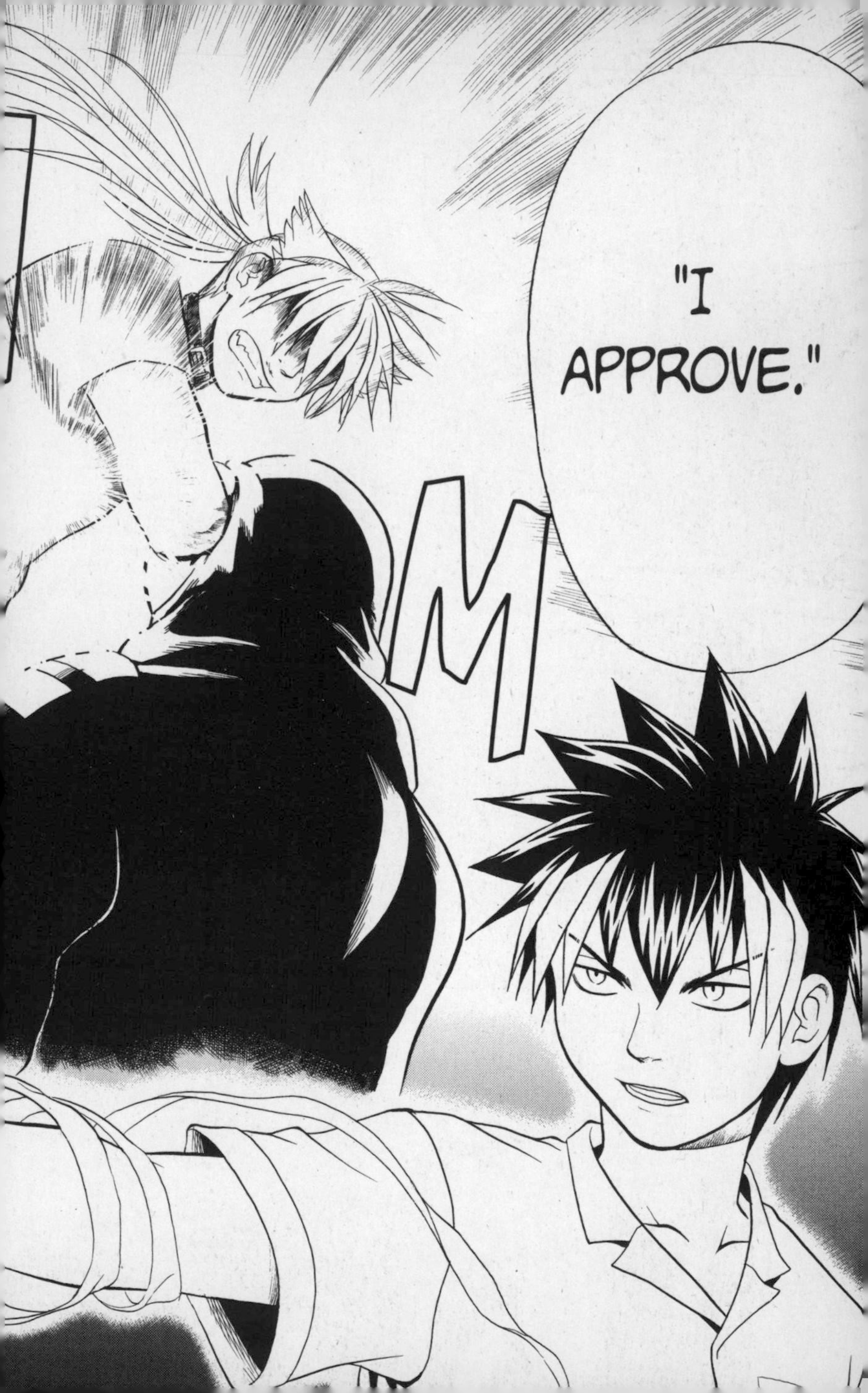
"I APPROVE."
M

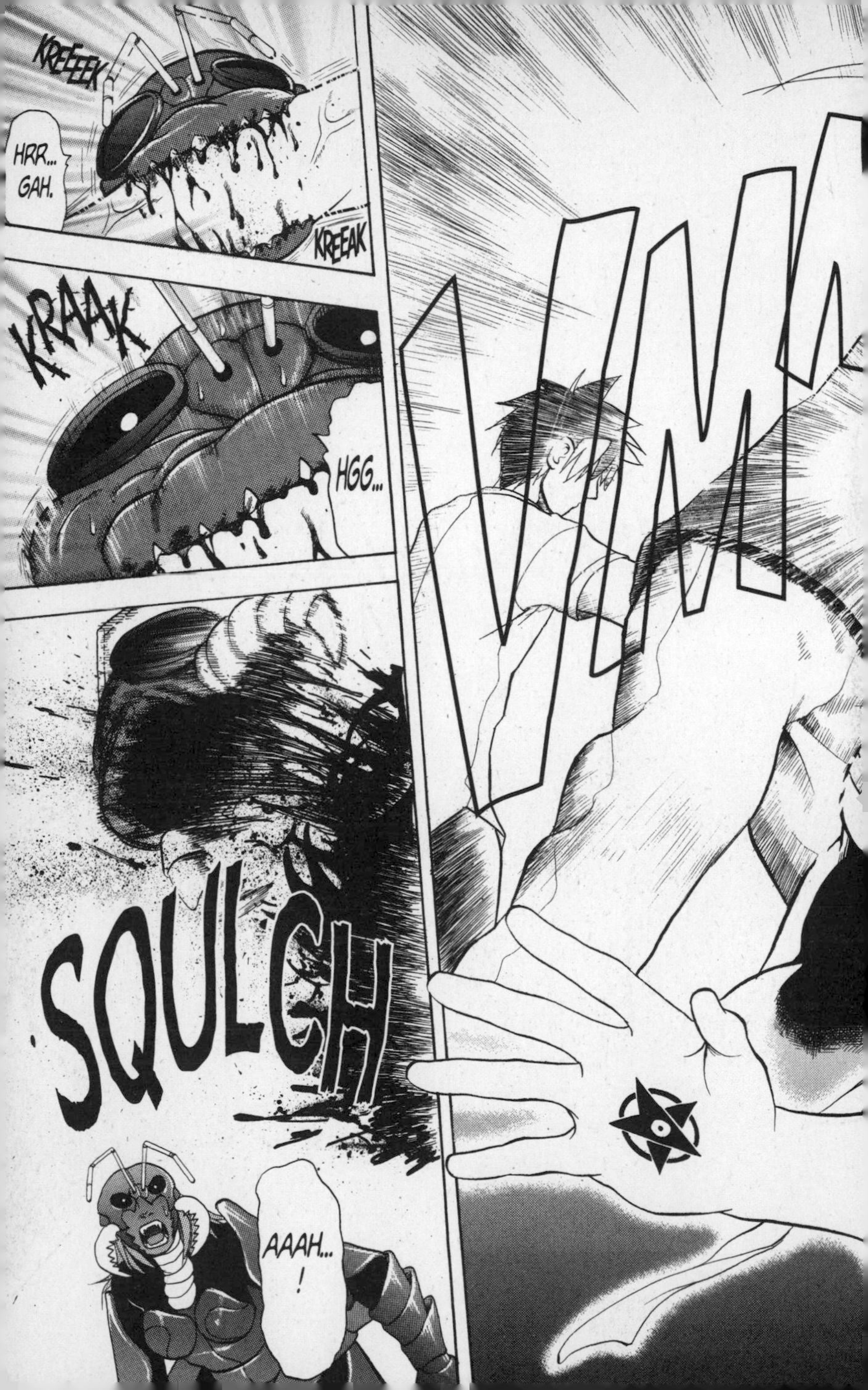
KREEEEK
HRR... GAH.
KREEAK
KRAAK
HGG...
SQULCH
AAAH... !

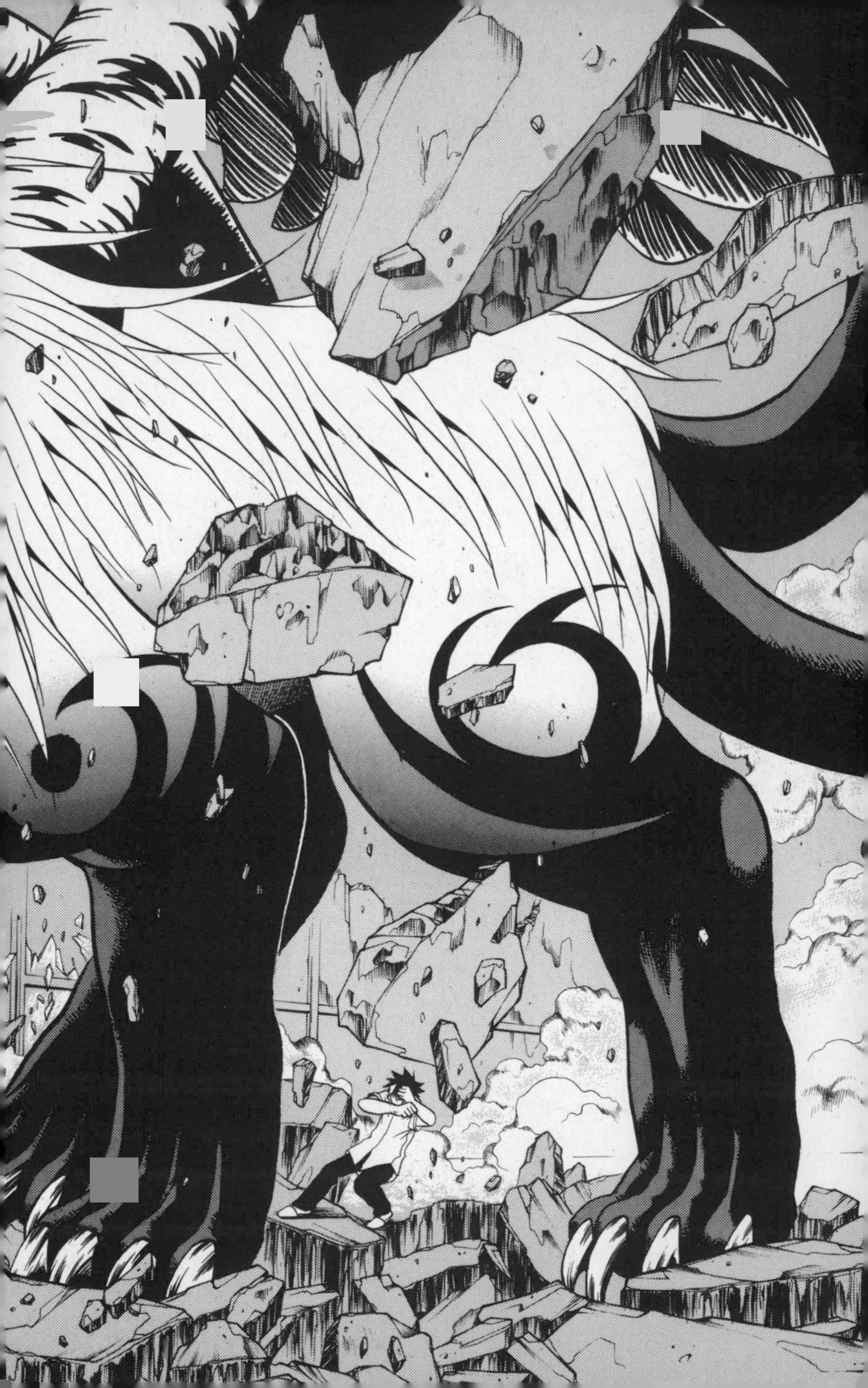

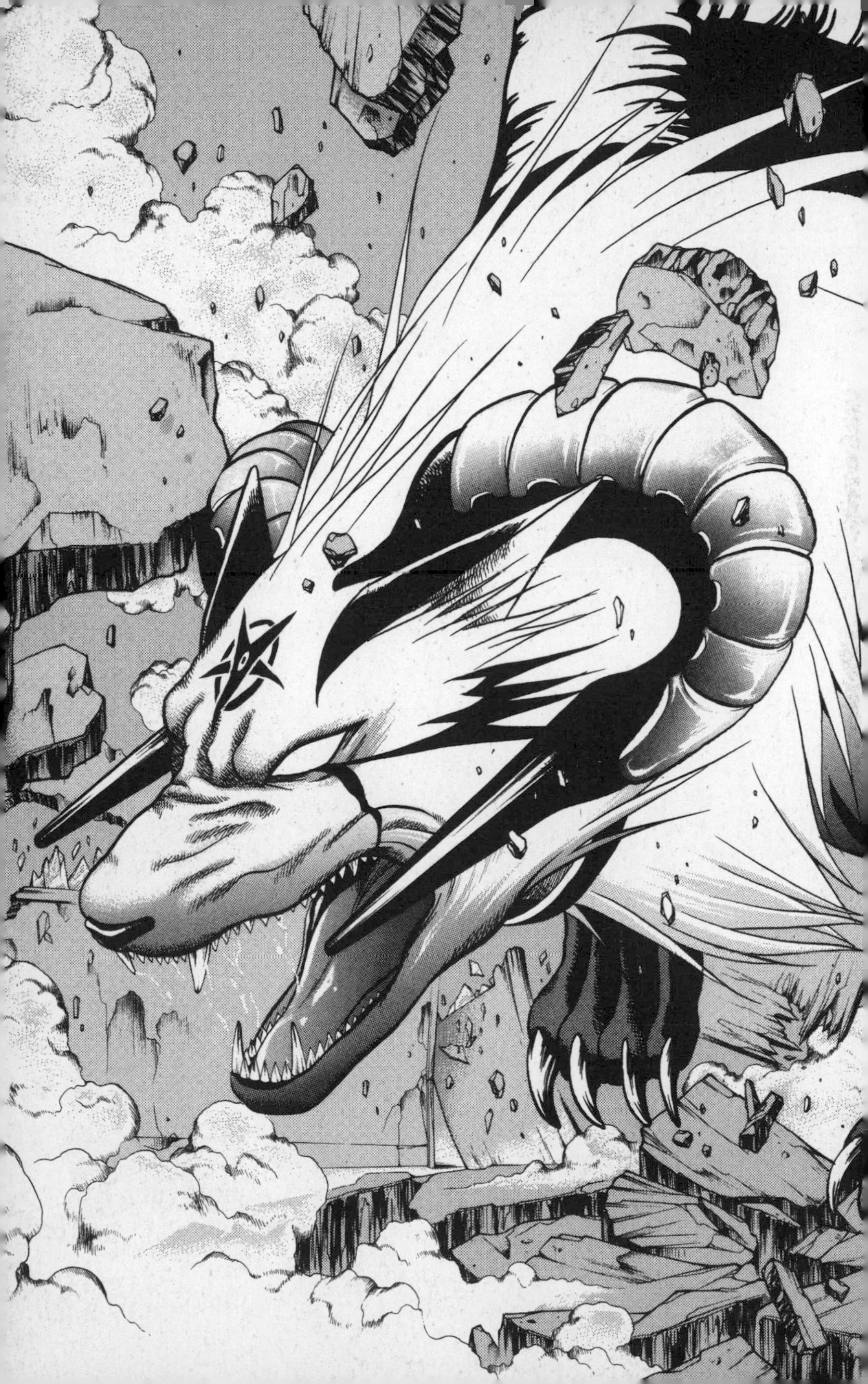

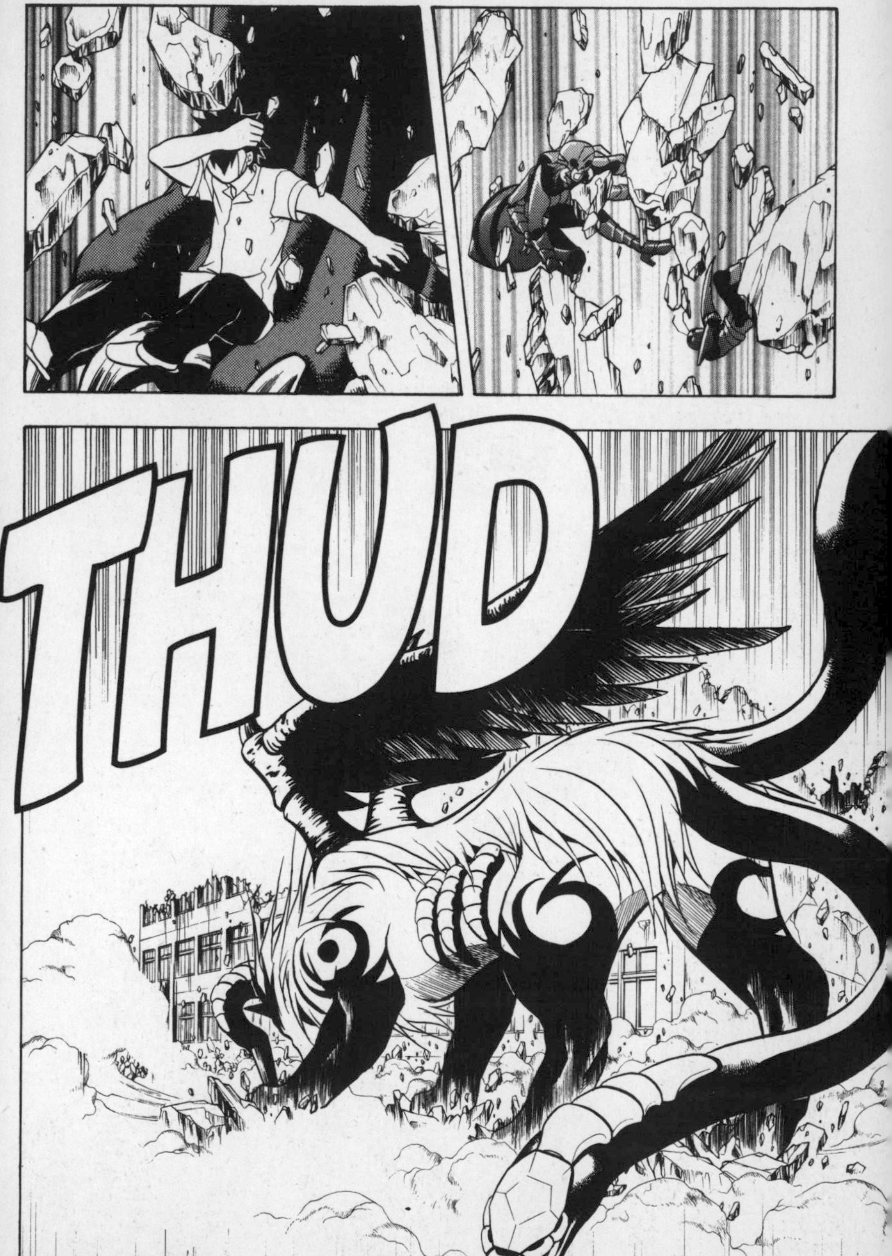
THUD

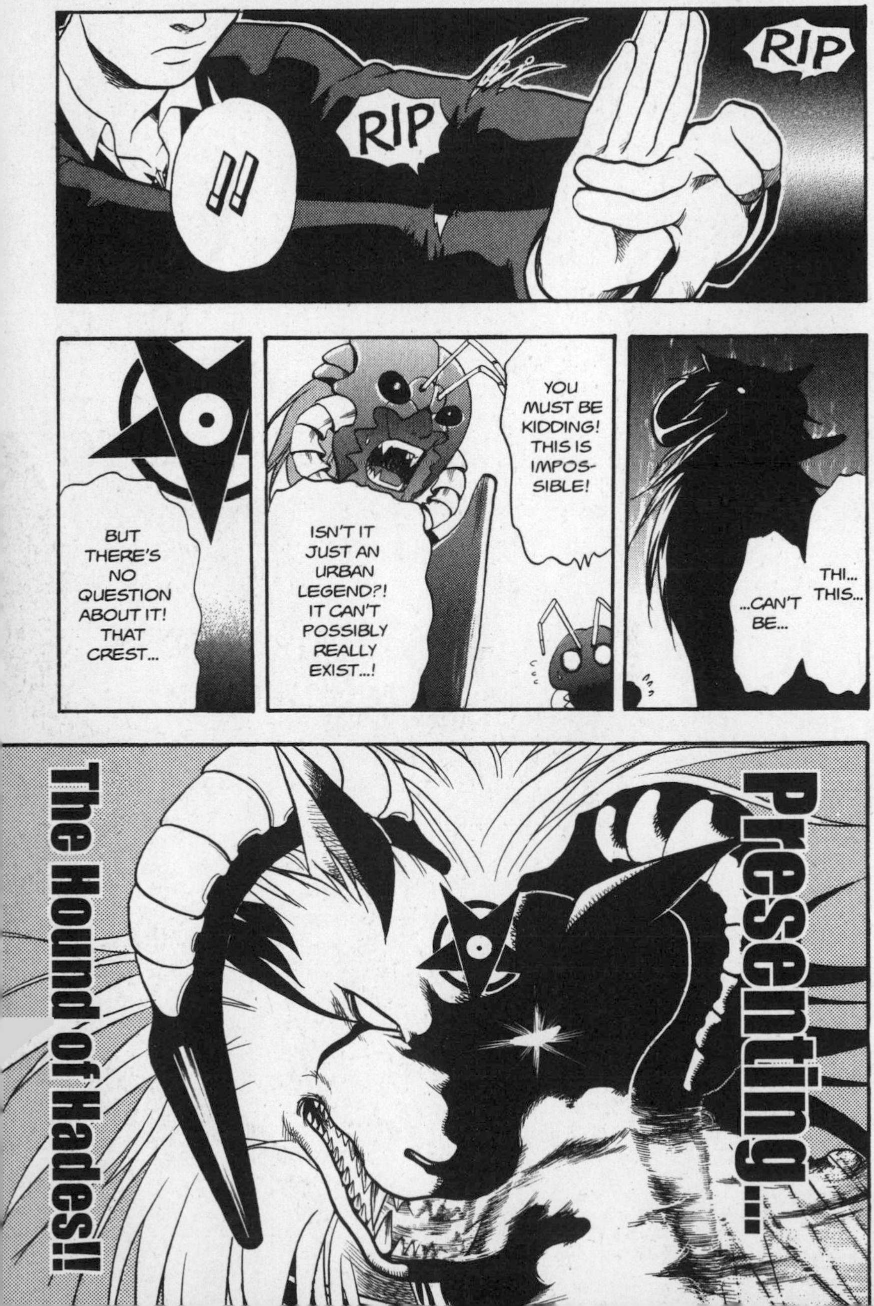
RIP
RIP
!!
THI... THIS...
...CAN'T BE...
YOU MUST BE KIDDING! THIS IS IMPOSSIBLE!
ISN'T IT JUST AN URBAN LEGEND?! IT CAN'T POSSIBLY REALLY EXIST...!
BUT THERE'S NO QUESTION ABOUT IT! THAT CREST...
Presenting...
The Hound of Hades!!

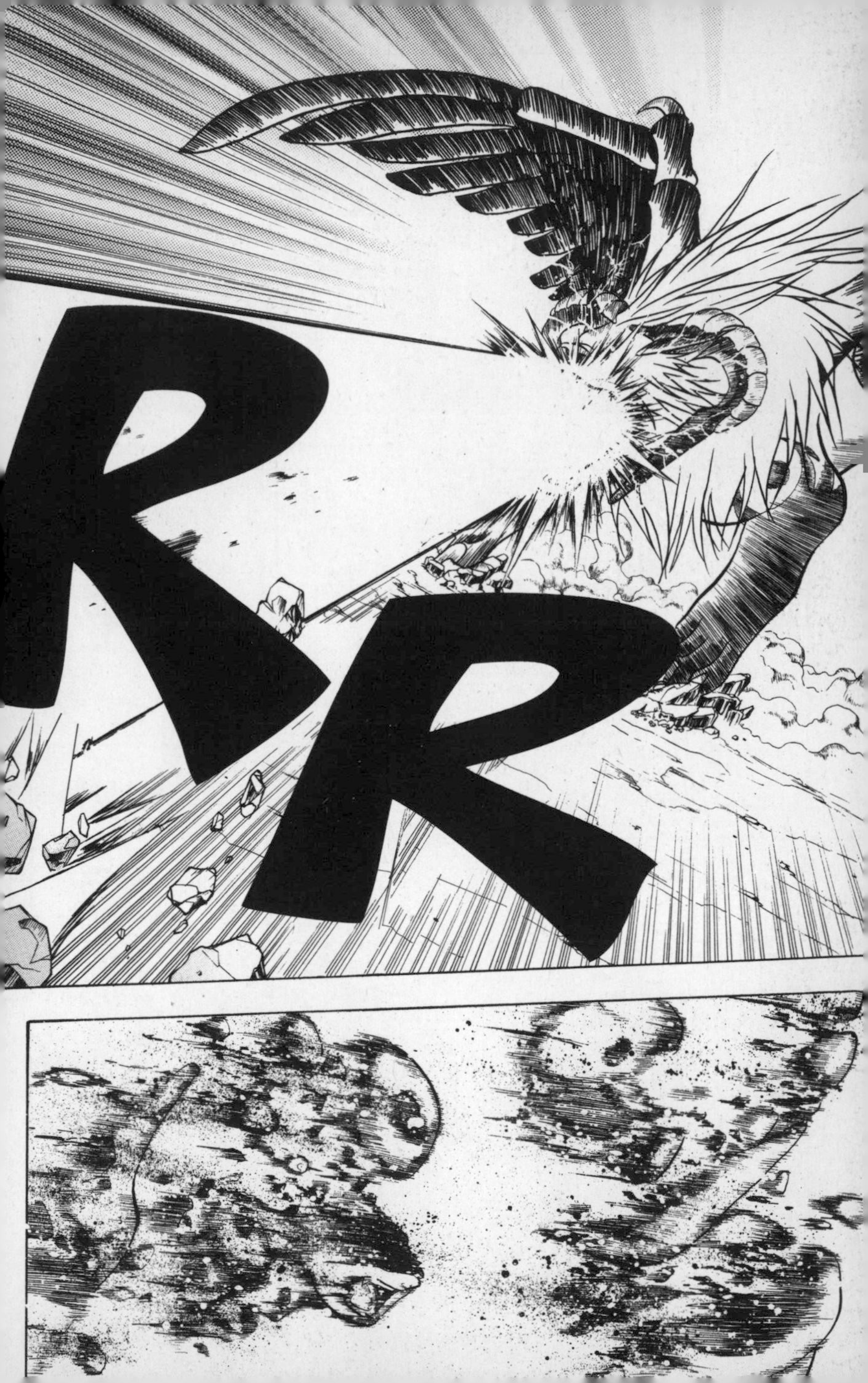
RR

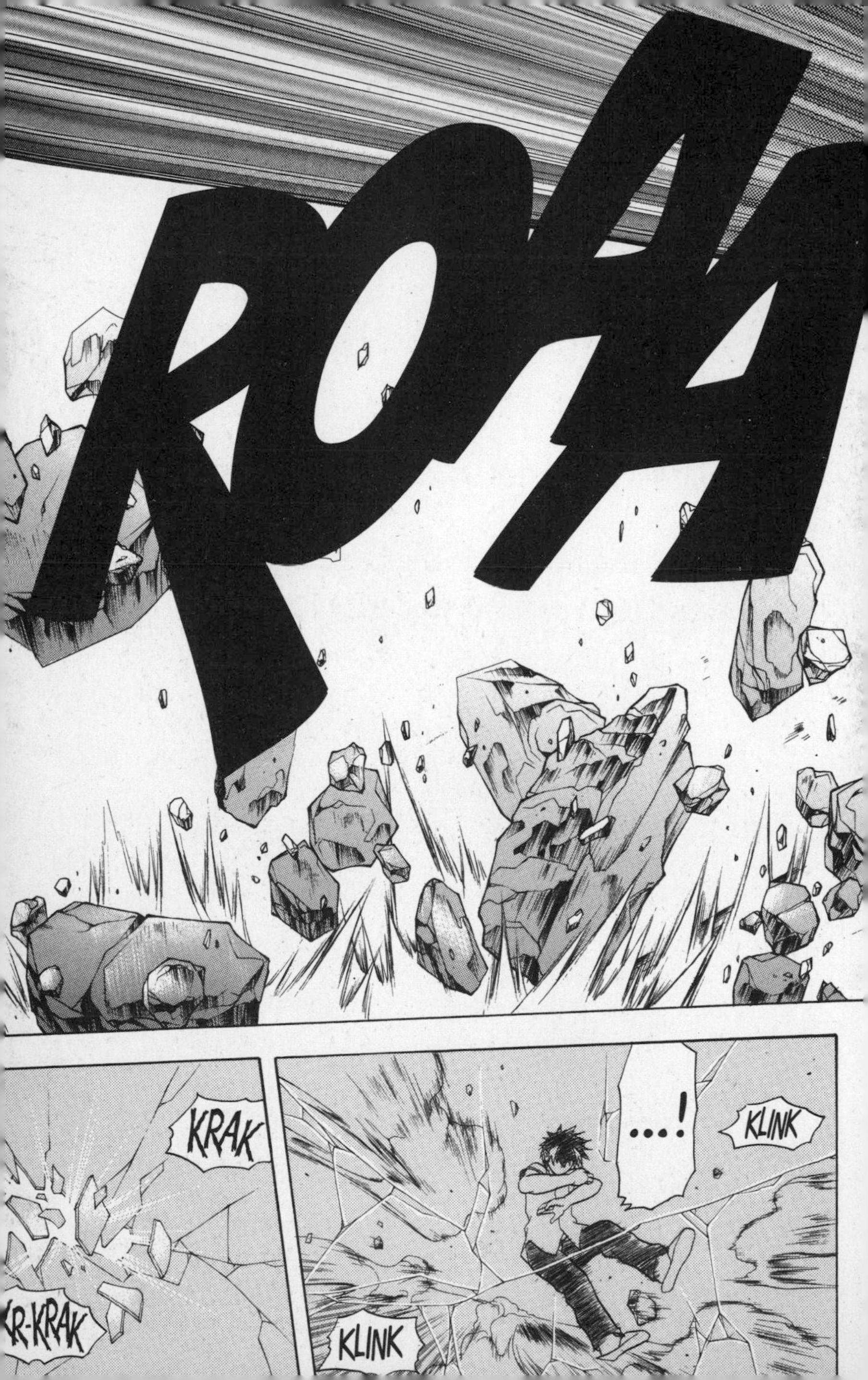
ROAA
...!
KLINK
KLINK
KRAK
R-KRAK

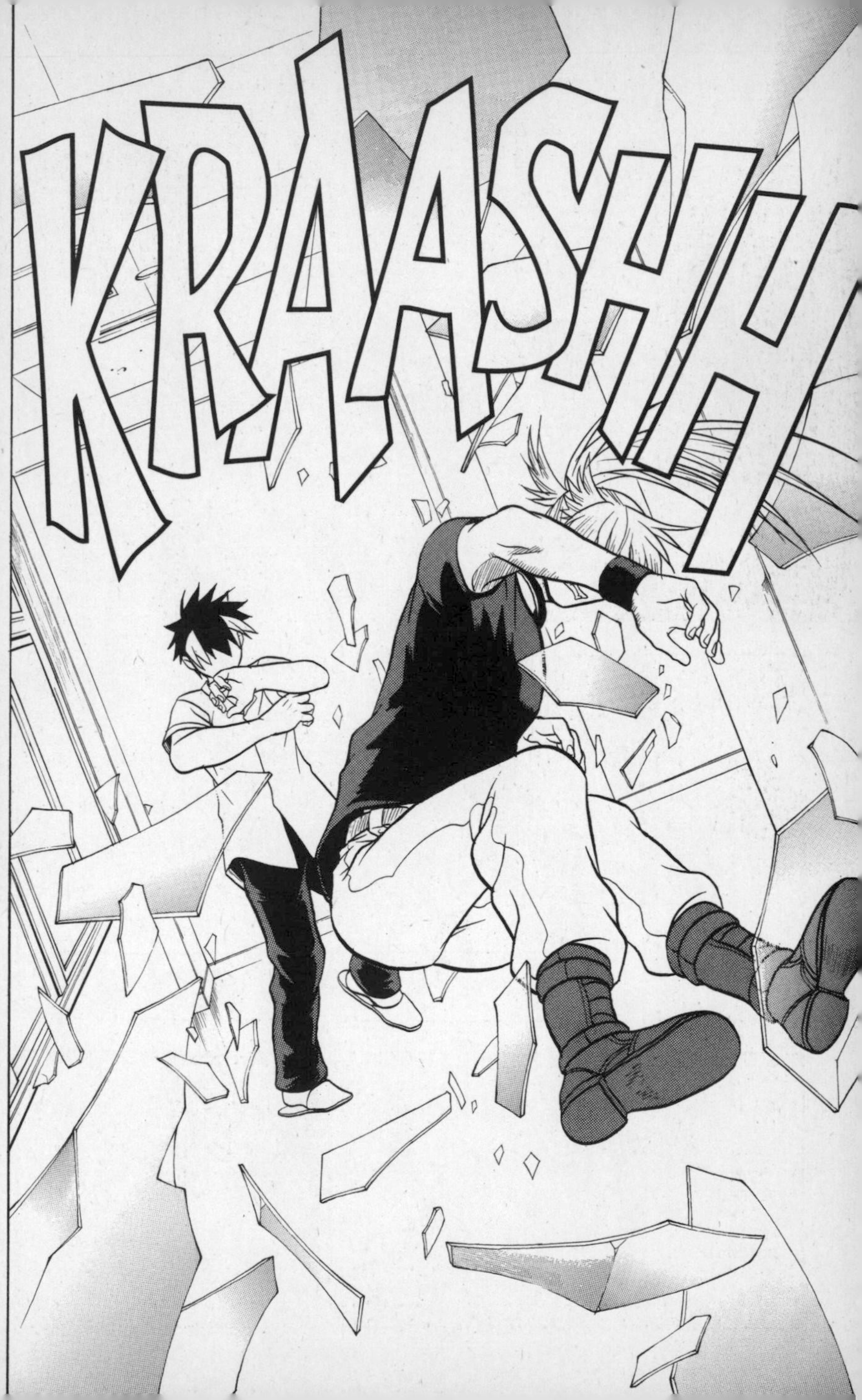
KRAASHH

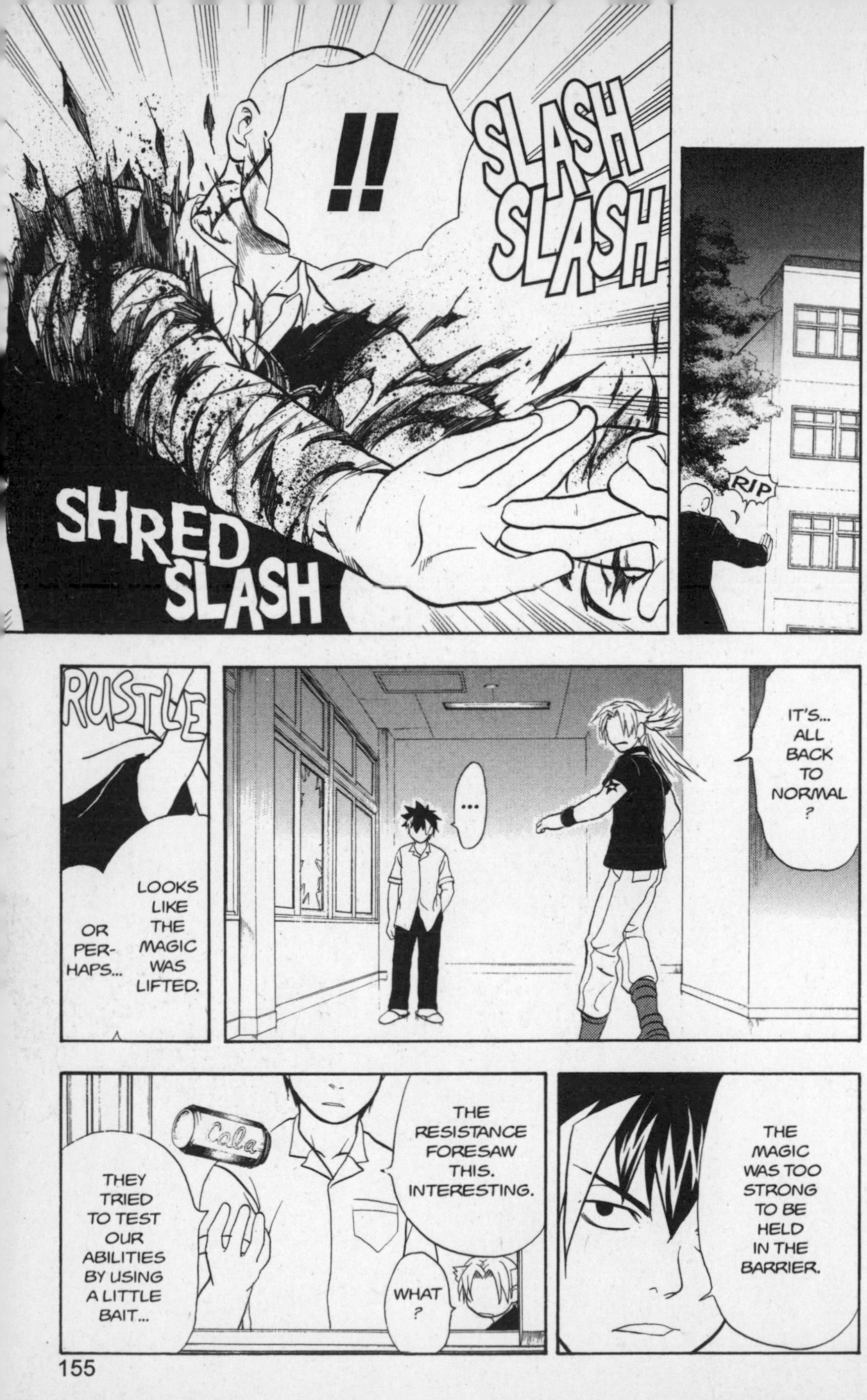
RIP
!!
SLASH SLASH
SHRED SLASH
IT'S... ALL BACK TO NORMAL?
...
LOOKS LIKE THE MAGIC WAS LIFTED.
OR PERHAPS...
RUSTLE
THE MAGIC WAS TOO STRONG TO BE HELD IN THE BARRIER.
WHAT?
THE RESISTANCE FORESAW THIS. INTERESTING.
THEY TRIED TO TEST OUR ABILITIES BY USING A LITTLE BAIT...
Cola

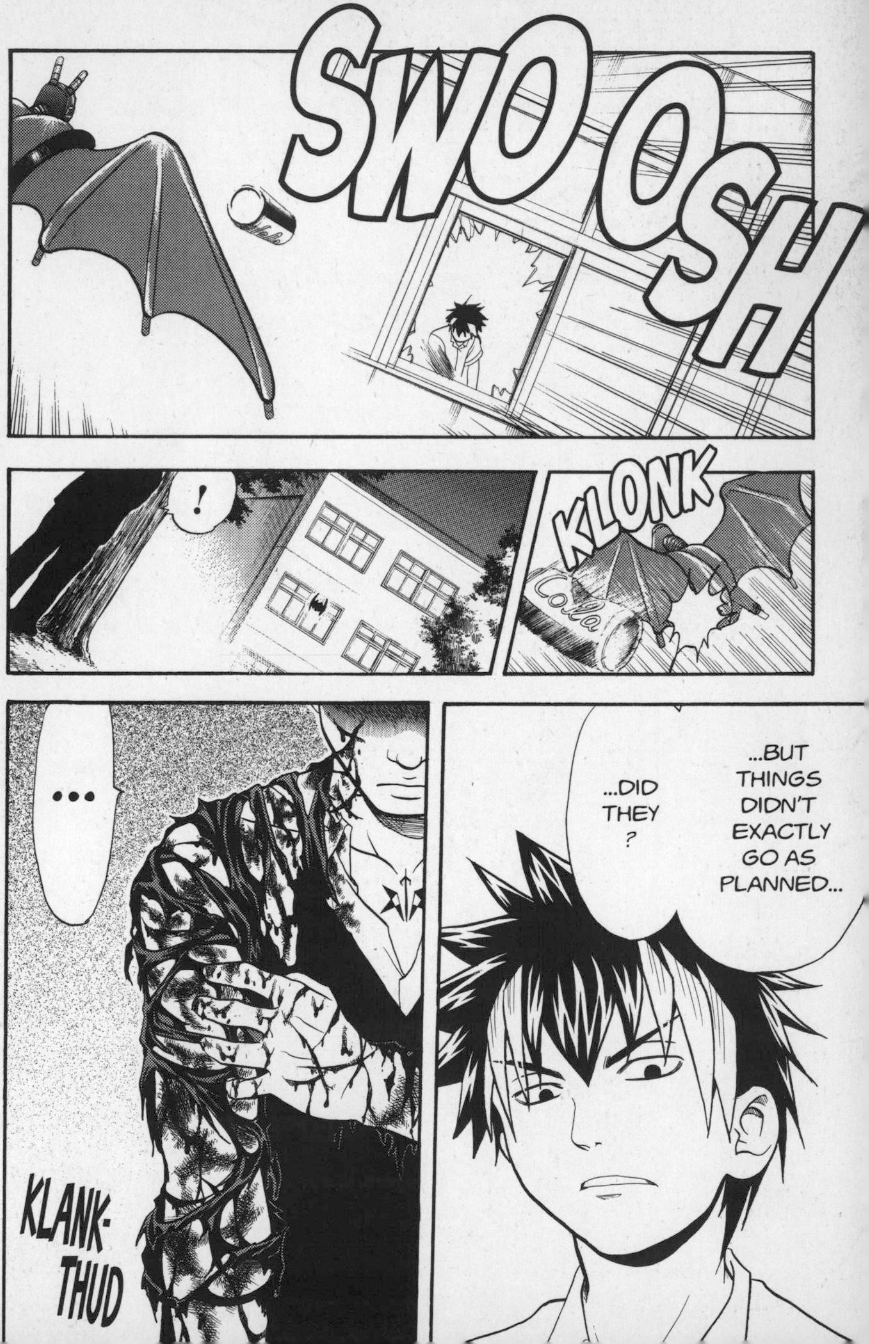
SWOOSH
KLONK
Cola
!
...BUT THINGS DIDN'T EXACTLY GO AS PLANNED...
...DID THEY?
...
KLANK-THUD

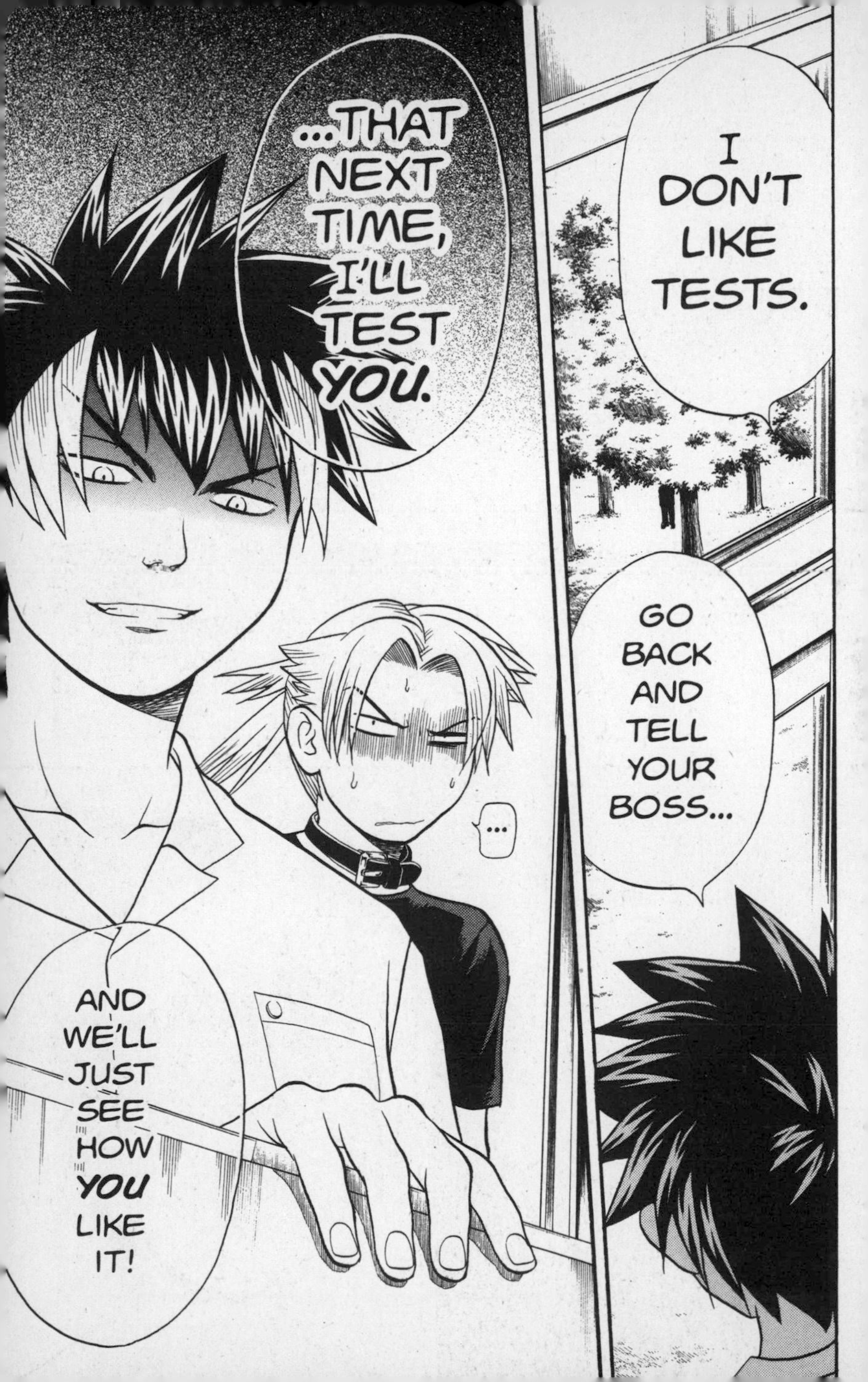
I DON'T LIKE TESTS.
GO BACK AND TELL YOUR BOSS...
...THAT NEXT TIME, I'LL TEST *YOU*.
...
AND WE'LL JUST SEE HOW *YOU* LIKE IT!

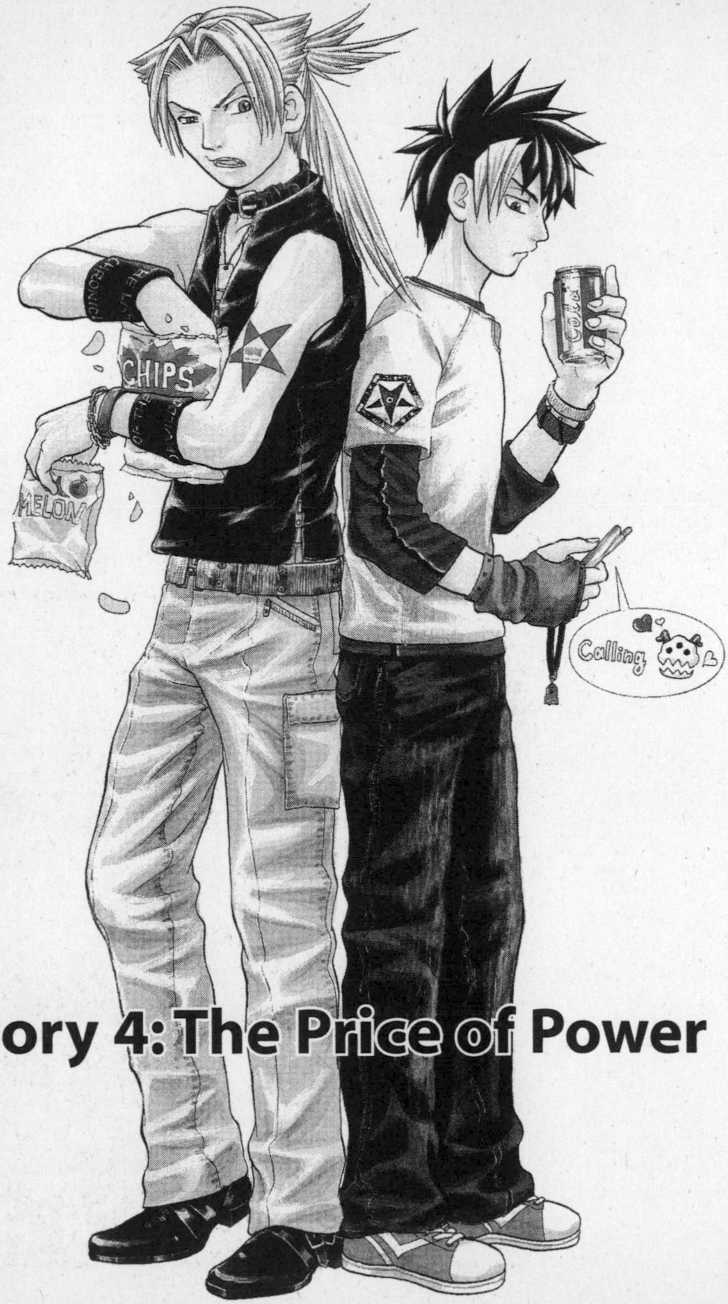
CHIPS
MELON
Calling

Story 4: The Price of Power

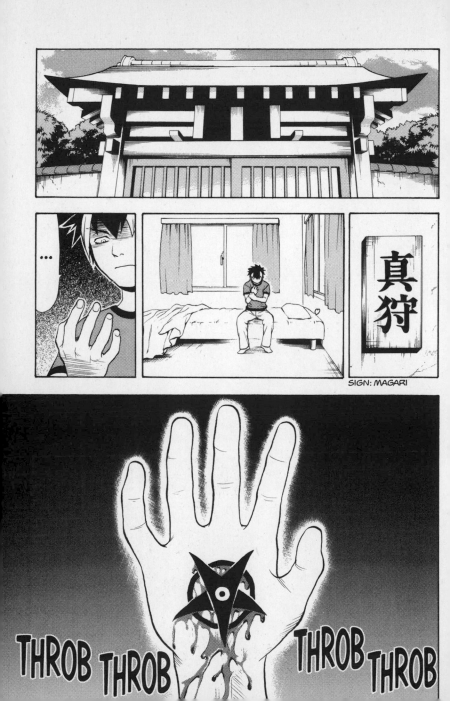

SIGN: MAGARI

THROB THROB THROB THROB

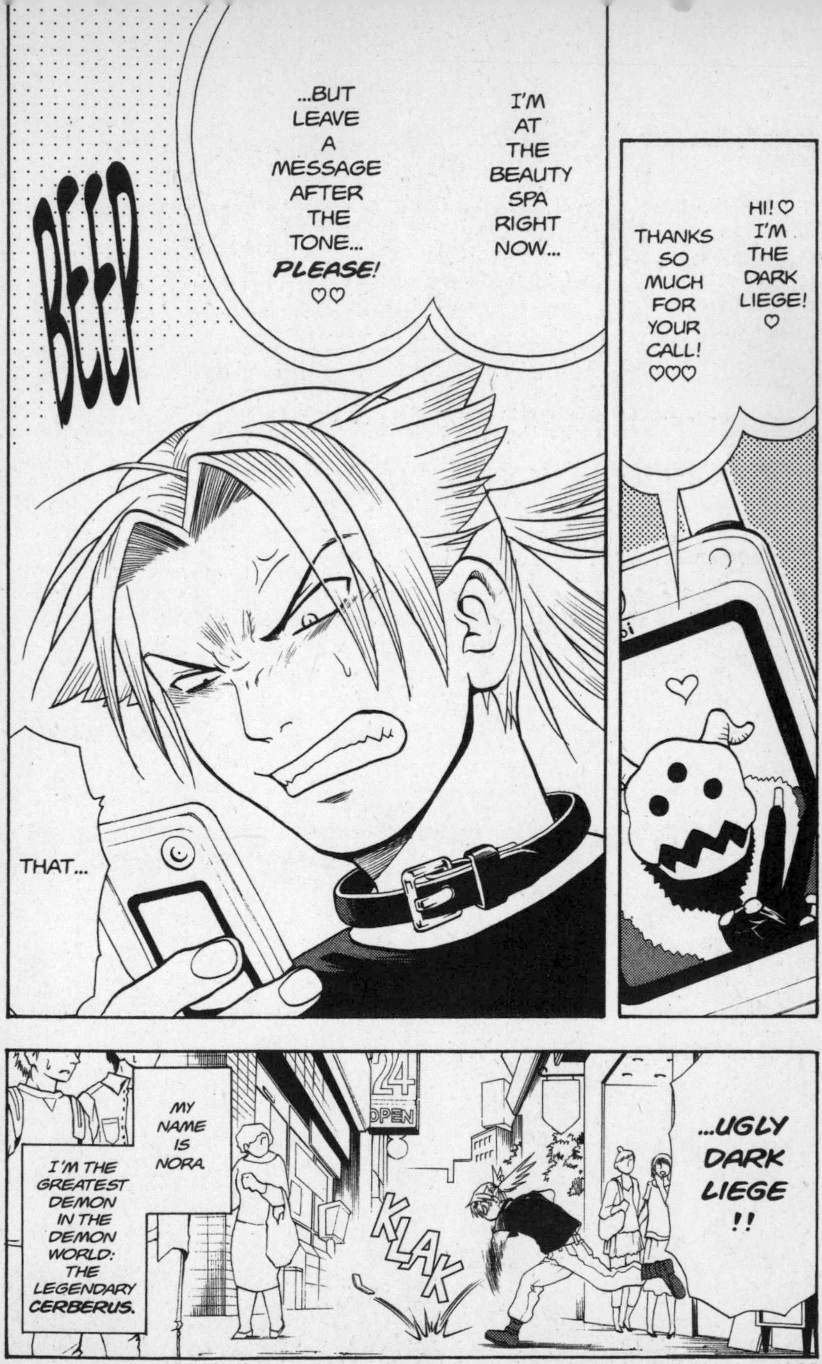
HI! ♡ I'M THE DARK LIEGE! ♡
THANKS SO MUCH FOR YOUR CALL! ♡♡♡
I'M AT THE BEAUTY SPA RIGHT NOW...
...BUT LEAVE A MESSAGE AFTER THE TONE... PLEASE! ♡♡
BEEP
THAT...
...UGLY DARK LIEGE!!
KLAK
MY NAME IS NORA.
I'M THE GREATEST DEMON IN THE DEMON WORLD: THE LEGENDARY CERBERUS.

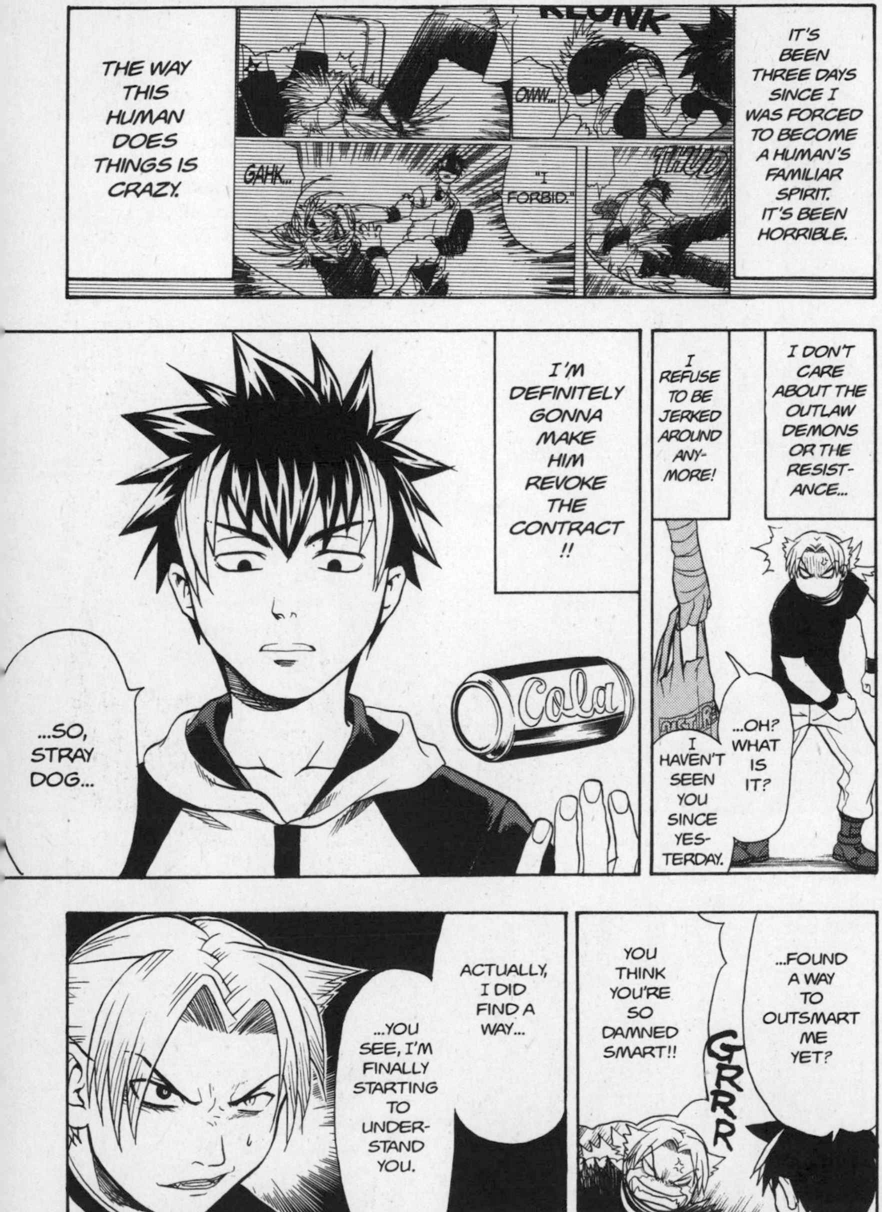
IT'S BEEN THREE DAYS SINCE I WAS FORCED TO BECOME A HUMAN'S FAMILIAR SPIRIT. IT'S BEEN HORRIBLE.
KLONK
OWW...
"I FORBID."
GAHK...
THE WAY THIS HUMAN DOES THINGS IS CRAZY.
I DON'T CARE ABOUT THE OUTLAW DEMONS OR THE RESIST-ANCE...
I REFUSE TO BE JERKED AROUND ANY-MORE!
...OH? WHAT IS IT?
I HAVEN'T SEEN YOU SINCE YES-TERDAY.
I'M DEFINITELY GONNA MAKE HIM REVOKE THE CONTRACT!!
Cola
...SO, STRAY DOG...
...FOUND A WAY TO OUTSMART ME YET?
GRRR
YOU THINK YOU'RE SO DAMNED SMART!!
ACTUALLY, I DID FIND A WAY...
...YOU SEE, I'M FINALLY STARTING TO UNDER-STAND YOU.

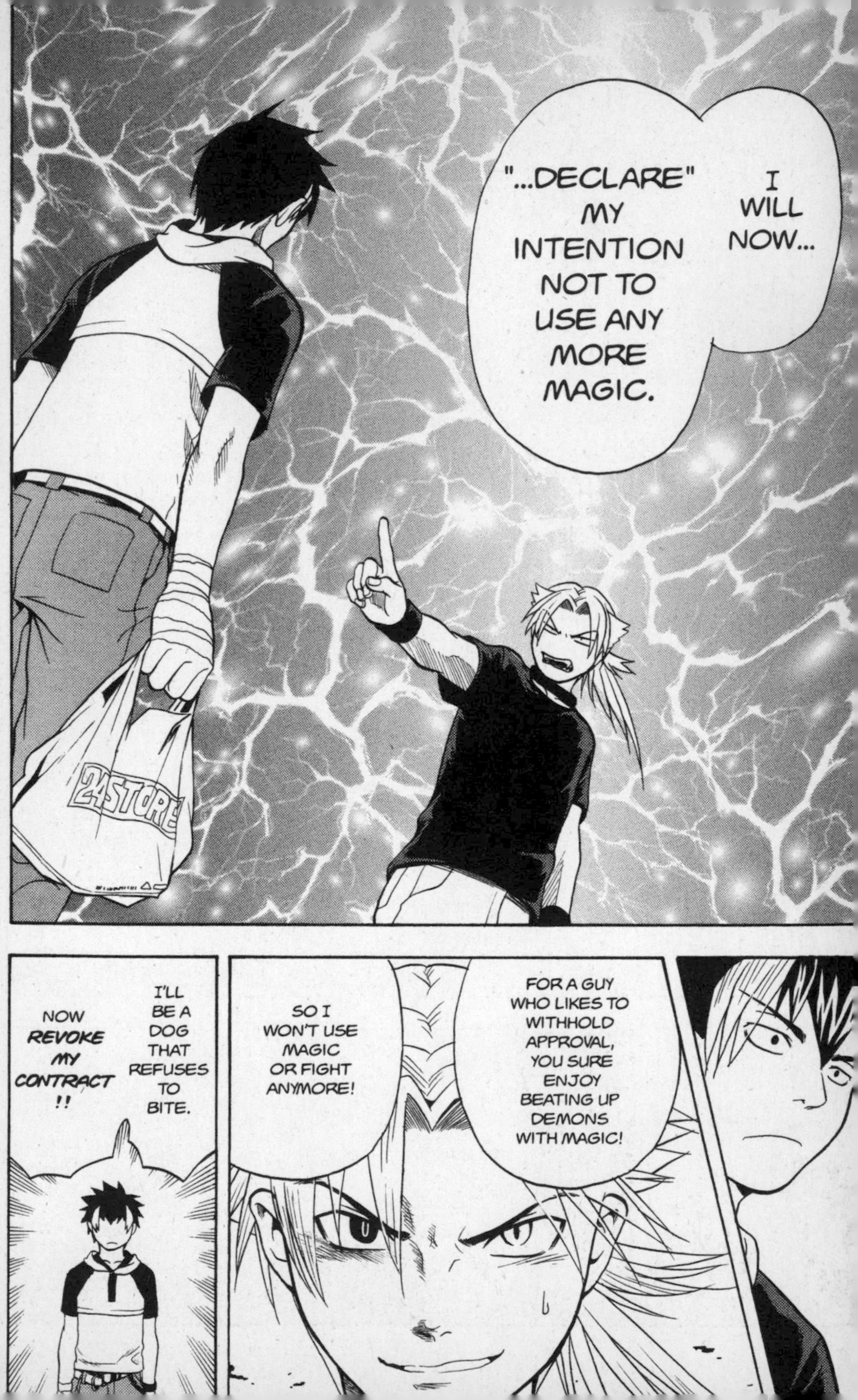
I WILL NOW...
"...DECLARE" MY INTENTION NOT TO USE ANY MORE MAGIC.
24STORE
FOR A GUY WHO LIKES TO WITHHOLD APPROVAL, YOU SURE ENJOY BEATING UP DEMONS WITH MAGIC!
SO I WON'T USE MAGIC OR FIGHT ANYMORE!
I'LL BE A DOG THAT REFUSES TO BITE.
NOW *REVOKE MY CONTRACT* !!

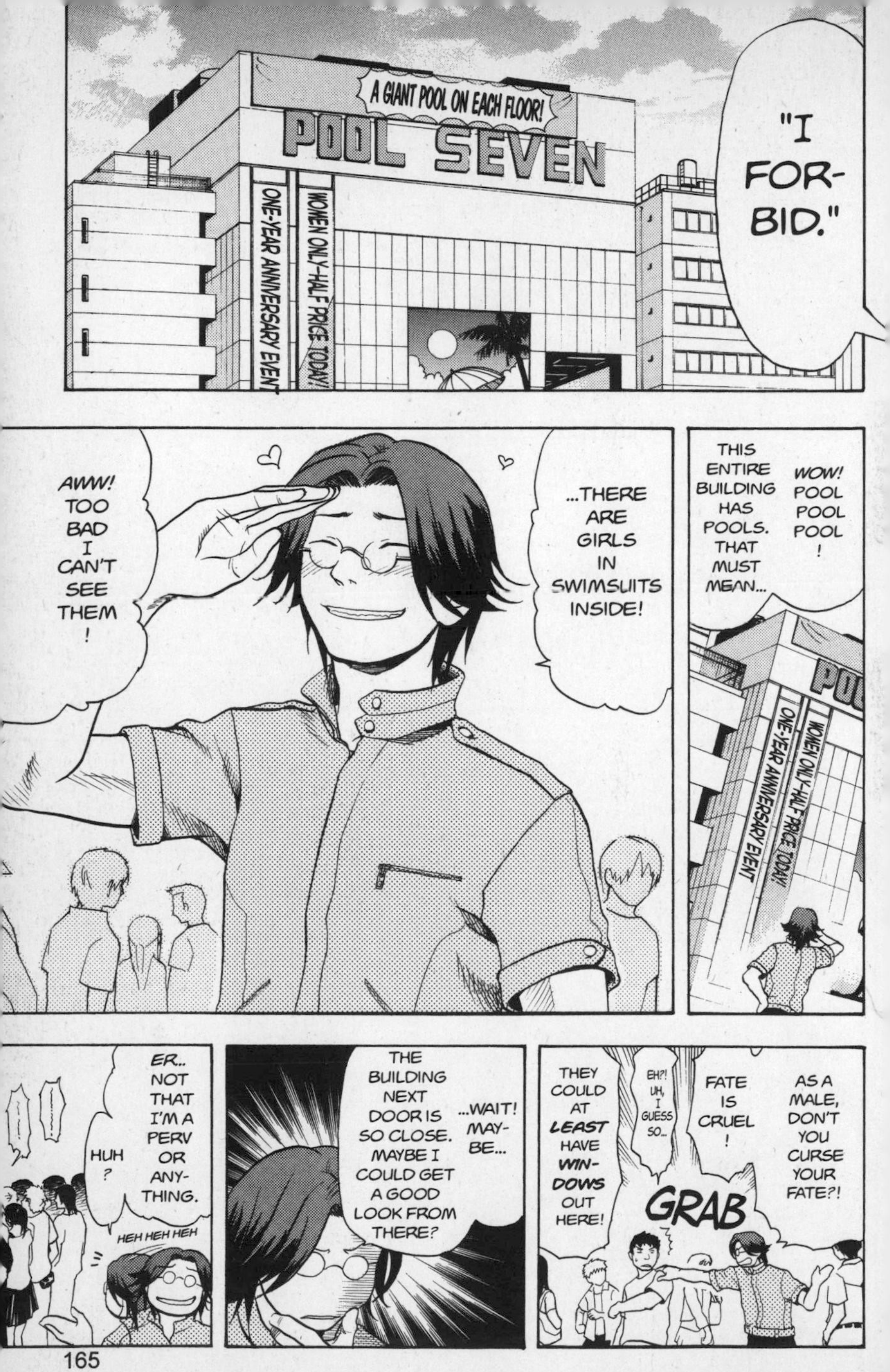
A GIANT POOL ON EACH FLOOR!
POOL SEVEN
WOMEN ONLY-HALF PRICE TODAY!
ONE-YEAR ANNIVERSARY EVENT
"I FOR-BID."
WOW! POOL POOL POOL!
THIS ENTIRE BUILDING HAS POOLS. THAT MUST MEAN...
WOMEN ONLY-HALF PRICE TODAY!
ONE-YEAR ANNIVERSARY EVENT
...THERE ARE GIRLS IN SWIMSUITS INSIDE!
AWW! TOO BAD I CAN'T SEE THEM!
AS A MALE, DON'T YOU CURSE YOUR FATE?!
FATE IS CRUEL!
EH?! UH, I GUESS SO...
THEY COULD AT *LEAST* HAVE *WIN-DOWS* OUT HERE!
GRAB
...WAIT! MAY-BE...
THE BUILDING NEXT DOOR IS SO CLOSE. MAYBE I COULD GET A GOOD LOOK FROM THERE?
ER.. NOT THAT I'M A PERV OR ANY-THING.
HUH?
HEH HEH HEH

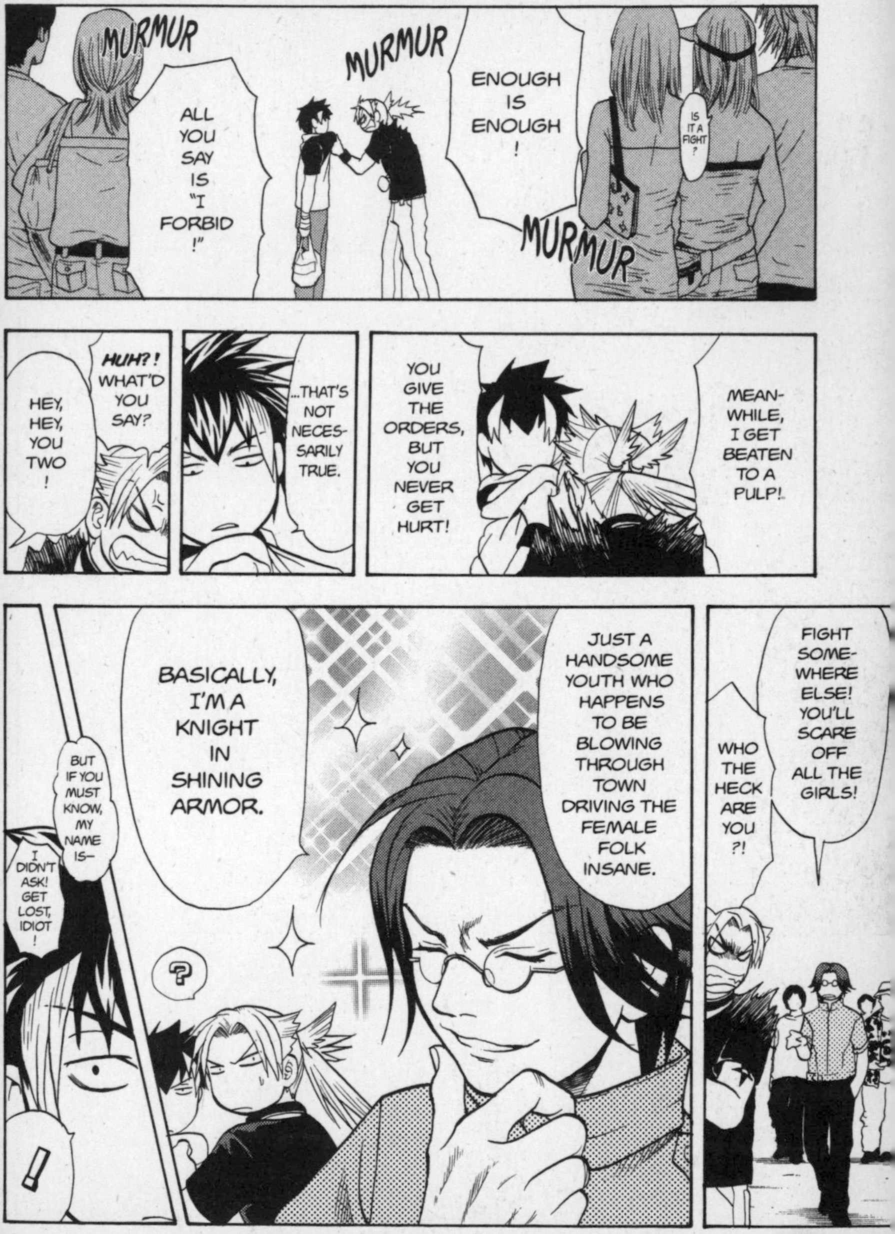
IS IT A FIGHT?
ENOUGH IS ENOUGH!
MURMUR
MURMUR
ALL YOU SAY IS "I FORBID!"
MURMUR
MEAN-WHILE, I GET BEATEN TO A PULP!
YOU GIVE THE ORDERS, BUT YOU NEVER GET HURT!
...THAT'S NOT NECES-SARILY TRUE.
HUH?! WHAT'D YOU SAY?
HEY, HEY, YOU TWO!
FIGHT SOME-WHERE ELSE! YOU'LL SCARE OFF ALL THE GIRLS!
WHO THE HECK ARE YOU?!
JUST A HANDSOME YOUTH WHO HAPPENS TO BE BLOWING THROUGH TOWN DRIVING THE FEMALE FOLK INSANE.
BASICALLY, I'M A KNIGHT IN SHINING ARMOR.
BUT IF YOU MUST KNOW, MY NAME IS—
?
I DIDN'T ASK! GET LOST, IDIOT!
!

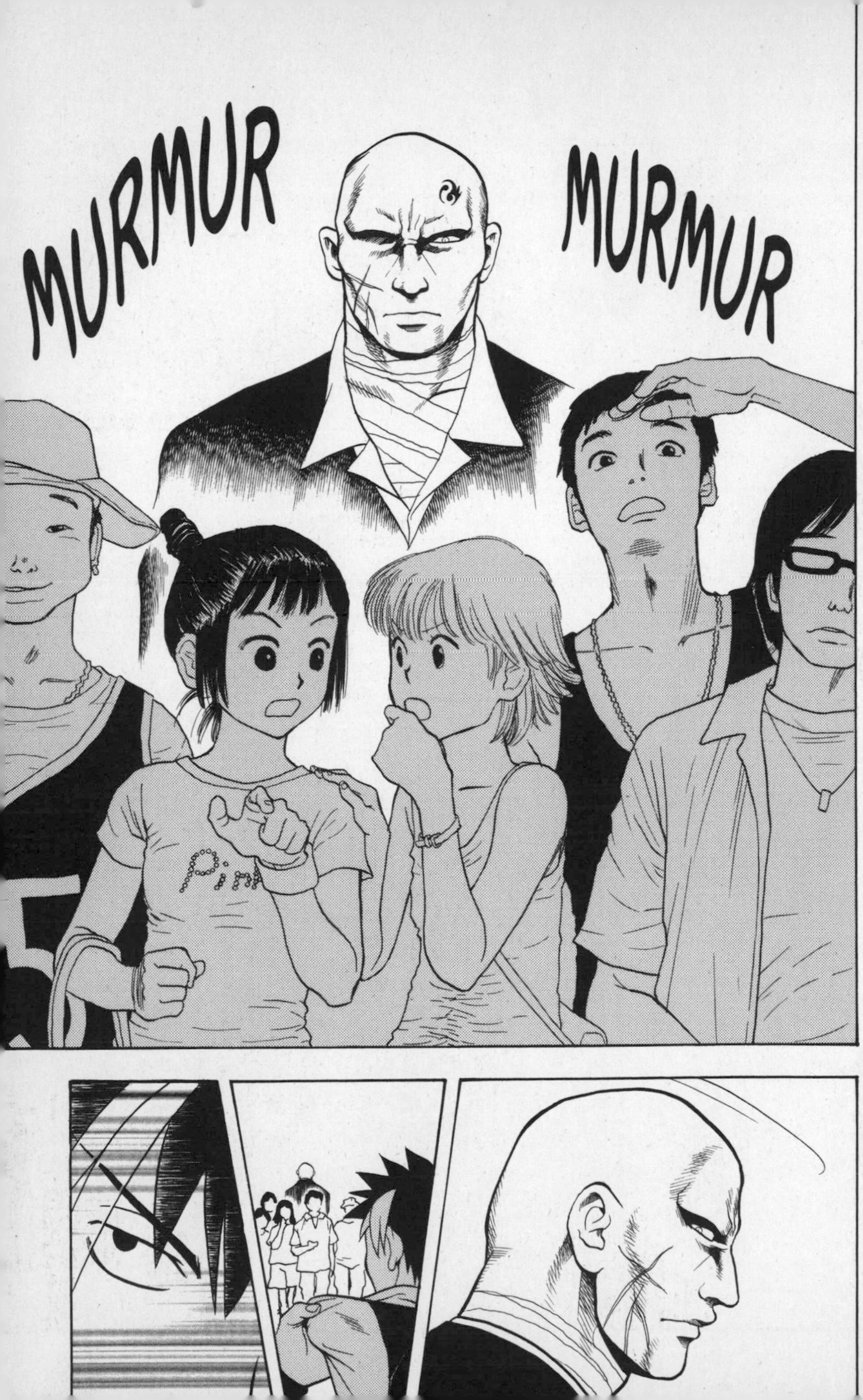
MURMUR
MURMUR

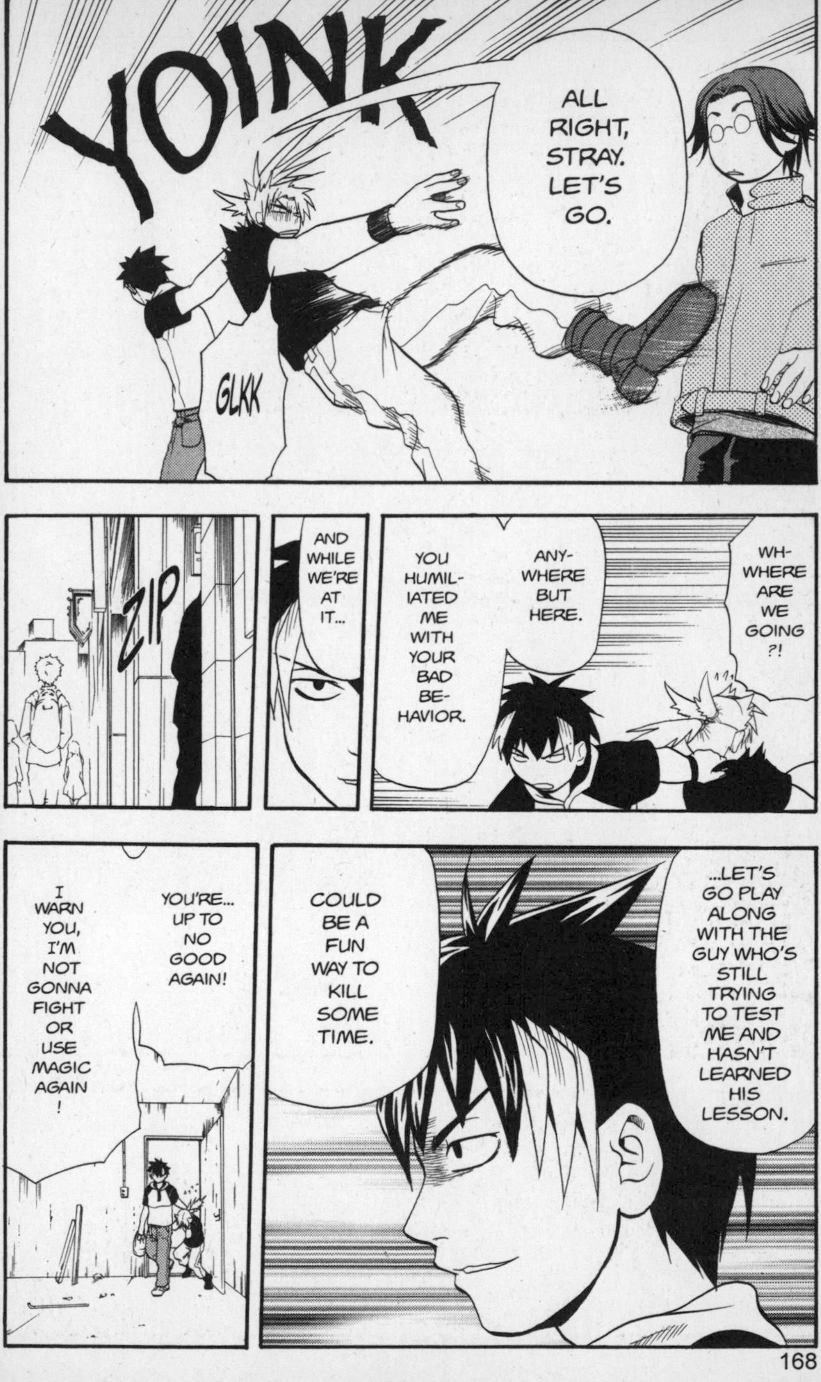
ALL RIGHT, STRAY. LET'S GO.
YOINK
GLKK
WH-WHERE ARE WE GOING?!
ANY-WHERE BUT HERE.
YOU HUMIL-IATED ME WITH YOUR BAD BE-HAVIOR.
AND WHILE WE'RE AT IT...
ZIP
...LET'S GO PLAY ALONG WITH THE GUY WHO'S STILL TRYING TO TEST ME AND HASN'T LEARNED HIS LESSON.
COULD BE A FUN WAY TO KILL SOME TIME.
YOU'RE... UP TO NO GOOD AGAIN!
I WARN YOU, I'M NOT GONNA FIGHT OR USE MAGIC AGAIN!

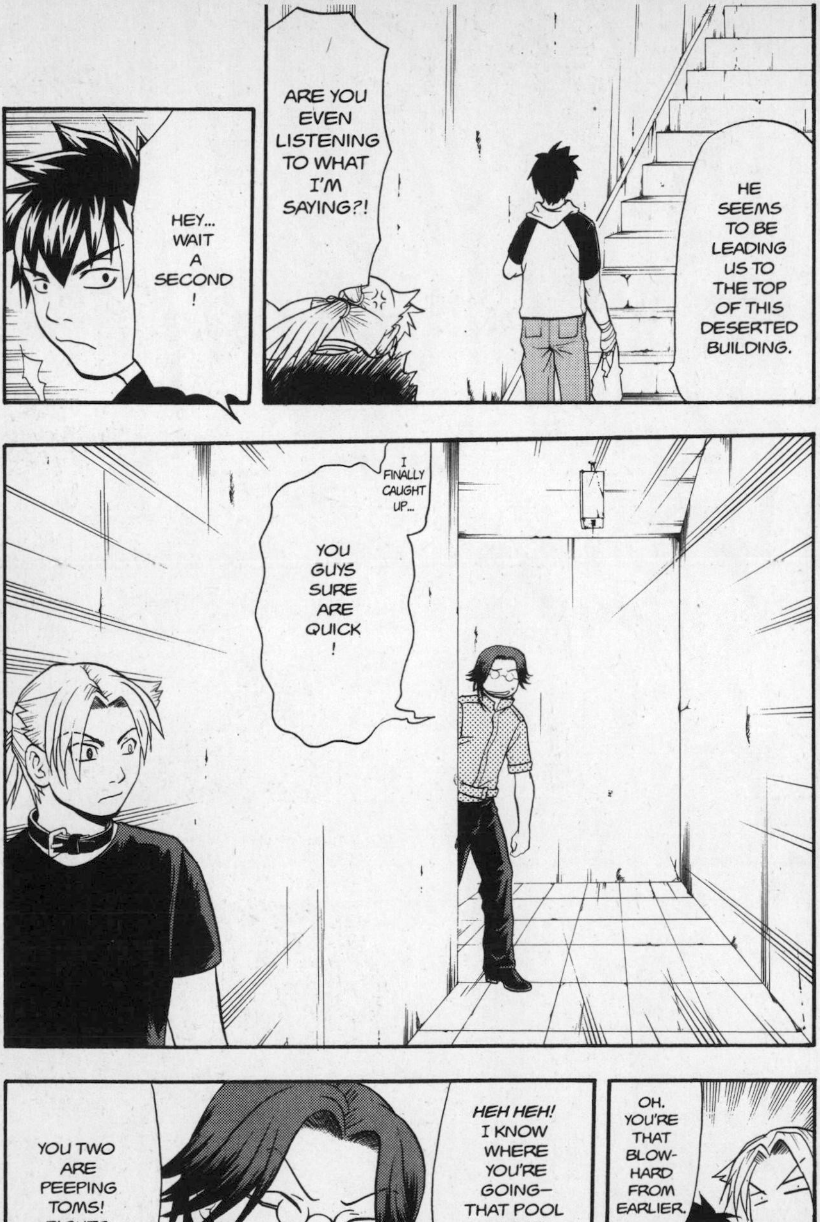
HE SEEMS TO BE LEADING US TO THE TOP OF THIS DESERTED BUILDING.
ARE YOU EVEN LISTENING TO WHAT I'M SAYING?!
HEY... WAIT A SECOND!
I FINALLY CAUGHT UP...
YOU GUYS SURE ARE QUICK!
OH. YOU'RE THAT BLOW-HARD FROM EARLIER.
HEH HEH! I KNOW WHERE YOU'RE GOING— THAT POOL IN THE BUILDING NEXT DOOR!
YOU TWO ARE PEEPING TOMS! RIGHT? RIGHT??

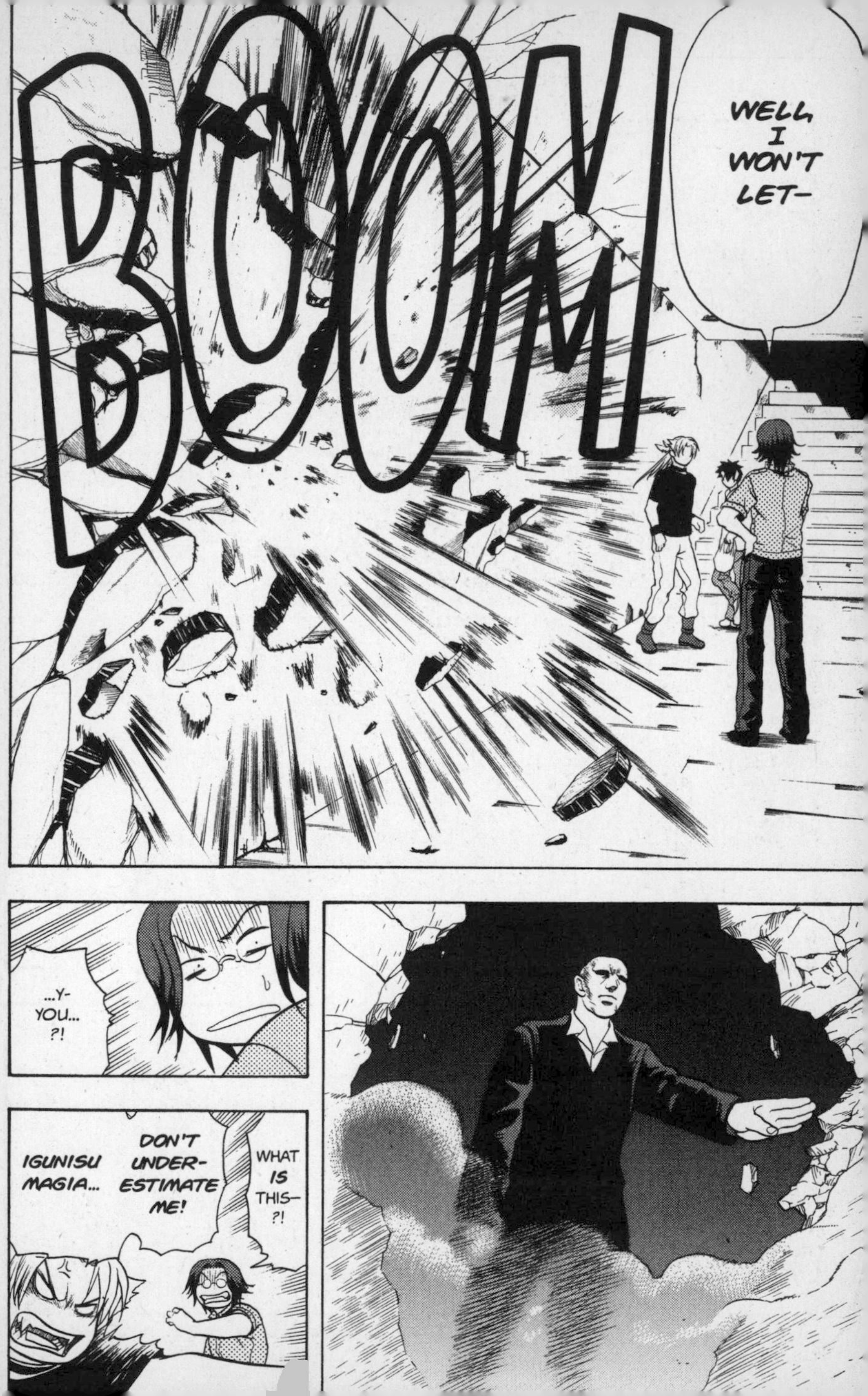
WELL I WON'T LET—
BOOM
...Y-YOU...?!
WHAT IS THIS—?!
DON'T UNDER-ESTIMATE ME!
IGUNISU MAGIA...

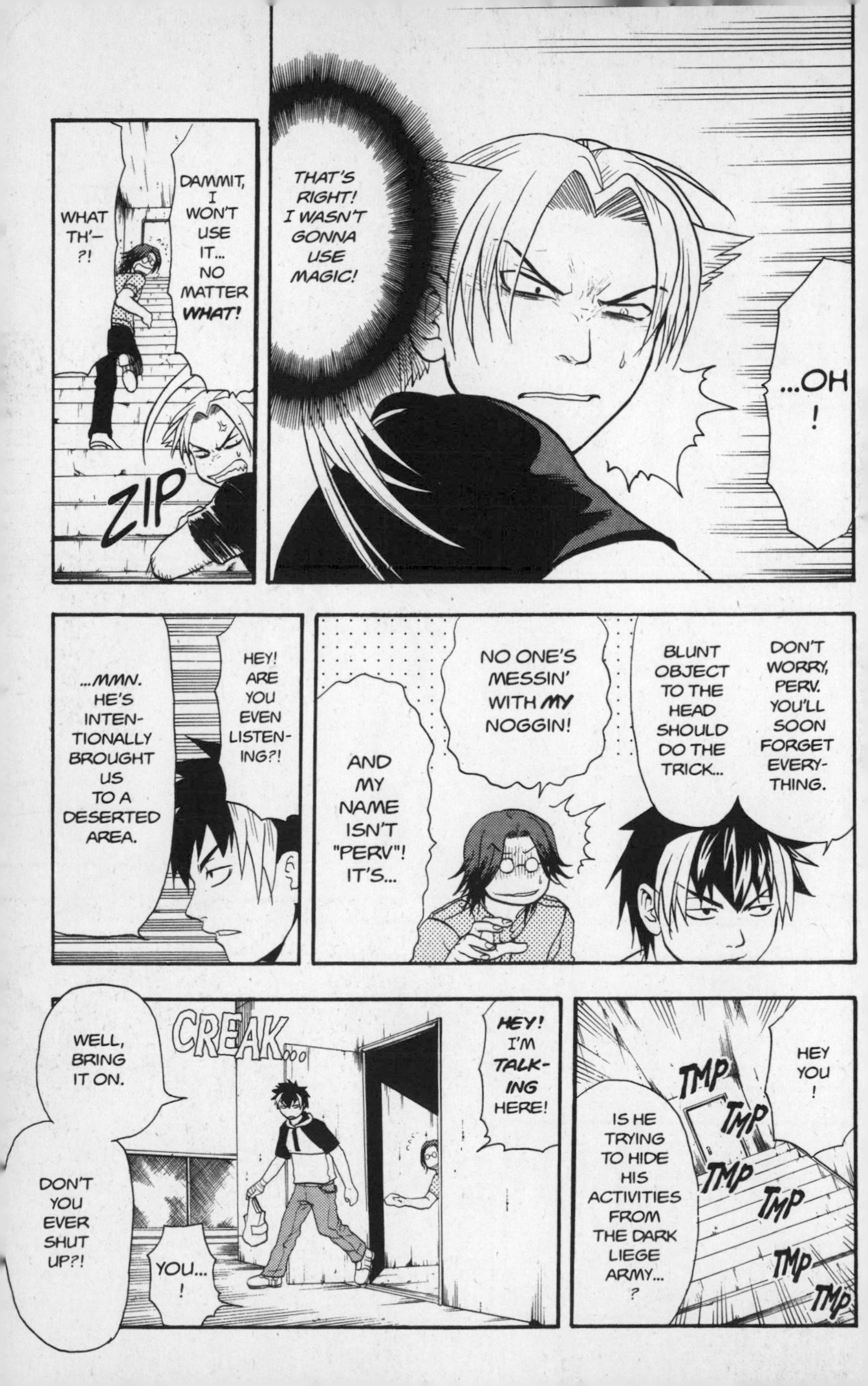
...OH!
THAT'S RIGHT! I WASN'T GONNA USE MAGIC!
DAMMIT, I WON'T USE IT... NO MATTER WHAT!
WHAT TH'—?!
ZIP
DON'T WORRY, PERV. YOU'LL SOON FORGET EVERYTHING.
BLUNT OBJECT TO THE HEAD SHOULD DO THE TRICK...
NO ONE'S MESSIN' WITH MY NOGGIN!
AND MY NAME ISN'T "PERV"! IT'S...
HEY! ARE YOU EVEN LISTENING?!
...MMN. HE'S INTENTIONALLY BROUGHT US TO A DESERTED AREA.
HEY YOU!
TMP TMP TMP TMP TMP TMP
IS HE TRYING TO HIDE HIS ACTIVITIES FROM THE DARK LIEGE ARMY...?
HEY! I'M TALKING HERE!
CREAK...
WELL, BRING IT ON.
YOU...!
DON'T YOU EVER SHUT UP?!

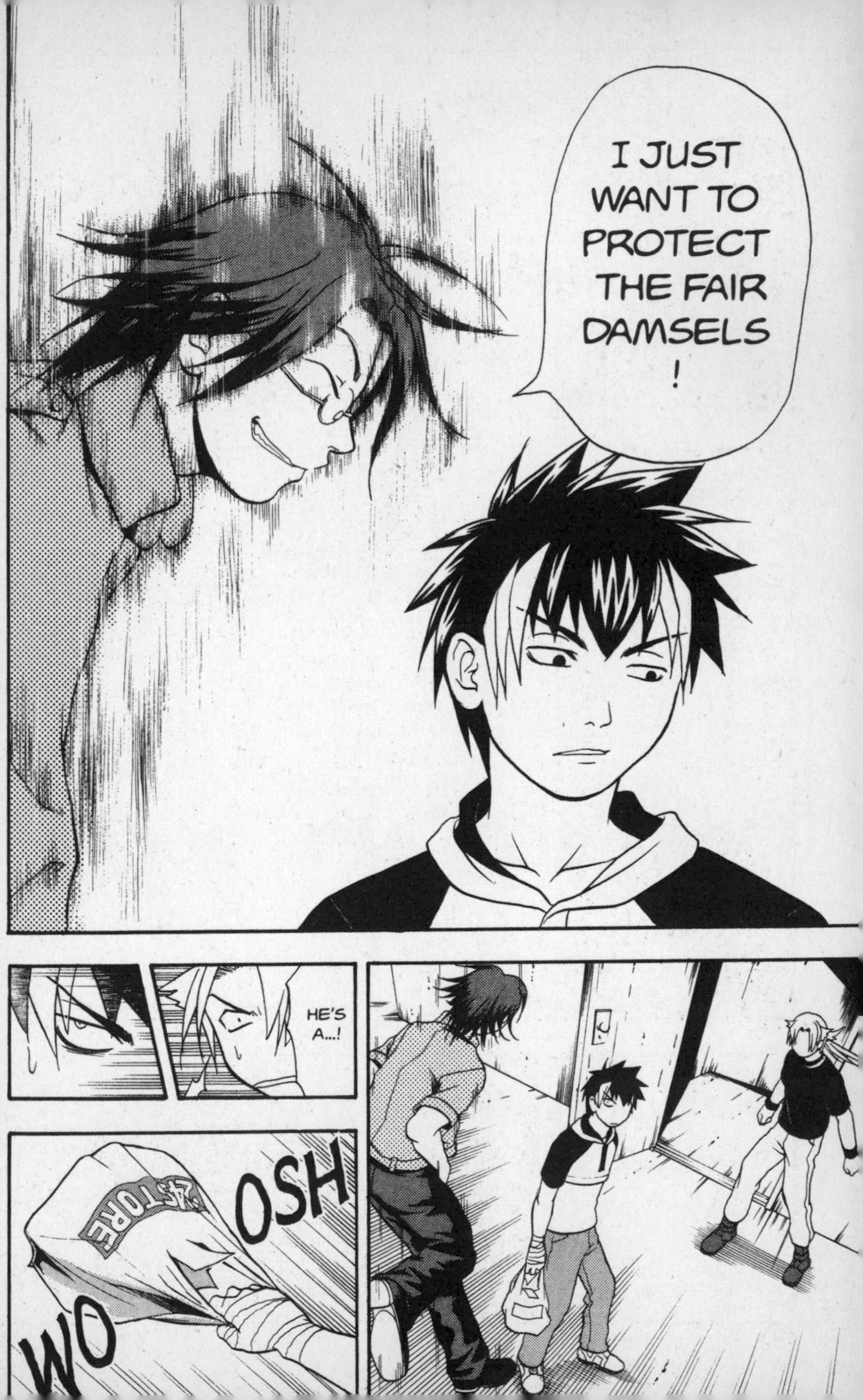
I JUST WANT TO PROTECT THE FAIR DAMSELS!
HE'S A...!
WOOSH

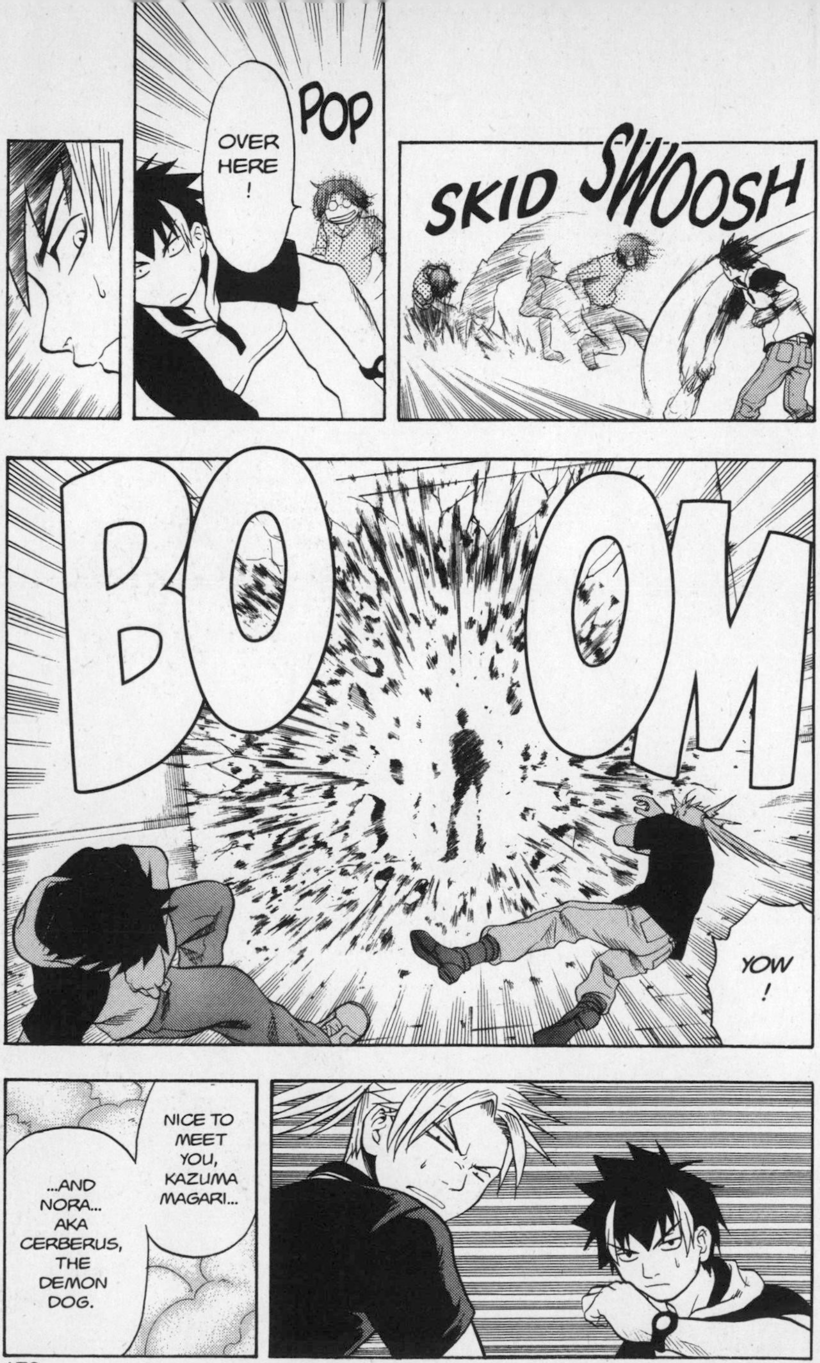
SWOOSH
SKID
POP
OVER HERE !
BOOM
YOW !
NICE TO MEET YOU, KAZUMA MAGARI...
...AND NORA... AKA CERBERUS, THE DEMON DOG.

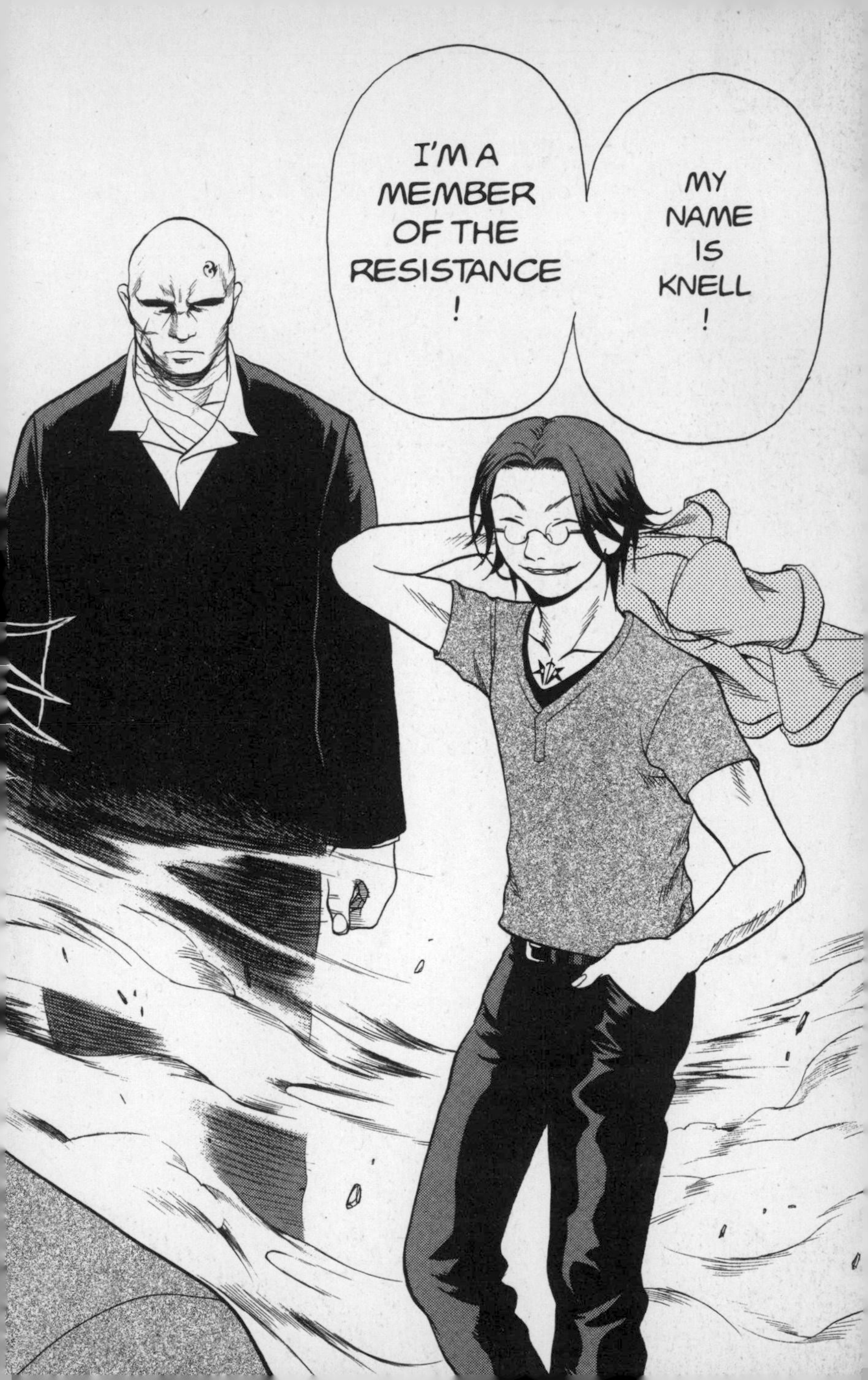
MY NAME IS KNELL!
I'M A MEMBER OF THE RESISTANCE!

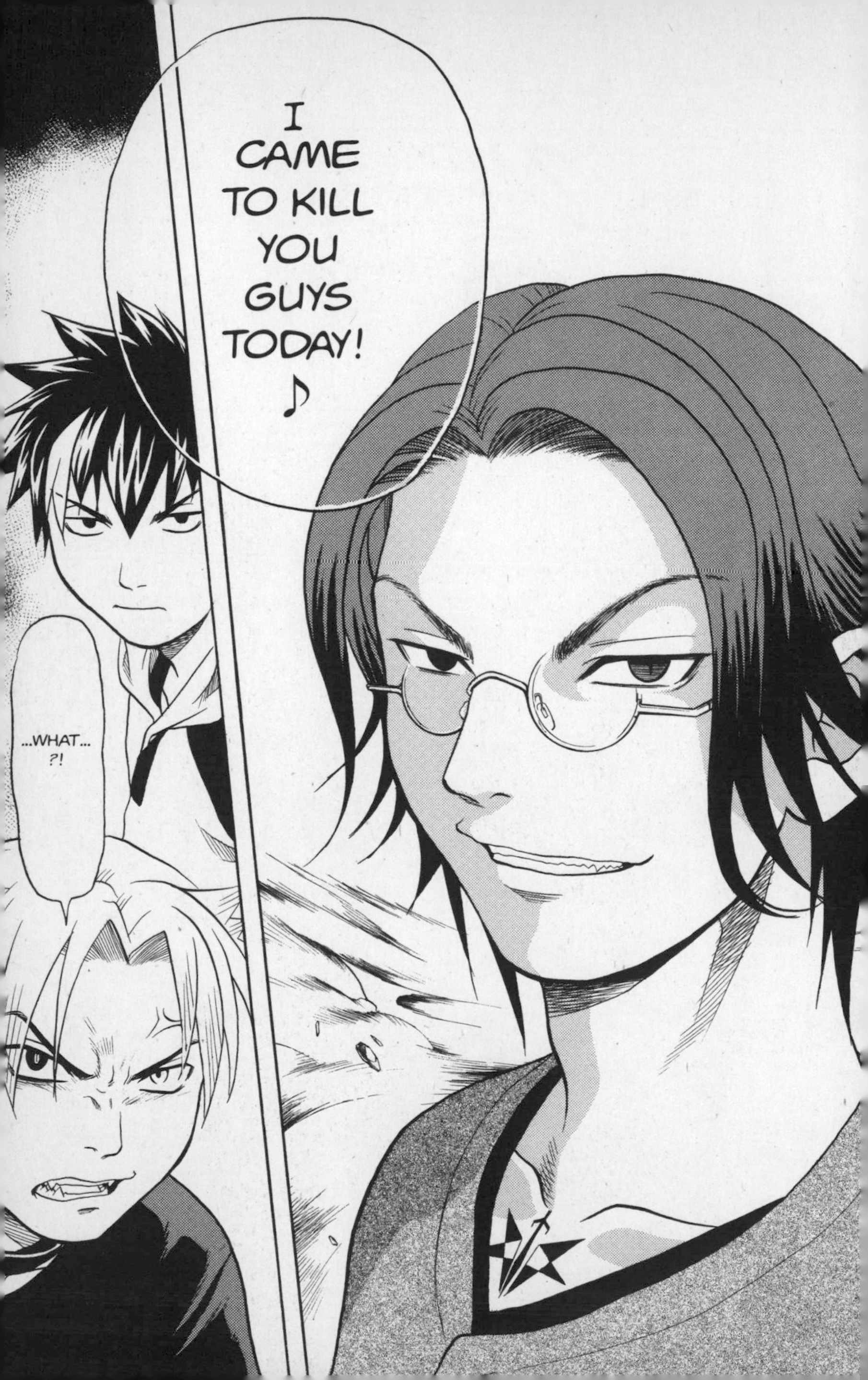
I CAME TO KILL YOU GUYS TODAY! ♪
...WHAT... ?!

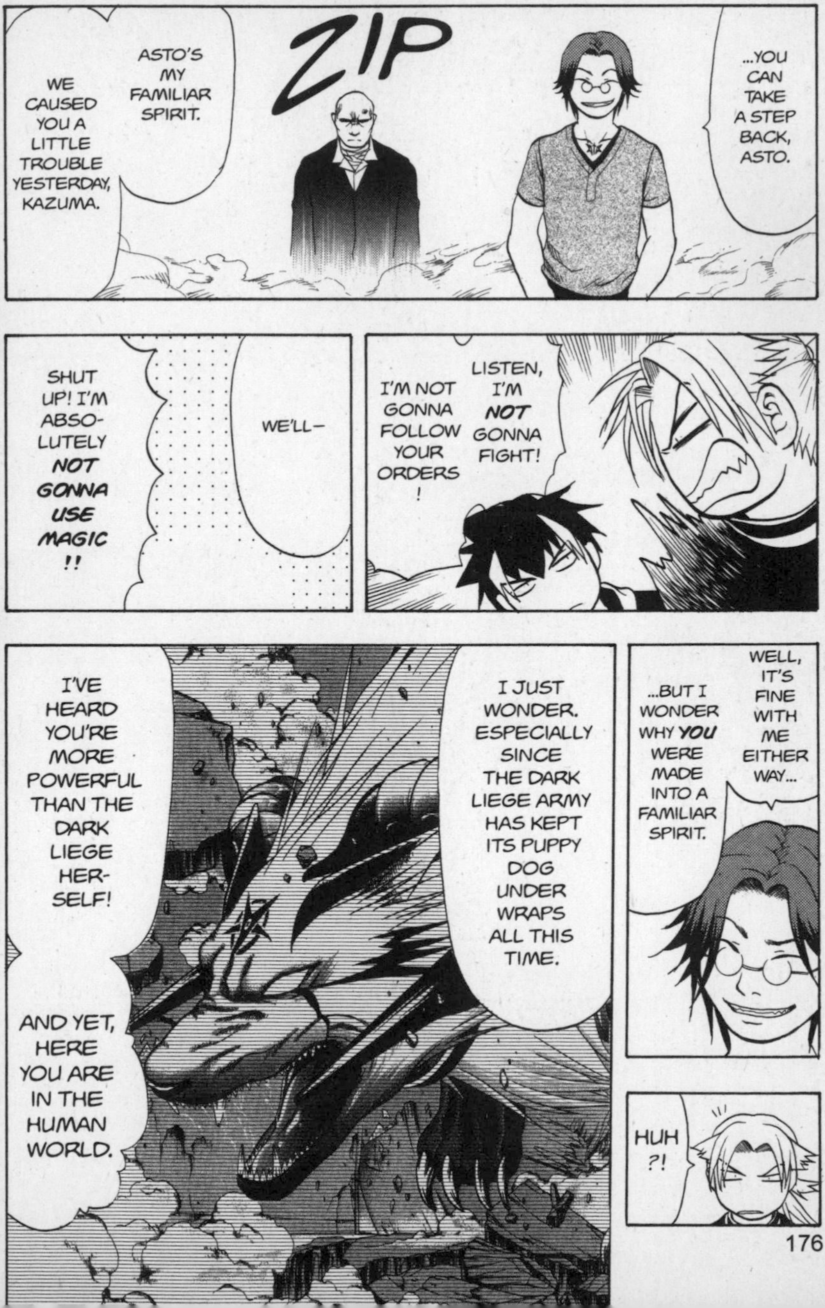
...YOU CAN TAKE A STEP BACK, ASTO.
ZIP
ASTO'S MY FAMILIAR SPIRIT.
WE CAUSED YOU A LITTLE TROUBLE YESTERDAY, KAZUMA.
LISTEN, I'M **NOT** GONNA FIGHT!
I'M NOT GONNA FOLLOW YOUR ORDERS!
WE'LL–
SHUT UP! I'M ABSOLUTELY **NOT GONNA USE MAGIC!!**
WELL, IT'S FINE WITH ME EITHER WAY...
...BUT I WONDER WHY **YOU** WERE MADE INTO A FAMILIAR SPIRIT.
HUH?!
I JUST WONDER. ESPECIALLY SINCE THE DARK LIEGE ARMY HAS KEPT ITS PUPPY DOG UNDER WRAPS ALL THIS TIME.
I'VE HEARD YOU'RE MORE POWERFUL THAN THE DARK LIEGE HERSELF!
AND YET, HERE YOU ARE IN THE HUMAN WORLD.

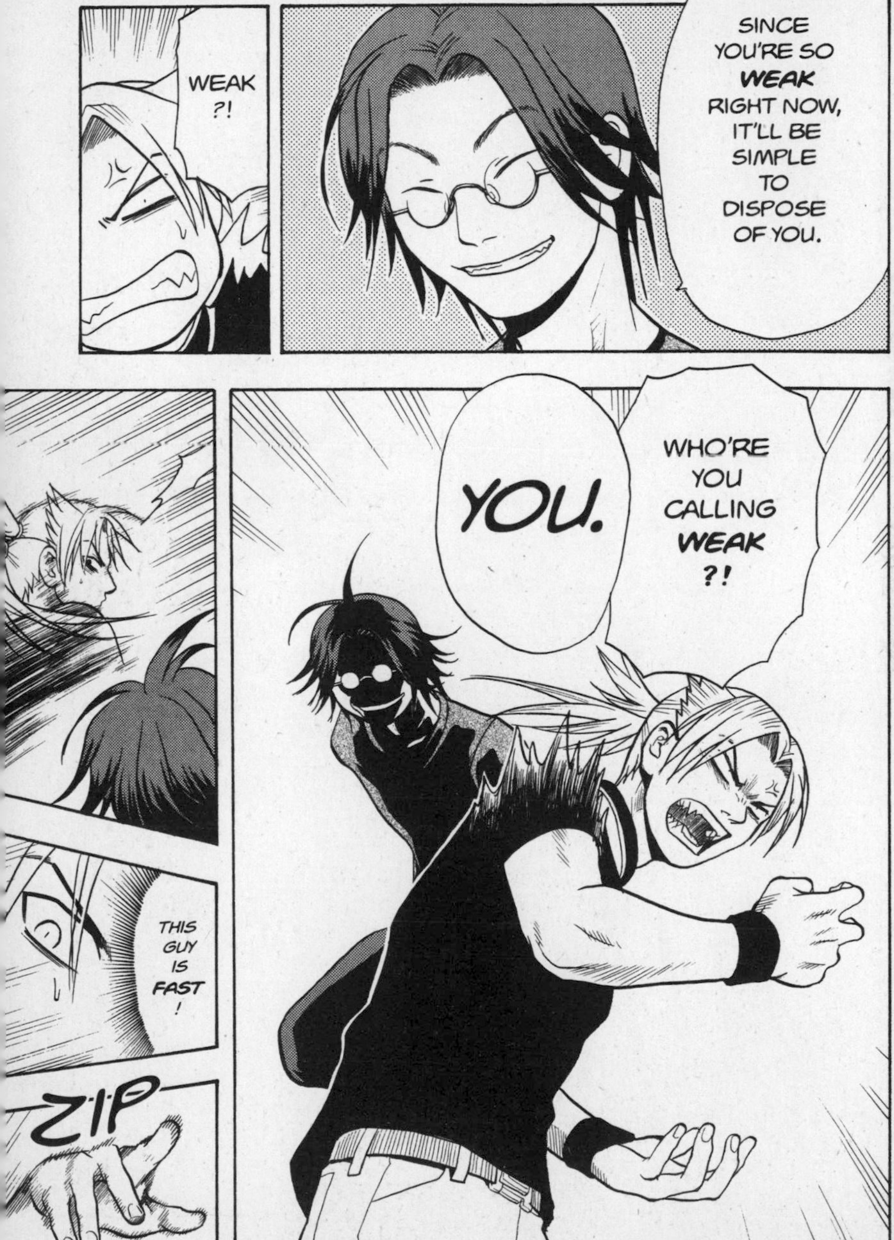
SINCE YOU'RE SO WEAK RIGHT NOW, IT'LL BE SIMPLE TO DISPOSE OF YOU.
WEAK ?!
WHO'RE YOU CALLING WEAK ?!
YOU.
THIS GUY IS FAST !
ZIP

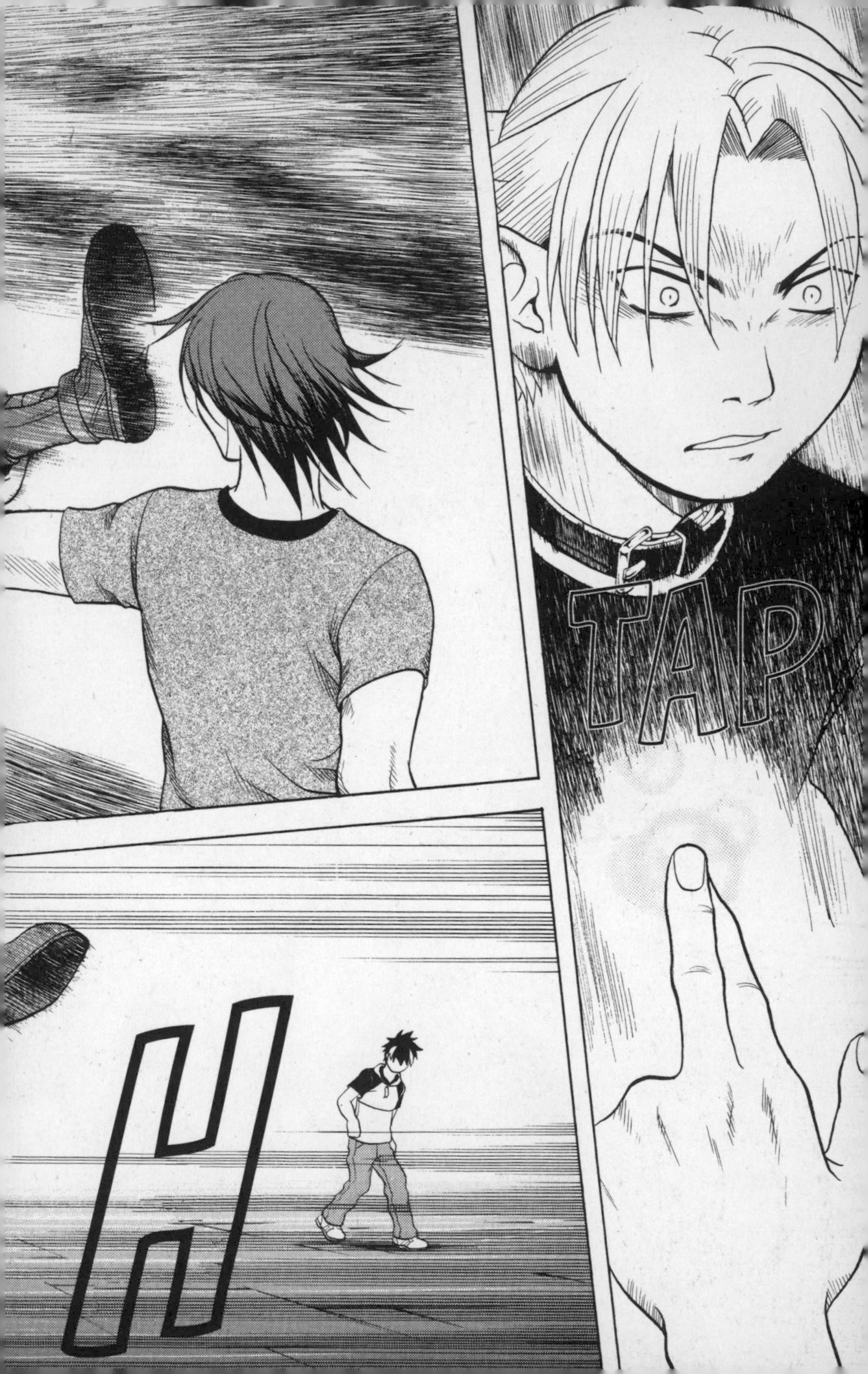
TAP
H

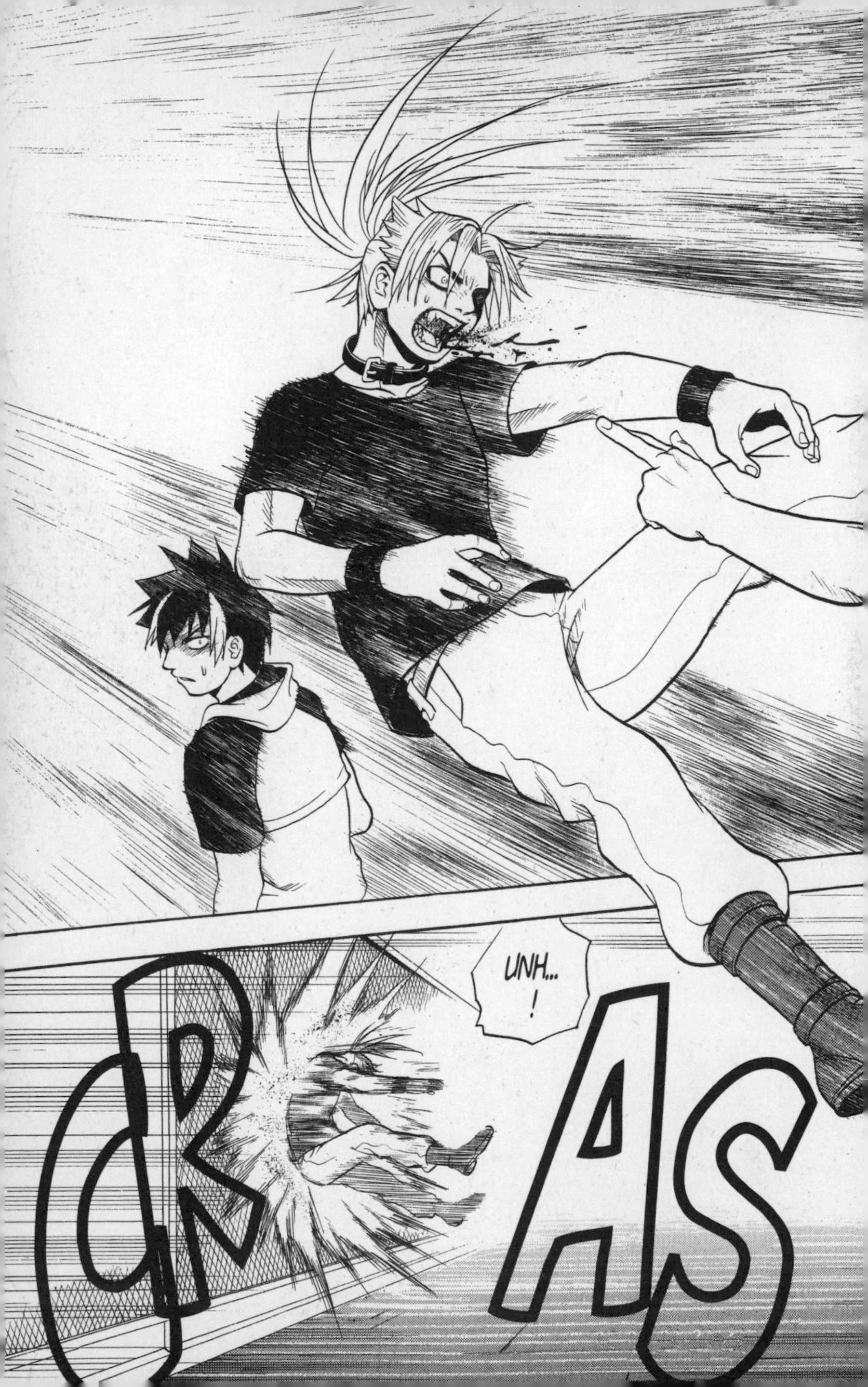
UNH... !
CRAS

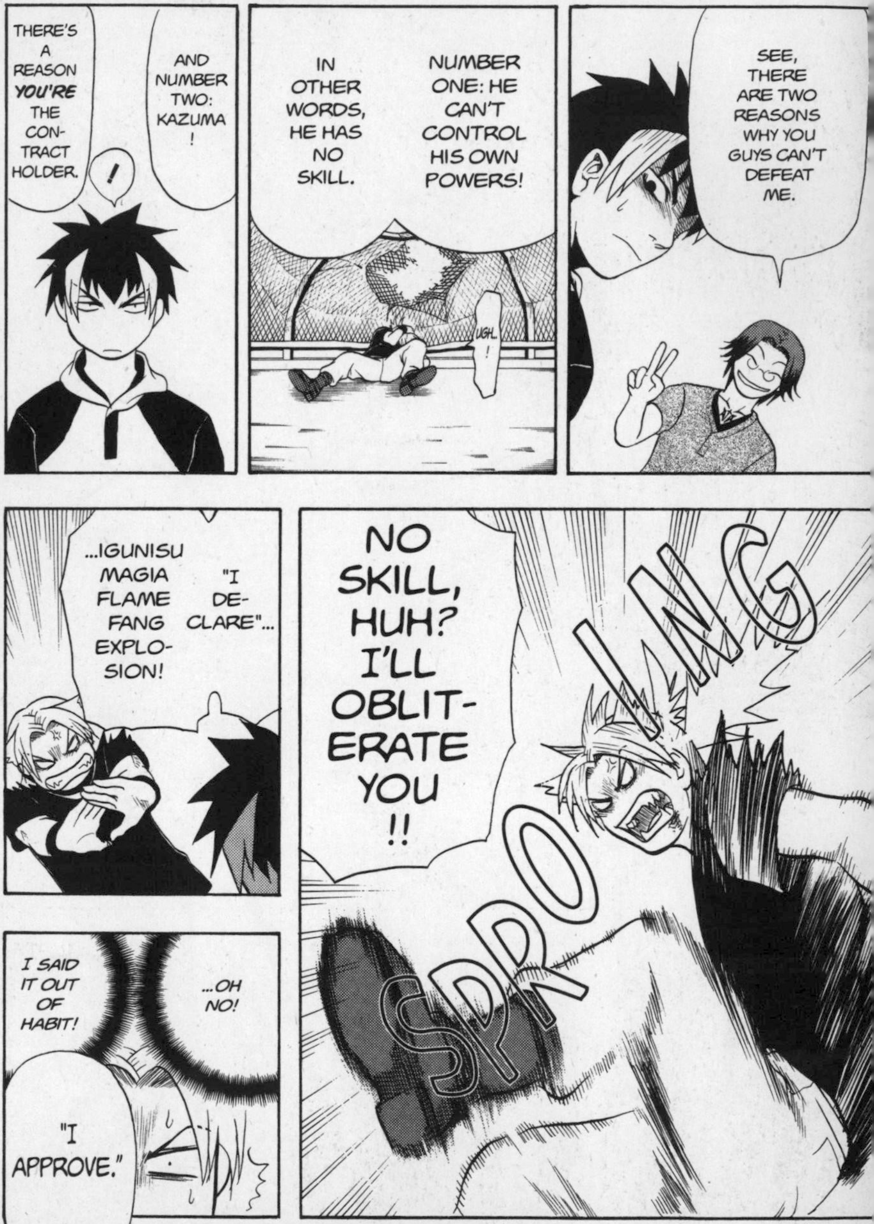
SEE, THERE ARE TWO REASONS WHY YOU GUYS CAN'T DEFEAT ME.
NUMBER ONE: HE CAN'T CONTROL HIS OWN POWERS!
IN OTHER WORDS, HE HAS NO SKILL.
UGH. !
AND NUMBER TWO: KAZUMA!
THERE'S A REASON YOU'RE THE CON-TRACT HOLDER.
!
NO SKILL, HUH? I'LL OBLIT-ERATE YOU!!
SPROING
"I DE-CLARE"...
...IGUNISU MAGIA FLAME FANG EXPLO-SION!
...OH NO!
I SAID IT OUT OF HABIT!
"I APPROVE."

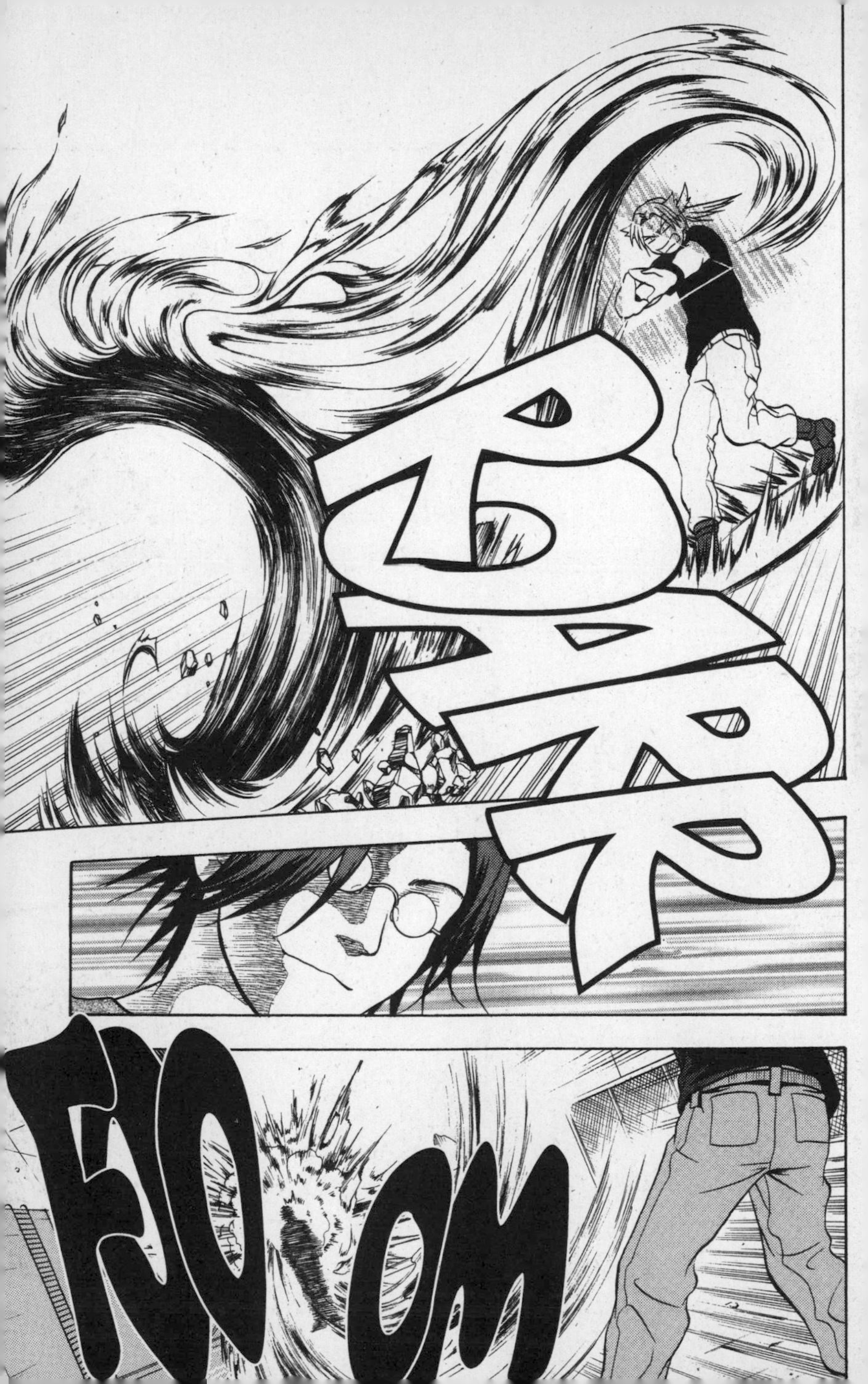
ROARR
FOOM

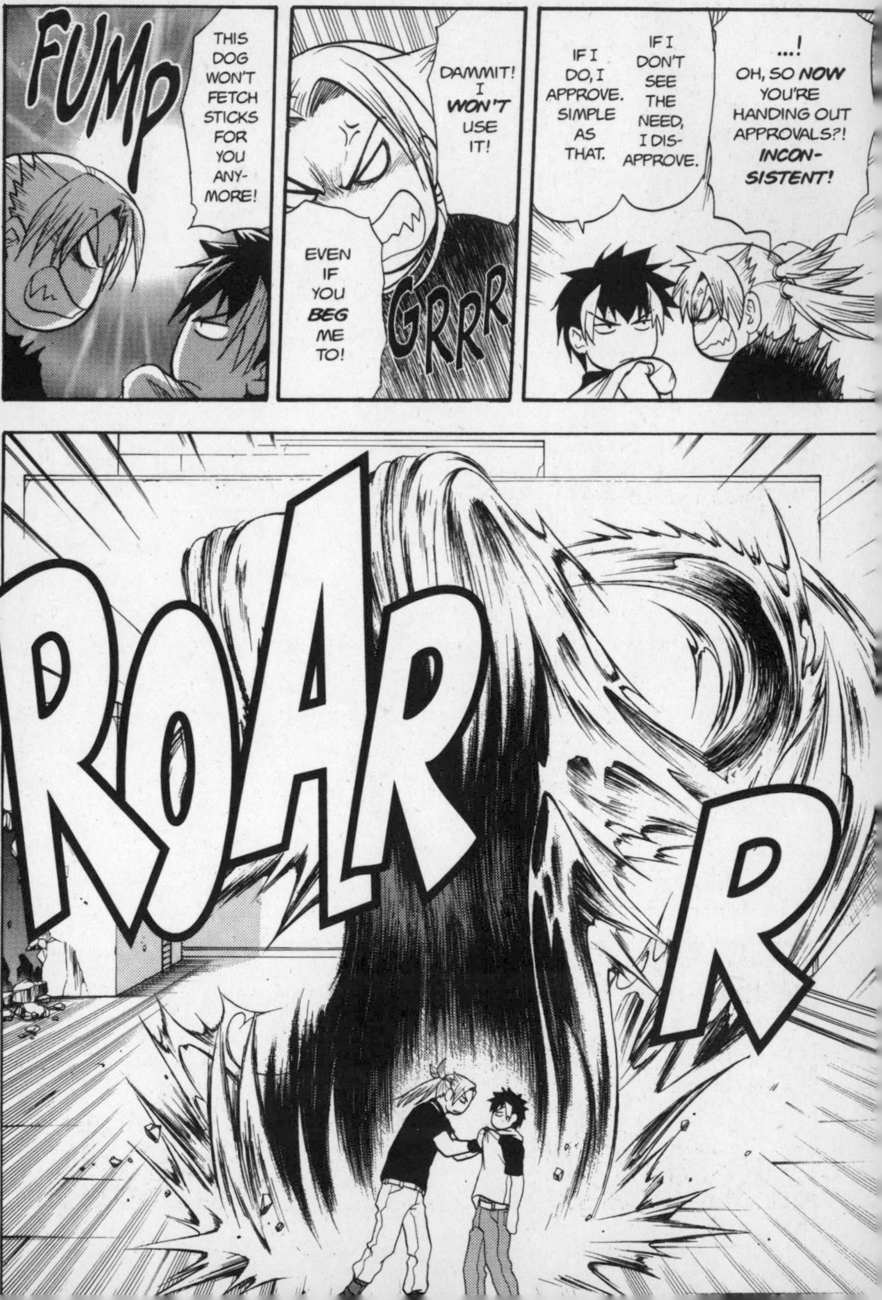
...! OH, SO **NOW** YOU'RE HANDING OUT APPROVALS?! ***INCONSISTENT!***
IF I DON'T SEE THE NEED, I DISAPPROVE.
IF I DO, I APPROVE. SIMPLE AS THAT.
DAMMIT! I ***WON'T*** USE IT!
GRRR
EVEN IF YOU ***BEG*** ME TO!
THIS DOG WON'T FETCH STICKS FOR YOU ANYMORE!
FUMP
ROAR
R

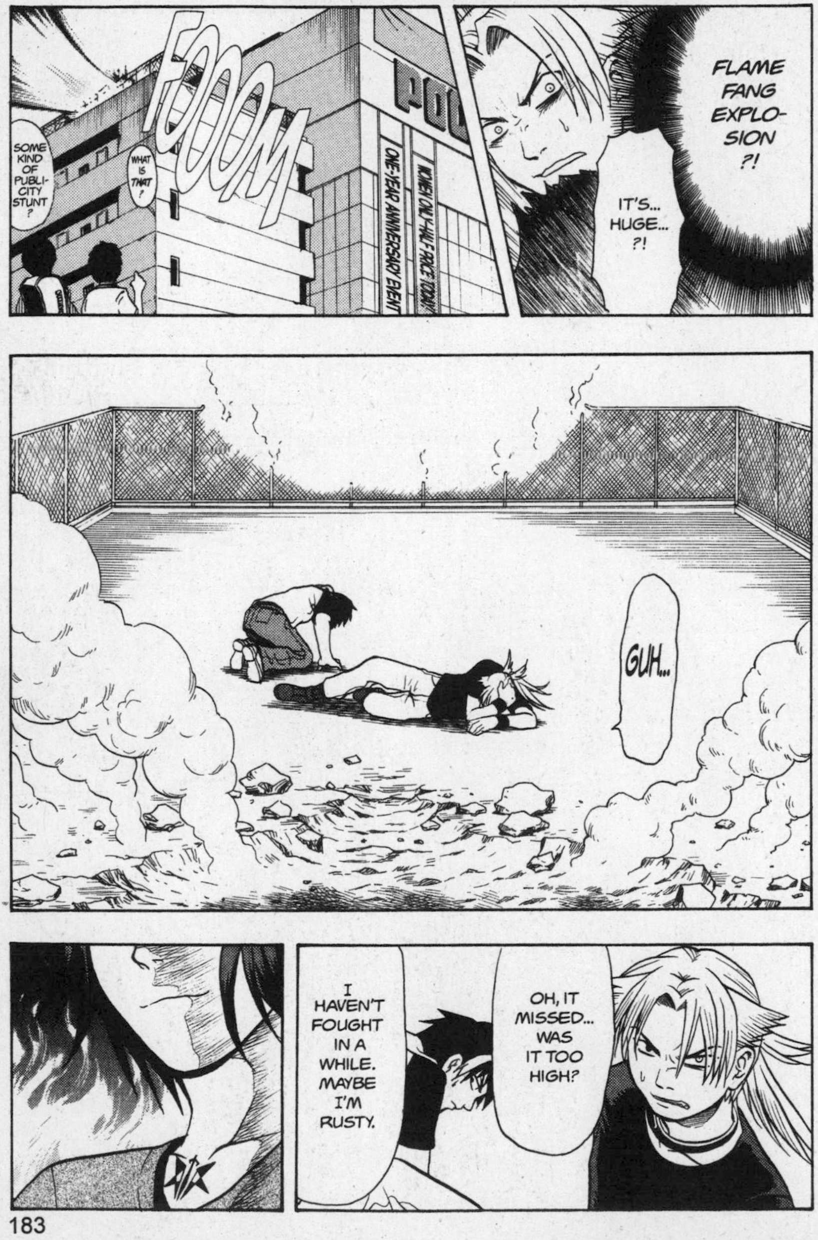
FLAME FANG EXPLOSION ?!
IT'S... HUGE... ?!
FOOOM
WOMEN ONLY HALF PRICE TODAY!
ONE-YEAR ANNIVERSARY EVENT
WHAT IS THAT?
SOME KIND OF PUBLICITY STUNT?
GUH...
OH, IT MISSED... WAS IT TOO HIGH?
I HAVEN'T FOUGHT IN A WHILE. MAYBE I'M RUSTY.

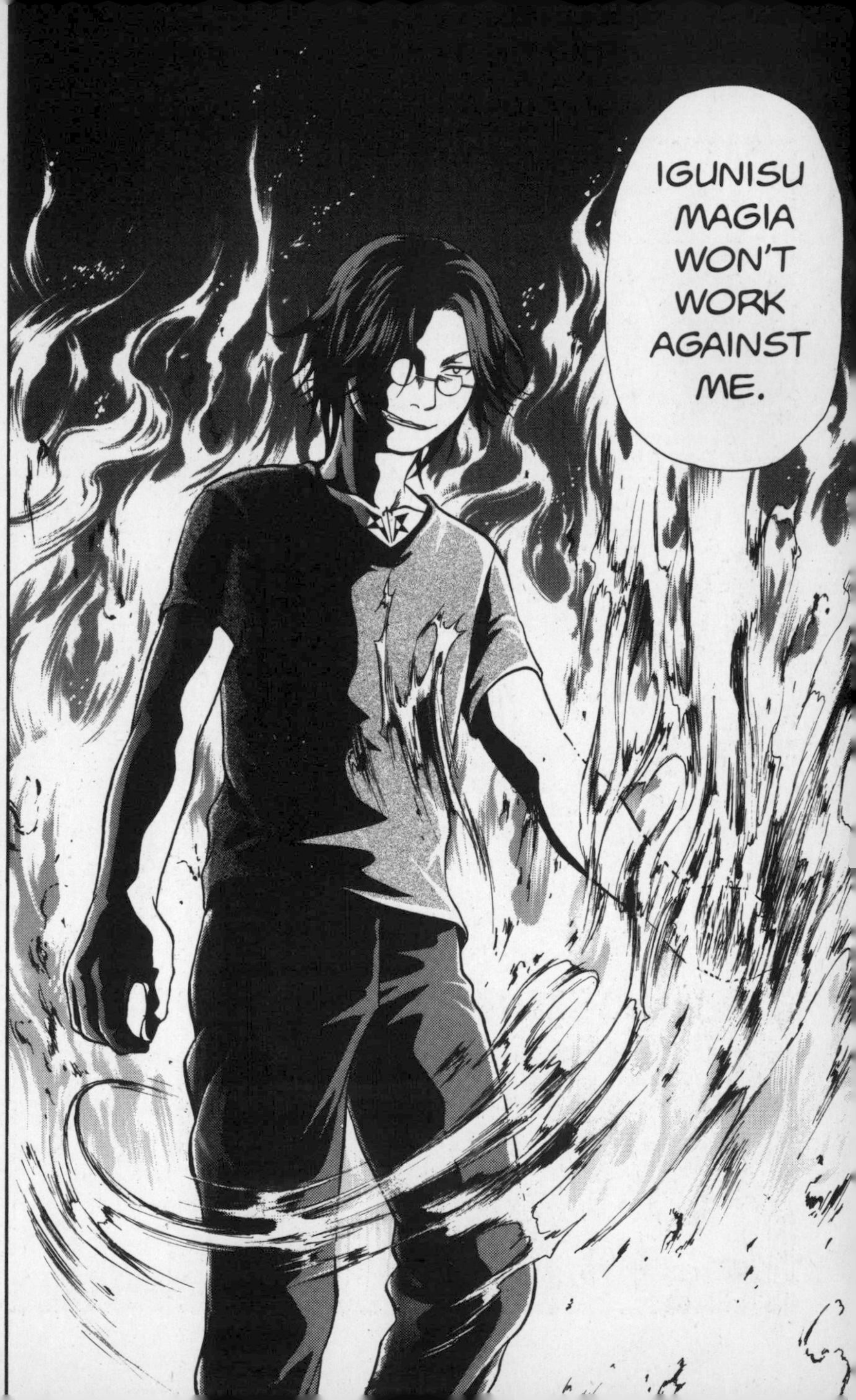
IGUNISU MAGIA WON'T WORK AGAINST ME.

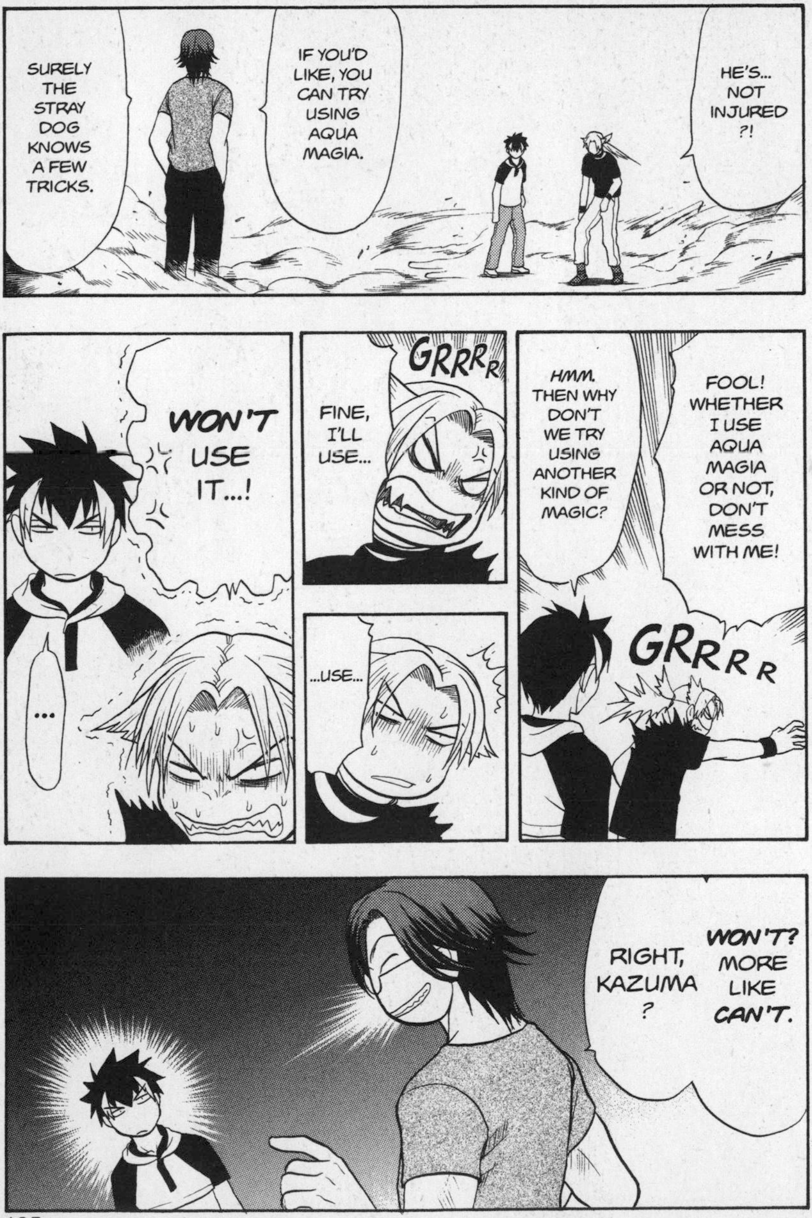
HE'S... NOT INJURED?!
IF YOU'D LIKE, YOU CAN TRY USING AQUA MAGIA.
SURELY THE STRAY DOG KNOWS A FEW TRICKS.
FOOL! WHETHER I USE AQUA MAGIA OR NOT, DON'T MESS WITH ME!
HMM. THEN WHY DON'T WE TRY USING ANOTHER KIND OF MAGIC?
GRRRRR
GRRRR
FINE, I'LL USE...
...USE...
WON'T USE IT...!
...
WON'T? MORE LIKE CAN'T.
RIGHT, KAZUMA?

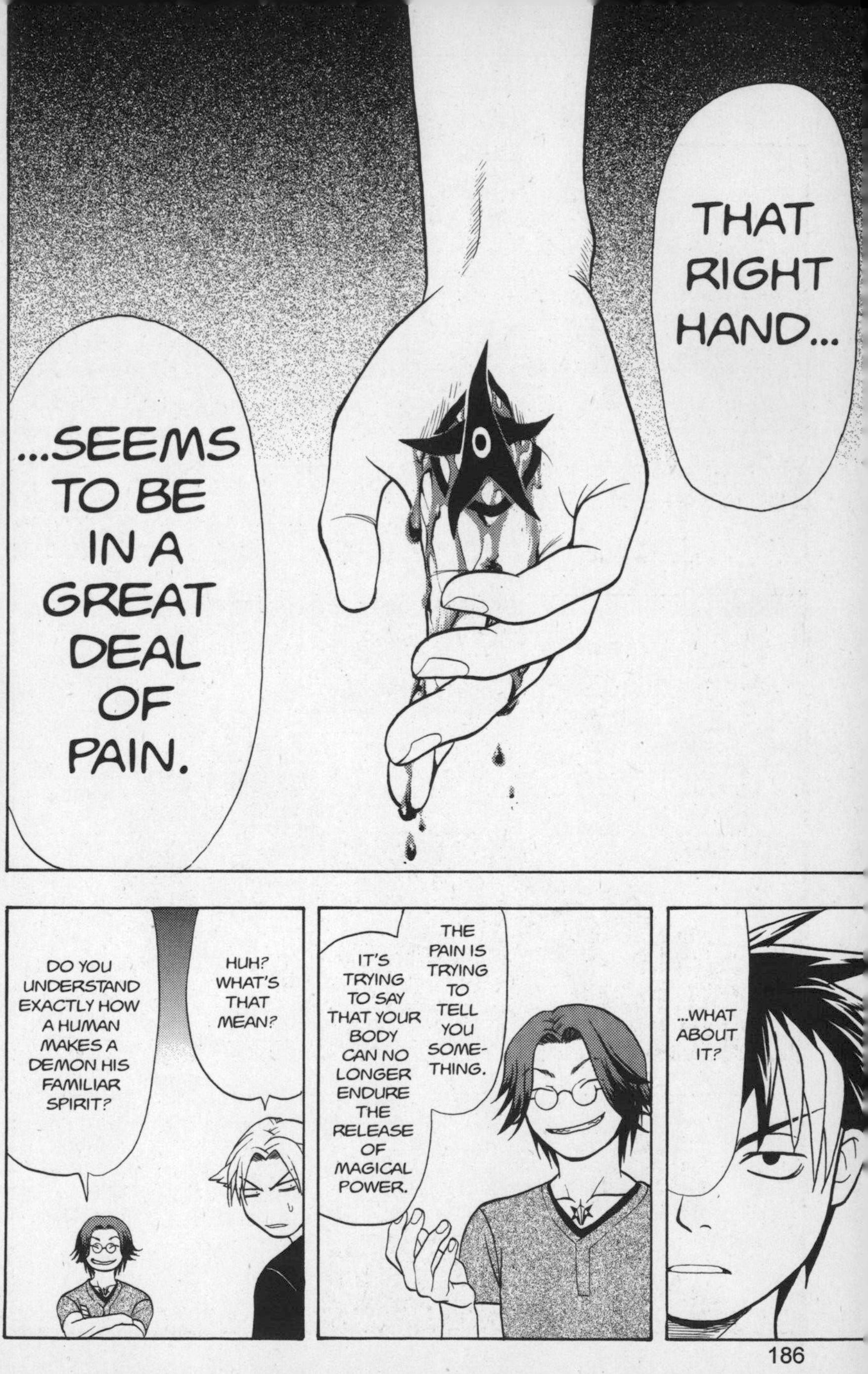
THAT RIGHT HAND...
...SEEMS TO BE IN A GREAT DEAL OF PAIN.
...WHAT ABOUT IT?
THE PAIN IS TRYING TO TELL YOU SOMETHING.
IT'S TRYING TO SAY THAT YOUR BODY CAN NO LONGER ENDURE THE RELEASE OF MAGICAL POWER.
HUH? WHAT'S THAT MEAN?
DO YOU UNDERSTAND EXACTLY HOW A HUMAN MAKES A DEMON HIS FAMILIAR SPIRIT?

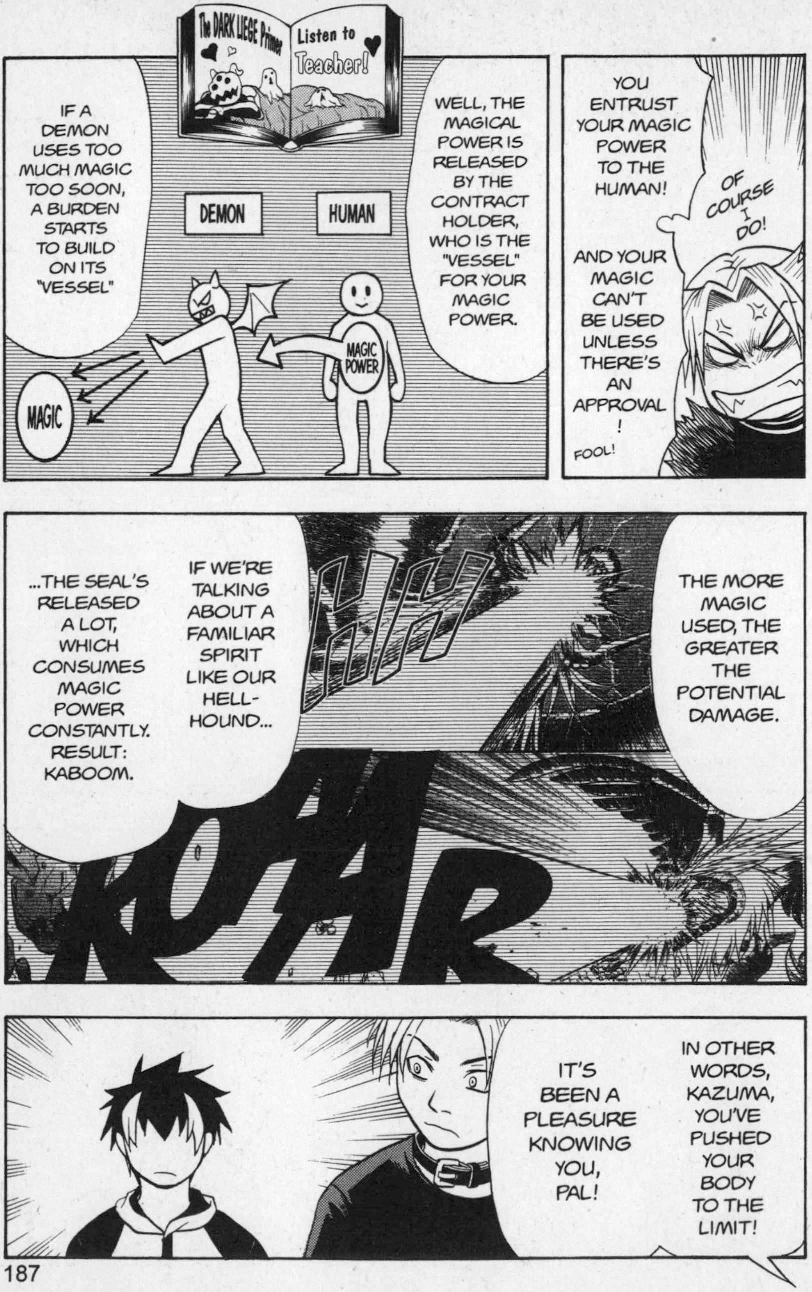
YOU ENTRUST YOUR MAGIC POWER TO THE HUMAN!
OF COURSE I DO!
AND YOUR MAGIC CAN'T BE USED UNLESS THERE'S AN APPROVAL!
FOOL!
The DARK LIEGE Primer
Listen to Teacher!
WELL, THE MAGICAL POWER IS RELEASED BY THE CONTRACT HOLDER, WHO IS THE "VESSEL" FOR YOUR MAGIC POWER.
HUMAN
DEMON
MAGIC POWER
MAGIC
IF A DEMON USES TOO MUCH MAGIC TOO SOON, A BURDEN STARTS TO BUILD ON ITS "VESSEL"
THE MORE MAGIC USED, THE GREATER THE POTENTIAL DAMAGE.
IF WE'RE TALKING ABOUT A FAMILIAR SPIRIT LIKE OUR HELL-HOUND...
...THE SEAL'S RELEASED A LOT, WHICH CONSUMES MAGIC POWER CONSTANTLY. RESULT: KABOOM.
IN OTHER WORDS, KAZUMA, YOU'VE PUSHED YOUR BODY TO THE LIMIT!
IT'S BEEN A PLEASURE KNOWING YOU, PAL!

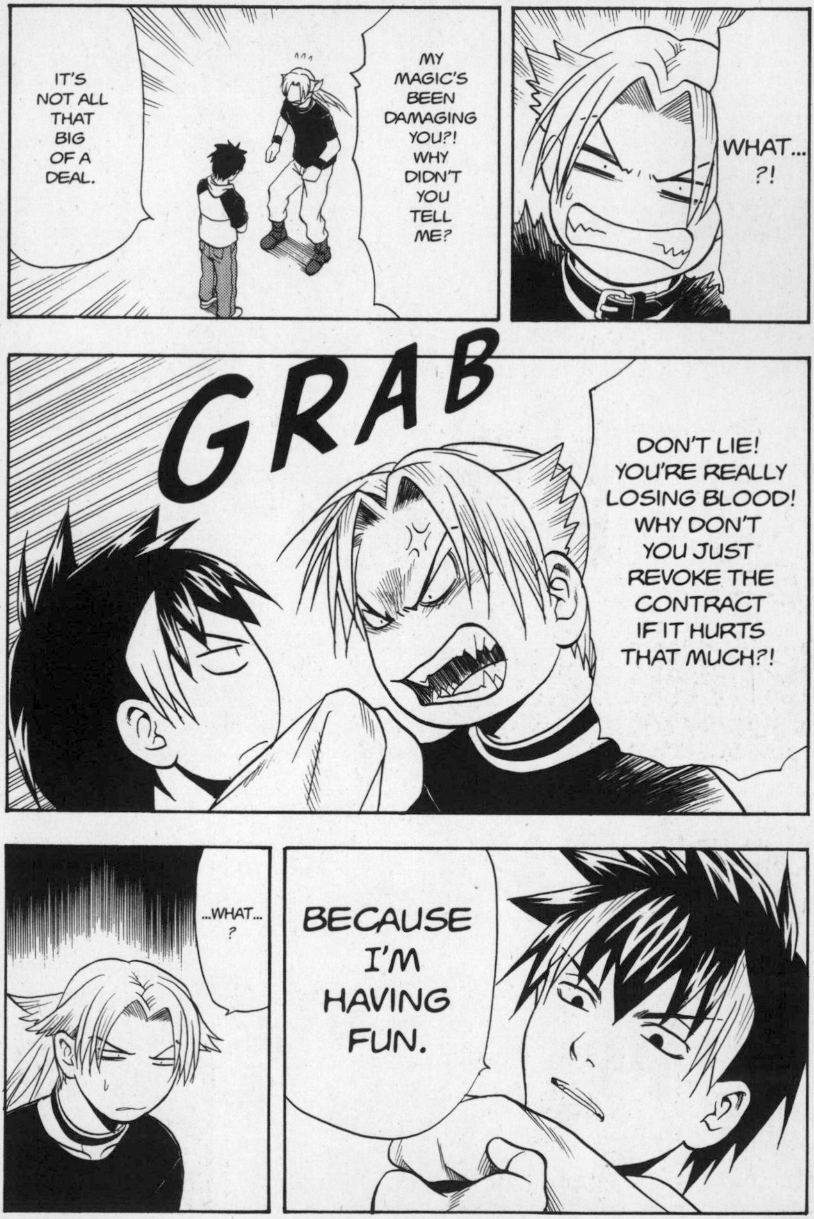
WHAT... ?!
MY MAGIC'S BEEN DAMAGING YOU?! WHY DIDN'T YOU TELL ME?
IT'S NOT ALL THAT BIG OF A DEAL.
GRAB
DON'T LIE! YOU'RE REALLY LOSING BLOOD! WHY DON'T YOU JUST REVOKE THE CONTRACT IF IT HURTS THAT MUCH?!
BECAUSE I'M HAVING FUN.
...WHAT... ?

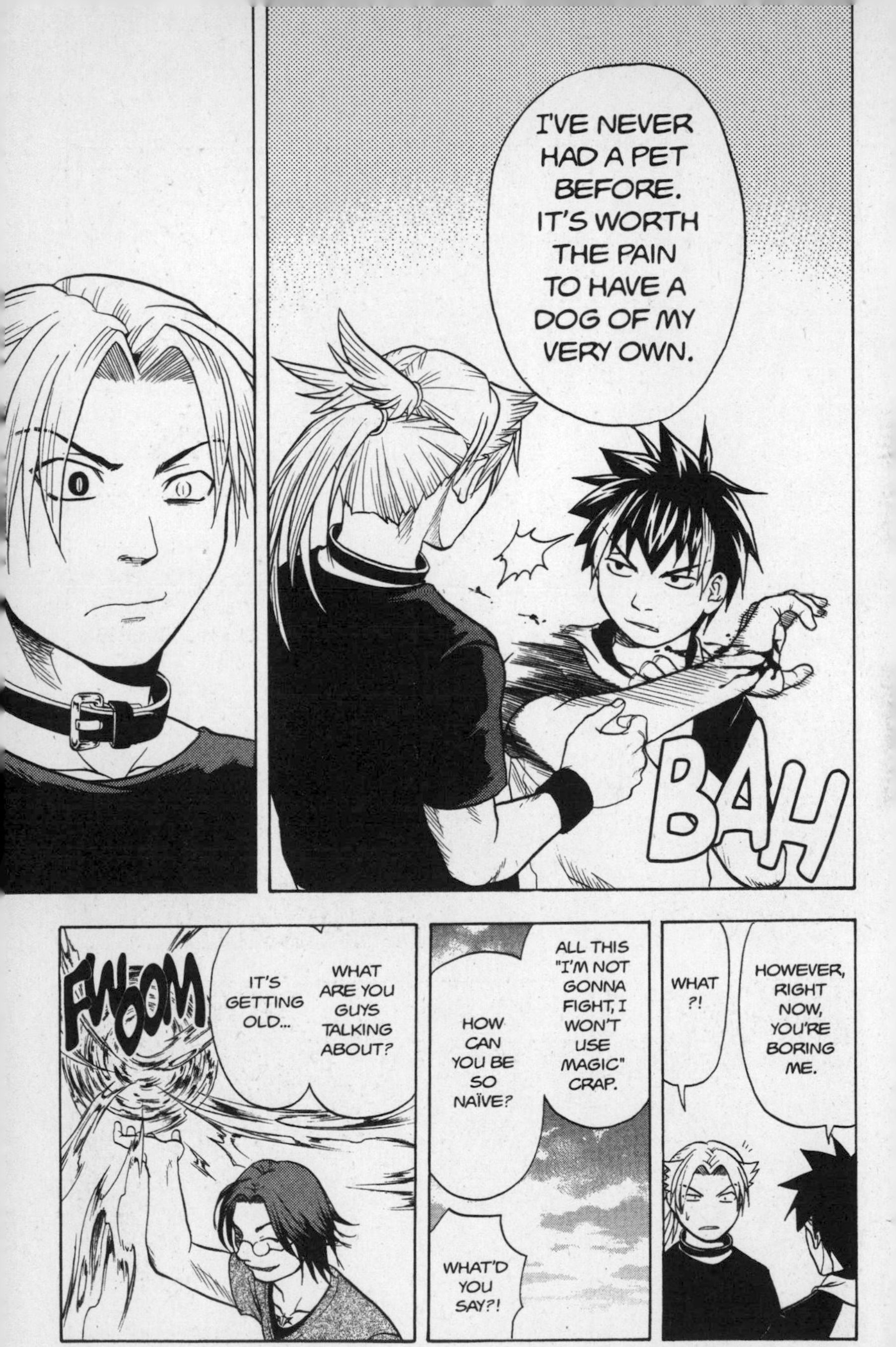
I'VE NEVER HAD A PET BEFORE. IT'S WORTH THE PAIN TO HAVE A DOG OF MY VERY OWN.
BAH
HOWEVER, RIGHT NOW, YOU'RE BORING ME.
WHAT ?!
ALL THIS "I'M NOT GONNA FIGHT, I WON'T USE MAGIC" CRAP.
HOW CAN YOU BE SO NAÏVE?
WHAT'D YOU SAY?!
WHAT ARE YOU GUYS TALKING ABOUT?
IT'S GETTING OLD...
FWOOM

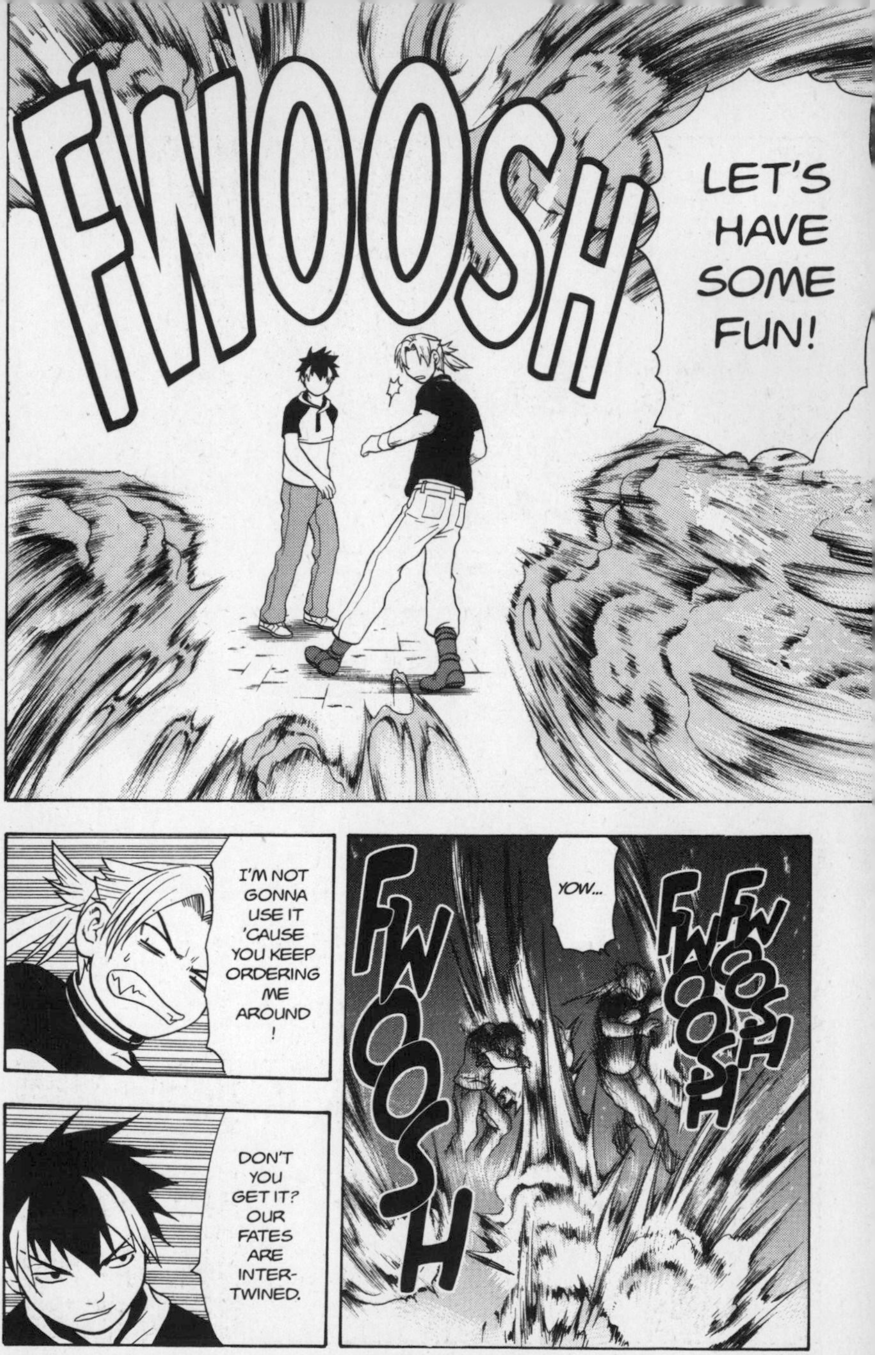
FWOOSH
LET'S HAVE SOME FUN!
FWFWOOSH
YOW...
FWOOSH
I'M NOT GONNA USE IT 'CAUSE YOU KEEP ORDERING ME AROUND!
DON'T YOU GET IT? OUR FATES ARE INTER-TWINED.

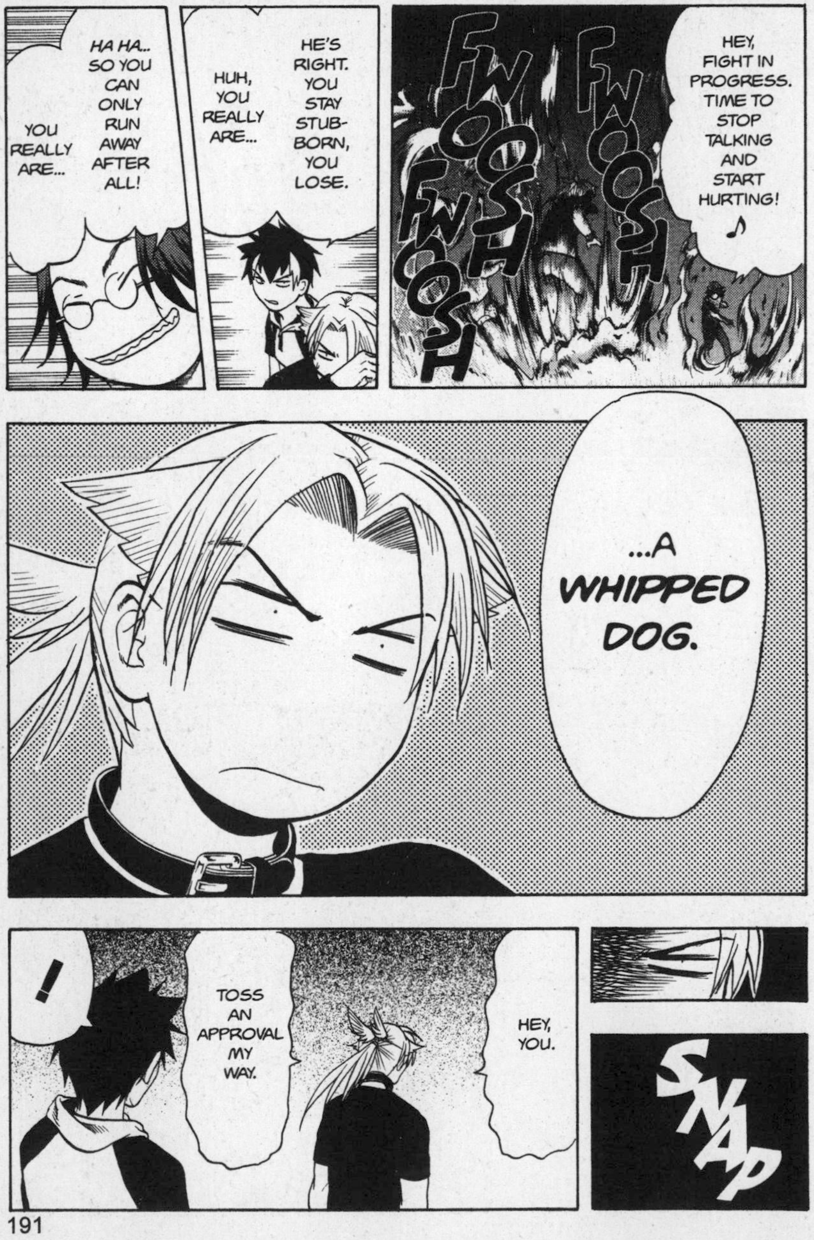
HEY, FIGHT IN PROGRESS. TIME TO STOP TALKING AND START HURTING! ♪
FWOOSH
FWOOSH
FWOOSH
HE'S RIGHT. YOU STAY STUB-BORN, YOU LOSE.
HUH, YOU REALLY ARE...
HA HA.. SO YOU CAN ONLY RUN AWAY AFTER ALL!
YOU REALLY ARE...
...A WHIPPED DOG.
SNAP
HEY, YOU.
TOSS AN APPROVAL MY WAY.
!

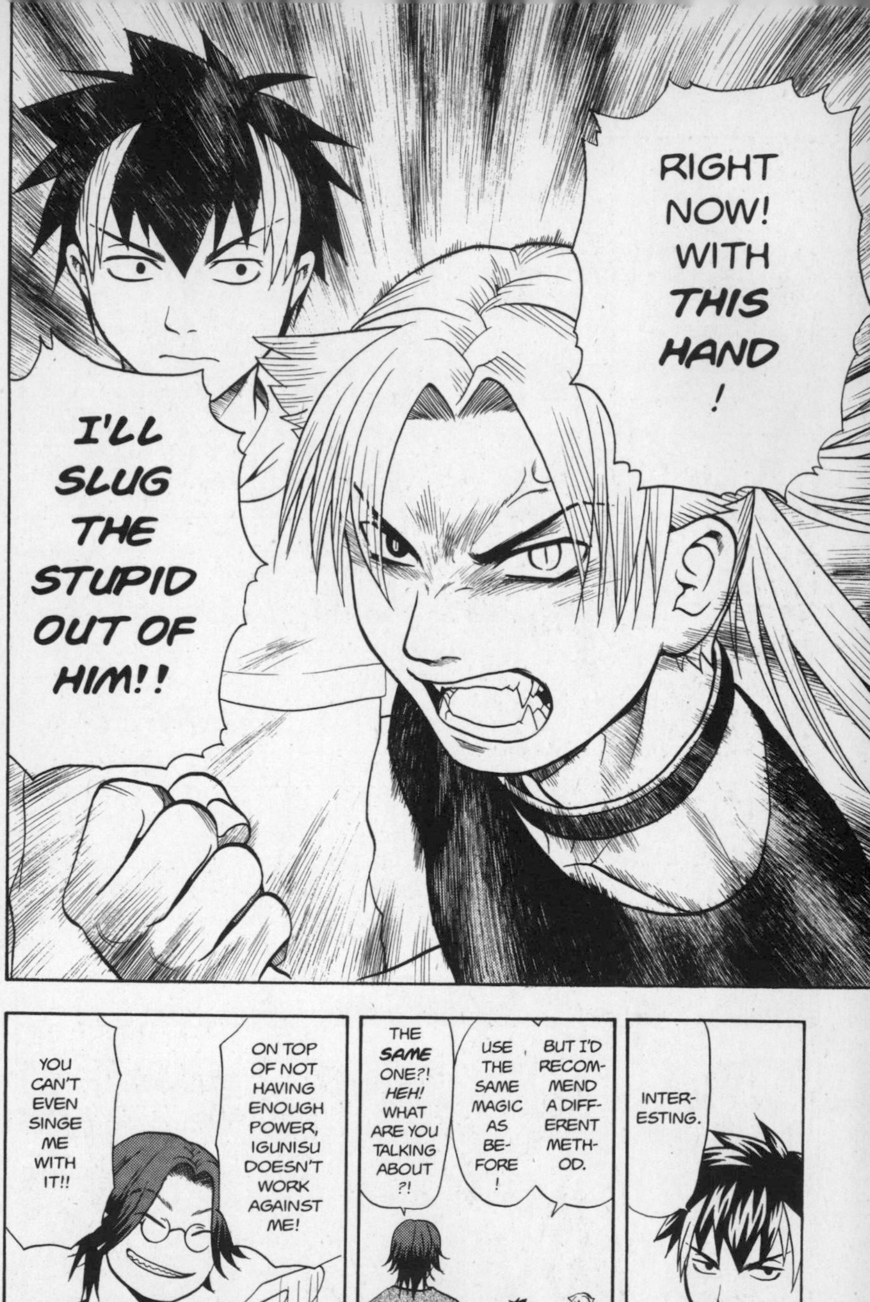
RIGHT NOW! WITH THIS HAND!
I'LL SLUG THE STUPID OUT OF HIM!!
INTERESTING.
BUT I'D RECOMMEND A DIFFERENT METHOD.
USE THE SAME MAGIC AS BEFORE!
THE SAME ONE?! HEH! WHAT ARE YOU TALKING ABOUT?!
ON TOP OF NOT HAVING ENOUGH POWER, IGUNISU DOESN'T WORK AGAINST ME!
YOU CAN'T EVEN SINGE ME WITH IT!!

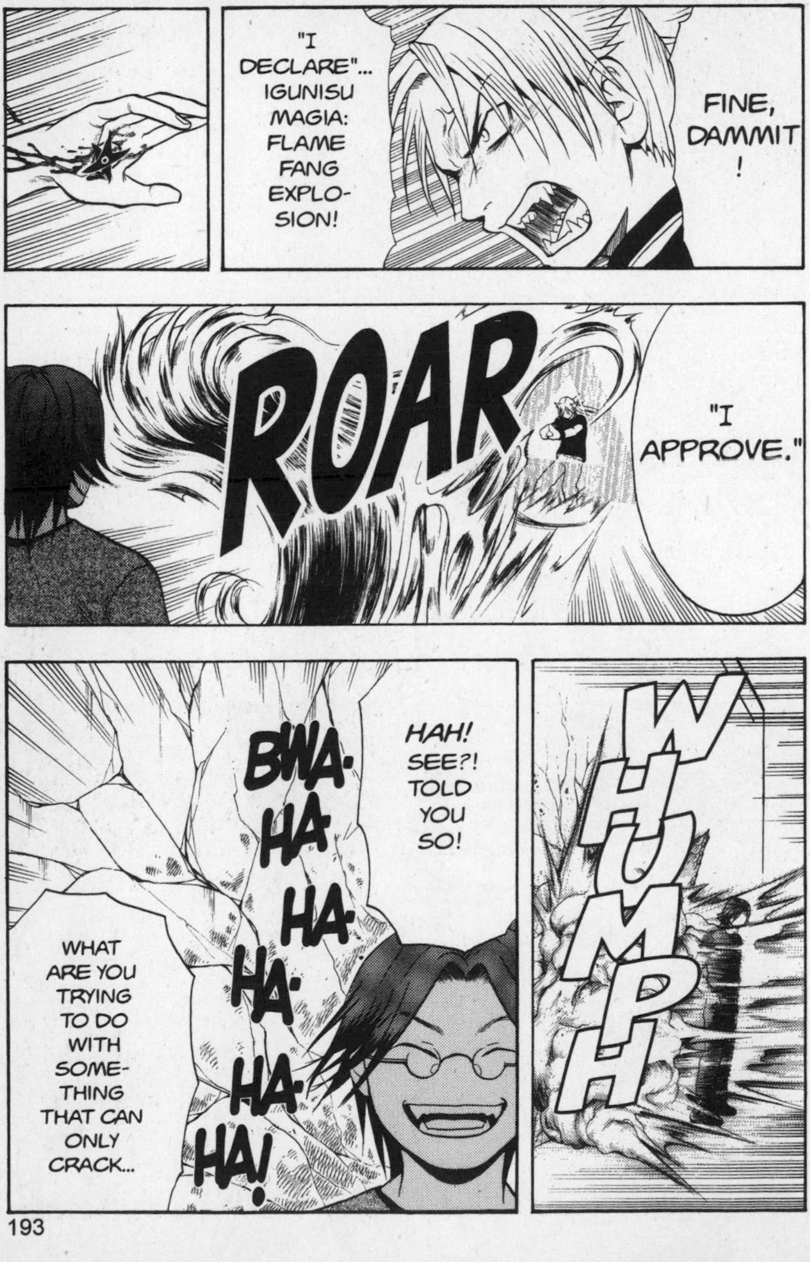
FINE, DAMMIT!
"I DECLARE"... IGUNISU MAGIA: FLAME FANG EXPLOSION!
"I APPROVE."
ROAR
WHUMPH
HAH! SEE?! TOLD YOU SO!
BWA-HA-HA-HA-HA-HA-HA!
WHAT ARE YOU TRYING TO DO WITH SOMETHING THAT CAN ONLY CRACK...

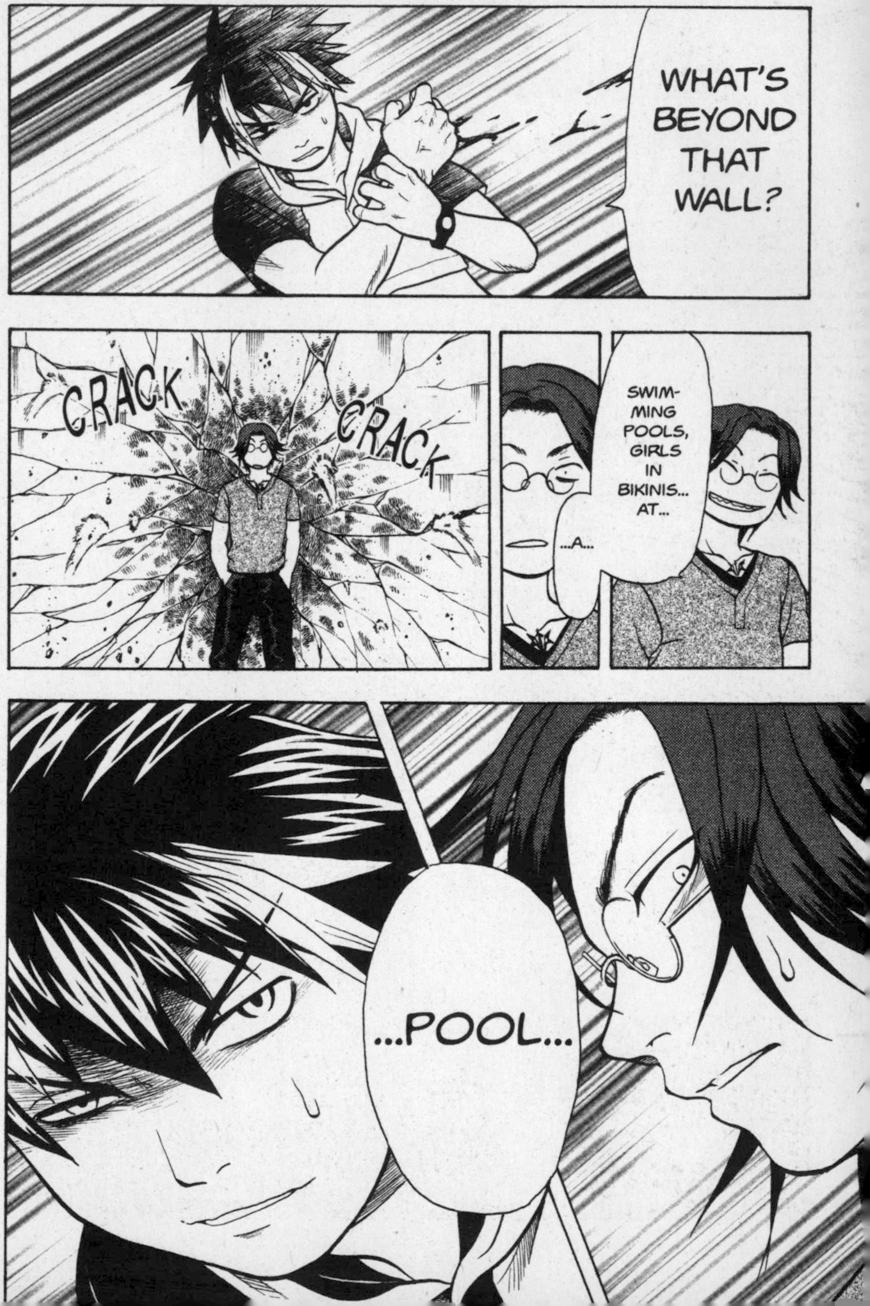
WHAT'S BEYOND THAT WALL?
SWIM-MING POOLS, GIRLS IN BIKINIS... AT...
...A...
CRACK
CRACK
...POOL...

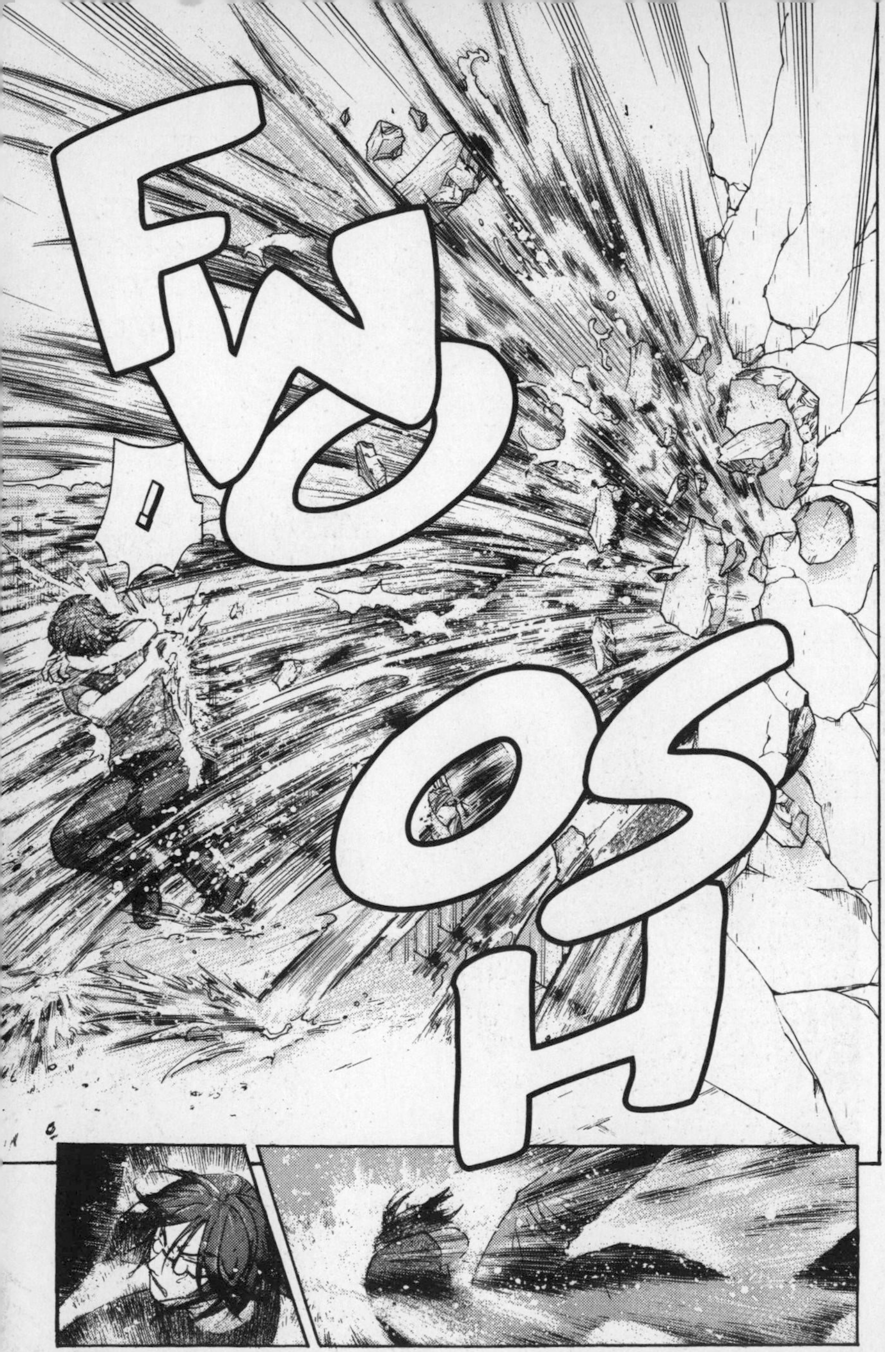
FWOOSH
!

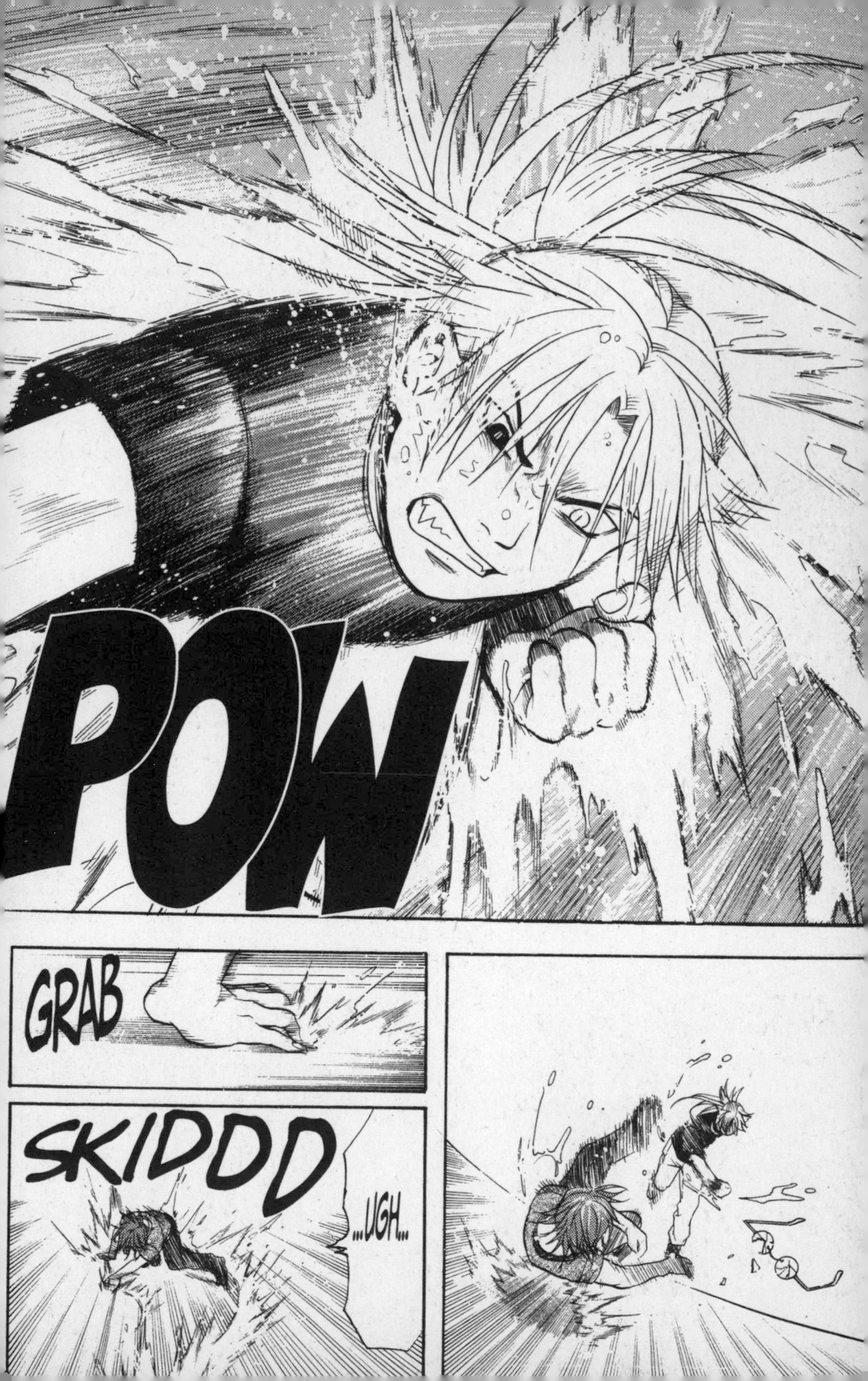
POW
GRAB
SKIDDD
...UGH...

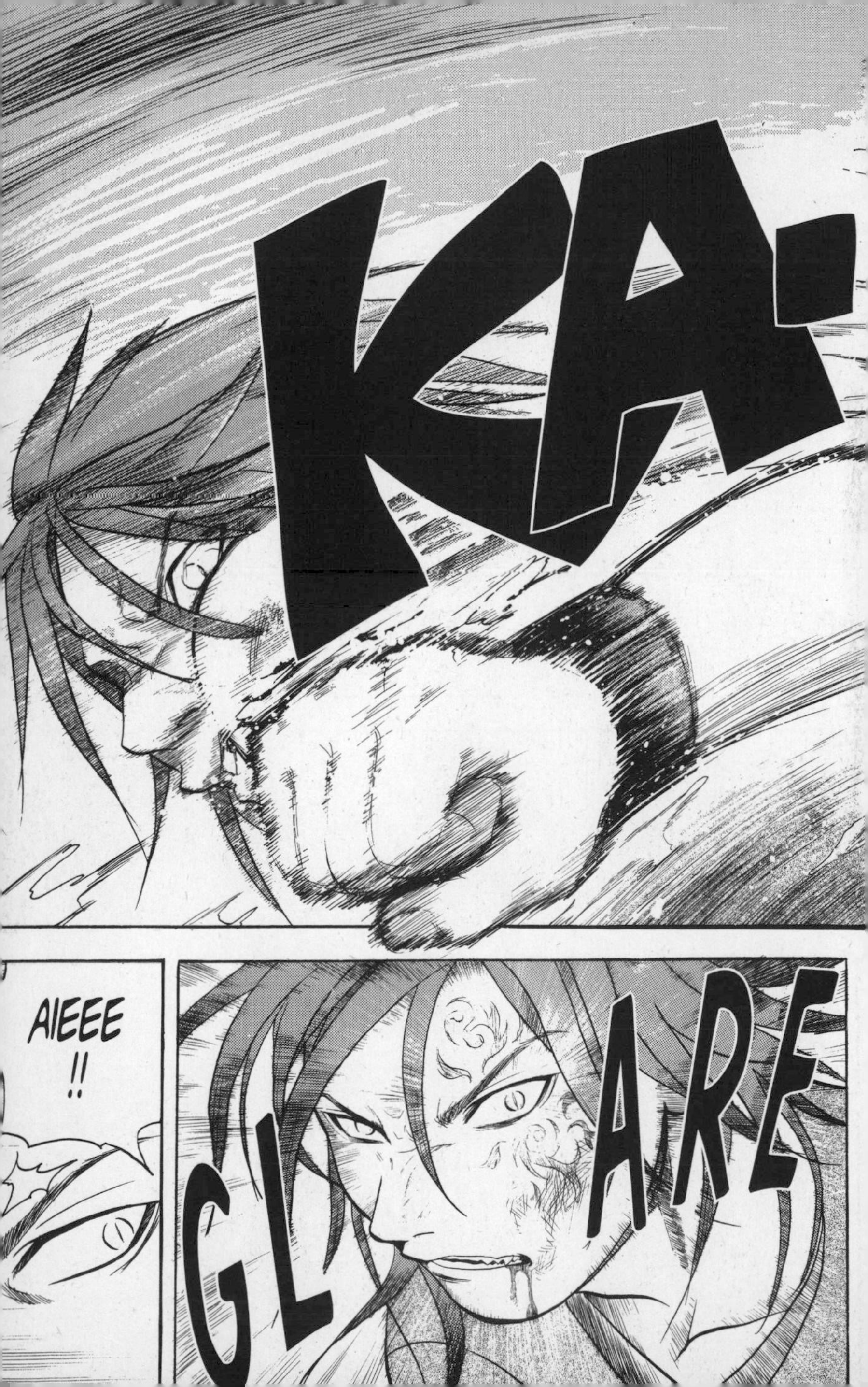
KA-
GLARE
AIEEE !!

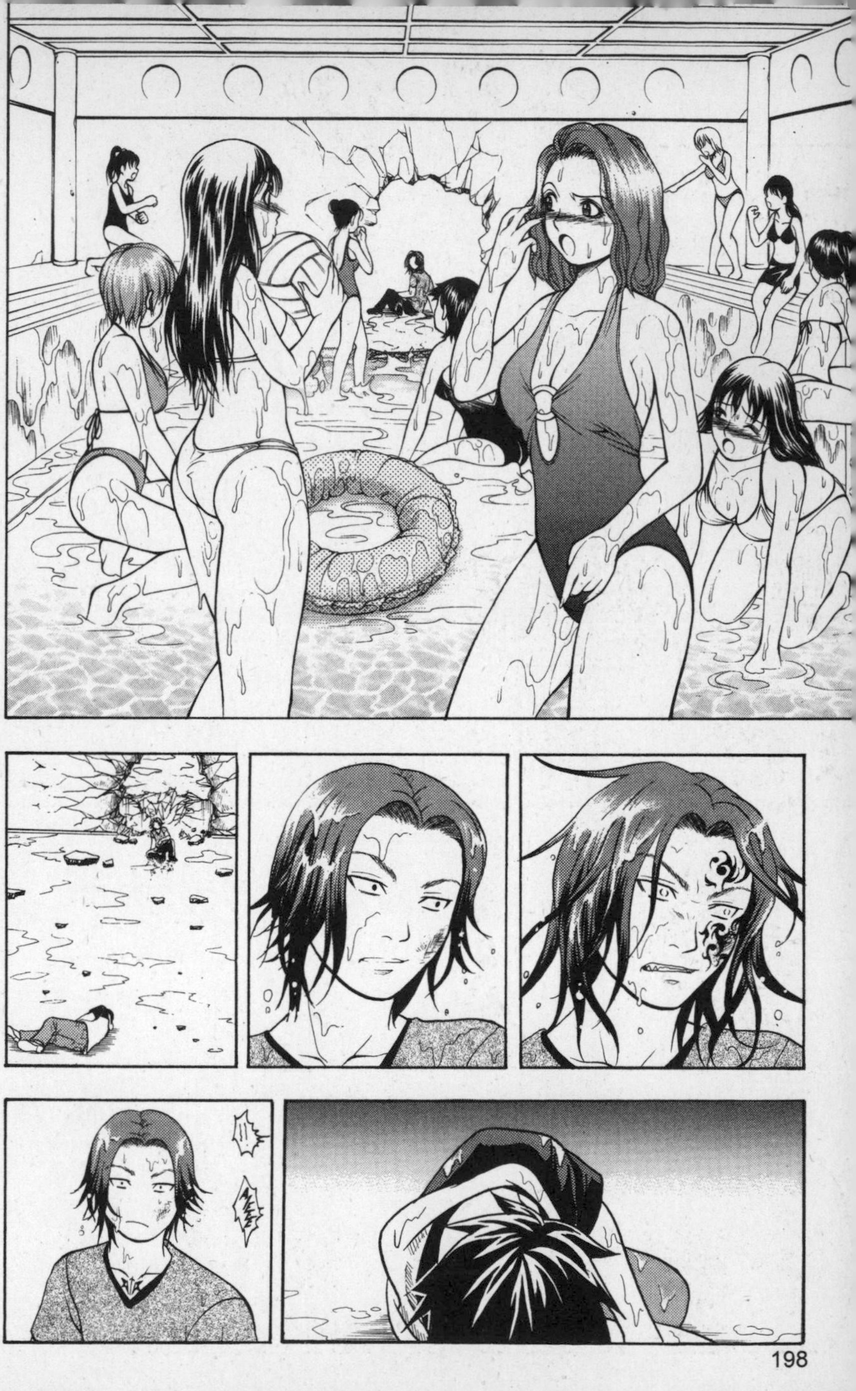
!!

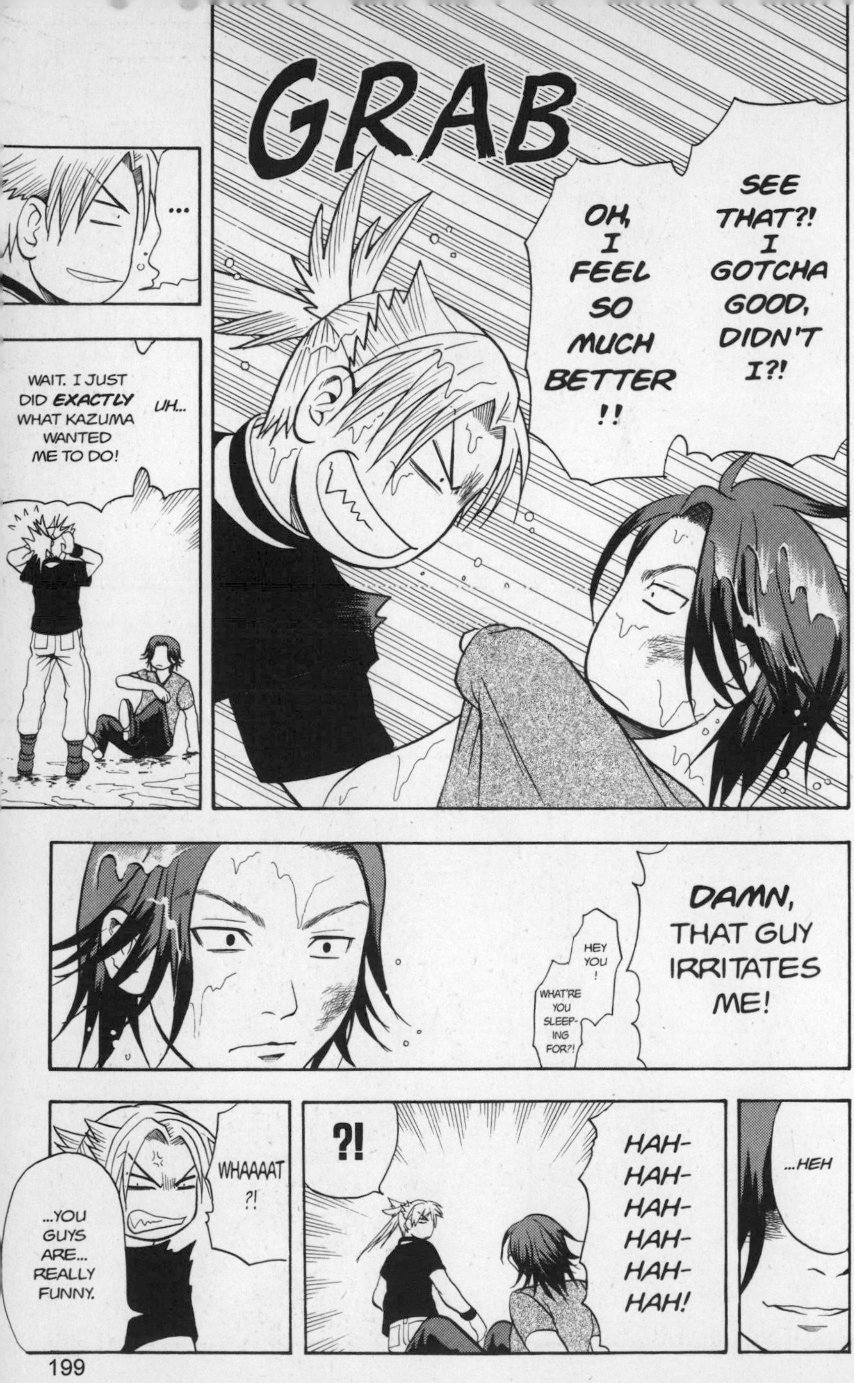
GRAB
SEE THAT?! I GOTCHA GOOD, DIDN'T I?!
OH, I FEEL SO MUCH BETTER!!
...
UH...
WAIT. I JUST DID EXACTLY WHAT KAZUMA WANTED ME TO DO!
DAMN, THAT GUY IRRITATES ME!
HEY YOU!
WHAT'RE YOU SLEEPING FOR?!
...HEH
HAH-HAH-HAH-HAH-HAH-HAH!
?!
WHAAAAT?!
...YOU GUYS ARE... REALLY FUNNY.

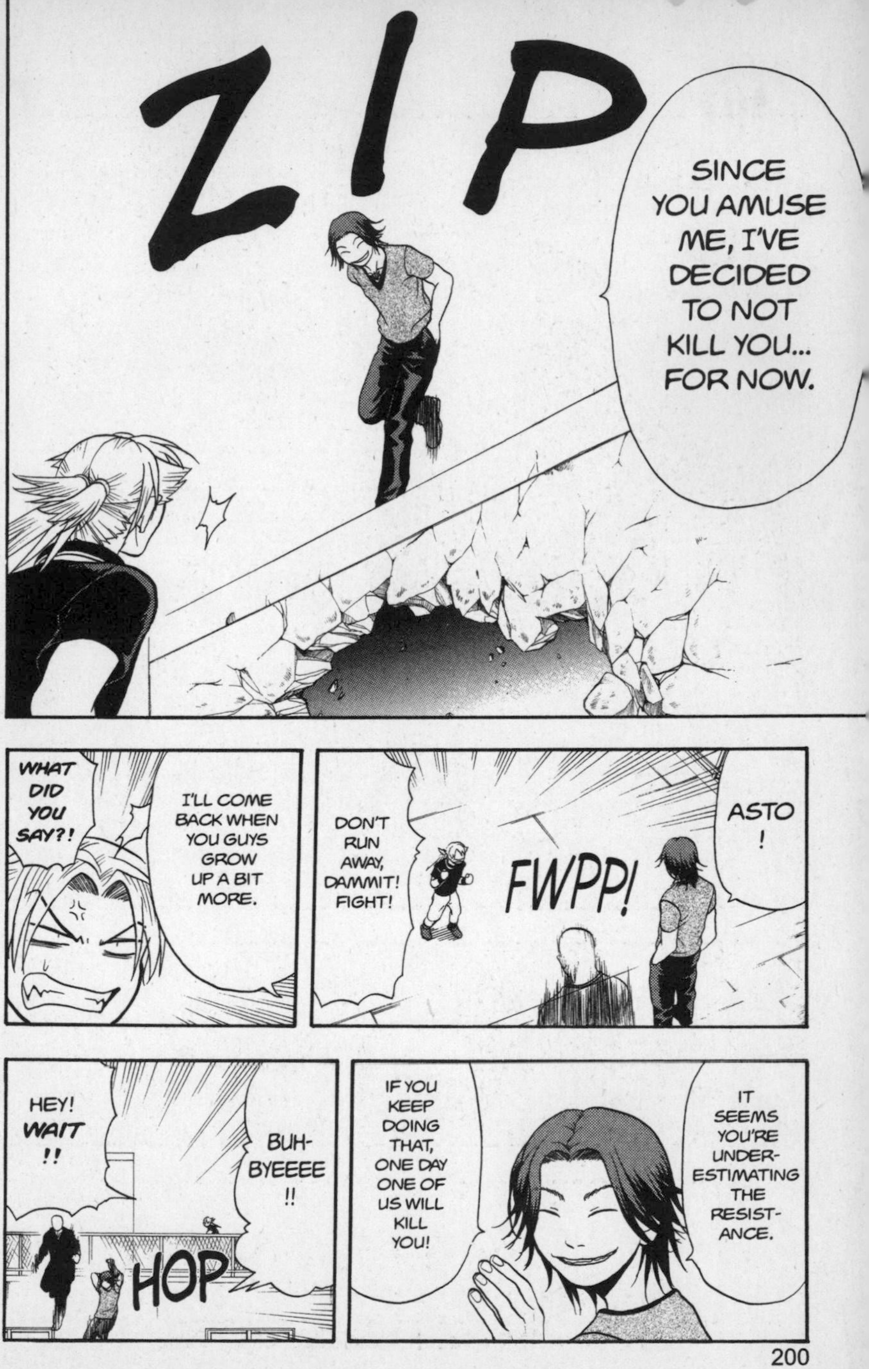
SINCE YOU AMUSE ME, I'VE DECIDED TO NOT KILL YOU... FOR NOW.
ZIP
ASTO!
FWPP!
DON'T RUN AWAY, DAMMIT! FIGHT!
I'LL COME BACK WHEN YOU GUYS GROW UP A BIT MORE.
WHAT DID YOU SAY?!
IT SEEMS YOU'RE UNDER-ESTIMATING THE RESIST-ANCE.
IF YOU KEEP DOING THAT, ONE DAY ONE OF US WILL KILL YOU!
BUH-BYEEEE!!
HEY! WAIT!!
HOP

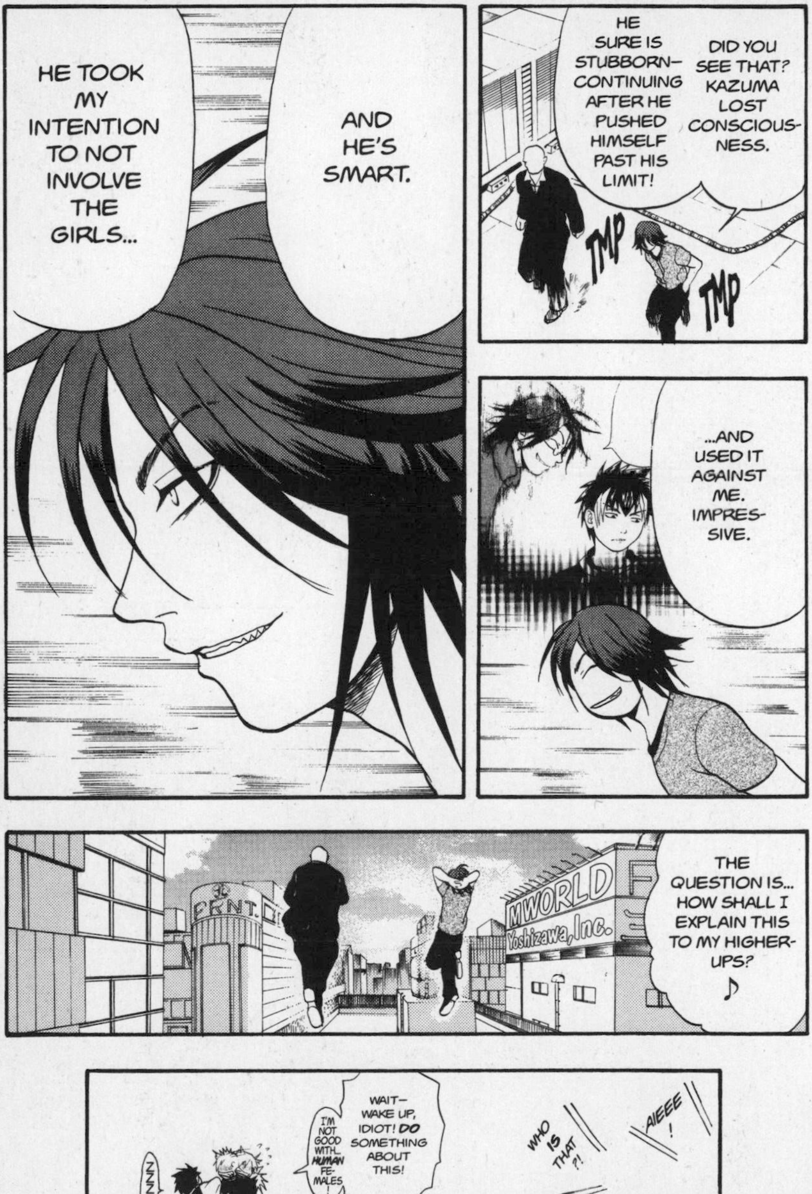
DID YOU SEE THAT? KAZUMA LOST CONSCIOUSNESS.
HE SURE IS STUBBORN—CONTINUING AFTER HE PUSHED HIMSELF PAST HIS LIMIT!
TMP
TMP
...AND USED IT AGAINST ME. IMPRESSIVE.
AND HE'S SMART.
HE TOOK MY INTENTION TO NOT INVOLVE THE GIRLS...
THE QUESTION IS... HOW SHALL I EXPLAIN THIS TO MY HIGHER-UPS? ♪
MWORLD
Yoshizawa, Inc.
PRNT.
AIEEE!
WHO IS THAT?!
WAIT—WAKE UP, IDIOT! DO SOMETHING ABOUT THIS!
I'M NOT GOOD WITH... HUMAN FEMALES!
ZZZ...

Volume 1: A Match Made in Hell—End

THIS ILLUSTRATION IS HOW I REPLIED TO THE FAN LETTERS I RECEIVED WHEN I DID THE NORA SHORT STORY. BELIEVE ME, I'VE BEEN CAREFULLY READING ALL THE FAN MAIL I'VE RECEIVED SO FAR! BUT EVER SINCE THE SERIALIZATION STARTED, I HAVEN'T BEEN ABLE TO WRITE PERSONAL RESPONSES. I'M HOPING TO FIND SOME OPPORTUNITY TO AT LEAST SEND A COOL GROUP RESPONSE. YOUR ENCOURAGEMENT REALLY GIVES ME A BUZZ. THANK YOU ALL SO VERY MUCH!

ALL-AROUND IMPRESARIO AND SUPER-TALENTED COOK, MR. H

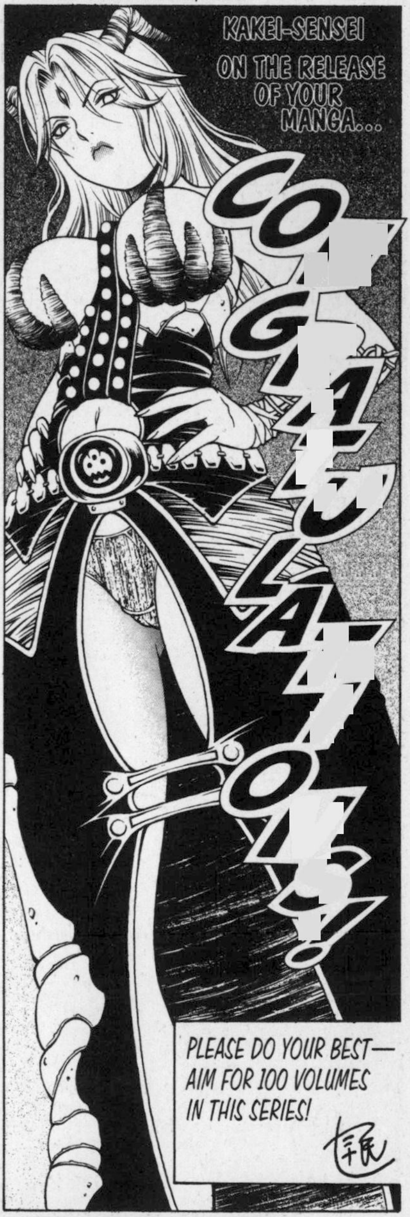
KAKEI-SENSEI
ON THE RELEASE OF YOUR MANGA...
PLEASE DO YOUR BEST—AIM FOR 100 VOLUMES IN THIS SERIES!

ALSO THANK YOU FOR DELICIOUS MEALS. I APOLOGIZE FOR MY SELFISHNESS, BUT I LOVE YOUR FOOD. —KAKEI

YOKOHAMA BAY STARS AND HONG KONG CINEMA FAN, MR. F.

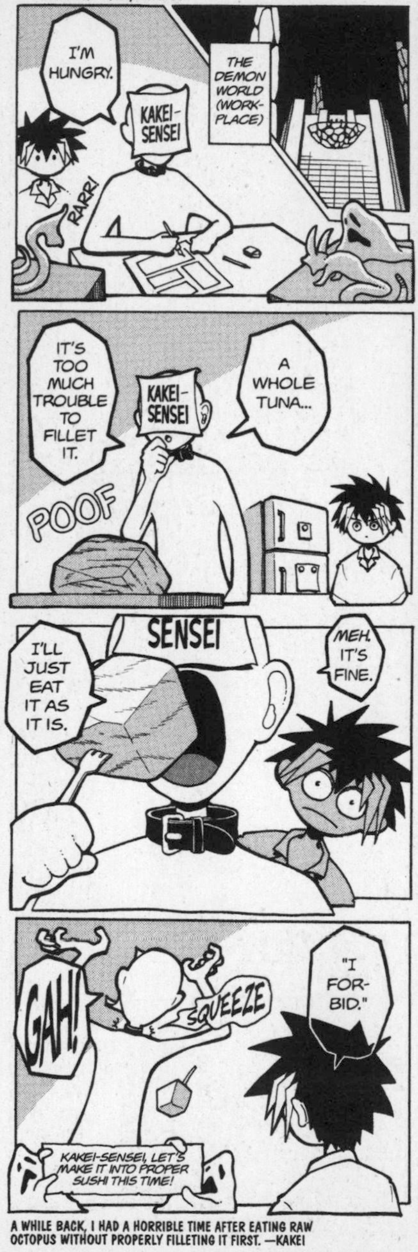
THE DEMON WORLD (WORK-PLACE)
I'M HUNGRY.
KAKEI-SENSEI
RARR!
A WHOLE TUNA...
IT'S TOO MUCH TROUBLE TO FILLET IT.
KAKEI-SENSEI
POOF
MEH. IT'S FINE.
SENSEI
I'LL JUST EAT IT AS IT IS.
"I FOR-BID."
SQUEEZE
GAH!
KAKEI-SENSEI, LET'S MAKE IT INTO PROPER SUSHI THIS TIME!

A WHILE BACK, I HAD A HORRIBLE TIME AFTER EATING RAW OCTOPUS WITHOUT PROPERLY FILLETING IT FIRST. —KAKEI

▼ CAT-LOVER AND MARTIAL ARTS FAN, MS. ASAKO

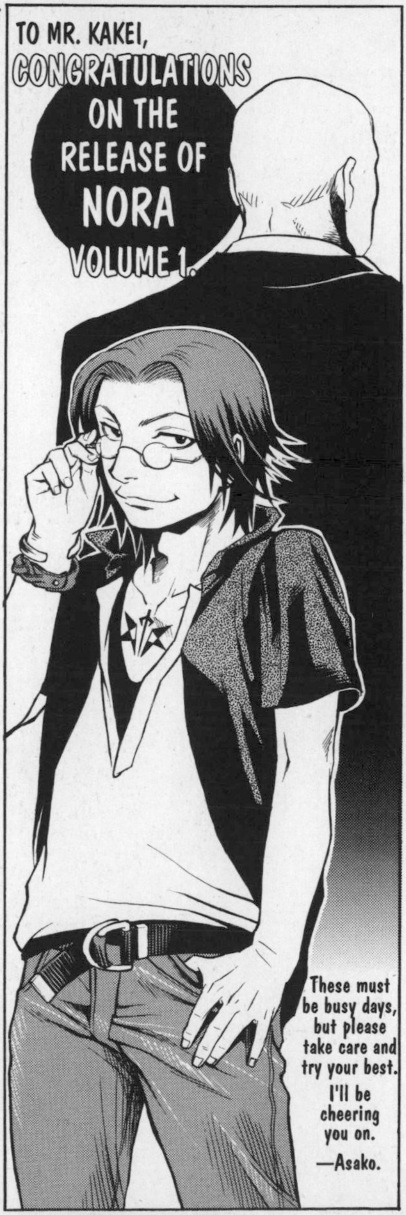
TO MR. KAKEI,
CONGRATULATIONS ON THE RELEASE OF NORA VOLUME 1.
These must be busy days, but please take care and try your best.
I'll be cheering you on.
—Asako.

ACTUALLY, I DON'T HAVE MUCH CONFIDENCE IN MY HEALTH HOLDING UP! —KAKEI

FASHIONABLE, PAINFULLY HONEST
▼ KANSAI NATIVE, MISS NAKAMICHI

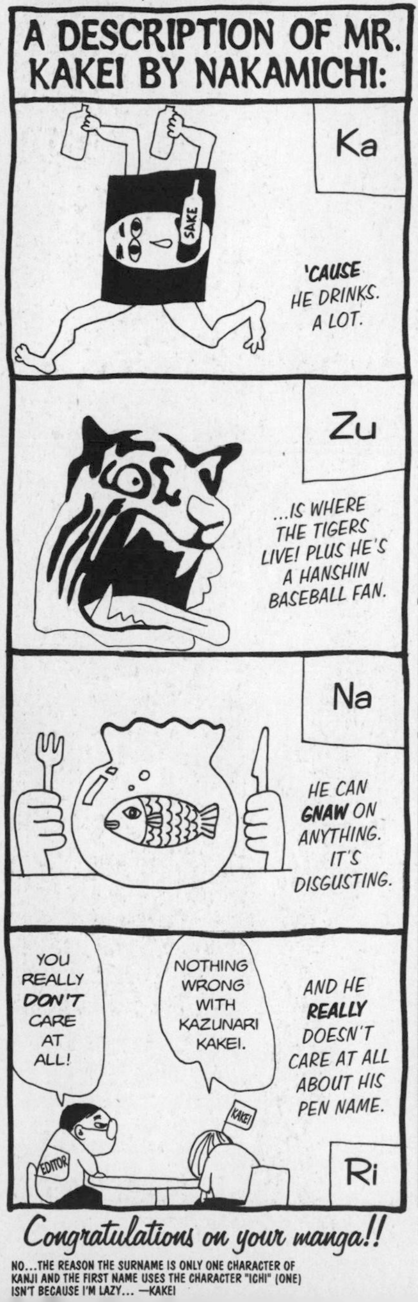
A DESCRIPTION OF MR. KAKEI BY NAKAMICHI:
Ka
'CAUSE HE DRINKS. A LOT.
SAKE
Zu
...IS WHERE THE TIGERS LIVE! PLUS HE'S A HANSHIN BASEBALL FAN.
Na
HE CAN GNAW ON ANYTHING. IT'S DISGUSTING.
AND HE REALLY DOESN'T CARE AT ALL ABOUT HIS PEN NAME.
NOTHING WRONG WITH KAZUNARI KAKEI.
YOU REALLY DON'T CARE AT ALL!
KAKEI
EDITOR
Ri

Congratulations on your manga!!

NO...THE REASON THE SURNAME IS ONLY ONE CHARACTER OF KANJI AND THE FIRST NAME USES THE CHARACTER "ICHI" (ONE) ISN'T BECAUSE I'M LAZY... —KAKEI

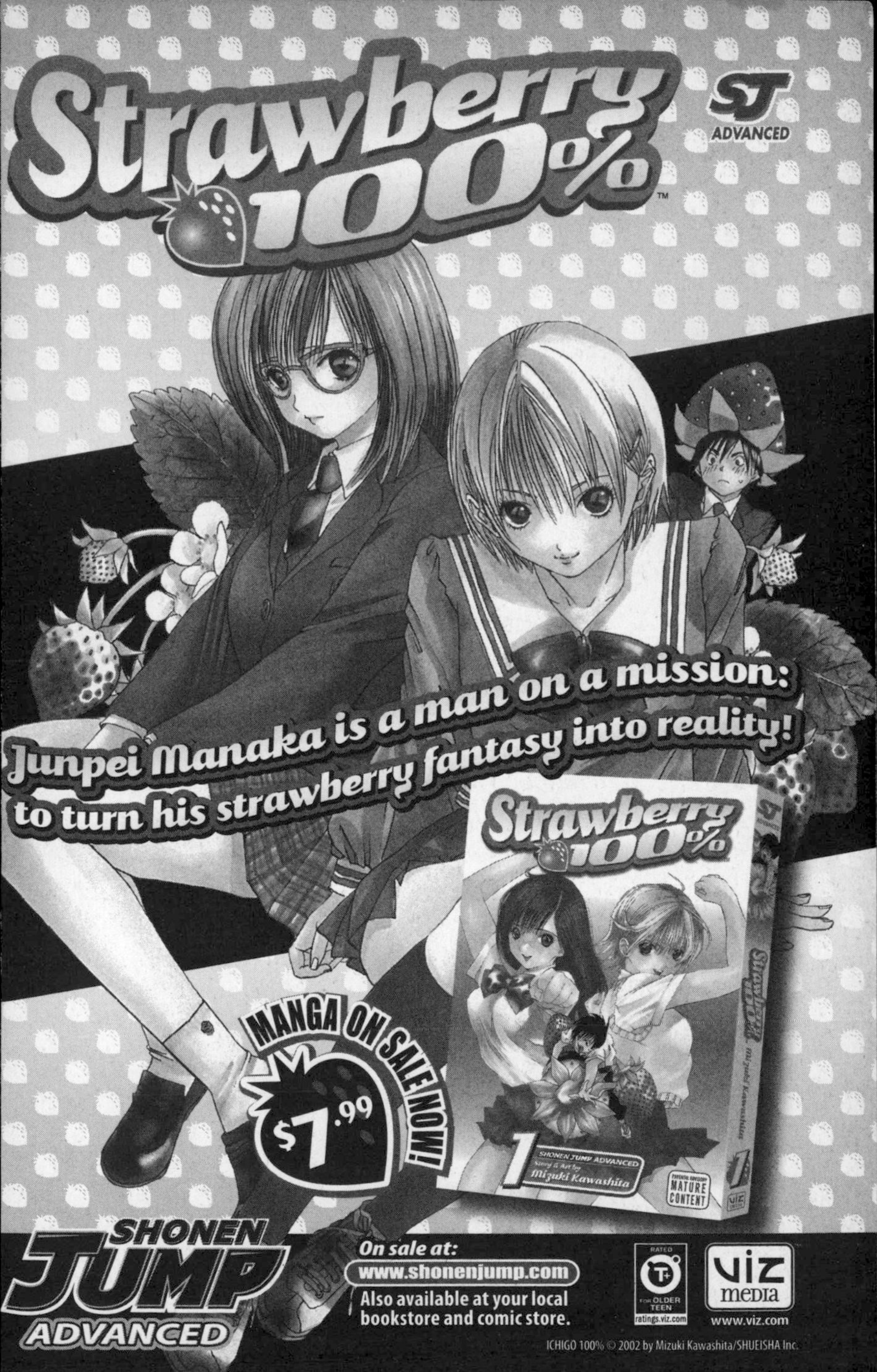
Strawberry 100%™
SJ ADVANCED
Junpei Manaka is a man on a mission: to turn his strawberry fantasy into reality!
Strawberry 100%
1
SHONEN JUMP ADVANCED
Story & Art by Mizuki Kawashita
MATURE CONTENT
MANGA ON SALE NOW!
$7.99
SHONEN JUMP ADVANCED
On sale at:
www.shonenjump.com
Also available at your local bookstore and comic store.
RATED T+ FOR OLDER TEEN
ratings.viz.com
VIZ media
www.viz.com
ICHIGO 100% © 2002 by Mizuki Kawashita/SHUEISHA Inc.

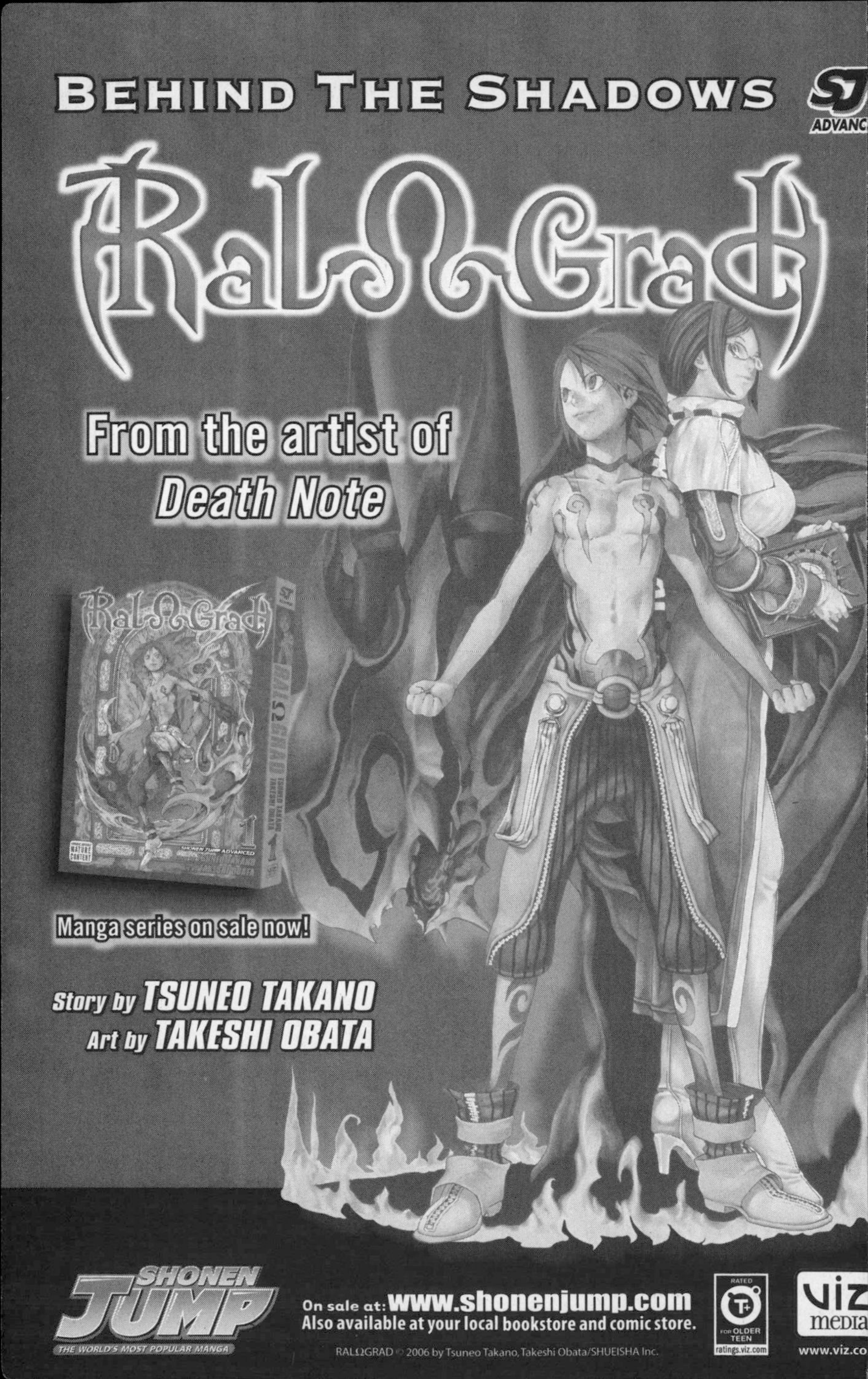
BEHIND THE SHADOWS
SJ ADVANC
RalΩGrad
From the artist of
Death Note
Manga series on sale now!
Story by TSUNEO TAKANO
Art by TAKESHI OBATA
SHONEN JUMP
THE WORLD'S MOST POPULAR MANGA
On sale at: www.shonenjump.com
Also available at your local bookstore and comic store.
RATED T+ FOR OLDER TEEN
ratings.viz.com
viz media
www.viz.co
RALΩGRAD © 2006 by Tsuneo Takano, Takeshi Obata/SHUEISHA Inc.

Check us out on the web!

www.shonenjump.com